Iwan Morgan is Professor of US Studies and Commonwealth Fund Professor of American History at University College London. He was awarded the British Association of American Studies Honorary Fellowship in 2014 in recognition of his contributions to the discipline over the course of his career. He is also a Fellow of Oxford University's Rothermere American Institute. His publications include *The Age of Deficits: Presidents and Unbalanced Budgets from Jimmy Carter to George W. Bush* (winner of the Richard Neustadt book prize), *Nixon* and *Beyond the Liberal Consensus: A Political History of the United States since 1965.*

'WOW! It's all here – and I mean *all of it* – in Iwan Morgan's superb biography of America's 40th president. I would never have believed how much I didn't know about a fellow Californian I first met in the spring of 1946. But when a distinguished historian with a wonderful way with words doubles as a prodigious researcher the pages are going to fly. Hey, the Gipper's back. Enjoy the ride.'

Alex Butterfield, former Deputy Assistant to President Nixon

'Iwan Morgan's *Reagan* is a fast-paced narrative, superbly organized and judiciously argued, about the life and times of America's 40th president. Before going elsewhere, both academics and general audiences should first read this exceptional volume as the introduction to this complex topic.'

Irwin F. Gellman, author of *The President and the Apprentice: Eisenhower and Nixon 1952–1961*

'Stands every chance of emerging as the standard life. Morgan has brought to its writing formidable but also thoughtful and critical research and a lively style… Morgan's greatest virtue is his fairness. He does justice to Reagan's authentic faith in the essential virtue of America and to the individual, non-ideological quality of his conservative faith. At the same time he is not afraid to point out the contradictions in Reagan's beliefs, the limitations of his political credo and the occasional mistakes and absurdities of his political career. Wise, fair and witty, Iwan Morgan's life of Reagan is likely to be accepted by both the admirers and the critics of the 40th president as both trustworthy and readable.'

Godfrey Hodgson, author of *The Myth of American Exceptionalism* and former Washington correspondent for *The Observer*

'Iwan Morgan has written a hugely valuable account of a highly consequential life. *Reagan* is engagingly written and exhaustively researched – the grounding in archival sources adds real depth to the portrayal of Reagan the person, performer, governor and president. Morgan's assessment of Reagan is nuanced and refreshingly non-partisan, giving credit and finding fault where each is appropriately due. Readers will come away appreciating the intriguing complexity of the man, and the immense impact of his career.'

Andrew Rudalevige,
T.B. Reed Professor of Government, Bowdoin College

'Iwan Morgan's highly intelligent and authoritative *Reagan* accomplishes the rare feat of elucidating President Reagan's complex personal psychology, his core values and his economic and political policies. In this concise and fair-minded portrait, Morgan shows us how this optimistic and pragmatic man became a consequential president who not only represented his times, but helped steer the course of history in a conservative direction. Morgan does not shy away from exploring Reagan's failures including his lack of empathy for AIDS patients and African-Americans.'

Will Swift, author of *Pat and Dick:*
The Nixons, an Intimate Portrait of a Marriage

'This is exactly what presidential scholars have been waiting for: a study of Ronald Reagan that avoids simplistic partisan judgements in developing an interpretation that is both critical and sympathetic. Lucid, fluent, perspicacious, and grounded in a keen appreciation of the broader themes of US history, this is an outstanding work by one of Britain's foremost historians of modern America.'

Mark White, Professor of History,
Queen Mary University of London

REAGAN

AMERICAN ICON

IWAN MORGAN

Published in 2016 by
I.B.Tauris & Co. Ltd
London • New York
www.ibtauris.com

Copyright © 2016 Iwan Morgan

ISBN: 978 1 78076 747 5
eISBN: 978 1 78672 050 4
ePDF: 978 1 78673 050 3

A full CIP record for this book is available from the British Library
A full CIP record is available from the Library of Congress

Library of Congress Catalog Card Number: available

Text design and typesetting by Tetragon, London

Printed and bound in Sweden by ScandBook AB

CONTENTS

LIST OF ILLUSTRATIONS

PREFACE

I n the late morning of 31 May 1988, a sunny and warm spring day in Moscow, Ronald Reagan and Mikhail Gorbachev took time out from their summit talks in the Kremlin to stroll together in the adjacent Red Square. This was a place associated with celebrations of the Bolshevik Revolution and May Day parades of Soviet military power. Now it was the setting for a display of mutual goodwill by the leaders of two countries hitherto locked in 40 years of Cold War antagonism. They stopped to talk to some Russian citizens also taking in the splendours of Red Square. Picking up a small boy there with his family, Gorbachev told him to shake hands with 'Grandfather Reagan'. As the walk continued within the Kremlin grounds, an American reporter put the question on the mind of every journalist present: 'Do you still think you're in an evil empire, Mr President?' After some thought, back came the reply: 'No [...] I was talking about another time and another era.'[1]

The symbolism of this moment was immense. The man who was the world's foremost anti-communist was engaged in a public display of warmth towards the leader of the state that he had denounced as an 'evil empire' in 1983. In that year of living dangerously, relations between the United States and the Soviet Union were at such a low ebb that the danger of nuclear confrontation was very real. Public opinion, in both America and Europe, feared that Reagan's hatred of communism was fanning the flames of conflict. Soviet leaders were of the same mind. Reagan's military build-up, his trenchantly hostile rhetoric, and his announcement of plans to construct an anti-missile shield in space to neutralize the USSR's offensive capacity caused them profound anxiety. Such was the depth of the Kremlin's insecurity that it put Soviet forces on high alert in November 1983 in the mistaken belief that the current NATO war-game exercise would be used to launch a real first strike against Russia. This war scare was the closest the world has yet come to unintended nuclear conflict but it was symptomatic of the tensions of the times. As Gorbachev later reflected, 'Never, perhaps, in the postwar decades was the situation in the world as explosive and, hence, more difficult and unfavorable as in the first half of the 1980s.'[2]

No one then could have anticipated that Ronald Reagan would negotiate a treaty to eliminate US and Soviet medium-range missile arsenals and lay the foundations for the end of the Cold War by the time he left office. These successes arguably stand out as the greatest achievements of any US president since World War II. Reagan was clearly not the trigger-happy, bellicose, rigidly anti-communist conservative that his many critics, both at home and abroad, had thought him to be. Instead, he had lived up to his oft-expressed dictum of 'peace through strength'. Fearing that America was losing the Cold War in the 1970s, he had rebuilt its military power with the intent not of attacking the Soviet Union but of negotiating nuclear-arms reduction with it from a position of strength. Visceral anti-communist Reagan certainly was, but he had an even greater hatred of nuclear weapons as a threat to mankind.

This was not the first time Reagan had confounded expectations about him. He had been doing so throughout a long life that spanned the twentieth century. Reagan had risen from modest circumstances in the small-town Midwest to become a radio star and then a film star amid the Great Depression of the 1930s. When his movie career hit the skids, he found resurrection in the new medium of television and as corporate spokesman for General Electric in the 1950s. Once a fervently liberal Democrat, he eventually became a strongly conservative Republican. At age 55, he embarked on another career by winning the governorship of California in his first ever run for office, defeating a two-term incumbent in what was thought to be a safe Democratic state. In office, he steered a largely pragmatic course in policy making while giving voice to anti-government ideas that established him as the nation's foremost conservative by the end of the 1960s. In defiance of conventional belief that a right-winger could not win the White House, he nearly wrested the Republican presidential nomination from incumbent Gerald Ford in 1976 and four years later defeated incumbent Democrat Jimmy Carter to become America's 40th president. For many pundits, Reagan's election victory was a revolutionary event that signalled the end of the New Deal political order established by Franklin D. Roosevelt in the 1930s. The transformative significance of his presidency turned out to be considerable but did not extend to sweeping away the foundations of the liberal state. To the disappointment of conservative ideologues, Reagan was too much of a realist to waste political capital fighting battles he could not win. There were occasions, however, when his sense of reality failed him, most notably in directing the illegal Iran–Contra operations that precipitated the greatest crisis of his presidency.

Ronald Reagan was one of a small band of leaders across the ages who changed the course of history through their remarkable qualities of vision, will, and character. It was not simply the case that he was in the right place at the right time. More fundamentally, he demonstrated the capacity to alter the course of affairs both in the United States and on the world stage in ways that no one else likely could have. It is impossible to understand what made America's 40th president so significant simply through examination of his White House tenure. Reagan would entitle his presidential memoir *An American Life* to signal that his rise from humble origins to national leadership validated his country's unique promise as the land of freedom and opportunity. Looked at somewhat differently, Reagan's life journey had put him at the heart of critically important developments in America's twentieth-century history. This odyssey moulded his character, values, and vision, which in turn helped him to shape America's history in the 1980s and beyond.

No American president could boast a curriculum vitae anywhere near as varied as Reagan's. The optimism, religiosity, and individualistic values that he was inculcated with as a child of the early twentieth-century small-town Midwest made him appear typical of what so many Americans thought of themselves. Careers in three forms of media during their golden ages – radio in the mid-1930s, movies from the late 1930s to the mid-1950s, and television from the mid-1950s to the mid-1960s – gave him unparalleled tuition in the political arts of communication, image-making, and performance. An avowed liberal when the New Deal order was at its peak in the 1930s and 1940s, he journeyed rightward within the emergent conservative movement of the 1950s and early

1960s in support of anti-statism at home and more assertive anti-communism abroad. When Reagan was elected governor of California, the state was in the forefront of the regional shift of economic, political, and demographic primacy from the old industrial heartland of the north-east to the new Sunbelt of the south-west and south. Finally, when American liberalism ran out of steam in the 1970s, he emerged as the only figure capable of uniting conservative and moderate voters into a winning coalition in the presidential election of 1980.

The first part of this biography deals with the making of the pre-presidential Ronald Reagan. The second part deals with his presidency and its significance. Each component of his life contributed in equal measure to making Reagan a great American icon. The 'Reagan era' has become synonymous with the 1980s, but understanding why this was so requires exploration of the making of Ronald Reagan prior to this momentous decade. More often than not, biographers develop a more positive view of their subject as a consequence of engaging in detailed study of a life. Accordingly, this volume comes to conclusions that once would have surprised the author, who shared the conventional left-liberal suspicion of Reagan's competence and conservatism in the 1980s. While acknowledging his achievements and unquestioned significance, it also pays due attention to his shortcomings. The Reagan this biography portrays is complex rather than one-dimensional; someone who benefited from having a variety of careers before entering politics; a deep thinker if not an original one; a conservative but also a pragmatist; a committed anti-communist who was dedicated to ridding the world of nuclear weapons; a passionate advocate of freedom who aligned the United States with repressive regimes for Cold War advantage in Latin America, Africa, and Asia; and an eternal optimist about his country's future who could not empathize with disadvantaged groups needing the assistance of government to get by in 1980s America.

ACKNOWLEDGEMENTS

I have received a great deal of assistance in researching and writing this biography. I should begin by thanking Joanna Godfrey at I.B.Tauris for commissioning the book, helping shape my vision for it, and supporting me at all stages of the project. It would have been impossible to undertake the study without help from archival staff at the Ronald Reagan Presidential Library in Simi Valley, California. The Warner Bros. Archive, held by the University of Southern California, and the Margaret Herrick Library of the Academy of Motion Picture Arts and Sciences provided vital detail on Reagan's Hollywood career. The Hoover Institution in Stanford University and the Richard Nixon Presidential Library furnished me with valuable documents. I am also grateful to Godfrey Hodgson for allowing me access to his papers at the Rothermere American Institute, University of Oxford.

Over many years I have benefited from discussing Ronald Reagan and his presidency with colleagues on both sides of the Atlantic too numerous to name, but they have my heartfelt thanks. It is also a pleasure to record how much I have learned about Reagan by teaching and talking with students about him over the last 40 years or so at City of London Polytechnic/London Guildhall University, the University of London School of Advanced Study, and University College London. I have been very fortunate that my latter years in the academy have been spent at UCL, where the Institute of the Americas xvi *Reagan*

and the History Department offer wonderful support and collegiality for the study of the Americas.

Finally, and most importantly, my family has kept me going in this venture. My grown-up children, Humphrey and Eleanor, managed to escape the full brunt of my Reagan obsession, but reminded me at times of flagging endeavour that there are other things in life. Above all, without daily support in ways too numerous to mention from my wife, Theresa, I can honestly say that the project would never have made it to completion.

ONE

Young Dutch

onald Wilson Reagan, America's 40th president, spent his youth in the small-town milieu of early twentieth-century Illinois. The second son of Jack and Nelle Reagan, he was born on 6 February 1911 in their rented first-floor apartment on Main Street in Tampico (population 849), located some 110 miles west of Chicago. With the new arrival weighing in at ten pounds, the delivery proved difficult and could have been life-threatening for mother and child but for the belated arrival of the local physician, who promptly advised the parents not to have further children. On first sight of the screaming baby, his father remarked, 'For such a little bit of a fat Dutchman, he makes a hell of a lot of noise, doesn't he?' These words were the basis for Ronald's nickname in youth. Thinking his actual name – and the diminutive 'Ronnie' that his mother favoured – insufficiently masculine, the boy wanted everyone to call him 'Dutch' as he grew up.[1]

The formative influences of family, Church, and community provided the lodestar for Ronald Reagan's odyssey from the small-town Midwest to the White House. His paternal forebears were the O'Regans, an impoverished potato-farming family in Doolis, County Tipperary, Ireland. He knew very little of this ancestry until the Irish government provided a family tree to mark his presidential visit in 1984. Among the highlights of that trip was seeing the handwritten record of great-grandfather Michael's baptism at age three days in 1829.[2] The bright and ambitious Michael eloped to London with Catherine

Mulcahy in October 1852. At the nuptials, he signed the marriage register as Reagan, its anglicized form forever more. Michael emigrated with his wife and three children to the United States via Canada in 1856. Taking advantage of the Homestead Act, he settled on undeveloped acreage in Carroll County, Illinois, working the land for four years to make it his own. His second son, John Michael (born 1854), helped on the farm before branching out to work in a grain elevator in nearby Fulton in 1873 and then claiming his own homestead four years later. Marriage to Jenny Cusick in 1878 produced three children. The youngest, born in 1883, was Jack (formally John Edward), Dutch's father. The American Dream did not work out for John Sr. Unable to make a go of the farm after a decade of toil, he resumed employment at the grain elevator, but a hard life took its toll. Jack's parents died of tuberculosis within six days of each other in 1889. He would keep this sad history from his own sons. Not until he was president did Ronald Reagan learn that some of his forebears were buried in a Fulton cemetery. When a local citizen finally informed him of this in 1986, he funded repairs to their dilapidated graves and family marker.[3]

Too young to work on his uncle's nearby farm like his siblings, the orphaned Jack was packed off to live with his aunt and her husband, a childless couple residing just over the Iowa border in Bennett. Growing up in a strict household and shown little affection, he became a dreamer, a prankster, and a tearaway who quit school at 12. In 1899, he fled back to Fulton, where charm, good looks, and the gift of the gab made him a success as a shoe salesman in a local emporium.[4] After marrying Nelle Clyde Wilson on 8 November 1904, Jack moved up in the world to become senior salesman in the clothing and shoe department of H. C. Pitney's General Store in nearby Tampico in early 1906. This would be the Reagans' home town for over eight years. Their first son, Neil – nicknamed 'Moon' because he was bulky and full-faced – was born in September 1908. When Dutch was not yet four, Jack's yearning to make something of himself launched the family into a series of job-related relocations that would take in five different places in northern Illinois within the space of six years. According to his younger son, his singular ambition was 'to own a shoe store… not an ordinary shoe shop, but the best, with the largest inventory in Illinois, outside Chicago'.[5]

Jack's primary motivation was to get people to look up to him rather than to become rich. Despite outward bravado, what likely drove him was a need for a sense of self-worth that reflected an unsettled and ultimately loveless upbring-ing. He first moved his family to Chicago in January 1915 to take a position as shoe salesman in the giant uptown Fair Store. Just over a year later, he headed for a new post in Galesburg that lasted till March 1918, when he moved on to nearby Monmouth. H. C. Pitney's offer of the manager's position in his gen-eral store brought Jack back to Tampico in August 1919, but the opportunity was short-lived. Pitney sold up a year later when the postwar collapse of farm commodity prices dented Corn Belt prosperity. As compensation, Jack was made manager of Pitney's new Fashion Boot shop in Dixon and promised a half-share of the business funded from sales commissions.[6]

Located on the Rock River, Dixon was larger (population 8,191) and more prosperous than Tampico. It was where Jack seemingly found his footwear Shangri-La. Talking up a Dr. Scholl's correspondence-course diploma, he advertised himself as 'a graduate practipedist [who] understands all foot troubles' and the possessor of X-ray equipment to match shoes with bone structure. Unfortunately for Jack, most Dixonites did not spend lavishly on footwear, preferring to rely on a cobbler to effect multiple repairs on the two pairs they habitually owned – one for work, one for dress. The Reagans had initially rented a roomy house on Hennepin Avenue (the restored version can now be visited as the future president's boyhood home), a middle-class south-side street. With his shop not the expected success, Jack moved the family to a smaller place on the north side in 1923, the first of four downward moves on the rental ladder. Heading in the same direction even faster, Fashion Boot ceased operations because of poor sales before the decade ended. By mid-1929 Jack was working for another Dixon shoe store; the next year he was a travelling shoe salesman, and in 1931 he was managing what his younger son called a 'hole-in-the-wall' shoe store in Springfield, Illinois, from which he received his notice on Christmas Eve.[7]

Jack's unsuccessful efforts to make something of himself meant that his family was almost perpetually hard up. Criticized for hostility to the poor as president, the adult Reagan would respond in self-defence, 'I was raised in poverty.'[8] The Reagans never owned their home, frequently found it difficult to make ends meet, and could afford only the cheapest cuts of meat. Until well into his teens, Dutch wore hand-me-down clothes that his older brother had outgrown. He later claimed never to have thought of his family as poor, not least because plenty of other townspeople were no better off. Such paeans to the fortitude of common folk in a pre-welfare age revealed a lack of understanding of what real poverty was in the 1920s. In its grip were southern sharecroppers – black and white – migrant workers, many female-headed families, sweatshop workers, and low-income senior citizens trying to get by without pensions and health-care protection. However tight money was for the Reagans, they were far from being impoverished in the manner of these groups.

Jack's history of falling short of his career ambitions owed much to alcohol dependency. His boozing may have had roots in his genes – his Irish forebears were prodigious drinkers and older brother William was certified insane with *delirium tremens* in 1919. Neither an abusive alcoholic nor a daily drunk, Jack was hard-working in dry periods but went on week-long benders once or twice a year. The bottle cost him his job in Chicago (where he was also arrested for public drunkenness), in Galesburg, and in Monmouth. In Dutch's recollection, his father's tendency to fall off the wagon at holiday time meant 'I was always torn between looking forward to Christmas and dreading it.'[9]

As soon as they were old enough to understand, Nelle explained to the children that Jack's drinking was a sickness rather than a moral failing. Dutch did not have to confront it directly until aged 11. One night in early 1922 he came home to find Jack passed out drunk on the front porch, 'arms spread out as if he were crucified – as indeed he was'. With no one else around, the still scrawny boy dragged his father indoors and put him to bed. The vivid memory of this episode stayed with him into old age. The adult Dutch would recall the experience as the 'first moment of accepting responsibility' that was an essential part of growing up.[10] The teenage Dutch always dreaded the social embarrassment of his father's next bout of public drunkenness, which would be widely known in Prohibition-era Dixon, but Nelle's teaching about the disease helped him endure the stigma. 'I always loved and always managed to maintain respect for Jack,' he would later write.[11] However, the self-absorption characteristic of alcoholics meant that the Reagan boys could not rely on Jack to take much interest in their youthful development. As compensation, Dutch found surrogate fathers to advise him about life's journey. The habit of relying on the counsel of older men whom he admired stayed with him far into adult life.

Some analysts regard Jack's alcoholism as the predominant source of the behaviour that his son reputedly displayed in adulthood – notably emotional reserve, retreat into a comforting world of make-believe, avoidance of conflict with those in his orbit, and craving for applause. One political psychologist went so far as to claim that it 'was a powerful and defining reality that Ronald Reagan was never fully able to surmount, not even as president of the United States'.[12] Contrary to such claims, Reagan displayed a pragmatic understanding of political reality as both governor and president, was resilient in pursuit of his core goals, and was prepared to risk unpopularity for doing what he considered right. Arguably, the negative influence of an alcoholic parent was most apparent in the adult Reagan's wariness about forming close relationships: 'I've been inclined to hold back a little of myself, reserving it for myself,' he admitted.[13] This caused pain for his children and disappointed friends wanting greater intimacy. 'There's a wall around him,' second wife Nancy commented. 'He lets me come closer than anyone else, but there are times when even I feel that barrier.'[14] It is also likely that the self-discipline, strong sense of responsibility, and competitiveness that Dutch manifested in his youth and adulthood reflected a determination to be different from Jack.

There were positive elements in Jack's influence, however. Reagan's trade-mark use of anecdotes as a politician owed much to his father, 'the best raconteur I ever heard'.[15] His celebrated humour, both in public and private, was another paternal legacy. Without doubt, he inherited silver-tongued skills to make bigger sales than his father ever dreamed of. Jack's detestation of bigotry, resulting from experience of anti-Catholicism, also rubbed off on his son. 'Among the things he passed on to me,' Reagan later wrote, 'was the belief that all men and [...] women are created equal and that individuals determine their own destiny [...] largely [through] their own ambition and hard work.'[16] Both his memoirs recounted (albeit with some differences of detail) one particular incident as evidence of his family's progressive racial views. During his undergraduate days at Eureka College, Reagan was part of a football squad that included two African Americans, who were refused hotel accommodation on one occasion when the team was playing away to another Illinois college in Elmhurst. In a gesture of solidarity, Reagan took the pair back to Dixon, where they were made welcome guests at his home. Believing himself free from racial prejudice, accusations to the contrary during his political career were guaranteed to raise his hackles more than anything else.[17]

Dutch grew up without bigotry but his awareness of racism was confined to the few examples he encountered rather than the everyday reality of it. Dixon's 12 African American families had to endure discrimination that was an unspoken and therefore unacknowledged part of life in virtually all-white Midwestern communities. Dutch was blithely unaware of what was all around him because he did not personally see African Americans as inferior. This was why he substituted the nation's ignorance for his own in remarking during the 1980 presidential debate with Jimmy Carter that America 'didn't even know it had a racial problem' when he was young. As one biographer concluded, '[A] youth unaware of evil must also be unaware of evil's effects.'[18] Significantly, the adult Dutch was much more willing to take a stand against anti-Semitism than to speak out about discrimination against African Americans. During World War II, he resigned from Lakeside Country Club in North Hollywood over its refusal to admit Jews and later joined the Hillcrest Club, the favoured haunt of Hollywood's Jews. The fact that African Americans were denied membership of both establishments did not register with him.[19]

Whatever Jack's contrary influences, far more important in the making of Dutch was his mother, born Nelle Clyde Wilson on a farm in North Clyde, Illinois, on 24 July 1883. Her paternal forebears, the Wilsons and the Blues, had left Scotland for Canada in the 1830s but fled to the United States following involvement in an abortive rebellion against Ontario's governing oligarchy. In 1839 the two families staked land claims in Whiteside County, northern Illinois, adjacent to Carroll, where the Reagans later settled. They were united by the marriage of John Wilson and Jane Blue in November 1841. Nelle was the youngest of seven children born to the Wilsons' youngest son Thomas and Mary Anne Elsey, an Englishwoman who had come to America as a 16-year-old orphan to work as a domestic. The marriage was not a happy one. Thomas absconded to Chicago in 1890, returning only at the behest of his dying mother four years later.[20]

Despite this, Nelle grew up in a loving extended family that practised temperance, found its primary satisfaction in weekly church attendance and regular Scripture reading, and allowed her to enjoy simple pleasures. A child of the farm who yearned for the small city, she found work as a seamstress in Fulton at age 19. In reaction to the unhappiness of her own parents, she was determined to marry for love. The beguiling Jack Reagan, with his dark

Irish good looks, would fulfil this need for the small-statured, auburn-haired, blue-eyed Nelle, who set her cap at him despite parental concern about his drinking. Her romantic side also found expression in naming her second son after William Ronald Wilson, an ancestor she mistakenly believed to have won the hand of a high-born lady who was consequently disowned by her family.[21]

Passionate about her sons getting the good education she never had, Nelle taught Dutch to read at the remarkably early age of five, thereby developing his capacity to memorize words quickly – to his later benefit in broadcasting, acting, and politics. Blessed with an engaging voice, she also trained her sons in the art of elocution, and her related enthusiasm for amateur dramatics implanted the performing bug in both of them. A competitive desire to keep up with Moon overcame Dutch's initial shyness about appearing on stage. In May 1920, he made his debut as a nine-year-old with a reading, 'About Mother', earning hearty applause that was music to his ears. 'I didn't know it then,' he later remarked, 'but, in a way, when I walked off the stage that night, my life had changed.'[22]

Nelle's most important influence was instilling in Dutch his characteristic optimism. From her he learned 'how to have dreams and believe I could make them come true'. As an adult he would display what political columnist George Will called 'a talent for happiness'.[23] According to behavioural research, how parents – especially the primary carer – explain adversity to their children influences their outlook on life. Mothers, in particular, incline their offspring towards optimism if they explain that setbacks are just temporary and pertain to specific issues rather than the inherent flaws of the child. Nelle delivered this in spades with her reassurances that everything happened for a purpose and every reverse contained the seeds of something better to come, so that in the end everything worked out for the best.[24] Another maternal legacy, Dutch's tendency to believe the best of people, was not always an advantage in politics. Nancy Reagan often felt it necessary to play the bad cop to ensure that White House subordinates were doing what her husband wanted. 'Sometimes it infuriates me, but that's how he is,' she remarked of his inherited trait of trusting everyone.[25]

Nelle's influence on Dutch intersected with that of the Disciples of Christ Church, into which she was inducted in the Tampico revival on Easter Sunday 1910. Even when things were tight at home, she would tithe to it what little the family could afford. Once settled in Dixon, she became a very active member of its First Church of Christ, serving as adult Sunday school teacher, missionary society leader, and choir director, among other things. A deeply spiritual person, she comforted sick neighbours with prayer, visited local sanatoriums, and conducted Bible readings on prison visits – her devotion to helping the incarcerated live better lives extended to accepting custody of those jailed for petty theft or drunkenness. Nelle was also the mainstay of dramas, entertainments, and recitations mounted for church audiences, with her dramatic readings being especially popular.[26]

Sharing his mother's piety, the young Dutch was an enthusiastic member of the Disciples community. Regular prayer was important to him in boyhood, remaining so for the rest of his life. As president, he made a serious point with humour when thanking a nun who had prayed for his re-election: 'I believe in intercessory prayer and know I have benefited from it. I have, of course, added my own prayers to the point that sometimes I wonder if the Lord doesn't say, "here he comes again."'[27] His early spirituality was primarily an emotional one. In historian Paul Kengor's assessment, he saw God as a 'rock of reliability', in contrast to his own father, and 'a permanent friend', to whom he could become close 'without fear of abandonment' when his family's frequent relocations made it impossible to form lasting associations.[28] Dutch had something of an epiphany as a five-year-old that foreshadowed the intellectual dimension his religiosity later acquired. In the attic of the family's rented house in Galesburg, he found a large encased collection of colourful birds' eggs and butterflies, which he would spend many happy hours examining. The experience, he later wrote, 'left me with a reverence for the handiwork of God that never left me'.[29]

The adult Reagan would call the Bible his favourite book, adjudging it 'the result of Divine inspiration' and believing in it absolutely. 'Inside its pages,' he asserted when president, 'lie all the answers to all the problems that man has ever known.'[30] As a boy, however, he was a voracious reader of adventure novels like *The Last of the Mohicans*, *The Count of Monte Cristo*, Zane Grey westerns, and Edgar Rice Burroughs tales about space explorer John Carter on Mars that engendered a lifelong fascination for science fiction. These stories could also be read as morality tales. In his mid-sixties Reagan reflected, '[A]s I look back I realize that my reading left an abiding belief in the triumph of good over evil.'[31] This was manifestly true of the book he read shortly after finding his father drunk on the porch.

That Printer of Udell's: A Story of the Middle West was a popular novel of Christian social commitment penned by Disciples minister Harold Bell Wright. It narrates the rise of Dick Falkner from poverty as a vagabond fleeing an abusive alcoholic father to find material improvement and spiritual fulfilment. He obtains gainful work as a printer in a small town, gets a night-school education, finds God through the Disciples, and develops a social-welfare plan to help other youngsters escape indigence. A commanding orator, Dick persuades wealthy citizens to endow a dormitory in return for its impoverished residents collecting and selling scrap wood to pay for their upkeep. Its success in saving the young from poverty and vice earns Dick election to Congress to do good deeds on a larger stage.[32] The themes of practical Christianity, the power of oratory, right triumphing over wrong, and communal problem-solving, all set in a milieu so familiar to him, had an immense impact on Dutch. When president, he would write to Harold Bell Wright's daughter-in-law that Dick Falkner became his role model: 'He set me on a course I've tried to follow even unto this day. I shall always be grateful.' Some 60 years earlier he had told Nelle, 'I want to be like that man.' This ambition inspired him to declare his faith and be baptized.[33]

The Disciples forbade parents from forcing the sacraments on children. In their credo, baptismal immersion had to be a personal commitment to the way of Christ. It signified that the old life was buried, the new life was born, and sins were forgiven. The 11-year-old Dutch underwent baptism at the Dixon Disciples church on 21 June 1922. Henceforth, he believed fervently in the divinity of Jesus as 'the promised Messiah, the Son of God come to earth to offer salvation for all mankind'.[34] Seeking to woo evangelical voters in the 1980 presidential election, Reagan described his baptism as a born-again experience that invited Christ into his life. When asked by prominent televangelist James Robison whether he truly knew the Saviour, he responded, 'Jesus is more real to me than my own mother.'[35]

Whether the young Dutch would have spoken similarly is doubtful, but his spiritual commitment following baptism was very real. As well as regular church attendance, he went to summertime big-tent meetings with his mother to hear religious lectures and Bible readings. At age 15, he began teaching Sunday school for young boys, many of whom would recall his fine speaking voice and capacity to make the Bible seem personally relevant. Beyond matters spiritual, Church of Christ doctrine strengthened Dutch's understanding of the importance of education, personal responsibility, and private charity. It also endowed him with an optimistic belief in human progress. Of particular importance to his political development, he absorbed the Disciples' conviction that America was a special place with a divinely ordained mission to serve as a beacon of freedom in the world.[36] When California governor, Reagan wrote to his old pastor and first surrogate father, Ben Cleaver, saying that his formative Christian beliefs still helped him meet the challenges of office. 'One thing I do know – all the hours I spent in the old church in Dixon [...] and all of Nelle's faith,' he declared, 'have come together in a kind of inheritance without which I'd be lost and helpless.'[37]

The final element in the trinity of influences that shaped Ronald Reagan was the small-town Midwest where he grew up. This was a milieu imbued with a mythical sense of being the most American part of the United States. Its notions of uber-authenticity helped to instil in Dutch a particular reverence for Independence Day, whose celebration he anticipated as eagerly as Christmas. As president, he recalled, 'To one who was born and grew up in the small towns of the Midwest there is a special kind of nostalgia about the 4th of July.'[38] For Dutch, these places also offered communal solidarity, a sense of security, and dependable rhythms of life. 'Almost everybody knew one another,' he later remarked, '[so] they tended to care about each other.'[39] His was a boyhood largely untouched by the class, racial, and ethnic divisions characteristic of bigger cities. After some years of moving from town to town, the Reagans put down roots in Dixon in 1920. Despite getting into playground scraps with new schoolmates who hurled insults at his father's Catholicism, Dutch soon gained acceptance and felt at home there. 'It was a good life,' he later wrote. 'I never have asked for anything more, then or now.'[40]

Some two years after his baptism in Dixon, Dutch had a different kind of revelation, one that literally changed his view of the world. Severe myopia had long made the school blackboard a blur but good grades earned through prodigious memory hid the condition from teachers. Unable to match Moon in reading roadside advertising billboards while on a Sunday-afternoon family drive in the summer of 1924, Dutch kidded around by putting on his mother's spectacles to view them. The world instantly became clear and colourful rather than full of indistinct blobs. Nelle immediately had him fitted out with 'huge black-rimmed spectacles' that he hated wearing in public, an aversion that proved lifelong.[41] Nevertheless the new glasses enhanced enjoyment of his two favourite pastimes – reading and seeing movies, particularly westerns, at Saturday matinees.

There were other changes for the teenage Dutch as he matured physically. Sport now competed with the Dixon Church for his time and energy. Myopia limited his success in team games requiring good hand–eye coordination like baseball and basketball. Even as a scrawny, short-sighted child, however, he loved the close-quarter physicality of football. Never a star player, his dogged-ness finally earned him a starting place on the Dixon High School team in the 1927–8 season, by which time he had reached his adult height of six foot. Always on the bench when a freshman at Eureka College, he developed into a solid performer as starting guard for the next three years. Lack of a winning season did not dim passion for a sport that he considered 'a matter of life or death'. The athletic pursuit in which Dutch truly excelled was swimming, for which his physique was perfect and 20/20 vision was not a requirement. A strong crawl stroke earned him a string of victories both at high school and college meets. Swimming also brought him steady employment as a lifeguard at Lowell Park, three miles north of Dixon, for seven consecutive summer vacations from 1926 until 1932.

Comprising 320 acres of wooded hills running down to a beach on one of the loveliest stretches of the Rock River, the municipally owned Lowell Park was a popular swimming spot, but treacherous currents made the river dangerous. Needing safety improvements after a spate of drownings, the beach concession-aires decided to hire a lifeguard. Dutch got the job that was better suited to his talents and qualifications – he had recently completed a life-saving course at the Dixon YMCA – than his previous summer employment as a construction worker. The pay was $15 a week in his first five years (the local average was around $22 in 1926), rising to $18, and eventually $20, plus all the hamburgers and root beers he wanted for free. Private swimming lessons for the children of affluent vacationers staying at the park's hotel provided a useful stream of supplementary income. On call for at least 12 hours, seven days a week, Dutch began his shift by helping pick up food supplies and then breaking a 300-pound block of ice for putting in coolers. He sometimes had 1,000 bathers or more to watch over, helped by a temporary assistant on public holidays, and made 77 rescues without a single drowning in seven years of duty.[42] Another was notched up some 40 years later – in June 1969 Governor Reagan dived fully clothed to rescue a seven-year-old black girl who had got into difficulties in the swimming pool at his Sacramento house where a party for staff families was being held. 'I guess it's just an old instinct that remains,' he told the press when the story got out.[43]

An important stage in Dutch's transition from youth to manhood, lifeguarding taught him the discipline of work, the rewards of public service, and the benefit of saving his pay. The formerly shy youth liked the limelight of being on the lifeguard stand that was 'like a stage. Everyone had to look at me.'[44] Often front-page news in the *Dixon Daily Telegraph*, his rescues turned him into a local hero. Needing to decide when a swimmer was in difficulty, he learned to rely on his own judgement and not to expect gratitude since most of those he helped would deny having been in danger.[45] Perhaps most importantly for the teenage Dutch, his new job made him attractive to the opposite sex for the first time.

An iconic 1927 photograph shows the athletic, willowy, and good-looking Dutch in his lifeguard uniform. Among the girls flocking round him at the beach was a high-school classmate on whom he had long cast yearning eyes without receiving any attention in return. Margaret 'Mugs' Cleaver was the clever, witty, and attractive daughter of Dixon's Disciples of Christ minister. As they got to know each other better during Lowell Park summers, Dutch's crush grew into something stronger. Despite having other boyfriends, Mugs in turn grew increasingly fond of the one-girl guy. By the middle of their senior year at North Dixon High, they had an exclusive relationship and talked of being in love. Jack's drinking, which Dutch tried to keep secret from his sweetheart, nearly destroyed the budding romance. On learning of it, the strait-laced Mugs thought of breaking things off but decided she did not want to lose Dutch. Considering them perfect examples of Christian youth, Disciples Church members assumed that the two would eventually become husband and wife.[46]

Life looked very good to Dutch during his last year of high school. He had found his first love, become a local celebrity, made it onto the varsity football team, and been elected senior class president. A blossoming acting talent made him both star and president of the Dramatic Club. Another father figure, drama coach B. J. Fraser, later characterized him as academically average but lifted out of the ordinary by extra-curricular activities that taught 'a lot of lessons about people, about what they want, what they think about life, the problems they run into'.[47] The next step for Dutch was to become one of the 2 per cent of high-school graduates nationwide who went on to study for a college degree in 1928. His sights were firmly set on Eureka College, where Mugs was also headed. Small wonder that the motto entered under his photograph in the class yearbook read: 'Life is just one grand sweet song, so start the music,' words that came from a self-authored poem.[48]

The only blip on Dutch's horizon was whether he could afford college. The $400 saved from vacation jobs would not cover freshman-year expenses. Setting off with Mugs in her coupé to make the 95-mile journey south to Eureka in early August, Dutch wondered if he would be going home alone next day on the Greyhound bus. Thanks to his reputation as a star swimmer, financial salvation was at hand. Athletics director Ralph 'Mac' McKinzie, soon to become another father figure, awarded Dutch a $90 half-scholarship. A dishwashing job at his Tau Kappa Epsilon fraternity house enabled him to pay for meals. A meagre sum of $35 had to cover other expenses for two semesters but straitened circumstances did not make him unique. Although the Wall Street Crash was still a year away, Corn Belt farmers and the Illinois small towns that depended on their prosperity were already in trouble owing to another sharp fall in commodity prices because of rural overproduction. As a result, Eureka's enrolment fell some one-third short of its recent 250 peak because of students not taking up places or dropping out to help hard-pressed families.[49]

The college was in the grip of crisis when Dutch arrived. Founded by anti-slavery Disciples in 1855 to train students for the Church of Christ ministry and teaching, Eureka was by now a liberal-arts institution. Putting its belief in the equality of everyone before God into practice, it was only the third college in America to admit female students on a par with males and there was no bar on admitting African Americans – Willie Sue Smith Stewart was the last survivor of Reagan's graduating class until her death in August 2011.[50] Eureka's financial wellbeing remained dependent on contributions from former students and Disciples congregations in Illinois, but donations declined alongside the rural economy. The fee shortfall from smaller enrolments and the need to excuse full payment by students like Dutch made things worse. Accordingly, college president Bert Wilson won trustee support for a solvency plan to save money by eliminating some courses and laying off faculty. A student strike to protest this retrenchment gave Dutch his first experience of political activism.

In his first memoir, published as a prelude to his first run for political office, Reagan allocated himself a leading role in a strike he depicted as a battle to safeguard Eureka's academic ideals against the college president's misman-agement. His account turned it into a morality tale that ended with Wilson's defeat and resignation. Reagan's narrative featured a rousing speech that he delivered in support of the strike motion to students gathered at the college chapel in the early hours of 28 November. In his recollection, its invocation of collective action in a just cause had such a moving effect on the audience that 'I could have had them riding through "every Middlesex village and farm" – without horses yet.' This reference to Henry Wadsworth Longfellow's poem about Paul Revere's ride to warn that the British were coming suggested that the speech was as much 'heady wine' for Reagan as his listeners in its combina-tion of selling skills and evangelism learned from Jack and Nelle respectively. He later remarked, 'Giving that speech – my first – was as exciting as any I ever gave.' The earliest manifestation of his greatness as a political orator it may have been, but the address did not pave the way for student victory as his memoir suggested. Though Wilson quit, his ouster was largely due to the manoeuvring of faculty opposed to him. This did not stop the trustees imple-menting his retrenchment plan in full. Reagan's faulty memory was a case of putting himself at the centre of an earlier battle between right and wrong just as he was gearing up for an election campaign to save California from the mismanagement of Governor Pat Brown.[51]

As well as being a cash-strapped academic backwater, Eureka was run in accordance with a stern moral code that held the 'Roaring Twenties' at bay. Illicit drinking, flapper styles, and petting parties, common on other campuses, were alien to it. Not wanting to appear strait-laced, the abstemious Dutch once got dead drunk on Prohibition alcohol while visiting friends off-campus in the spring of 1930. The resultant 'sense of helplessness' made him swear off booze for the rest of his college days.[52] Nevertheless, there was plenty of opportunity for more innocent fun that made Eureka life very enjoyable for the student body. The college held a special place in Dutch's heart long after he left, so much so that he delivered commencement addresses there in 1957, 1982, and 1992. Visiting during the final stages of the 1980 presidential campaign, he told students that they were better off at this small college than at the big, well-endowed universities 'because you will have memories, you will have friendships that are impossible on those great campuses and that are just peculiar to this place'.[53]

Significantly, Eureka's most famous alumnus never waxed lyrical about what it had taught him academically, even in his economics major. Half a century later, *Wall Street Journal* editorialist Jude Wanniski, the self-appointed proselytizer of supply-side economics, claimed that Ronald Reagan had been an easy mark for conversion as 'the only political leader on this entire planet who has a degree in economics from Eureka College before Keynesian economics was taught'. In fact, Dutch's economics teacher, Archibald Gray, emphasized the need for social justice in the distribution of wealth in capitalist society. Unsurprisingly, therefore, Reagan's post-presidential memoir specifically discounted the influence of his undergraduate studies on his conservative economic ideas, attributing them more to his life experience. He acknowledged getting a 'solid' liberal-arts education at Eureka, but more tellingly admitted to having been 'accused of majoring in extra-curricular activities'.[54]

During his four years at college, Dutch was a very big man on a very small campus. In addition to making the football starting team, he starred for and eventually coached the swimming team, won varsity letters for track, and was basketball team cheerleader. Outside the sports arena, he was president of the Boosters Club, editor of the student yearbook, a reporter for the *Pegasus* student newspaper, a member of the student senate, senior class president, and treasurer of the drama society. He won an acting award when Eureka came second in a nationally renowned college competition for one-act plays at Northwestern University in his senior year. So impressed was the host department with Dutch's performance in Edna St Vincent Millay's *Aria da Capo* that its head advised him to consider an acting career.[55]

Dutch was already thinking on these lines but had told no one because his prospects of breaking into show business amid the Depression appeared so bleak. The seeds of this ambition had been planted when he went with Mugs and her parents to see a touring company perform British playwright R. C.

Sherriff's anti-war drama, *Journey's End*, in Rockford, Illinois, in the summer of 1929. His first taste of professionally performed drama was a profoundly moving experience because he identified wholeheartedly with the main character, the war-weary Captain Stanhope. As he recalled:

> For two and a half hours I was in that dugout on the Western front –
> but in some strange way, I was also on stage. More than anything in
> life I wanted to speak his lines [...] If I had only realized it, nature was
> trying to tell me something – namely, that my heart is a ham loaf.[56]

Grades that were mostly bare passes proved sufficient for Dutch to graduate with honours. A photographic memory and pre-test cramming got him through a college not known for tough academic standards. His aversion to serious study exasperated Mugs Cleaver, a top-honours graduate. Around campus, she was known as 'Young Miss Brains', her beau as 'Mr Congeniality'. Mugs wrongly thought Dutch lacking in ambition, adventure, and curiosity. When a rising Hollywood star, he claimed to have deliberately underperformed as a student for fear of falling into a default career as athletics director at a small school like Eureka. 'To get a [college] coach's job,' he explained, 'you naturally had to have certain scholastic standing, so I was careful not to get it... I didn't want to take the chance of weakening when the time came.'[57] True or not, Dutch clearly considered his extra-curricular activities a better foundation than academic achievement for his future prospects. He may not have left Eureka with firm ideas about what job he wanted, but the skills honed on this small campus would serve him for the rest of his life. Chief among them were a talent for acting, a capacity for public speaking, and a projection of confidence that emanated from self-belief.

Nevertheless, even the optimistic Dutch found it hard to visualize good days ahead when graduating on 7 June 1932 with the Great Depression in full swing. Seeking to instil some sense of hope in a departing cohort shrunk to 45 by economic adversity, Eureka president Clyde Lyon exhorted his former charges not to let the future 'bully [you] into non-achievement'.[58] By then unemployment was around 23 per cent of the labour force, with more than 12 million people out of work – compared with respective figures of 3.5 per cent and 1.5 million people in 1929. Reduced to living in a rented apartment in Dixon, the Reagan family was sinking into the economic mire. As the only steady breadwinner, Nelle made $14 a week as a sales clerk and seamstress at a local store. Dutch still had the lifeguard job for the summer but would be unemployed when that ended. Just as things looked their worst, he began the upward trajectory of a career that would 'take me a long way from Dixon and fulfil all my dreams, and then some'.[59]

TWO

Rising Star

S hortly after graduation, Dutch told some Eureka friends, 'If I'm not making five thousand a year when I'm five years out of college, I'll consider these four years here wasted.' This was false bravado in bleak times, but he more than made good on that 'desperation shot', initially as a radio broadcaster and then as a movie star.[1] Attributing his early success to a kindly fate, Reagan remarked in 1980, 'When I look back now and think how easily I could have turned in different directions, I have to believe in that and I say a little prayer of thanks every night.'[2] Perhaps his rapid rise was providential but in more worldly terms it owed something to luck, perseverance, and talent in ascending order of significance.

His first job interview after graduation, for a position paying $12.50 weekly in the sporting-goods department of Dixon's new Montgomery Ward store, was unsuccessful. Thereafter, Dutch sought career guidance from Kansas City businessman Sid Altschuler, whose daughters he had taught to swim during summer visits to Lowell Park. The advice was to get into an industry that was doing well despite the Depression. Radio fitted the bill now that wireless sets were to be found in most homes. Dutch loved the play-by-play baseball and football broadcasts pioneered by the likes of Tommy Cowan and Quin Ryan. Getting an announcer's job that accommodated his passion for sport and show-business aspirations held considerable appeal. Thinking this a good choice, Altschuler counselled:

> The important thing now [is] getting in, so start knocking on doors, tell
> anyone who'll listen that you believe you have a future in the business,
> and you'll take any kind of job, even sweeping floors, just to get in.[3]

As the Mecca of Midwestern radio, Chicago had most doors to knock. Armed only with optimism, Dutch hitchhiked to the Windy City one hot day in late September 1932, but no station would interview someone without broadcasting experience. At the end of a dispiriting week, a sympathetic NBC assistant advised trying smaller cities 'out [...] in the sticks'. Ready to grasp any straw, Dutch drove off one October day in the now rarely used family Oldsmobile to try his luck in Iowa. He hit the jackpot on the first stop in Davenport's World of Chiropractic station, better known as WOC.[4] Station manager Peter MacArthur, a Scot with a heart of gold beneath a gruff exterior, said he wasn't hiring, but on a kindly whim let the crestfallen job-seeker give an impromptu mock football broadcast. Having recounted lots of imaginary plays to amuse friends at Eureka, Dutch had no difficulty doing a commentary featuring his own game-saving block against Western Illinois. MacArthur was sufficiently impressed to give him a $5 fee plus the price of a return bus ticket from Dixon for a trial broadcast helping the station announcer at the next University of Iowa football game. Played on 22 October, the match that ended in a long-forgotten 22–6 Iowa loss to Minnesota has a place in history as Ronald Reagan's professional media debut. Despite his inexperience, Dutch gained in confidence as the game progressed, doing well enough to be retained for Iowa's remaining home fixtures at $10 per game with travel expenses.

The end of the football season meant renewed unemployment – but not for long. In early 1933, MacArthur telephoned with the offer of a staff announcer's position at WOC at a $100 monthly salary. From this, Dutch gave Nelle $20 for household costs and Moon $10 to help finance his studies at Eureka, where he had enrolled in 1929 after his cost-accountant job at the Dixon cement plant became a casualty of economic downturn.[5] Things nearly ended in tears, however. Within a month, the station owner fired the callow broadcaster over MacArthur's objections for inadvertently failing to give a programme sponsor a free plug on air. Dutch endured the further ignominy of training his replacement, a schoolteacher planning a career change. Luckily, the putative successor resumed his more secure occupation on learning that WOC employees could be dismissed for so small a slip. This necessitated Dutch's supposedly temporary rehiring, but his growing assurance as an announcer, helped by MacArthur's coaching, ended talk of finding another replacement.[6]

Dutch took to broadcasting like a duck to water. His voice, with its capacity to project warmth, sincerity, and enthusiasm, was ideal for radio, which forever remained his favourite medium for public communication, even in the television age. His one weakness as a vocal performer was soon put right. Though adept at ad-libbing, he came over as wooden when reading prepared text, particularly for commercials. Memorizing a script and repeating it out loud before delivery produced a natural-sounding broadcast, a technique later useful for politics. More immediately, the practised ability to sound spontaneous combined with natural qualities of voice put Dutch on the road to radio stardom.

In May 1933 WOC relocated operations to its Des Moines sister station WHO, whose recent receipt of a federal permit to operate one of only 15 50,000-watt clear channels in the entire country made it a key affiliate in the NBC national network. MacArthur appointed his protégé its designated sports announcer on $200 a month, recognition that he had become a popular draw in his short time at WOC. Within 12 months the 23-year-old Dutch was a celebrity throughout the Midwest as the regional voice of sport. He was soon earning $75 a week from radio while making additional income from speaking engagements, guest newspaper columns, and public-address work at sports events.[7]

Dutch's new duties encompassed outside broadcasts, a weekly sports commentary, interviewing all kinds of celebrities who passed through Des Moines, and, eventually, news announcing. Despite never having attended a major-league baseball game, he became best known for reconstructing Chicago Cubs matches from pitch-by-pitch telegraph accounts. His only training was a visit to the Wrigley Field stadium to be shown the ropes by NBC's Pat Flanagan, a master of reconstruction. Advised to act out games rather than just narrate them, Dutch found he could produce several minutes of exciting imagery from the briefest of wire lines about the on-field action. Listeners in radioland thought he was at the game in person rather than in a studio 400 miles away. This inventiveness reached a peak when the telegraph went dead for seven minutes during a Cubs game with the St Louis Cardinals. Dutch had the batter make a series of foul-offs that kept the game going without affecting the score.[8] Small wonder, therefore, that his radio career engendered a lifelong skill in manipulation without appearing inauthentic on the public stage. For him, there was never a contradiction between inventing and embellishing a story for dramatic or political purposes while exuding utter conviction in the truth of his words.

Back home, the Reagan family's economic position was also much improved. In March 1933, new Democratic president Franklin D. Roosevelt launched the New Deal programme to rescue an economy now at rock bottom. Since 1929, GDP had fallen by 30 per cent, farm income by 70 per cent, and investment by 87 per cent. Jack Reagan's reward for Democratic loyalty in habitually Republican Dixon was a patronage job distributing welfare assistance for the newly created Federal Emergency Relief Administration (FERA). A temporary transfer followed to the Civil Works Administration (CWA), established to get the nation through the winter of 1933–4 by employing 4 million people on low-capital, labour-intensive, shovel-ready projects. Responsible for getting local works certified by regional headquarters in Chicago, Jack once overcame its cost-based opposition to constructing a municipal airport hangar by suggesting use of Dixon's now defunct streetcar rails, removed by another CWA operation, to save on steel-girder expense. His canniness did not end there. Employment of men from the same family in the relief bureaucracy was frowned upon, but Jack got recently graduated Moon appointed as district representative of the Federal Reemployment Bureau.[9]

As far as Dutch was concerned, Roosevelt was his family's saviour in its darkest moment: 'I was a child of the Depression, a Democrat by upbringing, and very emotionally committed to FDR,' he told daughter Maureen in 1960.[10] People who knew him at WHO recalled his delight in imitating the president's Fireside Chats, his excitement when FDR visited Des Moines on 3 September 1936, and his encyclopaedic knowledge of political facts and figures when arguing with any Roosevelt critic – such as station news director and future Republican congressman H. R. Gross.[11]

Just how far this adulation of FDR translated into ideological commitment to liberalism in the 1930s is unclear. Dutch was sensitive to the economic problems of his family, others he knew in Dixon, and college friends – some of whom he put up in Des Moines on their travels looking for work. There is no persuasive evidence of burning concern about unemployment and poverty beyond the familiar, however. Coloured by a midlife turn to the right, his later memories of the Great Depression must be treated with caution, but they offer nothing to support the self-image of having been a 'near-hopeless hemophilic liberal'.[12] What he recalled most strongly were the 'drab, dreariness' of the times and the 'human warmth' that fostered togetherness in the face of adversity.[13] There was no word about the widespread economic misery that blighted millions of lives. Des Moines was literally on the edge of a human catastrophe seemingly erased from his memory. A combination of heat, drought, and dust storms in the summers of 1934–7 created the Dust Bowl that forced many thousands of farm families to quit the central plains. The purpose of FDR's visit to Des Moines, when Dutch glimpsed his hero for the only time in his life, was to attend the Western Drought conference called to deal with the crisis. When Dutch moved to southern California in the summer of 1937, the sense of being in a paradise of plenty – articulated in a series of articles written for the *Des Moines Sunday Register* – obliterated awareness that thousands of people lived in ramshackle temporary dwellings and relied on soup kitchens for daily nourishment in downtown Los Angeles.

In later life, Reagan's memory of his father's experience as a minor federal bureaucrat became a means to legitimize his own conservatism. In reality, Jack's days on FERA/CWA were probably the most fulfilling of his life because he found new purpose in helping others. One sign of this was that he got his drinking under control. What stuck more in his son's recall was his frustration with heartless red tape that hindered getting people onto work relief. Proud of what he was doing, Jack drove himself so hard that he suffered a heart attack in the summer of 1934. Requiring a lengthy convalescence, he could no longer undertake his government job – or any other – aged just 51. Consequently, Dutch began sending home a weekly $25 cheque that 'removed all [Jack's] economic problems for the first time in his life'.[14] Loyalty to family ranked among his best traits but seemingly prevented recognition that few sons were able to provide comparable assistance to unemployed fathers during the Great Depression.

To get its relief operations going as speedily as possible, the New Deal initially channelled relief through pre-existing state and local bodies. When Jack railed against bureaucratic obstructions, his animus focused on these agencies, not on national administrators. In 1935, the federalization of work relief under the Works Progress Administration standardized administrative procedures, but it meant the end of Moon's patronage job. Neil consequently set out for Des Moines in the hope of brotherly assistance to get work there. Coming up trumps, Dutch persuaded WHO to hire him on the strength of his football knowledge. Moon soon found himself transferred to the newly reopened WOC station in Davenport, where he became programme manager with responsibilities for marketing in 1936. Though never his brother's equal as a broadcaster, he was now launched on what became a successful career in producing and advertising.

The only cloud over Dutch's life was the 'dear John' letter from Margaret, breaking off their engagement agreement made on graduation from Eureka and returning the ring he had given her. Wanting to see something of the world before settling down, Mugs had set off with her sister in 1933 for an extended visit to France, where she fell in love with American consular official James Waddell Gordon Jr. The couple married in Dixon in June 1935. Dutch was devastated, 'not so much [...] because she no longer loved me, but because I no longer had anyone to love'.[15] If that was the case, there was no rush to find a replacement. Fortified by a repeat dose of maternal advice that things always happened for the best, the jilted suitor got on with life. For the next few years, he was never short of female company, but there was only one steady relationship, and that showed no real sign of turning into a long-term commitment.

Dutch enjoyed Des Moines from the moment he arrived. With a population of 142,000, it afforded unaccustomed anonymity to frequent local watering holes (where he imbibed modestly) and fashionable nightspots. The sudden improvement in his economic status did not make him a spendthrift. It became a standing joke among his wide circle of friends that the term 'Dutch treat' was invented just for him. Indulgence of his fascination for horses, stemming from his boyhood love of westerns, did not bust the budget. Aware of his sparing ways with money, a WHO colleague advised applying for a reserve commission in the 14th US Cavalry Regiment, stationed just outside Des Moines at Fort Dodge, as a way of learning to ride without the expense of owning a mount. Once enrolled on a two-year Army correspondence course in March 1935, Dutch could saddle up at the military post to his heart's content. After successfully completing his written assignments, he tricked his way through the eye test that was part of the physical examination by memorizing the letter chart. Dutch was appointed second lieutenant on 25 May 1937, but a change of workplace meant assignment to the 323rd Cavalry in Los Angeles.[16]

The thought of transferring his broadcasting celebrity into a cinematic one was never far from Dutch's thoughts. Only in Hollywood, not the theatre, could he earn more from acting than broadcasting. Interviewing stars who passed through Des Moines fuelled hope of becoming one of them. A visit to southern California whetted Dutch's appetite for its golden possibilities. Desperate to escape Iowa's record cold, he persuaded WHO to send him to cover the Chicago Cubs at 1936 spring training on Catalina Island, where he had a wonderful time hanging out with the players, swimming in the Pacific, and basking in an unseasonable heatwave.[17] The popularity of his radio reports earned a return visit in 1937 and the opportunity for entrée into the movie world.

The kind of luck that got Dutch into radio held good for his cinematic hopes. Des Moines native Joy Hodges, a successful big-band singer in Los Angeles, had hinted at Dutch's Hollywood potential during their WHO interview on one of her visits home. When Dutch looked her up on his return to California, she agreed to arrange an interview with the Bill Meiklejohn agency that represented her.[18] Fortunately for him, this outfit wanted to fatten its client portfolio in readiness for a lucrative takeover by the giant Music Corporation of America (MCA), which was planning a move into Hollywood. Assured by Hodges that the next Robert Taylor was at hand, Meiklejohn knew on seeing Dutch's soft and crinkly face that he was nothing of the kind. The better pitch to his mind was the next Ross Alexander, slotted by Warner Bros. to play good-looking, carefree leads until a welter of personal problems drove him to suicide in January 1937.[19]

The screen test arranged with Warners did not go well. The unflattering camera made Dutch's head look too small and his shoulders too wide, problems later mitigated by wearing shirts with specially tailored collars and a Windsor-knotted tie. Even so, studio boss Jack Warner decided that Dutch's wholesome quality merited the offer of a six-month trial. Holding out for a better deal, Meiklejohn warned that Dutch had another offer awaiting him, neglecting to mention it was his old one in radio. This prompted Warner to agree a seven-year contract with a six-month cancellation option, at a starting salary of $200 a week and incremental pay rises if he was kept on. Getting the glad tidings on returning to Des Moines, Dutch telegrammed his new agent, 'Sign before they change their minds.'[20]

Before leaving Des Moines, Dutch splashed out on purchases that he thought fitting for a movie actor – a pipe, a brown suit, and a $600 beige Nash convertible, in which he motored out to the coast to begin his new career on 1 June 1937. The first day on the studio lot was given over to hairstyle, facial, and wardrobe makeover. Such transformations often included a new name that better fitted the movie persona for which an actor was being groomed. Thus, Archibald Leach became Cary Grant, Spangler Arlington Brugh became Robert Taylor, and Marion Morrison became John Wayne. Ronald Reagan was among the group of stars – Clark Gable and James Stewart were others – to keep their real name because it fitted their studio image. No moniker for a star, 'Dutch' was effectively consigned to history, replaced forever more by Ronald (or Ron or Ronnie). Fearful of being saddled with something that did not sound right to him, Reagan was the one to propose using his real name.[21] It proved a smart decision – the derision he encountered on entering politics for being a movie actor would have been even greater if he'd had a stage name.

Warner Bros. (its preferred designation) was one of Hollywood's eight major studios and one of the so-called 'big five', with its own chain of metropolitan cinemas. It operated on the business principle of vertical integration by controlling the production, distribution, and exhibition of movies. Harry Warner was the brother in charge of financial operations as head of the New York office and Jack Warner held executive control of movie operations. As the first to commit fully to sound films, Warner Bros. briefly became the most profitable studio, but the Depression-induced collapse of movie-ticket sales in 1931 forced its sell-off of some 25 per cent of assets. After four years of large losses, it returned to net profitability in 1935, but could not unseat Metro-Goldwyn-Mayer (MGM) as top studio.

The financial wellbeing of every major studio depended primarily on the box-office returns for its A-features, which relied in turn on the popularity of the stars appearing in these movies. Accordingly, each of them invested heavily in the creation of stars, but without ever being able to delineate the qualities needed to become one. 'It's a crackpot business,' commented one film historian, 'that sets out to manufacture a product it can't even define, but that was old Hollywood.'[22] In reality, the making of stars was a matter of seeing what worked with audiences, with the consequence that their number was relatively small. The largest studio, MGM, carried a maximum of 100 performers on its payroll, of whom no more than 30 might be considered 'stars'. Second in this regard, Warner Bros. based its production and marketing strategies on star vehicles keyed into 'house-style' genres: gangster movies and crime dramas, featuring James Cagney, Edward G. Robinson, and, later, Humphrey Bogart; crusading biopics, often with Paul Muni in the lead; backstage musicals, usually with Dick Powell and Ruby Keeler; swashbucklers with Errol Flynn and Olivia de Havilland; and 'women's pictures' featuring Bette Davis.[23] Despite this galaxy, Jack Warner was always on the lookout for newcomers like Reagan to cast in inexpensive movies and assess their potential for bigger things.

With fascism on the march in Europe in the late 1930s, the studio began producing a new genre of movies that affirmed the democratic values of Americanism to promote, in Harry Warner's words, 'renewed consciousness of our national life'.[24] In brother Jack's eyes, the all-American good-guy persona of his new signing showed promise of becoming a box-office draw for this patriotic message. For the time being, however, Reagan had to learn his trade in the B-movies that were shot in three weeks, lasted about one hour, and were put on double bills with A-movies to draw audiences into studio-owned theatres. These productions afforded little scope for artistic subtlety, trotted out familiar storylines, and served as a warm-up for the big picture.

Within weeks of arriving in Hollywood, Reagan took the lead in *Love Is on the Air* (1937), playing a version of himself as a radio personality who uncovers a crime syndicate. Studio publicity built him up as an 'all-round athlete', 'broad-shouldered with a slender waistline', and possessing a 'contagious smile'. All this added up to 'great promise of a happy future in pictures'.[25] The newcomer moved and spoke well on screen but without much comic flair and showed little heat towards leading lady June Travis (despite intensive off-screen courting of her during the shoot). Still, the critics gave his performance the thumbs-up for having considerable charm. A particularly enthusiastic reviewer urged female readers of her column, 'Run, don't walk […] and beg, borrow or steal a look at Ronald Reagan.'[26] This reaction persuaded Warners to continue his contract. Even so, his starring roles remained stuck in B-movies for nearly three years, interspersed with small parts in bigger productions. Reagan's capacity to memorize lines quickly and willingness to follow direction made him ideally suited to the assembly-line production of these films. Frequently cast in action adventures, he became in his own words 'the Errol Flynn of the B pictures'.[27]

While awaiting his big breakthrough, Reagan adapted to life in Hollywood – without yet being fully of it. Lack of status and working in constantly changing crews made it difficult to form new friendships. His social environment was more Midwestern than Californian. A group of old fraternity buddies came out to join him in the vain hope of finding steady work in the film business. Once his contract was renewed, Reagan brought his parents to live in Hollywood, renting a ground-floor apartment for them near his own on Sunset Boulevard. Nelle immediately threw herself into the life of the local Disciples of Christ Church. Under her influence, Reagan renewed his own churchgoing that had fallen into abeyance in Des Moines. Before long, Neil arrived with wife Bess, a Des Moines native he married in 1935, to try his luck in Hollywood. Minor roles followed in B-movies, but it was as CBS senior producer in the 1940s and 1950s and then senior advertising executive with McCann Erickson that he found fame and fortune.

Despite a reputation as best-behaved male in Hollywood, Reagan began to enjoy the social perks of minor stardom as time passed. He dated a string of starlets – mostly on studio-arranged appearances at film premieres and other events. Although some of these public duets turned into private ones, Jack Warner put a stop to anything that did not match Reagan's wholesome image. A budding romance with Susan Hayward ended when the studio boss objected that the Brooklyn-born beauty's toughness and confident sexuality made her unsuitable for Reagan. Shortly after Reagan's election as president, one-time starlet Ila Rhodes claimed that the pair had been briefly engaged in 1939 until Warner vetoed the match on account of her exotic image. The two certainly had a fling, but none of their old Hollywood friends remembered it being more than that.[28]

Reagan was initially more interested in career advancement than relationship building. Of his first 20 films, half were B-movies, most – but not all – of poor quality because 'the studio didn't want good, they wanted them Thursday'.[29] The most popular, particularly with younger matinee audiences, were the four in which he played Secret Service Agent Brass Bancroft. Warners made the series to boost confidence in law-enforcement agents as patriots with a strong sense of duty. Studio publicity for the first – *Secret Service of the Air* (1939) – depicted its star as 'representative of all that was admirable in young American manhood'. It received a bigger budget than usual for a B-movie in order to film the aerial sequences. Reagan was saddled with a weak script, a 12-day shoot, and having to do his own fist-fight stunts that gave him two real black eyes. More seriously, he suffered permanent hearing impairment from a blank gunshot being fired too close to his head.[30] Nevertheless, the Brass Bancroft movies had a benefit that Reagan could never have predicted. They instilled an ambition in a ten-year-old cinemagoer in Montgomery, Alabama, to join the Secret Service. In 1981 Agent Jerry Parr's quick thinking was instrumental in saving the 40th president's life following an attempted assassination.[31]

Warners showed faith in Reagan's prospects by giving him small roles in big-star vehicles. The contacts made through these minor appearances would be important for his career development. It was an amazing stroke of fortune that the most powerful columnist in Hollywood, with an estimated 20 million daily readers for her syndicated reports in William Randolph Hearst's newspaper empire, was a former Dixon resident. A bit-part in *Hollywood Hotel* (1937) brought Reagan into the orbit of Louella Parsons, making a cameo appearance in the movie based on her own radio show. Thereafter she took a personal interest in promoting her home town's favourite son. Another booster was Pat O'Brien, with whom Reagan worked on *Submarine D-1* (1937) – a part that ended up on the cutting-room floor, *Cowboy from Brooklyn* (1938) and *Boy Meets Girl* (1938). Taking a shine to the younger man because of his Irish ancestry and lack of airs, O'Brien became another father figure. Through him, Reagan got a seat at the 'Irish table' in the Warners commissary, where he rubbed shoulders with the likes of Humphrey Bogart, James Cagney, and Errol Flynn.[32]

The best of Reagan's early parts was in *Brother Rat* (1938), a popular comedy about three cadets. One of the few A-films without a big-name draw, it brought him together with his future wife, who played his love interest. Only 21 years old, Jane Wyman had already divorced one husband, a travelling salesman she had married when 16, and her second marriage to dressmaker Myron Futterman, a man 15 years her senior, would end the same way in December 1938. A cherub-faced beauty with a button nose that made her look even younger than she was, she had signed for Warners in 1936 with the ambition of becoming a serious actress but got typecast in 'dumb blonde' parts that only called for sex appeal.[33]

Born Sarah Jane Mayfield in St Joseph, Missouri, in January 1917, Wyman was reared by foster parents, both strict disciplinarians, after the divorce of her birth parents in 1921. Being falsely blamed by her best friend for a classroom prank that resulted in suspension from school brought the little girl's feelings of insecurity from parental abandonment to the surface. 'I could never trust or confide in anyone again,' Wyman later told a movie magazine. '[I]t followed me through my formative years, poisoned my life and my whole outlook until I met Ronnie.'[34] Sensing the always-optimistic and ever-trusting Reagan was her best hope for emotional security, she transformed herself to win him. The night-clubbing good-time girl became an enthusiast for his favoured pursuits of golf, swimming, and skating during filming of *Brother Rat*. Reluctant to become entangled with a married woman, Reagan's romantic interest in Wyman heated up once she became divorced. With Jack Warner orchestrating things, studio publicity played up the couple's growing attachment in the hope of boosting their screen popularity. Wyman's determination to get her man was also revving up. To overcome Nelle's doubts about her son marrying a divorced Hollywood actress rather than a homebody, she attended Christian Church services and eventually taught a Sunday-school class.[35]

According to unverified reports, Wyman overdosed on sleeping pills when her matrimonial hopes looked as if they would be unrealized. She was certainly hospitalized in October 1939 after completing a sequel movie, *Brother Rat and a Baby*, but official records attributed this to recurrence of an old stomach disorder.[36] What is clear is that Reagan proposed marriage when visiting her in hospital, sealing the deal with a 52-carat amethyst ring. As thanks for getting the news scoop on their engagement, Louella Parsons took the couple on a 'Hollywood Stars of 1940' nine-week national tour that gave up-and-coming performers exposure to a wide public. The charter plane carrying the group to the east was buffeted by violent snowstorms, which eventually forced it to touch down at Chicago, from where the journey was completed by train. After this stomach-churning experience Reagan vowed never to fly again, a promise that he kept for more than a quarter of a century.[37] Once their tour was over, the happy couple tied the knot at Wee Kirk o'the Heather wedding chapel on 26 January 1940, hosted a reception at Louella Parsons' home, and honeymooned in Palm Springs. They returned to set up home in Jane's apartment overlooking Sunset Strip that was part of her divorce settlement.

On 4 January 1941, the day before her 24th birthday, Wyman gave birth to their first child, Maureen Elizabeth. Seeing the opportunity to boost itself as the studio that brought such a wholesome couple together, the Warner Bros. publicity machine went into overdrive to portray the Reagans as an ordinary family with an average middle-class suburban home. A press release, entitled 'The Hopeful Reagans. They Are Looking Forward to More of Everything Good – Including Children', catalogued their furniture, fittings, and household equipment before quoting Mr Norm, alias Ronald Reagan:

> [Our] home life is just like yours or yours or yours. We do the same foolish things that other couples do, have the same scraps, about as much fun, typical problems and the most wonderful baby in the world.[38]

Making them the representatives of the American Way also fitted the studio's increasingly patriotic message amid growing threat of war but was far removed from material reality. Few newly-weds had the wherewithal for the $15,000, seven-room, shingled, ranch-style dream home the Reagans were having built in Hollywood Hills. The project came to fruition in 1942 once the Federal Housing Administration approved government insurance for the $125-a-month mortgage.

In other ways the Reagans were like most newly-weds in having to adjust to each other in marriage. One thing Wyman never came to terms with was her husband's pontificating on almost every subject under the sun. 'You ask him what time it is,' she let slip to gossip columnist Earl Wilson, 'and he'll tell you how the watch was made!' Reagan's oft-expressed opinions on politics drew even more scathing comments in private. Wyman reportedly told actor Robert Cummings when they worked on *Princess O'Rourke* (1943): 'He gives me a pain in the ass. That's all he talks about!'[39] Reagan, for his part, liked being the focus of studio publicity, something that his wife considered an intrusion. After one of Wyman's harangues about this, he reportedly snapped, 'We'll lead an ideal life if you'll just avoid doing one thing: *Don't think.*'[40] The tight control that Reagan kept on family purse strings also caused friction – since Wyman was by her own admission a spendthrift. 'If there was anything I wanted, I'd go and buy it, and think about whether I could really afford it afterward but Ronnie has a phobia about bills,' she told *Silver Screen* magazine.[41]

Meanwhile, the Reagans' respective movie careers were not proceeding apace – Wyman's was stuck in the doldrums but her husband's was on the up. In 1940, he appeared as Notre Dame's tragic football star, George Gipp – popularly known as 'the Gipper' – in *Knute Rockne, All American*. Reagan's claim that he got the part because Hal Wallis, head of Warner A-movie production, saw an old photograph of him in college football uniform was pure hokum.[42] The truth was much more complex – and more fortuitous. With every studio keen to make a picture about the great football coach killed in a plane crash in 1931, the Rockne family entrusted Warner Bros. to film his story. Like Jack Warner, scriptwriter Robert Buckner thought the choice of lead actor fundamental to the movie's success. The one they had in mind as best able to capture Rockne's 'driving personality' was James Cagney.[43] However, the Catholic Church and the University of Notre Dame, unofficial partners in the project, objected to casting a star with a gangster image on screen and in real life a leftist supporter of the anti-Franco cause in the Spanish Civil War. Their preference was Spencer Tracy but MGM would not loan him for a rival studio's biggest film of the year. By default the Rockne role fell to Pat O'Brien, who promptly lobbied for his protégé to play George Gipp. 'A helluva lot of people you have under contract don't know a football from a cantaloupe. This guy does,' he recalled telling Jack Warner. So keen was O'Brien on the casting that he offered to do a screen test with Reagan, a very unusual step for a star.[44]

In line with their anti-Nazi sentiments, the Warner brothers expected that the United States would eventually join the conflict against fascism already started in Europe. The Rockne biopic made football an obvious metaphor for war. While its protagonist personally embodies all-American values, the teams he coaches to victory suggest that the properly trained army of God's chosen nation will consign any opponent to defeat. On screen for just ten minutes, Reagan gave an electrifying performance. His athleticism captivated audiences, making his character's premature death from streptococcal infection in pre-penicillin 1920 all the more shocking to them. On his deathbed, he whispers to Rockne, 'Some day when things are tough, maybe you can ask the boys to go in there and win just one for the Gipper.' This became the best-remembered scene in the movie, its impact enhanced by the sense that many of the nation's young men could soon die fighting a real war. As one movie historian noted, Reagan's portrayal of Gipp made him an icon of prewar America: 'Culturally, he became the poster-boy for self-sacrifice, teamwork, humility, and ultimately, the American Way.'[45] The role remained very much a part of his life for the next 50 years. The inspirational connotations of 'Win one for the Gipper!' made it the unofficial slogan for Reagan's later campaigns for governor and president. One of his last official duties in the White House was to greet the champion Notre Dame football team, who presented him with Gipp's letter sweater.[46]

Knute Rockne, All American was a big hit, one of the few films of the era to break the million-dollar mark for initial theatrical release. The movie had 'the greatest premiere' in the studio's history to date at Notre Dame in October 1940.[47] It was the highlight of 'National Knute Rockne Week', a publicity gimmick concocted by Warner Bros. but one receiving White House endorsement through the presence of Franklin D. Roosevelt Jr at the screening. Reagan's participation in the festivities received huge publicity: he broadcast a quarter of Notre Dame's home game to a radio audience of millions; he was interviewed by the *Saturday Evening Post* – the nation's biggest-circulation weekly magazine – and his re-enactment with O'Brien of scenes from the movie for a local audience went out nationwide on CBS radio. His performance as Gipp also got him the best reviews of his career to date, with *Variety* calling it 'remarkably fine […] [for its] capacity to stir the emotions deeply'.[48]

Elevated to stardom, Reagan was put to work immediately on another A-movie, *Santa Fe Trail* (1940), in the supporting role of George Armstrong Custer to Errol Flynn's lead as Jeb Stuart. This was originally conceived as a tribute to the construction of the Santa Fe railroad. On Jack Warner's insistence, the secondary storyline became the main one to better reflect the studio's preparedness-for-war message. It focused on the pursuit and capture of abolitionist John Brown, the perpetrator of murderous attacks on slave-owners in Kansas who was later hanged for seizing the federal arsenal at Harpers Ferry in 1859 with the intent of sparking a slave insurrection in Virginia. Far more concerned with the present and immediate future, the film played fast and loose with the past. Stuart and Custer are shown as brothers-in-arms in support of the Union, glossing over their later involvement on different sides in the Civil War. Raymond Massey endowed John Brown with a demented charisma that clearly referenced Hitler. Although Flynn and Massey garnered the best reviews, *Santa Fe Trail* advanced Reagan's stardom and was among those films, he later remarked, 'that cause me no shame'. Premiered on 28 December 1940, it became a huge hit, out-grossing *Knute Rockne* by more than a third.[49]

After this success, Reagan's B-movie days were behind him, but his father did not savour his success for long. Although Jack now had a paid job answering his son's fan mail, his resumption of heavy drinking suggested unhappiness in Hollywood. Perhaps the Freudian dimensions of the father/son role-reversal – he was now the one being looked after by Reagan on his home territory – unsettled him. Invited to be part of the Warner Bros. entourage for the *Knute Rockne* premiere, Jack managed to stay dry during the Notre Dame celebrations but got smashed with Pat O'Brien on the return train journey from South Bend. The assertion in Reagan's presidential memoir that he had finally sworn off alcohol before his death from a heart attack on 18 May 1941, just short of his 59th birthday, does not ring true. This more accurately testifies to a son's desire to present his father in the best light despite deep disappointment in him. Nevertheless, Reagan was now free from fear of humiliation by Jack's 'black curse'. Though it would not have immediate effect, his father's passing also removed one of his strongest ties to the Democratic Party.[50]

Doubtless Jack's absence was sorely felt when Reagan and Nelle made a triumphant visit back to Dixon to celebrate 'Louella Parsons Day' on 14 September 1941 in the company of the columnist and a host of Hollywood celebrity friends. Marked by a local public holiday, the event became as much a celebration of Reagan as of Parsons. 'Welcome home Dutch' banners were everywhere; an adoring crowd of some 35,000 people (many had come from nearby small towns and farms) shouted 'We love Dutch' at the formal ceremony of welcome, and his newest movie, *International Squadron*, was given its world premiere at the local cinema that he frequented as a boy. As a further boost, Reagan joined Parsons on a nationwide CBS radio hook-up the next day to celebrate their homecoming. The print media, especially the Hearst press, went overboard to proclaim their rise in the world as proof that the American Dream was real. According to the *Chicago Herald-American*, the Dixon celebrations constituted 'a slice of Americana in the heart of the country where a simple beginning is a stepping stone to success'.[51]

Reagan's burgeoning career did not allow much time to grieve for Jack. The seven films he made in 1941–2 included another western, *The Bad Man* (1941), made on loan to MGM. Ironically the aerophobic star appeared as a heroic American airman serving in the RAF in two movies that identified with Britain's cause in the war against Nazi Germany. *International Squadron* (1941) opened with a map of the United States, showed planes crossing the Atlantic as the titles rolled, and then superimposed over the RAF symbol the message that the film was dedicated to its brave men. *Desperate Journey* (1942), with Errol Flynn in the lead, went on release after America entered the war. Like *International Squadron*, its tale of shot-down airmen making their escape home with valuable secrets about Germany's rocket capacity emphasized duty, sacrifice, and teamwork in wartime. The movie's portrayal of Nazis as fundamentally stupid and incompetent did little to educate Americans that the war in Europe would be long-lasting, however.

Two other films made in 1941 but released when the United States was at war presented greater challenges for Reagan's acting skills. In *Juke Girl*, he played a Dust Bowl-displaced farmer who champions downtrodden migrant fruit pickers in Florida. Worried that Nazi propaganda would exploit the depiction of class exploitation, the newly established Office of War Information persuaded Warners to limit its foreign release, particularly in Latin America. Nevertheless, Reagan won uniformly complimentary reviews for what a number of trade papers rated an outstanding performance.[52] Even more controversial was *Kings Row* (1942), which gave Reagan his finest role, in a production costing $1,082,000, far surpassing any of his previous films. The very opposite of a paean to American values, the rationale for making it was the commercial one that sex and sin were good for profits. The film was based on Henry Bellamann's popular 1940 novel that depicted homosexuality, incest, infidelity, insanity, pre-marital sex, sadism, and suicide as part of everyday life in a turn-of-the-century small town. The author apparently modelled the fictional community of Kings Row on his home town of Fulton, Missouri, a place somewhat smaller than Dixon (and later the venue for Reagan's 'America the Beautiful' commencement address at William Woods College in 1951).[53]

The most lurid parts of the book's storyline did not feature in the movie at the insistence of the Production Code Administration (PCA), the self-polic-ing body that Hollywood producers had established in 1934 as an alternative to government censorship. Reagan lamented its mid-1960s demise out of belief that voluntary restraint had underwritten Hollywood's 'Golden Era', when movies had sparkling dialogue rather than the routine profanity of contemporary films.[54] He may not have felt the same had the PCA vetoed his key scene in *Kings Row*, something given serious consideration. Despite strong opposition from the American Medical Association it did not prohibit a sadistic doctor's needless amputation of both the Reagan character's legs after a workplace accident in vengeance for courting his daughter. Making for another memorable movie line is the scream of horror – 'Where's the rest of me?' – at his awful discovery.

Reagan carried off the scene very convincingly in a single take after meticulous preparation that included talking to physicians and amputees about how to approach the moment of revelation. It was a scene he played time and again in his mind. On the day of filming, he lay down for a time on the bed that prop men had created to allow his real legs to be placed through two mattress holes into a supporting box below. As Reagan recalled, 'I spent almost that whole hour in stiff confinement, contemplating my torso and the smooth undisturbed flat of the covers where my legs should have been.' This readied him to film the scene without rehearsal. His success in carrying it off in one take was a perfect expression of what would later be called 'method acting', whereby performers connect their feelings with those of their characters. As film historian Marc Eliot suggests, Reagan had touched 'both ends of his "self," the external, expressive performance side and the internal, emotional engine that fuelled it'.[55]

A quarter of a century later, Reagan used 'Where's the rest of me?' as the title of his first memoir, written to boost his imminent candidacy for California governor. Its evocation of incompleteness was meant as a metaphor for being unfulfilled by acting. At the time, however, he basked in the glory of a performance that seemingly promised a golden Hollywood future. Reagan had only ranked 74th in the Gallup poll of the 100 most popular stars in January 1942. Only 10 per cent of those polled said that his name on the marquee made them want to see a film (Errol Flynn's draw was over three times greater). By July, the number had jumped to 24 per cent following the release of *Kings Row* in early February and *Juke Girl* in late May.[56]

Word had got out about Reagan's performance in *Kings Row* months before the film's release. Seizing the moment, Lew Wasserman, the top man in MCA's Hollywood agency that now represented the rising star, pressed Warner Bros. to renegotiate his client's contract or risk him going freelance when the present one ended in 1944. Anxious to retain its hot property, the studio agreed a weekly salary of $1,650, almost three times the current one, in November 1941. Wasserman also got Jane Wyman, another MCA client, a substantial pay rise to strengthen her husband's ties to the studio.[57] Reagan now seemed en route to Errol Flynn's big-money league, a source of personal as well as financial satisfaction. A longstanding rivalry had started between them when filming *Santa Fe Trail* due to Flynn's insistence on upstaging his co-star. For one outdoor production photograph, Reagan found himself virtually hidden in the second row directly behind Flynn, a slight that did not go unanswered. Female lead Olivia de Havilland remembered him quietly kicking the dirt at his feet into a mound that he stepped on to tower over Flynn when the camera clicked.[58]

Thinking themselves set for the future, Reagan and Wyman expressed gratitude to Jack Warner for his generosity. 'The more we see of the movie industry,' they wrote, 'the more we are convinced we work in the right place.'[59] Shortly afterwards, however, call-up for military service dealt Reagan's movie career a setback from which it never recovered. Despite a heroic screen persona, the future president was a reluctant enlistee. This was hardly unusual as many Hollywood stars were loath to abandon lucrative careers to go off to war. Revoking his reserve status, the Army initially called him to active service in the summer of 1941. With *Kings Row* still shooting and other Reagan movies planned, Warner and Wasserman collaborated to secure a deferment until the studio could change its production schedule to adjust for his loss. Further deferments kept Reagan making movies, but time eventually ran out on him.[60]

Hoping to keep him at work, Warner leaked to Hollywood journalists that his new top star would team up with Ann Sheridan, his co-star in *Kings Row* and *Juke Girl*, in a new film entitled *Casablanca*. Reagan missed the chance of playing in one of the all-time great movies, but as idealist Victor Laszlo, eventually played by Paul Henreid, rather than Rick Blaine, immortally portrayed by Humphrey Bogart. Whether Warner really intended to cast him or was just spinning a yarn in the hope of another deferment is unclear. If the former, it is difficult to envisage *Casablanca* becoming a classic that has only improved with age had Reagan, Sheridan (in Ingrid Bergman's part of Ilsa), and Dennis Morgan (Rick) taken the starring roles. In refusing to play ball with the studio on this occasion, the War Department may have been the saviour of an iconic movie loved by generations of viewers. It instructed Reagan to report for duty on 19 April 1942. Wyman threw a leaving party attended by some top stars, a sure sign of her husband's rising status in the snobbish film community. By the time of his return to civilian life more than three years later, the world had changed and so had Hollywood. Reagan would have to find a new film persona to fit different times, but he never did.

THREE

Falling Star

I n 1942 Ronald Reagan was among Hollywood's fastest-rising stars, but thereafter his career went into decline and his earlier successes faded from popular recall. Instead of great lines in top movies, what stuck in popular memory from his postwar films was a chimp upstaging him in *Bedtime for Bonzo* (Universal, 1951). Dissatisfied with roles at Warner Bros., he worked for other studios in the early 1950s without ever reviving his cinematic stardom. Meanwhile his personal life underwent a parallel downturn with the collapse of his marriage to Jane Wyman. Despite these setbacks, the postwar years were vitally important in Reagan's political development. With his movie career going nowhere, he became influential in Hollywood politics as president of the Screen Actors Guild (SAG). His political metamorphosis from liberal to conservative also began in this era. Moreover, marriage to actress Nancy Davis in 1952 established one of the most important husband–wife partnerships in American history.

Going off to war in April 1942, Reagan went no further than San Francisco, where he assisted in loading troop transports for Australia. Army doctors assessed him as unfit for active duty because his eyesight was so bad at '7/200 bilateral' that a tank could advance within seven feet of him before he could have identified it as Japanese. Accordingly, he returned to Los Angeles in May to join the newly established First Motion Picture Unit (FMPU) of the Army Air Corps, located at the old Hal Roach studios in Culver City. The FMPU recruited some 1,300 Hollywood actors, scriptwriters, cameramen, and directors serving in uniform to make nearly 400 'shorts' over the course of the war, many of them training films, some morale boosters, and others propaganda for air power.[1]

In addition to being FMPU's personnel officer and then intelligence officer, Reagan had acting roles in many of its productions, like *Rear Gunner* (as a gunnery instructor), *Identification of a Japanese Zero* (as a pilot), and *For God and Country* (as a Catholic priest). At Jack Warner's behest, he never appeared as a high-ranking officer in order to preserve his everyman image. His radio voice was often put to good use as a narrator, notably in *Beyond the Line of Duty* (1942) that additionally featured FDR's voice. Despite being absent from Hollywood, he also rode high for a time in film-star popularity polls, even topping the important *Box Office Records* survey for the 1942–3 movie season. The success of *Kings Row*, which grossed $3 million on domestic release, was largely responsible for this. To keep Reagan in the spotlight, the Warner Bros. publicity machine ensured that stories about his military service regularly featured in movie magazines. Virtually all of these, notably a *Modern Screen* cover story of early 1943, conveyed the impression that he was away at war, not back in Burbank – and neglected to mention that he went home most weekends.[2] Meanwhile, moviegoers got regular sightings of Reagan in FMPU films shown as first features or between first and main features in cinemas nationwide. They also saw him in one studio movie that became his greatest commercial hit.

Reagan was disappointed that his *Kings Row* performance was overlooked in the 1942 Academy Award nominations. James Cagney took the best actor Oscar for playing vaudevillian George M. Cohan in Warners' flag-waving musical, *Yankee Doodle Dandy* (1942). Following that success, the studio made Irving Berlin's Broadway hit *This Is the Army* into a movie in 1943. With net profits promised for its relief fund, the Army cooperated fully in its making. Reagan was released to play non-singing lead Johnny Jones, a Broadway producer's son who enlists after Pearl Harbor only to find himself charged with organizing an Army show. At its spectacular finale, the cast of 350 real soldiers marches off the stage, supposedly going directly to war.

Loss of income was the most immediate effect of war service for Reagan. *This Is the Army* grossed $10 million on its domestic run, but military pay was all he got for starring in it. Commissioned a lieutenant, his monthly salary of $250 a month ($280 after promotion to captain in 1943) did not cover the mortgage on the new house, upkeep of his family, and an allowance for Nelle. Wyman's earnings now paid most of the bills, a reversal of financial roles not easy for Reagan to accept. With his fan mail now second in volume only to Errol Flynn's on the Warner lot, he solved the problem of supporting Nelle by getting the studio to employ her at $75 a week answering his letters – repayable from his salary on return to commercial movie-making.[3]

Despite not seeing combat, what Reagan did during the war was important. *Rear Gunner* boosted Air Corps recruitment, helping to overcome its shortage of gunners. Other films that Reagan acted in or narrated improved pilot identification of enemy planes, explained how flyers should deal with interrogation if captured, and boosted popular morale after Pearl Harbor.[4] In addition, he participated in launching the fourth War Loan Drive in New York in January 1944. As part of this assignment, he played a fatigued soldier in a front-line foxhole in a national radio broadcast that featured contributions from General Dwight Eisenhower, Admiral Chester Nimitz, and secretary of the Treasury Henry Morgenthau (who effusively praised Reagan's contribution to the bond drive's success).[5]

This did not stop political adversaries in postwar Hollywood exploiting Reagan's absence from the front line. An anonymous letter (from 'a wounded veteran') published in a trade journal in the summer of 1946 ridiculed him as a 'cutting room commando' who had 'fought the war from the polished nightclub floors of Hollywood'. Fellow actors, including Audie Murphy – America's most decorated soldier in World War II – came to his defence in a signed letter to the same publication.[6] There is no doubt, however, that Reagan felt some shame at not having been in action. This was evident when *Brother Rat* co-star Eddie Albert, who saw combat as a marine, gave him a netsuke taken from a dead Japanese soldier during the bloody battle of Tarawa in 1943. 'I [...] explained what it was,' he recalled, 'and he was appreciative – but I've never forgotten the way he looked. Like I'd humiliated him.' Another war hero, Richard Todd, his British co-star in *The Hasty Heart* (1949), regarded Reagan as 'a frustrated soldier'.[7] In view of the martial analogies peppering his accounts of the Hollywood Red Scare, it is probable that battling communists within the film industry met an emotional need to be on the front line against America's enemies.

Everything seemed set fair for Reagan, with military discharge on 11 July 1945. Lew Wasserman had got him a new, million-dollar, 35-picture limit, seven-year contract with Warner Bros. One studio executive commented that the price was worth it for a 'very talented artist' and proven box-office draw.[8] Reagan later wrote about returning to civilian life:

> [A]ll I wanted to do [...] was to rest up awhile, make love to my wife, and come up refreshed to a better job in an ideal world. (As it came out, I was disappointed in all these postwar ambitions.)[9]

The first role under the new contract was as a heroic veterinarian in *Stallion Road* (1947), a part that required a lot of riding. Needing to brush up on his equestrian skills in preparation for this, Reagan worked hard to become an accomplished horseman with the help of former Italian cavalryman Nino Pepitone. A sign of new affluence, he bought a black thoroughbred mare called Tar Baby from his coach to ride in the movie. The spending spree did not stop there. Once filming was over, Reagan fulfilled a longstanding ambition in buying an eight-acre horse ranch in the San Fernando Valley where he kept a stable of three mounts.[10] His top billing could not turn *Stallion Road* into box-office gold. A dull plot, revolving round an anthrax scare, and a weak script co-written by a frequently inebriated William Faulkner did nothing to help.

Reagan only appeared in nine more movies for Warner Bros. because the studio no longer knew how to use its expensive star. The all-American roles he played in prewar days were unsuited to the more cynical postwar era when noir thrillers became a flourishing genre. Nor were the youthful roles of his early screen days now suitable for a star looking the middle-aged man he was. The wholesome sex appeal he once displayed did not evolve as he matured. A co-star in four of his 1950s movies, Rhonda Fleming, remarked: 'Ronnie wasn't Errol Flynn – his sex appeal wasn't obvious. That electric something just didn't project [...] He did not exude sex.'[11] Perhaps aware of his limitations as a screen lover, Reagan wanted to play cavalry westerns set in the post-Civil War years – in his description 'a phase of Americana rivalling the Kipling era for color and romance' – in the hope that his horsemanship and athleticism would bring box-office success.[12] To his dismay, Jack Warner seemed to see him as more Cary Grant than John Wayne. As a consequence, Reagan found himself cast in a curious mix of dramatic, romantic, and light comedy roles, in few of which he felt comfortable.

The critical and box-office disaster of *That Hagen Girl* (1947) did irreparable damage to Reagan's chances of getting the lead in big pictures at Warner Bros. Another exposé of the unpleasant side of small-town life, this was meant to usher former child star Shirley Temple, now 19 years old, into adult stardom in the role of an adoptee facing nasty gossip about her paternity. Jack Warner ordered a reluctant Reagan to play the man wrongly suspected of being Temple's father who ends up falling for her. Reagan tried in vain to get the script changed so that he was paired off with a woman his own age and Temple got her high-school beau. Audiences were unready to accept Temple in a nubile role, especially as the love interest of someone twice her age. Reagan himself harboured doubts that 'I wanted to be a party to presenting her to America for the first time as a young lady'.[13] In a typically damning review, one trade paper commented that the movie was 'the kind of heart-searing melodrama which flourished in the silent era [...] Today, it just doesn't strike a responsive audience note.' Three decades later, when it was fashionable to ridicule Reagan's movies, two film critics nominated *That Hagen Girl* as one of the 50 worst films of all time.[14] Though very far from being that, it was bad enough for Jack Warner to decide that Reagan lacked the star power to carry a movie.[15]

Adding to his woes, Reagan came close to death after contracting viral pneumonia, the disease that killed George Gipp, during filming. Undertaken without a stunt double, one scene that had him jumping into an icy cold lake to rescue the Temple character from attempted suicide required several takes. Awaking with a fever the following morning, he called off work but his condition worsened over the next five days. He was rushed into Cedars of Lebanon hospital on 24 June 1947 and his life hung in the balance. He later maintained that only the exhortations of a friendly nurse to keep breathing got him through the worst night of the fever.[16]

Whenever given decent parts by Warner Bros., Reagan turned in good performances, such as when playing a soldier on leave in wartime New York in *The Voice of the Turtle* (1947), a soldier recuperating from malaria in *The Hasty Heart* (1949), and a county prosecutor fighting the Ku Klux Klan in *Storm Warning* (1951). Next to *That Hagen Girl*, his biggest commercial flop was *Night unto Night* (completed in early 1947, but not released until 1949 after extensive recutting). The critically panned movie cast Reagan as a terminally ill biochemist contemplating his imminent end, a role for which reviewers deemed him unsuitable. Viewed some 70 years later, however, his performance appears dignified and realistic in contemplation of death in a movie that has somewhat improved with age. Paradoxically, a pair of films that did not test Reagan's acting ability in the least did well at the box office – Virginia Mayo looking good in a white swimsuit ensured the healthy profitability of *The Girl from Jones Beach* (1949) and her legs did the same for *She's Working Her Way through College* (1952). Without doubt Reagan's best performance in his postwar movies was as baseball great Grover Cleveland Alexander opposite Doris Day, top-billed for marquee appeal as his wife, in *The Winning Team* (1952). Three weeks of preparatory training under the eye of several professional players made him believable when throwing from the mound. The maturity and vulnerability he displayed as the alcoholic sports star who pitched the St Louis Cardinals to victory over the New York Yankees in the 1926 World Series also showcased his acting skills to good effect. However, the highly fictionalized biopic was too clichéd and conventional – habitual problems of the genre – to light up the box office.

Meanwhile, Jane Wyman's career was heading upwards. Salvation from her dumb-blonde typecasting at Warners came through loan-outs to other studios. Her breakthrough part was for Paramount in Billy Wilder's Oscar-winning movie about an alcoholic, *The Lost Weekend* (1945). Though not nominated for an award, Wyman perfectly captured the anguish required for her role as the drunk's fiancée. MGM hired her to play alongside Gregory Peck as the matriarch of an impoverished farm family in *The Yearling* (1946), for which she received an Academy Award nomination for Best Actress. Finally recognizing her talent, Warner Bros. gave her an Oscar-winning part in *Johnny Belinda* (1948), the first Hollywood movie to deal seriously with rape – a subject long prohibited by the Production Code.

The rise of Wyman's star alongside the decline of Reagan's spelled trouble for their marriage. The family dynamic had already changed during the war when Wyman started, in Maureen's words, 'making more than her share of family decisions, financial and otherwise'.[17] Postwar career success further diminished the emotional need that had initially drawn Wyman to Reagan. The almost non-stop patter about his growing involvement in Hollywood politics bored her to distraction. She later confided to a friend that it was 'exasperating to […] have someone at the breakfast table, newspaper in hand, expounding on the far right, far left, the conservative right, the liberal left, the middle of the roader'.[18] Wyman herself was hardly easy to get along with. Getting an Oscar became an obsession to prove her calibre to Hollywood. She spent several months learning sign language in preparation for *Johnny Belinda* and put wax in her ears to get the sense of being deaf. She had always immersed herself fully in every part she played, even the dizzy ones. It was unfortunate, as her daughter recalled, that the breakthrough roles of 1945–8 'consisted mostly of one depressingly serious part after another […] [in which she was] always struggling to survive'. This did not make for a happy household because 'we had to live with Mother's wide personality swings for months at a time'.[19]

A family tragedy might have brought the Reagans close once more but cruel circumstance prevented them bonding over it. Doubting that Wyman could bear another child after what had been a difficult birth with Maureen, the couple adopted a day-old baby boy, whom they named Michael Edward, in March 1945. In fact, she did get pregnant again but the baby, a girl they named Christine, was born premature on 26 June 1947 and survived only a few hours in an incubator. This was just when Reagan was battling for his life against pneumonia in a different hospital. Wyman had to go through the ordeal alone and return home while her husband remained on the critical list.[20]

It was widely believed that Wyman began an affair with co-star Lew Ayres during location shooting for *Johnny Belinda*. She claimed to find him a cerebral rather than a romantic soulmate who talked with rather than at her. Whether or not their relationship went further, it was another nail in the coffin of her marriage. Reagan himself had little doubt that the two were intimate but was willing to overlook it in the hope of reconciliation with Wyman. 'Right now Jane needs very much to have a fling,' he told Louella Parsons, 'and I intend to let her have it.' He also told columnist Hedda Hopper, 'If this thing comes to a divorce, I think I'll name *Johnny Belinda* as co-respondent.'[21]

There were several attempted reconciliations before Wyman filed for divorce on grounds of 'extreme mental cruelty', the standard rationale for Hollywood terminations. Granted on 29 June 1948, the uncontested decree became final on 16 July the following year. The financial settlement gave Wyman custody of the children, $500 a month for their support, alimony if illness or injury stopped her working, and half the proceeds from sale of their home. In addition to getting the other half, Reagan kept the ranch and horses. Though long on the cards, the divorce left him emotionally devastated. 'The plain truth,' he recalled, 'was that such a thing was so far from even being imagined by me that I had no resources to call upon.' Whatever its problems, Reagan had not wanted to end the marriage. Years later when president, he remarked, 'I was divorced in the sense that the decision was made by somebody else.'[22]

Reagan's personal life nearly went off the rails after the break-up. Never prudish about sex, he thought a man's desire for an attractive woman was 'an instinct as much a part of him as hunger and thirst'.[23] His behaviour now lived up to that conviction in full. Checking into a Hollywood Hills apartment, he began squiring a succession of attractive women around town, running up large nightclub bills of $250 a month in the process. 'Never thought we'd come right out and call Ronnie Reagan "a wolf," but leave us face it.' *Silver Screen* commented. 'Suddenly every glamour gal considers him a super-sexy escort for an evening.'[24] According to film historian Marc Eliot, Reagan's rage over his divorce found expression in 'dating everything that moved, sleeping with and then discarding them'. Among his supposed conquests were Doris Day, Ava Gardner, Rhonda Fleming, Marilyn Monroe, Patricia Neal, and a host of lesser starlets. Similar claims were made by investigative journalist Kitty Kelley.[25] A good number of those named as being amorously involved with him strenuously denied it, particularly Fleming and Neal. Day was one of his many lovers, however. Another was Piper Laurie, the 19-year-old playing his daughter in *Louisa* (Universal, 1950), later to write an acerbic account of losing her virginity to him.[26] British star Patricia Roc had fonder memories of their liaison, which began in Hollywood and continued while Reagan was filming *The Happy Heart* in London, but remembered him being very upset about his divorce.[27]

Although beset with professional and personal difficulties, Reagan was taking the first steps towards what would eventually become a new career in politics. World War II had come close to radicalizing him in a way that the Depression had not. Though not in combat, he felt deeply involved in the fight against fascism. According to Ed Meese, a top aide to Reagan as governor and president, making movies for the war effort 'gave him almost a religious view of America – something holy and worth dying for'. Leftist writer-director Bernard Vorhaus remembered being surprised by the depth of his political knowledge and progressive commitment when they worked together for FMPU.[28] As FMPU intelligence officer, Reagan spent weeks processing raw footage from the liberation of Ohrdruf and Buchenwald concentration camps, captured on film by one of the unit's combat-camera teams. The horrific scenes made an indelible impression on him. When sons Michael and Ron turned 14, he would make them watch Holocaust documentary footage so they could understand the horrors of Nazism.[29]

'[H]ell-bent on saving the world from neo-Fascism' on return to civilian life, Reagan joined groups variously wanting to ban the atomic bomb, end US support for the corrupt nationalist regime in China, and promote one-world ideals in support of the United Nations. Most of these organizations were imbued with the wartime spirit of unity between left-liberals and communists. With the US–Soviet alliance rapidly disintegrating after victory in Europe, however, the Communist Party of the United States (CPUSA) brought many such groups under its surreptitious control for use as platforms to condemn American foreign policy. Unaware of what was happening, Reagan remained an outspoken advocate for their causes, leading the Federal Bureau of Investigation (FBI) to suspect him of being a communist sympathizer. He later acknowledged, 'I was not sharp about communism,' but the scales soon fell from his eyes.[30]

Reagan's activities in the Hollywood chapter of the American Veterans Committee (AVC), a group supporting social justice for returning servicemen, brought about his first brush with communists. He served on its board, helped in recruitment drives, and put his voice in its support. The first address he gave, also the occasion of his last public appearance in uniform, was on United America Day, 8 December 1945, at a ceremony honouring slain Japanese American war hero, Sergeant Kazuo Masuda. Reagan's words made unspoken reference to recent attacks on returning Nisei veterans:

> Blood that has soaked into the sands of the beaches is all of one color. America stands unique in the world – a country not founded on race, but on a way and an ideal. Not in spite of, but because of our polyglot background, we have had all the strength in the world. That is the American way.[31]

Over 40 years later Reagan would quote these words when signing the Redress Act of 1988 granting restitution to Japanese American civilians interned in World War II.[32]

In other public remarks, Reagan was forthright in attacking not only the Ku Klux Klan but also police violence against African American veterans in the south as fascist stains on America.[33] Despite the unmistakeable evidence of communist influence in the AVC Hollywood chapter, a strong commitment to helping veterans kept Reagan working for the organization throughout 1946. He eventually resigned in early 1947 after being warned by the FBI that he risked being tarred as a red through continued association with it.[34]

Reagan's next run-in with communists was in the Hollywood Independent Citizens Committee of the Arts, Sciences and Professions (HICCASP), formed in 1945 to unite progressives of every ilk in support of domestic reform and peaceful cooperation abroad with the Soviet Union. Well-received speeches given on its behalf earned Reagan a seat on the executive in June 1946, but an unsuccessful effort to counter communist influence made his tenure a brief one. The board meeting of 2 July ended in furious dispute after liberal members proposed that HICCASP issue a statement repudiating communism, a motion endorsed by Reagan. Now reassured of where he stood, a group of liberals enlisted his help in drafting an anti-CPUSA resolution at the apartment of his one-time co-star, Olivia de Havilland. Their statement asserted that communist nations could 'live together in peace and good will' with 'capitalist democratic nations' but rejected communism as 'desirable for the United States'. This provoked another donnybrook with communist members when submitted to the board on 5 July. Reagan's proposal to put it to a vote of the entire membership was rejected out of hand. Instead, a smaller executive committee, packed with communists and their sympathizers, produced an alternative statement avowing HICCASP's support for FDR's ideals but saying little about communism. Seeing no way to save the organization from becoming a communist front, disillusioned liberals resigned from it in droves. Despite being the target of vitriolic slurs for his anti-communist stance, Reagan stayed on for several months in order to report on developments to the de Havilland group – and to brother Neil, now an FBI informer on HICCASP.[35]

Reagan's greatest confrontation with communism resulted from his leadership role in the SAG. Formed in 1933 as an American Federation of Labor affiliate, SAG aimed to protect actors against salary cuts, restrictive contracts, excessive work hours, and benefit restrictions. A rising star, Reagan was invited onto its board as an alternate in July 1941, but war service interrupted his tenure. Following demobilization, he regained a position in the same capacity, becoming a fully fledged board member in February 1946, vice-president in September that same year, and finally president in March 1947. No master of detail when US president, Reagan was good at grappling with the nitty-gritty of SAG affairs. His intensive, time-consuming engagement in defeating what he considered a communist plot for control of the film industry was instrumental in his marriage break-up. As he admitted to Louella Parsons, 'Perhaps I should have let someone else save the world and have saved my own home.'[36]

The trigger for the Hollywood Red Scare was the arcane jurisdictional battle between the International Alliance of Theatrical Stage Employees (IATSE) and the Conference of Studio Unions (CSU) to represent film-industry craft workers. A byword for corruption and extortion in 1930s Hollywood, a now-reformed IATSE enjoyed a cosy relationship with the studios. Labour activist Herbert Sorrell had launched CSU in 1941 with the aim of uniting all Hollywood locals within a democratic membership-oriented union. Leftist in political outlook, it gained support from progressive groups of all stripes, including communists. Fearful of CSU's potential to force better pay and conditions for every kind of studio worker, the Association of Motion Picture Producers (AMPP) – the group that set common labour policy for the studios – exploited union jurisdictional disputes with the aim of strangling its development. AMPP's refusal to recognize the transfer of set decorators from IATSE to CSU sparked a prolonged strike in 1945, one the National Labor Relations Board ultimately helped to resolve in Sorrell's favour.[37]

Observing neutrality in the initial jurisdictional dispute, the SAG executive advised actors to cross picket lines and continue working. When Sorrell called a new strike in July 1946, it delegated an emergency committee that included Reagan to broker a settlement. The group assisted in negotiating the so-called 'Treaty of Beverly Hills' whereby the studios and CSU agreed terms, but this was a short-lived truce. Unbeknown to SAG, AMPP had reached a secret deal with IATSE to drive CSU out of Hollywood. In September it approved IATSE jurisdiction for set erection in the knowledge that CSU carpenters and painters would refuse to work on 'hot' sets. As intended, this provoked Sorrell into calling a new strike. With every studio proclaiming determination to stay open at all costs, the dispute became a life-or-death struggle for CSU.[38]

Like all Hollywood liberals, Reagan was initially sympathetic to CSU but the 1946–7 strike produced a change of heart – in part because of direct exposure to labour violence. Sorrell concentrated his resources on Warner Bros. in the hope of breaking a link in the producers' chain of resistance. CSU pickets fought pitched battles with police, studio guards, and IATSE thugs outside the studio gates. While making *Night unto Night*, Reagan was among the employees bussed through the lines to report for work. Although there were two sides involved, he saw only the CSU supporters throwing rocks at incoming vehicles and committing other forms of violence. As Neil Reagan commented, this was 'the first time' his brother witnessed 'a bunch of pickets swing three-foot lengths of log chain at people's heads who were just trying [...] to go to work'.[39]

More significant in turning Reagan against CSU was his belief that it was communist-controlled. The man who did much to convince him of this was Roy Brewer, IATSE chief representative in Hollywood. A complex mix of ardent New Dealer and fervent anti-communist, Brewer had long claimed that the CSU's drive to organize all studio workers under its umbrella was intended to give Moscow a hold over the American movie industry. This was the message that he pitched at Reagan in their frequent meetings to discuss ways of settling the IATSE–CSU dispute. As the strike dragged on, the initially sceptical actors' leader came to share Brewer's concern that there was a Soviet conspiracy at work. 'The Communist plan for Hollywood,' he later declared, 'was remarkably simple. It was merely to take over the motion picture business [...] for a grand world-wide propaganda base.'[40] Following CSU's eventual defeat, Brewer and Reagan strengthened their partnership by co-founding in late 1948 the Labor League of Hollywood Voters, a Democratic group dedicated to resisting communist infiltration of the film industry. They were still in communication with each other 40 years later about the Hollywood Reds who were 'still under the bed'.[41]

The efforts of CPUSA supporters within SAG to change its position on the strike added grist to Brewer's warnings. John Garfield, Sterling Hayden, and Howard Da Silva spearheaded a group wanting a pro-CSU stand that would have required actors not to cross picket lines. Accompanied by actor friend William Holden, Reagan gatecrashed one of its meetings to explain why he would advocate continued neutrality in a report soon to be submitted to the

SAG membership. The next day, while on a location shoot, he received an anonymous telephone warning that if he took this line, a squad would 'fix you so you won't ever act again'. Reagan later discovered on the Hollywood grapevine that CSU goons intended to throw acid in his face. Warner Bros. immediately arranged for the Burbank police to give him a .32 Smith & Wesson pistol, which he wore in a shoulder holster wherever he went and kept by his bedside at night for the next seven months.[42]

Assembling to discuss continued neutrality in the strike at the Hollywood Legion Stadium on 2 October 1946, SAG members had to pass through some 2,000 placard-waving CSU members lined outside. Despite the intimidating circumstances, Reagan delivered a powerful address declaring that actors had no business taking sides in a jurisdictional dispute between other unions. A secret ballot of the membership produced a 2,748–509 majority in favour of remaining neutral. This success raised Reagan's profile as a strong anti-communist voice within SAG. Conservative columnist Hedda Hopper later remarked: '[He] always struck me as being quiet, unassuming, and not the two-fisted fighter we needed […] I was never more wrong.' Jesuit priest George Dunne, a CSU supporter, was of similar mind for different reasons. '[T]his is a dangerous man,' he commented, 'because he's so articulate, and because he's sharp.'[43]

Although Reagan continued to search for a settlement, his impartiality was fast disappearing. The failure of independent arbitration, the growing violence, and CSU's refusal to abide by studio-obtained injunctions limiting pickets to eight per gate convinced him that Sorrell had no interest in ending the strike. Speaking publicly in mid-November, Reagan declared that the CSU leader 'stands to gain by continued disorder and disruption in Hollywood', words that as good as accused him of subversive intent.[44] Sorrell's supporters in SAG consequently denounced the leadership as 'anti-union, anti-labor, anti-democratic'. They gathered the requisite number of signatures for a petition demanding a meeting of the entire membership to reconsider the union's stand on the strike. Held on 19 December 1946, this assembly produced a ten-to-one majority vote of confidence in the SAG board, with Reagan once more the foremost spokesman for continued neutrality. One of the opposition, Alexander Knox – recipient of an Oscar nomination for his lead role in the presidential biopic *Wilson* (20th Century Fox, 1944) – accused him of 'talk[ing] out of both sides of his mouth'. An enraged Roy Brewer swore to run the Scots Canadian actor out of

Hollywood for these remarks, a promise later fulfilled.[45] The meeting was the last roll of the dice for the pro-CSU faction. Although the strikes continued far into 1947, SAG's stand on members crossing picket lines proved critical in the eventual defeat and collapse of Sorrell's organization. According to Reagan, CSU 'dissolved like sugar in hot water', but as biographer Edmund Morris notes, the better analogy was 'crushed to powder' by studio power, red-baiting, and SAG neutrality.[46]

Reagan's role in the labour dispute made him popular with most SAG members for keeping them working. It marked the end of his association with the Hollywood Left, however. CSU supporters variously denounced him as a bosses' man, an opportunist seeking advantage only for actors, and a scab. Conversely, Reagan saw himself as a soldier in the battle for Hollywood's soul. He often cited Sterling Hayden's explanation for the failure of the communist plot in testimony admitting his past to the House Un-American Activities Committee (HUAC) in 1951: 'We ran into a one-man battalion named Ronnie Reagan.' Continuing the martial theme in his presidential memoir 40 years later, he remarked, 'I knew from the experience of hand-to-hand combat that America faced no more insidious or evil threat than that of Communism.'[47]

Father George Dunne recalled Reagan's insistence in their only face-to-face meeting in early 1947 on 'interpreting everything in terms of the Communist threat'. His own investigation for the Catholic archdiocese of Los Angeles concluded that 'the strike is not Communist inspired nor Communist directed'.[48] Max Silver, a party organizer in Los Angeles, later acknowledged CPUSA's interest in making Sorrell's union its creature, but the project made little headway.[49] Complex factors pertaining to the nature of Hollywood unions, their jurisdictional rivalries, and their relations with the studios were behind the strikes. A congressional subcommittee – the Kearns Committee – that investigated the dispute placed principal responsibility for it on collusion between the producers and IATSE. For Reagan, however, everything boiled down to a conspiracy 'to communize the world'.[50]

This outlook fuelled Reagan's determination to expunge communist influence in the actors' union. Having formed his own production company, Robert Montgomery resigned as SAG chair on conflict-of-interest grounds in March 1947. Reagan was elected to complete his unfinished term, going on to serve five yearly terms in his own right. On 10 April, he enlisted alongside Jane

Wyman as FBI informer to report on SAG's communist members. This was not his first interaction with the agency. During the war he had supplied it with information on German sympathizers and anti-Semites in the film business.[51] Reagan's postwar dealings with the FBI were sufficiently regular for him to be given the codename T-10, something he never acknowledged until *San Jose Mercury* reporter Jack Sirica obtained a copy of his FBI file (#100-382196) under the Freedom of Information Act in 1985. The identities of those he named as suspected CPUSA supporters are redacted from this, but they likely did not include anyone not already known for this association. Former party members who named names were the FBI's main source of information on Hollywood Reds. Seeing CPUSA as a fifth-column agent of Soviet aggrandizement amid worsening Cold War tensions, Reagan never regretted his decision to turn informer. '[T]he so-called "Communist Party,"' he wrote during the Korean War, 'is nothing less than a "Russian–American Bund" owing allegiance to Russia and supporting Russia in its plan to conquer the world […] They are traitors practicing treason.'[52]

Despite his growing anti-communism, Reagan did not engage in indiscriminate red-baiting lest Hollywood seem a hotbed of subversives. He distinguished himself in this regard as a friendly witness before high-profile HUAC hearings in Washington DC in October 1947. Now controlled by Republicans and conservative Southern Democrats following liberal Democrat reverses in the 1946 midterm congressional elections, the committee seized on the reports of communist influence within AVC, HICCASP, and the movie unions as an opportunity to embarrass the entire progressive left. Hollywood had survived previous inquisitions by HUAC and Jack Tenney's California Senate Fact-Finding Subcommittee on Un-American Activities. Now the film industry's reputation for Americanism came into question just as it was beginning to feel insecure about the rising challenge of television. Instead of standing up to HUAC, studio bosses – with Jack Warner to the fore – gave assurances of their determination to drive out the Reds. Testifying as former and current presidents of SAG, however, Robert Montgomery, George Murphy, and Reagan downplayed communist influence in the film business.[53]

The last to speak, Reagan made his appearance wearing a white gabardine suit and horn-rimmed spectacles, respectively intended to convey his goodness and gravitas. In a nuanced testimony he admitted that communist members had sought to disrupt SAG, but insisted that 'within the bounds of our democratic rights […] we have done a pretty good job in our business of keeping those people's activities curtailed'. He also denied that communists had ever been able 'to use the motion picture screen as a sounding board for their philosophy or ideology'. While decrying CPUSA, his testimony ended with a ringing avowal: 'I never as a citizen want to see our country become urged, by either fear or resentment of this group, that we ever compromise with any of our democratic principles.'[54]

Reagan's role as resistance leader against the Hollywood inquisition was short-lived. A group of hostile witnesses subpoenaed to appear before HUAC undid whatever good impression was made by preceding friendly witnesses. The so-called Hollywood Ten's histrionic refusal to answer questions about their suspected communist affiliations got them cited for contempt of Congress, leading eventually to their conviction and imprisonment. Their highly publicized testimony turned moviegoers against anyone in the film community suspected of being Red or radical. Box-office receipts declined by 20 per cent in the two months following the HUAC hearings. Under pressure from financial backers, studio chiefs issued on 3 December 1947 the so-called Waldorf Statement that gave birth to the Hollywood blacklist. As well as firing the Hollywood Ten, the producers pledged never knowingly to employ a communist or member of any group that advocated the American government's overthrow. All the Hollywood guilds were encouraged to play their part in getting rid of subversives. Initially hostile to the blacklist, Reagan urged the SAG board to issue a counter-statement condemning studio discrimination against employees on the basis of their beliefs, a recommendation his colleagues voted down lest the union appear to be defending communists. Instead of resigning on a point of principle, their chastened leader joined George Murphy to draft a private letter to the studio chiefs supporting their new policy.[55]

By its early 1950s peak, the Hollywood blacklist featured over 200 actors, writers, and directors who refused to cooperate with HUAC. More extensive and insidious were the 'greylists' generated by conservative organizations, notably the American Legion and American Business Consultants. As well as suspected CPUSA sympathizers, these included liberals and radicals with any connection to communist front groups. The only way to get off either type of list was to recant in public and name others who were real or suspected communists. Clearance agencies were set up, the first under IATSE's Roy Brewer, to assist the process of rehabilitation. Without doubt, there were dedicated communists in Hollywood, many radicalized by the threat of Nazism in the 1930s, but their numbers were unlikely to have exceeded 300. Neither HUAC nor the Tenney subcommittee turned up substantive evidence of them using films as vehicles for communist ideas. According to one of the Hollywood Ten, screenwriter Edward Dmytryk, any such effort would have fallen foul of every studio's final control over movie content. In his recall, the furthest that communist supporters dared go was in trying to insert 'liberal propaganda' into movies they were involved in making.[56]

Despite building his later political career on the defence of freedom, Reagan did nothing of note to fight the Hollywood purges. Instead, he was in denial about the existence of producer blacklists and greylists. This was the first manifestation of the trait displayed as governor and president to believe sincerely in something that he wanted to be true while adapting to the contrary reality. It was certainly the case that HUAC and conservative organizations were the nominal creators of the blacklists, but every studio kept copies. When HUAC undertook a second Hollywood investigation in 1951, the Reagan-led SAG executive employed specious logic to explain its position regarding those subpoenaed to testify. Actress Gale Sondergaard, wife of director Herbert Biberman – one of the Hollywood Ten now in prison – decided to plead the Fifth Amendment to avoid answering questions about her political past. In an open letter, she asked SAG's support against being blacklisted for this, but the response offered no such hope:

> The Guild Board believes that all participants in the international Communist Party conspiracy against our nation should be exposed for what they are – enemies of our country and of our form of government. [...] The Guild as a labor union will fight against any secret blacklist created by any group of employers. On the other hand, if any actor by his actions outside of union activities has so offended American public opinion that he has made himself unsaleable at the box office, the Guild cannot and would not force any employer to hire him. That is the individual actor's personal responsibility and it cannot be shifted to this union.[57]

Reagan stood by repentant communists willing to name former associates to HUAC, such as Sterling Hayden, but abandoned the likes of Sondergaard to her fate – 20 years elapsed before any studio would re-employ her. Among the many others to see his career suffer was Alexander Knox, whom Roy Brewer got greylisted for his one-time baiting of Reagan. It took two years for this actor to prove his loyalty to his persecutor's satisfaction, but most of his movie work would henceforth be in British productions.[58] SAG itself was only willing to challenge the supposedly non-existent blacklists and greylists in the case of individuals mistakenly named in them. It was in this way that Reagan met the woman who became his second wife.

Nancy Davis endured a difficult childhood without becoming emotionally scarred. She was born Anne Frances (but was always known as Nancy) Robbins in New York in July 1921 to actress Edith Luckett and car salesman Kenneth Robbins, who deserted his wife and daughter soon afterwards. Resuming her stage career as their only means of financial support, Edith left two-year-old Nancy in the care of an aunt and uncle. She eventually found the love of her life in Loyal Davis, an unhappily married Chicago neurosurgeon. In 1929, with their divorces finalized, the pair tied the knot and brought Nancy to live with them. Giving up the stage, Edith dedicated herself to supporting her new husband's rise to pre-eminence in his field. Nancy adored the stepfather who had given her a new life that included an expensive education at Chicago's Girls' Latin School and Smith College in Massachusetts. In 1935, she took Davis' name when Kenneth Robbins agreed to her adoption. Inheriting Edith's love of acting, Nancy found her mother's friendship with many stage and screen personalities helpful in opening career doors for her. After graduation in 1943, she appeared in theatrical productions, including some on Broadway, before landing a film contract with MGM in 1949. In her late twenties and not a classic beauty, she was typecast in character roles as the responsible woman in the 11 movies she made. Holding no illusions about stardom, her ambition was to make a marriage partnership akin to that of Edith and Loyal Davis. Like her mother, she was ready to give up her career to help a husband go on to great things. In her eyes, Ronald Reagan, now Hollywood's most eligible bachelor was perfect for the part.[59]

'My life didn't really begin until I met Ronnie,' Nancy later declared (almost exactly the words he used about her in a letter written in 1984).[60] The fateful encounter took place on 15 November 1949. This was just after the *Hollywood*

Reporter published Nancy Davis' name among the 208 co-signatories of an *amicus curiae* legal brief on behalf of the Hollywood Ten. The well-connected Nancy could easily have got MGM to clear up the matter. Instead she asked family friend Mervyn LeRoy, her director in *East Side, West Side* (1949), to enlist the SAG president's personal help in escaping the greylist. Reagan soon telephoned back with the good news that it was a case of mistaken identity – the name on the list was another Nancy Davis. Feigning continued concern, Nancy asked via LeRoy to arrange for her to have a full explanation in person. The knight errant consequently asked her out for dinner, a get-together that lasted long into the night. Nancy was an interested listener of Reagan's tales of his SAG battles with communists and laughed at his jokes, both a turn-off for Jane Wyman. She recalled her feelings as 'pretty close' to love at first sight – perhaps a subtle reference to a previous effort to engineer a meeting. Another influential friend, the wife of MGM production head Dore Schary, had thrown a dinner party to which both were invited, but Reagan's early departure on SAG business had foiled Nancy's hopes of getting him to escort her home. For the target of her wiles, their first real date was not so significant. Years later, he wondered whether bells had rung, but said, 'I had buried the part of me where such things happened so deep, I couldn't hear them.'[61]

The two became involved in a non-exclusive relationship. Reagan's dating of other women hurt Nancy, but she was willing to bide her time in the knowledge that he was 'in no hurry to make a commitment' after the painful break-up with Wyman. Fan-magazine efforts to marry them off as Hollywood's newest perfect couple annoyed him. To stay in Reagan's orbit, Nancy got herself elected onto the SAG executive as a replacement in late 1950. Two years of dating brought the pair ever closer. Sensing the moment was right, Nancy decided 'to give things a push' by telling Reagan that she was planning a return to Broadway. Rather than risk losing her, he popped the question. They became engaged on 21 February 1952 and married in a private ceremony on 4 March. By then, Nancy was pregnant with their child Patti, born on 22 October 1952. An enduring love match, the marriage restored equilibrium and optimism to Reagan's life, not least because his new wife was in his words 'her mother's daughter' who would put his career before her own rather than outstrip it. Remembering Nelle's teaching that everything worked out for the best in the end, he often told Nancy: 'You see my mother was right. If I hadn't been divorced, I never would have met you.'[62]

Nancy anticipated helping her new husband to advance his movie career but the gap between his status as Hollywood negotiator–politician and star was widening inexorably. Reagan's repeated re-election as SAG chair owed much to his success in getting Hollywood studios to agree better terms for actors. In 1949, he won them compensation for overtime and being recalled for close-up shots after a movie's completion. SAG executive secretary Jack Dales commented on his negotiating style: 'He was two men [...] aggressive fighter across the table, then in conference among ourselves in our caucuses [...] most realistic.'[63] As television grew in the early 1950s, Reagan's remit also extended to advancing actors' rights in the new industry. The greatest challenge he faced was the resistance of the newly formed Alliance of Television Film Producers (ATFP) to pay actors' residuals for reruns of television programmes in which they starred and sales of these to markets abroad. It was not his toughness as a negotiator that settled this issue but a Faustian bargain struck with MCA.

Having started out in the film capital as a talent agency, MCA branched into producing television versions of popular radio shows through its Revue subsidiary in 1950. This put it in violation of SAG's prohibition on actors being represented by organizations also engaged in production. The conflict of interest was self-evident – an agent was supposed to get top money for a client but a producer had to keep down costs in the name of profits. However, MCA Hollywood chief Lew Wasserman put a deal to SAG – if allowed to continue production enterprises, MCA would break the ATFP's united front on television residuals. As a longstanding MCA client, Reagan should have recused himself from the negotiations, but the benefits of the deal outweighed whatever doubts he had. Not only would Revue pay residuals, but also its Hollywood-based productions would break New York City's stranglehold on television programme-making. With Reagan supporting the proposal, the six other members (Nancy included) attending the SAG board meeting of 14 July 1952 approved an unprecedented blanket waiver – time-limited initially but made permanent two years later – for MCA to operate production and representation arms, something that no other organization would ever receive.[64]

The SAG–MCA deal turned out to be a real game-changer. It was the first step in Hollywood becoming the capital of television production. As Revue profits boomed, film studios overcame a common disdain for television to produce their own programmes for the medium. AFTP resistance to residuals crumbled in the face of Revue's advantages in getting top stars, many of them MCA clients, to appear in its productions. On the other hand, as the US Justice Department later commented, the waiver 'vaulted MCA to the head of the television industry with advantages that its competitors could never hope to equal'.[65] The SAG deal was the foundation of an immense expansion that saw it rise within a decade to pre-eminence as a Hollywood corporation. The vast profits from its combined enterprises gave 'the Octopus', as MCA became known, far-reaching and acquisitive tentacles. Its purchases included the entire backlog of Paramount and Universal films for showing on television, Decca Records, and in 1962 outright ownership of Universal Pictures.[66]

The question of whether Reagan had struck a corrupt deal with Wasserman dogged him for years, culminating in a 1962 appearance before a federal grand jury in the Justice Department's investigation of MCA's monopolistic practices. In an effective rehearsal for his performance before Iran–Contra inquisitors 25 years later, Reagan's testimony asserted no memory of involvement in the waiver negotiations. 'One of the reasons perhaps why this doesn't loom so importantly to me,' he declared, 'is I personally never saw any harm in it [...] those were times of great distress in the picture business, I was all for anyone that could give employment.'[67] This was an early display of Reagan's capacity to retreat into forgetfulness when breaking the rules in what he deemed a just cause. The waiver had saved Hollywood television production in his eyes, but MCA was in reality its principal beneficiary.

Alongside his SAG work, Reagan was in demand as a spokesman for the Motion Picture Industry Council (MPIC), formed in 1948 by producers, talent guilds, and craft unions to promote a better image of Hollywood. After serving as president for one term in 1949, he remained on its executive into the mid-1950s. Involvement in MPIC was another important staging post in Reagan's political development. Appearances before prestigious civic groups honed his capacity to communicate beyond Hollywood. Despite their fraying professional relationship, Jack Warner acknowledged that he was a very effective speaker for the industry. Reagan also learned to convey an image of gravitas when addressing non-Hollywood organizations. Until the late 1940s, he had shown preference for sports coats and slacks, but thereafter he increasingly wore a suit and tie on the public podium.[68]

It was on one of his MPIC missions that Reagan met Christian evangelist Billy Graham, later an important political ally. At a Southern Baptist fundraiser in Dallas in 1953, the Hollywood star debated with W. A. Criswell, pastor of Graham's home church, whether the movie industry was 'of the Devil'. Reagan's success in convincing a critic that Hollywood turned out wholesome films representing the best American values impressed Graham. 'Ron had not only changed a man's mind,' he recalled, 'but he had done it with charm, conviction, and humour – traits I would see repeatedly as I got to know him.'[69] The encounter was also early evidence of Reagan's ability to connect with the evangelical constituency that later became a significant source of his electoral support.

In terms of personal development, the most important speech Reagan gave in his emerging role as public speaker was the commencement address delivered at William Woods College, a Christian Church higher-education establishment in Fulton, Missouri, on 3 May 1952. Entitled 'America the Beautiful', this was his first public declaration that the United States was a divinely ordained nation, an idea with roots in Disciples doctrine. The most famous passage avowed:

> I, in my own mind, have thought of America as a place in the divine scheme of things that was set aside as a promised land [...] I believe that God in shedding his grace on this country has always [...] kept an eye on our land and guided it as a promised land.[70]

This notion suffused his rhetoric for the next 40 years, receiving its most famous expression in his farewell address as president in 1989. It came to underlie a fundamentally conservative vision that identified Americanism with free enterprise, anti-communism, and a small state.

At the time he gave the speech Reagan was still on the political odyssey that took him from left-liberalism to the right. Battling Hollywood Reds had turned him into an anti-communist, but a liberal one. In 1947 he joined the newly formed Americans for Democratic Action, the bailiwick of Cold War liberals, and helped organize the California chapter. Though elected to the national board in 1948, he only served a year and thereafter kept a low profile in an organization that encountered producer hostility for opposing the blacklists. Two deaths, Jack Reagan's in 1941 and – more particularly – Franklin D. Roosevelt's in April 1945, may have severed his strongest personal ties to the Democratic Party, but he was a prominent Hollywood supporter of Harry S. Truman in the 1948 presidential election. In the 1950 US Senate election in California, he delivered radio spots for Democrat Helen Gahagan Douglas, a fellow Hollywood liberal, in her unsuccessful campaign against Republican Richard Nixon. Some Douglas supporters actually worried that his 'far-out liberal' reputation would harm her cause. This did not stop local Democrats asking him to enter the congressional race for California's newly formed 22nd district in 1952. Two years later they asked him to run for a Senate seat. The answer in both cases was negative because his support for the party was weakening.[71]

There were clear signs that Reagan's liberalism had crested with Truman's election. His stay in Britain making *The Hasty Heart*, just when a Labour government was trying to build a New Jerusalem, sewed doubts about big-government benevolence. He recalled having seen 'firsthand how the welfare state sapped incentive to work' – possibly a reference to the frequent tea breaks that brought an obligatory halt to filming at Elstree Studios. The red tape, the rationing, and the perceived inefficiencies of newly nationalized industries were further bugbears of his first trip abroad. Reagan appeared incapable of understanding that Britain was grappling with postwar reconstruction problems far more daunting than America's. Fed up with the poor fare on offer, even at the Savoy, he got 12 steaks sent over from New York – only for the hotel's inadequate refrigeration to spoil most of them.[72]

While still a registered Democrat, Reagan backed the winning Republican presidential ticket of Dwight Eisenhower and Richard Nixon in 1952. The single most significant factor that precipitated this deviation was antipathy to high taxes, henceforth a constant theme of his political life. The 1945 Warner Bros. contract had put Reagan in the top marginal bracket of the federal income tax that had been made significantly more progressive in World War II. When alimony payments also began to hit his pocket, he grew very resentful of Uncle Sam's claim on his earnings. The Truman administration's 1950 proposal to eliminate tax loopholes, which enabled movie executives and stars to evade as much as two-thirds of what they ought to pay, caused further angst. Though never enacted, Reagan considered it evidence of Democratic hostility to the deserving rich in general and his own profession in particular. Frequently railing against heavy levies on the film industry in his MPIC addresses, he told the Kiwanis International in 1951 that no other business had been picked out for 'such discriminatory taxes'. If government could do this to Hollywood, he warned, the pocketbooks of ordinary people would be its next target.[73]

While his personal and political lives were taking their future shape, Reagan was also trying to resurrect his film career. He had grown disillusioned with Warner Bros. for not giving him decent parts. Having to go all the way to London just to play second lead to Richard Todd in *The Hasty Heart* was a particular grievance. Another was the failure of any studio executive to visit him in hospital when he was laid up for six weeks with a triple fracture of his leg after a collision with another player in a charity baseball game in July 1949. The damage from the injury required medical treatment for several years. The final straw was Jack Warner's decision to cast Errol Flynn in *Ghost Mountain*. Instrumental in getting Warner Bros. to purchase the option on this western, Reagan had expected to play the starring role.[74] For its part, the studio was furious about a newspaper interview that made public Reagan's dissatisfaction with the movies he was getting. Voicing determination to choose his own roles henceforth, he declared, 'With the parts I've had, I could telephone my lines in and it wouldn't make any difference.'[75]

Already going cold on a highly paid star who was no longer 'clicking at the box office', Warner Bros. executives had no intention of risking Reagan in his present state of mind in 'a picture of heavy costs'. In the summer of 1950 the studio indicated its readiness to end his current contract if he could do better elsewhere.[76] Riding to the rescue, MCA negotiated a non-exclusive, five-year, five-film deal with Universal Studios that would bring Reagan $75,000 a movie and a continuing stipend for making three films before final expiry of his association with Warner Bros. Although this arrangement would net just half his previous income, he took it in the vain hope of getting good parts. In late 1952, with things not working out anywhere near his expectations, he ended his lengthy tenure as SAG chair – the longest in the organization's history – out of concern that it was hurting his screen career. The producers, he later told a reporter, 'stop thinking of you as an actor. The image they have of you [is] [...] the guy who sat across the conference table beefing. And that's death.'[77]

In addition to the three movies made for Warner Bros., Reagan starred in three for Universal and three as a freelancer for Paramount from 1950 to 1953. The only one that was memorable – for the wrong reasons – was *Bedtime for*

Bonzo. Though nowhere near as bad as mockers later made out, the chimp was the real star and the human leads looked wooden by comparison. The two westerns that Reagan made – *The Last Outpost* (Paramount, 1951) and *Law and Order* (Universal, 1953) – only showed that he was no John Wayne. While he looked good on a horse, one-dimensional plots, poor dialogue, and pedestrian direction hampered both films. The other movies were entirely forgettable, his appearances in them dictated by the need for money. Reagan had always held forth about politics when making pictures – director Irving Rapper remembered him getting so carried away on his soapbox that he sometimes missed 'Action!' calls on the set of *The Voice of the Turtle*. The habit intensified when making movies in which he had no interest. Co-star Rhonda Fleming remembered him being more animated treating all and sundry to his views on world affairs between takes than when filming his scenes in the woeful *Hong Kong* (Paramount, 1952).[78]

Jack Warner had praised Reagan as a tower of strength in the struggle to keep studio production going in the 1946–7 strike, but had no sentimentality about his worth as a star. When his contract ended, there was no word of gratitude or parting gift to mark his nearly 15 years of service. Reagan drove off the Warner lot for the last time at noon on 28 January 1952. Within two hours, his name was removed from his personal parking bay. Two weeks earlier, Universal had decided not to take up the option on the remaining films of its contract because of Reagan's objections to the parts he was to play. Despite his hopes of freelance offers, producers hardly beat a path to his door. MCA pulled strings to get his Universal contract reactivated for *Law and Order* at his previous $75,000 fee, but there were no further reprieves.[79]

As 1953 drew to a close, Reagan's career was on the skids and he was short of cash, with two families to support and a new home and ranch to pay for. In September, he agreed to do a Korean War movie for MGM, *Prisoner of War* (1954), at a fee of only $30,000. A low-budget film, it effectively put him back in the B-movies whence he had come. Co-star newcomer Robert Horton, (soon to play Reagan's old part in a television version of *Kings Row*) expressed surprise that such a big name was in the picture too. 'I know it's a dog,' was the reply, 'but I'm not in a position *not* to do it.' A rushed production to capitalize on the topicality of the recently ended conflict resulted in a sub-par movie that bombed at the box office.[80] Just when his financial prospects looked their bleakest, there was the further blow of a demand to settle deferred federal tax payments. Reagan's famous optimism was now undergoing an even greater challenge than that posed by the Wyman divorce. At least Nancy had rescued him from that particular dip. It was difficult to see resurrection from his current predicament, but he soon rose phoenix-like from the ashes of his film career to achieve undreamed-of success in new fields.

FOUR

Right Star

As 1954 dawned, Ronald Reagan was a washed-up, hard-up movie actor preparing to appear in a Las Vegas revue to pay his bills. Before long, however, he renewed himself as a television star and corporate spokesman. Meanwhile, his political transition from liberalism to conservatism and from Democrat to Republican came to completion. An unrivalled capacity to deliver a popular conservative message brought him to national attention. His television address in support of Barry Goldwater's doomed candidacy was the brightest spot in an otherwise dismal 1964 presidential campaign for the GOP. As a consequence, Reagan found himself being urged by wealthy backers and conservative activists to seek election as California governor on the Republican ticket two years hence, a remarkable ascent for a man whose prospects had looked bleak a decade earlier.

The two-week appearance compèring a show in the Last Frontier hotel and casino in February 1954 was Reagan's career nadir. Only desperate need for money induced him to play the engagement that MCA had arranged as part of its efforts to break into Las Vegas, then a somewhat seedy gambling town with mob connections. Despite being a non-smoker (he gave up his pipe after the divorce), Reagan was already reduced to doing magazine advertisements for Chesterfield cigarettes. The $30,000 fee for the Las Vegas gig, which only required 15 minutes onstage nightly, matched what he received for his most recent film, *Prisoner of War*. Even so, it was insufficient compensation for the loss of dignity Reagan felt when appearing before a drink-fuelled crowd and performing the slapstick routine that ended the show. Other cabaret offers were soon forthcoming, but he told MCA, 'Never again will I sell myself so short.'[1]

Salvation was at hand in the job hosting *General Electric Theater*, an anthology drama series airing on Sunday evenings on CBS. Other than occasional guest appearances, television was a medium that Reagan had hitherto shunned for fear that people would not pay to see him in films if they saw him for free on the box. Although saving his movie career was no longer a consideration, he still rationalized his new one on artistic grounds. 'Television,' he declared,

> is now being produced in much the same manner that the film industry turns out their product. For a long time [...] TV was handled by strictly radio people. In short you were getting nothing but radio – with a picture.[2]

In other words, television had changed, not him.

MCA's television arm, Revue Productions, made the series for General Electric (GE). Wasserman may well have seen Reagan's five-year contract as payback for assistance in securing the 1952 waiver, but the sponsor was getting good value for money. The star was a personable host for the weekly dramas, a good performer whenever he acted in them, and an outstanding corporate spokesman – when the show was out of season, he was required to spend 16 weeks a year making public relations visits to GE plants across the country. Debuting on 26 September 1954, *General Electric Theater* made 19th spot in the ratings in the first season. Viewing figures remained high for most of its eight-year run, aided by audience retention from CBS's hugely popular preceding programme, *The Ed Sullivan Show*, and lack of competition in the nine o'clock slot until the western series *Bonanza* aired on NBC in September 1959. MCA's immense client portfolio enabled it to book top stars – including some 40 Oscar winners – for the show. In return, these big names received a share of the profits that their episode generated after five showings (some dramas were still being shown somewhere in the world when Reagan's presidency ended).[3]

As well as introducing each weekly drama, Reagan plugged the company's futuristic manufactures at the end. His trademark slogan, 'At General Electric, progress is our most important product,' became so well known that daughter Maureen's schoolmates would endlessly quote it at her. A single show brought him before a bigger audience than in cinemas over a whole year. Small wonder, therefore, that a 1958 opinion survey named him among the most recognized men in America. As well as reconnecting with older viewers familiar with his movies, Reagan became known to younger ones, many of whom would later vote for him. In Garry Wills' words, they were 'the first television generation, being introduced to the man who would use television better than any other politician'.[4] The GE contract also relieved Reagan of financial worries. It brought him a guaranteed annual salary of $125,000, soon raised to $150,000, with extra for appearing in a total of 41 of the weekly dramas (four alongside Nancy). To his disgust, higher earnings also increased his income taxes – until MCA resolved this problem by making him part-owner of the show in March 1959. Henceforth, Reagan got 25 per cent of the eventual proceeds, but received less income from the first run that just covered costs – so he paid less in taxes.[5]

Although the work was demanding, Reagan derived benefits of a different kind from acting as GE's roving spokesman. He spent the equivalent of two full years from 1954 to 1962 on the road visiting every one of the company's 139 plants in 39 states and meeting more than 250,000 of its employees. In the first year, Reagan did two tours of eight weeks each, a physically exhausting schedule that kept him too long from home. Thereafter, he did more frequent tours of shorter duration – the longest being 21 days – but would still lose some three pounds in weight for every week away.[6] At first, Reagan was essentially a goodwill ambassador in the cause of corporate loyalty in GE's far-flung empire. The typical schedule for these visits was a hectic one – Reagan would begin by meeting plant managers, then speak with groups of selected workers, thereafter walk round the entire plant making random stops to chat with employees, and finally attend an evening event designed to strengthen company links with the local community. His standard patter interspersed praise for the corporation with Hollywood stories, jokes (in the vernacular for all-male audiences, sanitized for others), and warnings about the internal and external threat from communism. He also learned that railing against federal bureaucracy was a sure-fire way of getting applause.[7]

All this was perfect training for Reagan's later electoral campaigns. Instead of the long discourses inflicted on Hollywood friends, he became skilled in packaging his remarks when brevity was required. He also learned to conserve his voice, assess what stories and jokes worked with different audiences, deal with occasional hecklers, and fill his glass mostly with water at evening receptions while others were getting merry. Perhaps most importantly, he reconnected with ordinary Americans, who were to become his bedrock constituency. The tales of woe he heard from GE employees of all kinds about government red tape and taxes made a powerful impression. Ed Langley, an occasional travelling aide, recalled him saying:

> When I went on those tours [...] I was seeing the same people that I
> grew up with in Dixon, Illinois. I realized I was living in a tinsel factory
> [in Hollywood]. And this exposure brought me back.[8]

It all added up, in the GE official's estimate, to a rediscovery of 'the native conservatism of working America'.[9]

This was one reason why Reagan later characterized his tours as 'almost a postgraduate course in political science for me'.[10] Another was the changing nature of his duties following their integration into the 'Employee and Community Relations Program'. Founded in 1947 by GE vice-president Lemuel Boulware, this was ostensibly a civic project to educate the company's workers and the citizens of communities that were home to its plants about the issues of the day. In reality, it was intended to develop support for GE's conservative agenda of smaller government, lower taxes, restriction of union power, and Cold War militarism (it was a beneficiary of big defence budgets).[11] On learning that Reagan was adept at delivering the right message, Boulware changed the tour format for 1956 to provide more opportunity for doing so. Adapting without difficulty, Reagan read voraciously in preparation for the new mission while travelling by train to GE locations, a practice he sustained during rest periods at home. His increasingly conservative instincts acquired intellectual foundation through studying the works of economists like Friedrich Hayek and Henry Hazlitt, author of the bestselling *Economics in One Lesson* (1948), journals of the right – notably as a charter subscriber to William Buckley's *National Review* (which Boulware helped found in 1955), and GE publications that promoted Boulwarism to company employees.[12]

Initially just horror stories of government interference, the talks that Reagan delivered for the Boulware programme soon became more noteworthy for their ideological rationale. This was in line with the advice received from GE president Ralph Cordiner: 'You'd better get yourself a philosophy, something you can stand for and something you think this country stands for.'[13] The big idea that Reagan fixed upon became the organizing principle of his emergent conservatism. Through making American freedom the core of his belief system he could link the twin menaces of big government and communism as the main threats to liberty. This was essentially the message on which Reagan built his political career. As president, he invoked the need to defend freedom more often than any of his predecessors, making it the watchword of the so-called 'Reagan Revolution'. More than any other American political figure of the twentieth century, he endowed freedom with a conservative meaning, in the process appropriating for the right what had once been a liberal concept.

As historian Eric Foner observed, 'No idea is more fundamental to Americans' sense of themselves as individuals and as a nation than freedom.'[14] Nevertheless, it acquired different meanings at various stages of US history based on changing understanding of the benefits of government. Over the course of the nation's first century and a half a strong national state was variously interpreted as the agent or enemy of freedom. Seizing the opportunity to redefine freedom amid the Great Depression, Franklin D. Roosevelt espoused a 'broader definition of liberty under which we are moving forward to [...] greater [economic] security for the average man', and extolled the federal government as its principal guarantor in the form of the New Deal. Conversely, FDR identified entrenched economic inequality and 'the privileged few' advocating unrestricted private enterprise as freedom's greatest enemies. The liberal understanding of freedom gained further elaboration in Roosevelt's portrayal of World War II as a struggle against human slavery under fascism. In the 1941 State of the Union Address, he anticipated the postwar emergence of a new world order based on four 'essential human freedoms': freedom of speech, freedom of worship, freedom from fear, and freedom from want. The inclusion of the last of these embodied liberal belief that freedom based on economic security was a fundamental American ideal worthy of universal application.[15]

Reagan initially understood the meaning of freedom within this Rooseveltian framework. As a conservative evangelist, he promulgated it in anti-statist terms that emphasized restoration of the free market, opposition to confiscatory taxation, and removal of all obstacles impeding the right to contract freely for goods and services. He still adhered to FDR's wartime concept of the free world locked in a worldwide struggle with slavery, but now identified communism as the source of oppression. The idea that America had a divinely ordained mission to serve as a beacon of freedom for people elsewhere found a regular place in his rhetoric, usually accompanied by invocation of Abraham Lincoln's image of it as 'the last best hope of man on earth'.

Impressed with Reagan's first-year performances for Boulware's programme, GE began using him to spread the word to other parts of the corporate community. He appeared before state chambers of commerce, national business conventions, and politically influential groups like the Executives' Club of Chicago. The standard theme of these addresses, in line with the argument propounded by Austrian political economist Friedrich Hayek in *The Road to Serfdom* (1944), was that communism could emerge in democracies through the 'creeping socialism' of government's ever-expanding role in the economy.[16] In a 1962 speech entitled 'Losing freedom by installments', he warned: 'A government can't control the economy without controlling the people [...] when a government sets out to do that, it must use force and coercion to achieve its purpose.'[17] Confident that blue-collar America was also receptive to this message, Reagan started delivering it to plant workers. In January 1959, for example, the *GE Schenectady News* carried an interview with him under the heading: 'Reagan sees a loss of freedom through steady increase in taxes.'[18]

The GE spokesman's message also found interested listeners in the corridors of political power. On receiving a copy of 'Business, ballots, and bureaus', a diatribe against tax-and-spend government delivered to business leaders at New York's Waldorf Hotel in June 1959, Vice-President Richard Nixon sent a letter of congratulation. In reply, Reagan avowed, '[T]here is a groundswell of economic conservatism building up which could reverse the entire tide of present day "statism."' Clearly intent on enlisting the charismatic wordsmith to speak in support of his 1960 presidential campaign, the most consummate of Republican politicians responded: 'You have the ability of putting complicated technical ideas into words everyone can understand. Those of us who have spent a number of years in Washington too often lack the ability to express ourselves in this way.'[19]

Reagan's rise as a star of the right coincided with the abrupt termination of his movie stardom. Lew Wasserman had got him the lead alongside Barbara Stanwyck in RKO's *Cattle Queen of Montana* (1954). RKO's eccentric owner, billionaire Howard Hughes, mistakenly thought that a new Technicolor western with well-known stars would help him sell the virtually bankrupt studio as a going concern, but a weak screenplay limited its box-office appeal. One of Reagan's own favourites among his films, it would be the last movie he viewed before leaving the White House.[20] Hughes tried again with *Tennessee's Partner* (1955), a well-acted western featuring Reagan alongside John Payne, but its 'buddy' theme did not click with audiences in the manner of heroic westerns featuring the likes of John Wayne and James Stewart. Two years elapsed before Reagan got a new picture. Columbia's *Hellcats of the Navy* (1957), a clichéd World War II movie about maverick submariners engaged on a hazardous mission to sink the Japanese merchant fleet, barely recouped costs. No studio risked the fading star in another movie until he got fifth billing as a psychotic villain in *The Killers* (1964), a made-for-television production released in theatres because it was deemed too violent for the box. 'I'm weary […] of being the good, the sweet, the colorless charm boy,' Reagan had remarked back in 1950. 'I'd make a good louse and I hope they're not out of style before I get a chance to find out.'[21] When his wish came true, it gave him cause for regret. Reagan was uncomfortable that a scene in his movie swansong showed him viciously slapping co-star Angie Dickinson.

As a politician Reagan faced derision for being a failed actor. Governor Pat Brown of California invited voters in the 1966 gubernatorial election to compare his own achievements in office with his rival's record in 'such film epics as *Bedtime for Bonzo*'.[22] The Soviets later got in on the act. Georgi Arbatov, Moscow's top US expert, ridiculed Reagan as a B-movie actor in a press conference at the time of the Geneva summit. During a private moment in these talks, the US president took the opportunity to inform Mikhail Gorbachev that he had appeared in A-films – and was delighted to learn that his Soviet counterpart had seen *Kings Row*.[23] Reagan resented mockery of his movie career as disrespectful both to himself and to fellow actors. To his mind, he had done well in a noble profession that had promoted American values in Hollywood's golden age. His political career embodied the ideals that he had represented on screen. As Garry Wills put it, he played the same part in movies and in government: 'He always acted like Ronald Reagan. It is a heartwarming role.'[24]

During his political career, Reagan developed a nice line in self-deprecating humour about his time in movies, but this was a defence mechanism. His memoirs convey the real disappointment he felt about declining cinematic stardom. In the first, he wrote of the 'heartache' of the film business: 'Probably the most tragic thing is to be denied the chance to practice your profession when someone handing out the parts decides against you.' In the second, he lamented not getting the action roles he craved: 'When I'd ask Jack [Warner] to put me in a western, he'd cast me in another movie in which I'd wear a gray-flannel suit.'[25] The screen persona of most stars vastly outshines their real-life one, but the opposite was true of Reagan. As biographer Anne Edwards observed, 'He could not have helped but feel that his potential had never been realized, that the power and charisma he exuded in his SAG dealings and his speech givings should have been transferred to his image on film.'[26] This raises the question of why Reagan did not enjoy the same success in movies as in politics if he was playing himself in both.

For some commentators, Reagan's inability to get to the top, even with MCA behind him, was down to lack of star quality. 'Lew Wasserman nurtured talent,' asserted Hollywood journalist Dennis McDougal, 'but he didn't create it.' Others regard Reagan as perfectly competent in romantic and light-comedy roles, but little else. According to Garry Wills, he 'failed in Hollywood because he was not satisfied with his proper rung, with the range he commanded, but attempted heavier roles he could not sustain'.[27] Neither assessment is wholly satisfactory. Reagan showed real talent in rising out of B-movies to become a star in the A-pictures of his early-1940s halcyon days. In the postwar era, what he yearned for were action roles, but his failure to get good ones owed much to the travails of the studio system. The rise of television was not the only commercial problem facing the film industry. The Supreme Court's industry-transforming antitrust judgement, *US v. Paramount, Inc.* (1948), required the separation of film production from distribution and exhibition. Compelled to divest their cinema chains, the major studios could no longer count on automatic block-bookings for their films. Henceforth, movies needed guaranteed box-office appeal if they were to get widespread exhibition, making them more dependent than ever on the marketability of their stars. Trapped in a catch-22 situation, Reagan needed a good picture to revive his stardom on return from war service, but the predictably limited ticket sales for the modest movies given to him convinced Warner Bros. that he no longer had star power.

In terminating the big studios' stranglehold over movie exhibition, the Paramount ruling encouraged the rise of independent film production. With their share of Hollywood output falling by more than a half in the decade following this judgement, the majors significantly reduced the number of actors, writers, and directors under contract. Liberated from studio control, some stars could now command big money as freelancers, but Reagan's box-office decline prevented him benefiting from the transformation of Hollywood. Despite preaching the virtues of the free market in his political career, he would always express reservations about the judicial decision that terminated the Hollywood oligopoly. A company man to his core, he resented the mortal blow that forced the studios 'to take all the risk with an excellent chance of no return'. Reagan was still carping 40 years later that the anti-monopoly ruling had unnecessarily destroyed 'the stability of the industry'. In his mind, each studio's drive to turn out great pictures that outsold rival productions ensured the competitiveness of the classic Hollywood system. The outcome of judicial intervention was a risk-averse business reluctant to take a chance 'on people and stories'.[28] This was an instance of Reagan rewriting history to leave out the bad bits. The studios of Hollywood's golden age undoubtedly produced many great films, but their record also included exploitation of employees, ruthless disloyalty to those accused of communist sympathies, discrimination in the employment and on-screen representation of non-whites, and monopolistic practice to throttle competition from independent producers and exhibitors.

An actor friend offered another explanation for Reagan's unfulfilled movie career. 'If Nancy Reagan instead of Jane Wyman had been Ronald Reagan's first wife,' James Stewart remarked, 'he would never have gone into politics. Instead she would have seen to it that he got all the best parts, he would have won three or four Oscars, and been a real star.'[29] However tongue-in-cheek this was meant, it testified accurately to Nancy's intense ambition for her husband. Paradoxically, their cinematic careers went down in the same ship – *Hellcats of the Navy*, the first film in which they co-starred and the last real movie that either of them made. Aside from this attempted comeback and occasional appearances on *General Electric Theater*, Nancy's job from the moment of her marriage was Ronald Reagan.

Building her life around his, Nancy supported her husband's ambitions, urged him to aim high (and was a shrewd judge of when the time was right to do so), celebrated his successes, and offered reassurance when he was down. In turn he became emotionally dependent on her, the inverse of his early relationship with Jane Wyman. Whatever his initial reluctance to commit to marriage, she became the love of his life, as he was hers. On location in Glacier Park making *Cattle Queen of Montana* in July 1954, he wrote a letter to 20-month-old Patti that was clearly meant for Nancy. He recounted how the beautiful night scene had 'filled me with a longing so great that it seemed I'd die of pain if I couldn't reach out and touch your Mommie'. The very next day, he wrote direct to Nancy, 'I just see you in all the beauty there is because in you I've found all the beauty in my life.'[30] After nearly two decades of marriage, Reagan described his feelings for Nancy to a reporter: 'How do you describe coming into a warm room from out of the cold, never waking up bored?' Eschewing imagery, Nancy simply said, 'He was all I had ever wanted in a man, and more.' Cynical political reporters considered their publicly displayed affection for each other as just a practised Hollywood act, but eventually accepted it as real. 'I guess they came to think,' Nancy remarked, 'that nobody could be faking it that well – or for that long!'[31]

Though not responsible for her husband's conservatism, Nancy certainly facilitated it. While Reagan was away on GE tours, she became involved in charitable activity that brought her into the orbit of influential wives of powerful men. Befriended by Betsy Bloomingdale, wife of department store heir Alfred Bloomingdale, she gained entrée into an exclusive circle of couples who liked to socialize together. As a consequence, the Reagans became friendly with Armand Deutsch of Sears Roebuck and wife Harriet, mega-rich publishers Walter and Lee Annenberg, realtor Jack Wrather and wife – former actress Bonita Granville, automobile-dealership magnate Holmes Tuttle and wife Virginia, and oil-rich Henry and Grace Salvatori.

Calling themselves 'the Group', their numbers grew in time to include Rexall drug magnate Justin Dart and his wife, the former actress Jane Bryan, who had starred in three movies with Reagan – *Brother Rat* (1938), *Girls on Probation* (1938), and *Brother Rat and a Baby* (1940), philanthropists Earle and Marion O'Brien, bakery executive Ed Mills and wife Grace, and oil tycoon Cy Rubel and wife Henrietta.[32] As well as being rich, the men were mostly Republican and conservative. Major fundraisers for the GOP, Tuttle, Salvatori, and Dart were especially important in promoting Reagan's rise in politics. Nancy's own family connections further helped in this regard. Following retirement with Edith to Phoenix, Arizona, Loyal Davis introduced his son-in-law to Barry Goldwater and other influential figures in this new epicentre of western conservatism. The former neurosurgeon, an avowed right-winger, also tutored him on the evils of socialized medicine.

Needing to count the pennies when first married, the Reagans had moved out to Pacific Palisades, an up-and-coming area close to the ocean, in 1952. Their two-storey, seven-room house would have cost double its $23,000 price if located in Beverly Hills. Once their financial situation improved, they relocated a short distance in 1956 to what became their longstanding home. It was newly constructed to their specifications on a spectacular site carved into a steep, deeply wooded slope of the Santa Monica Mountains. Virtually hidden from the street below and with a massive iron gate to further guarantee privacy, the house offered an unlimited view across the city to the ocean. GE stocked it with all the latest electrical appliances, some not yet available in stores. A special panel had to be built on the side of the house for all the wiring and switches. Reagan loved the plethora of up-to-date gadgets. Nancy, in contrast, 'wasn't wild about having my home turned into a corporate showcase', but accepted it in the interests of his 'first steady job in years'.[33]

Pacific Palisades had the further advantage of being close to Yearling Row, the 290-acre ranch in Malibu Canyon that Reagan had bought for $65,000 in March 1951 with the proceeds from the sale of the smaller Northridge ranch and some of the horses stabled there. As well as paying for his dream home, the GE earnings financed construction of his dream ranch house on this land. Whatever reservations Nancy felt about a place named partly after Jane Wyman's 1946 film *The Yearling* (the 'Row' came from Reagan's *Kings Row*), the family spent a lot of time there. To even things up in the nomenclature stakes, the first filly born at the ranch to Tar Baby, now kept for breeding rather than movie-making, was named Nancy D. When fully grown, the mare succeeded its mother as Reagan's personal riding horse.[34]

In 1957, Reagan was named 'Hollywood Father of the Year', but his record as a parent would come in for critical media scrutiny during his presidency.

All four of his children attested that his infatuation with Nancy left little room for them in his affections and that his emotional remoteness made it hard to confide in him.[35] Whatever Reagan's imperfections, the letters written to his children at various stages of their lives suggest a loving father.[36] However, like most successful men of his era, he did not give them enough time. As the main carer, Nancy was probably over-protective, over-indulgent, and over-cautious. Looking back, she admitted being more successful as a wife than as a mother.[37] The Reagans may have made mistakes aplenty with their children, but this did not make them unique – then or now. Their approach to parenting was in keeping with the practice of the time and its shortcomings. The task was made more difficult through having to juggle their own children's needs with those of the Reagan–Wyman marriage when blended families were not commonplace.

One of the most painful consequences of Reagan's divorce was only getting to see Maureen and Michael at weekends. As Nancy became a bigger part of his life, she often came along on days out with the children, who both liked her (naming Tar Baby's foal Nancy D was Maureen's idea). Accordingly, they had time to adjust before their father remarried. However, Patti's birth inevitably left them feeling neglected, as she became the focus of attention. Meanwhile Maureen and Michael had to cope with bewildering changes in their life with Wyman – her sudden second marriage to musical arranger Fred Karger that lasted just two years (the pair remarried in 1961, divorcing again in 1965), their conversion to Catholicism at her insistence (and over Reagan's objections) in 1954, and the much disliked Catholic boarding schools she chose for them.[38]

Maureen felt lonely and excluded from both her parents' lives on being sent to Marymount College in Westchester County, New York. When she applied for a federal job on graduation, an FBI background check quoted a school administrator's opinion that her emotional insecurities made it difficult for her 'to achieve goals set by herself or others'. Working in Washington DC, she became involved with a policeman ten years her senior, in her words 'as a way to feel emotionally connected to another person'. Exploiting his FBI contacts, a worried Reagan got the agency to run a background check on the man, something it had no jurisdiction to undertake. The pair got married in a simple ceremony that Reagan and Nancy, but not Wyman, attended. From the outset, Maureen was subjected to extreme violence that lasted nearly two years until she found the courage to walk out, something only revealed in her

1989 memoir. It was not Reagan's reserve but Maureen's sense of shame that prevented her confiding in him. With domestic violence little understood at this time, wives were often made to feel guilty for provoking it.[39]

Already sensitive about his adoptive status, Michael's sense of self-worth suffered further damage when at age eight he was sexually molested and photographed nude by a summer-camp counsellor, something he did not tell his parents until 1987. Such were his inner demons, he was sent on psychiatric advice to live with the Reagans in 1959, but Nancy had difficulty coping with his moodiness, particularly when her husband was away on GE duties. Fortunately, Loyal Davis found Michael a place in a Phoenix boarding school, where he was happy. The close relationship that developed with Edith while there gave him a sense of being loved. However, Reagan's failure to recognize him in hat and gown at his graduation ceremony, the result of not wearing spectacles, became a new source of grievance. Despite success as an ocean boat racer and radio talk-show host in the 1970s, Michael remained emotionally volatile until he revealed what troubled him.[40]

Of all their children, Patti caused the Reagans greatest concern. When very young, she was attention-seeking and prone to throw tantrums, especially after the birth of brother Ron in 1958. The Reagans had not planned such a gap between children, but Nancy suffered two miscarriages.[41] So long the centre of their affections, Patti resented the new arrival. Her parents also made the mistake of not telling her that she had step-siblings. Only when Michael came to live did they explain that he was her half-brother. When Maureen told Patti soon afterwards that they were half-sisters, the news caused her considerable distress.[42] Things got worse as Patti went through her teens and entered womanhood. Gifted in the performing arts, she did not do well scholastically but made it to Northwestern University in 1970. To the chagrin of her parents, she soon quit college to co-habit with Eagles guitarist Bernie Leadon.

Patti blamed many of her difficulties on unresolved problems with her father. She once said, 'I never knew who he was, I could never get through to him.'[43] This was more or less what Reagan thought about her. As a 14-year-old, she burst into tears on being told of his election as California governor, saying, 'Oh no! How can you do this to me?' When Patti was in her twenties, Reagan wrote to his old Dixon pastor, Ben Cleaver: 'I am something of an embarrassment to Patti [...] She is typical of the generation gap, finds much wrong with the world, and can't really see that some of us are trying to help.'[44] Nancy later remarked that their mother–daughter relationship was 'one of the most painful and disappointing aspects of my life'. In her mind there was little she could have done to make things better between them. 'Some children are just born a certain way,' she concluded, 'and there's little you can do about it.'[45]

Inheriting his father's optimism and good humour, Ron (formally Ronald Prescott to avoid the Jr tag) had a good relationship with his parents, but they had to accept his independent mind. When 12, approximately his father's age in accepting baptism into the Church of Christ, he declared himself an atheist. Reagan always found his subsequent refusal to attend church hard to accept. Ron went through a difficult patch in his teens but this was a case of temporary rebellion rather than permanent alienation. A series of disciplinary infractions got him expelled from one high school. A relationship in his teens with a much older woman also shocked his mother and father. He still made the grades to get into Yale, but left in his first semester to become a ballet dancer, a long-held ambition never discussed with his parents. Overcoming disappointment that none of their children would earn a college degree, the Reagans helped Ron choose a ballet school (with Gene Kelly's guidance). They were proud when he earned a place with the famed Joffrey Ballet in New York, a significant achievement for a late starter.[46]

As well as meeting the challenges of parenthood, Reagan had to cope with the decline and eventual death of his beloved mother. The day after turning 79, Nelle died in her sleep from a cerebral haemorrhage on 25 July 1962. Osteoporosis and creeping senility, later classified as Alzheimer's disease, had not stopped her doing good works well into her seventies. She regularly drove from West Hollywood to visit inmates of the Olive View tuberculosis sanatorium in the San Fernando Valley. Worried about her getting lost, Reagan personally distributed photos of his mother to every gas station on the route with contact instructions if she showed up in a confused state.[47] Nelle's worsening condition finally induced her sons to place her in a Santa Monica rest home in 1958. Since her death was not sudden like Jack's, Reagan bore it with greater stoicism, but always considered her spirit to be close by. When president, he admitted taking comfort in the belief that 'maybe she's still giving me a hand now and then'.[48]

As the 1960s dawned Reagan continued to make strides in his public life. With another battle looming over residuals in late 1959, fellow actors called on him to serve another term as president of SAG. This dispute was over studio payments to actors when their old movies were shown on television. As part-owner of *General Electric Theater*, something not known to the SAG board, Reagan should have recused himself on conflict-of-interest grounds, but returned to duty at Lew Wasserman's urging. The recent acquisition of Universal's and Paramount's old movies gave MCA an important stake in the dispute. When talks broke down, SAG struck all the major studios on 7 March 1960, except MCA-connected Universal, which had agreed to abide by any industry-wide deal. In an ironic reversal of the late-1940s labour wars, the IATSE-organized studio employees looked set to cross the actors' picket lines. Forgetting his own past, Reagan denounced their president Richard Walsh as 'a lousy damn strike-breaker!' Wasserman got mob-connected Hollywood fixer Sidney Korshak to sort Walsh out. Nevertheless, the first strike in SAG's history would drag on for six weeks before a compromise settlement was reached with the producers on 18 April.[49]

The SAG executive accepted a one-time payment of $2.65 million for all film residuals to invest as seed money in a new pension-welfare fund for members, and 6 per cent of the gross, minus distribution costs, of post-1960 films and shows sold to television. The membership voted 6,399–259 to accept what looked like the best terms that could have been obtained. Shortly afterwards, on 9 June, Reagan submitted his resignation to the board on grounds that he was about to become a producer. This was another untruth that a job well done perhaps excused in his mind. Veteran actors remembered his second SAG coming with anything but fondness, however. As television money for the pre-1960 movies poured into studio coffers from all over the world, some accused Reagan of a sell-out. In 1981, a top star of the 1930s, Mickey Rooney, sued the major studios in an unsuccessful class action on behalf of fellow actors for residual payments on these films. The bitterness felt against Reagan was a factor in SAG's decision the same year to deny him its lifetime-achievement award.[50]

Once free of union duties, Reagan went off to help Richard Nixon in the 1960 presidential race against John Kennedy. This was the first time that he campaigned openly for a Republican ticket, a conversion attributed to the Democrats having changed, not him. 'By 1960,' he later wrote, 'I realized the real enemy wasn't big business, it was big government.'[51] Only the Nixon team's insistence that his attacks on JFK would have more effect if he remained a Democrat deterred Reagan from changing party registration. Now firmly ensconced on the right, his visceral antipathy to the Democratic candidate was evident in a handwritten letter to Nixon. Denouncing Kennedy's nomination acceptance address as 'a frightening call to arms' for un-American ideals, he declared:

> Under the tousled boyish haircut it is still old Karl Marx – first launched a century ago. There is nothing new in the idea of a government being Big Brother to us all. Hitler called his 'State Socialism' and way before him it was 'benevolent monarchy.'[52]

Reagan journeyed further rightward when Dalton Trumbo, one of the Hollywood Ten, was openly credited for the screenplay of two blockbuster movies released in 1960, *Exodus* and *Spartacus*. This signified the effective collapse of the blacklist. Of course, it was an open secret in Hollywood that Trumbo had produced scripts for other movies under a pseudonym – including the Audrey Hepburn smash *Roman Holiday* (1953). This did not stop Reagan dashing off a letter criticizing *Playboy* publisher Hugh Hefner for letting Trumbo pen anti-blacklist sentiments in an article for his magazine.[53] The conviction that 'Communists are crawling out of the rocks in Hollywood' inspired a personal campaign against the danger of renewed infiltration. This put Reagan on platforms organized by radical-right conspiracy groups like the John Birch Society, the Church League of America, and the Christian Anti-Communist Crusade. Fellow speakers included southern segregationists like Orval Faubus and Ross Barnett, respectively governors of Arkansas and Mississippi. Ignoring their racism, Reagan praised them as staunch anti-communists and defenders of states' rights against federal encroachment.[54]

The 'creeping socialism' of Kennedy administration initiatives also fuelled strident rhetoric. Reagan assailed federal aid to education as 'the foot in the door' to control of schools, attacked unemployment insurance benefit increases as 'a prepaid vacation plan for freeloaders', and damned Social Security expansion as socialistic.[55] 'Ronald Reagan speaks out against Socialized Medicine' was a disc sponsored by the American Medical Association in opposition to health-care legislation under consideration by Congress (much reproduced on the conservative blogosphere during the battle against enactment of Obamacare in 2010). In the recording, he warned that 'one of the traditional methods of imposing statism or Socialism on a people has been by way of medicine'.[56] Explaining away the absence of socialist doctrine in the actual proposal, Reagan told some friends, 'It comes about through the rules and regulations the Department of Health, Education and Welfare puts into effect to administer the bill.'[57] Material from the Liberty Amendment Lobby, an organization demanding repeal of the progressive income tax, also found its way into his speeches. In one address, he declared, 'We have received this [...] direct from Karl Marx, who designed it as the prime essential of a socialist state.' The same speech foreshadowed one of the goals he pursued as governor and later president – to starve the liberal state of revenue as a way of controlling spending. 'Here is the main battleground,' it concluded. 'We must reduce the government's supply of money and deny it the right to borrow.'[58]

In Reagan's mind, the Kennedy administration engaged in underhand tactics to silence him.[59] The summons from the Robert Kennedy-headed Justice Department to testify before a grand jury in the investigation of MCA in February 1962 planted the seeds of suspicion. Wanting to see if the Reagans had received any pay-offs for approving the MCA waiver, it then despatched a federal marshal to the *General Electric Theater* set with a subpoena demanding their income-tax returns for 1952–5. Embarrassing as this was, nothing sinister was afoot. Federal authorities did file a civil suit against MCA in July 1962, but soon dropped the case when it sold the talent agency that was now a minor part of corporate business.[60] Nor was Kennedy pressure at work in the termination of his GE contract in March 1962. The company's image had taken a battering from a federal investigation of price-fixing and cartelization in the heavy-equipment sector of the electrical industry. Although Ralph Cordiner was still CEO, new personnel charged with restoring GE's good name wanted Reagan to confine his road tour to assisting in this task. It was his refusal to give up the role entrusted him by the now retired Lemuel Boulware, combined with the precipitous decline in *General Electrical Theater* viewing figures from competition with *Bonanza*, that sealed his fate.[61] Misplaced resentment about being the victim of a Kennedy vendetta explains Reagan's lack of demonstrable sorrow at JFK's assassination on 22 November 1963. As most of the nation grieved, he and Nancy went ahead with a prearranged party for conservative Hollywood friends on the Sunday evening after the tragedy.[62]

Reagan lacked regular employment for two years after finishing with GE. The producer income he received for reruns of the *General Electric Theater*, the money from guest-star roles in other series, and occasional fees for public speaking kept him going. This dry period ended when Neil Reagan, now an advertising executive with McCann Erickson, used his contacts with soap-manufacturer sponsor Boraxo to get his brother a job as weekly host and occasional actor on the long-running *Death Valley Days* western series in 1964. This was a reversal of fraternal roles from WHO radio days in Des Moines, but Reagan accepted the favour with gratitude.

The new job allowed plenty of time for giving speeches in the 1964 presidential-election campaign, a critical one in the development of the Republican Party. The GOP was in the midst of tumultuous internal debate over its political identity. In every presidential election since 1936 it had nominated moderate candidates – mainly from the north-east – to run for the White House in the belief that the New Deal political tradition was too strong to overturn. Dwight D. Eisenhower, the only Republican to win the presidency since FDR, once remarked, 'Should any political party attempt to abolish social security, unemployment insurance, and eliminate labor laws and farm programs, you would not hear of that party again in our political history.' Associated with the GOP right early in his career, Richard Nixon moved to the centre as his presidential ambitions took shape. In common with Eisenhower, acceptance of New Deal-inspired initiatives while drawing the line against federal expansion into new areas was his formula for national electoral success. However, New Deal rollback was precisely what grassroots activists, mainly based in the Midwest, west, and south-west, now advocated. These anti-establishment conservatives decried the moderate approach of 'me too' statism as the reason for the party being so long out of power. Convinced that the tectonic plates of American politics were shifting against liberal excess, they rallied behind Senator Barry Goldwater's presidential candidacy, which developed into a crusade to eradicate the legacy of Franklin D. Roosevelt.[63]

An early Goldwater enthusiast, Reagan was much taken with the Arizonan's (actually ghostwritten) tract, *The Conscience of a Conservative*, published in 1960. This defined conservatism as a philosophy prioritizing 'the dignity of the individual human being' that was fundamentally at odds with 'dictators who rule by terror and equally those gentler collectivists who ask our permission to play God with the human race'. It also pronounced the communist aim to conquer the world to be the 'central political fact of our time'.[64] In 1962, Reagan had finally registered as a Republican while supporting Richard Nixon's campaign to win the GOP nomination for the California governorship against a right-wing rival – a race the former vice-president won before going down to heavy defeat at the hands of Democrat Pat Brown in the general election. Two years later Reagan supported Goldwater in his battle for the Republican presidential nomination against Governor Nelson Rockefeller of New York, the champion of the party's moderate wing. The divisions evident within the California GOP in the previous gubernatorial race reached new intensity in the 1964 presidential primary. Reagan caused the moderate wing deep offence with his verbal assaults on Rockefeller as the false voice of Republicanism.[65]

Once Goldwater became the GOP nominee, Reagan changed tone with the aim of generating support for the Arizonan beyond the conservative camp. The reassuring message in his speeches that there was still time for America to save itself from the drift to socialism contrasted with the angry, pessimistic, and divisive words that poured forth from the candidate. With everything pointing to a Democratic landslide, an undeterred Reagan gave a version of the basic talk given for so many years on the GE circuit – known to his admirers as 'the Speech' – to a $1,000-a-plate Goldwater fundraiser at the Ambassador Hotel's Cocoanut Grove in Los Angeles in early October. The perfectly delivered, self-written exposition of long-held ideas, laced with historical references and well-rehearsed but fresh-sounding lines that stuck in the memory, held the audience spellbound. At the end there was a stunned silence before a wave of tumultuous applause broke out, bringing everyone in the room to a standing ovation. Columnist Hedda Hopper, a comrade-in-arms in the Hollywood Red Scare, gushingly described it as 'the finest political speech I ever heard [...] Ronnie caught fire and was marvellous.' Also present at an event that raised over $430,000 were Holmes Tuttle and Henry Salvatori, who both realized that Reagan was far better at delivering the conservative message than the Republican presidential candidate. They were soon on the telephone urging Goldwater to let him record the address for a national television audience.[66]

Unaware of the change in Reagan's rhetoric, Goldwater aides did not want him making things worse for a campaign already in deep trouble. However, their boss approved the broadcast after reviewing the taped version recorded before an invited audience in a Los Angeles television studio.[67] Even so, the screening remained in doubt because the virtually broke Goldwater organization could not pay for it. The cavalry came to the rescue in the person of John Wayne as chair of The Brothers for Goldwater (TBG). The conservative movie star handed over a cheque for $60,000 to fund a slot on NBC on 27 October, a week before the election. This outcome owed much to Reagan's GE connections. The idea to finance the broadcast came from TBG's chief fundraiser, GE employee J. J. Wuerthner, acting on the suggestion of Lemuel Boulware, and the chair of the Goldwater Finance Committee that authorized payment to NBC was none other than Ralph Cordiner.[68]

The 27-minute televised address showcased Reagan's perennial theme – the twin threat posed to American freedom by big government and communism. Just like FDR's radio Fireside Chats, he succeeded in speaking to Americans on television as though he was in their sitting rooms. When he started talking, the camera shifted focus from his head to his body and back up to the eyes, which remained fixed on the unseen viewers' faces for the duration. Reagan conveyed passion not anger, reasonableness not hate, patriotism not paranoia, in stressing the urgency of 'A time for choosing', as the speech became known, between founding values and the alien ideals of Washington collectivism and Soviet totalitarianism. The issue of the election was

> whether we believe in the capacity for self-government or whether we abandon the American Revolution and confess that a little intellectual elite in a far-distant capital can plan our lives better for us than we can plan them ourselves.

The stirring finale avowed:

> You and I have a rendezvous with destiny. We will preserve for our children this, the last best hope of man on earth, or we will sentence them to take the last step into a thousand years of darkness.[69]

Once Reagan finished, a Goldwater official took his place on the podium to plead for donations to keep the campaign going. The speaker himself went to bed that night worried about how viewers would respond to his words. A late-night call woke him with the reassuring news that the Goldwater head-quarters switchboard could barely cope with incoming messages of support and promises of help. Money was soon rolling in as well, a flow that continued thanks to repeat showings of the speech on local stations round the country, and did not stop with Goldwater's defeat. All told, it may well have generated as much as $8 million for Goldwater and Republican coffers, an astonishing sum for the time.[70]

The speech could not save Goldwater from overwhelming defeat by 486 to 52 Electoral College votes and 61.1 to 38.5 per cent in the popular vote, the largest margins since FDR's victory in 1936. Thanks to this landslide, Lyndon B. Johnson's coat-tails helped the Democrats win massive majorities in both houses of Congress. This opened the way for the enactment of the Great Society, the greatest outburst of liberal reformism since the New Deal. Many pundits interpreted the result as consigning right-wing Republicanism into oblivion. As the electoral dust settled, Reagan's television address became a campaign footnote that disappeared from mainstream media memory. Journalist Theodore White considered it unworthy of mention in his 1965 bestseller, *The Making of the President 1964*. For conservatives, however, 'A time for choosing' remained a battle cry for a cause far from dead and buried.

Closer examination of the result showed that the GOP right had good reason not to give up on its quest for power. In the 1928 presidential election, Alfred E. Smith had lost by comparable margins to Herbert Hoover but trailblazed FDR's success through attracting a new constituency of northern, big-city, ethnic voters into the Democratic column. In 1964, Barry Goldwater played a similar role as the first Republican since the 1870s Reconstruction era to carry the five Deep South states, where many white voters rebelled against the national Democratic Party's liberalism. California, which had overtaken New York as the largest state in 1962, had gone to Johnson by more than a million votes. Nevertheless, Hollywood actor (and Reagan's buddy) George Murphy had scored a stunning victory in its Senate election over the hotly favoured Pierre Salinger, former Kennedy–Johnson press secretary. Meanwhile, Goldwater had carried his own state of Arizona. A new Republican base was emerging in what political analysts would soon dub the Sunbelt, the region stretching from the south-west to the old south. It carried the party to the White House in five of the next six elections.

In the immediate aftermath of the 1964 campaign, recrimination, not hope, was what exercised California Republicans. Reagan took aim at moderates like Senator Thomas Kuchel for not getting behind Goldwater in the election. 'We will have no more of those candidates who are pledged to the same goals as our opposition,' he told the Los Angeles County Young Republicans.[71] Once the disappointment subsided, he acknowledged that the conservative message needed a better apostle than Goldwater. The outcome, Reagan declared in *National Review*, was not a rejection of the candidate's philosophy, but a mark of liberal success in portraying him as wild-eyed rightist. 'Time now,' he asserted,

> for the soft sell to prove our radicalism was an optical illusion. We represent the forgotten American – that simple soul who goes to work, bucks for a raise, takes out insurance, pays for his kids' schooling, contributes to his church and charity and knows there just *'ain't no such thing as free lunch.'*[72]

This was an appropriation of Rooseveltian rhetoric for Reaganite ends. FDR had used the 'forgotten man' term in a 1932 speech to highlight Democratic concern for those 'at the bottom of the economic pyramid'. Reagan now employed it to portray Republicans as the ones sympathetic to the individualistic values of ordinary Americans.

Critics later derided Reagan for being 'Goldwater with a smile', but he was following the blueprint charted by George Murphy, whom he later characterized as his 'John the Baptist'. Once a Democrat, Murphy had changed party affiliation in 1939. Hitherto a fierce critic of big government, he modified his tone to win Democratic and Independent support in besting Salinger by more than 200,000 votes. Television was crucial in his success. Regular showings of Murphy's old movies had implanted a good-guy image in the minds of viewers. Moreover, the less-than-telegenic Salinger made the error of agreeing to debate a seasoned actor on the box. He may have won the encounter in substantive terms, but came a poor second in visual impact. As Murphy commented, 'The impression you make on people is very important.'[73]

Many California conservatives thought that Reagan could emulate Murphy to stop Pat Brown winning a third term as California governor in 1966. With

Tuttle, Salvatori, and Cy Rubel in the lead, rich backers began lobbying him to run. They visited him at home, telephoned repeatedly, offered to fundraise for him, and promised to get him a team of political consultants.[74] The thought of giving up the good life in southern California for the vicissitudes of the campaign trail held little appeal at first. Some Republicans had earlier floated the idea of a gubernatorial run in 1962, but Reagan saw himself as an actor who enjoyed giving speeches. '[W]hile I'm highly honored,' he wrote to friends, 'I don't think I'm right for the part.'[75] Slowly but surely Reagan's admirers wore down his resistance. The thought of what might lie beyond had already occurred to him. When corresponding with her father some time earlier, Maureen mentioned he could be governor one day, to which he replied, 'I *could* be president.'[76] For the time being, Sacramento rather than Washington DC beckoned. Though the decision to run was still some months away, the stars were in alignment for Reagan's life to take a new course at the end of 1964.

FIVE

California Governor

On hearing that his former employee was running for California governor, Jack Warner famously quipped: 'All wrong. Jimmy Stewart for Governor, Reagan for best friend.'[1] The butt of the joke loved the line and quoted it often over the course of his political career. In fact the casting turned out to be right because Reagan proved a capable chief executive of the nation's biggest state. There was a fundamental paradox at the heart of his governorship, however. Reagan quickly adapted to the reality that compromise was an essential part of governing in Sacramento. The pragmatism he displayed led one historian to conclude that his time in office made 'a shambles of his ideology'.[2] Far from acknowledging this, Reagan's rhetoric ceaselessly avowed commitment to the philosophical principles that his compromises had violated. As a consequence, he was firmly established as the nation's foremost conservative when he left Sacramento.

It was in the early summer of 1965 that Reagan finally decided to run for governor. For months previously the message coming from wealthy backers was that he alone could save the feeble California GOP from wipeout. Meanwhile, a groundswell of support for his candidacy had gained momentum in the conservative counties of southern California. In April a poll of registered GOP voters placed him a commanding first among prospective gubernatorial nominees.[3] Initially sceptical of his prospects, Nancy now urged entry into a race that would mark her own transformation from supportive wife to trusted advisor and self-appointed enforcer. Proving herself a natural politician, she impressed campaign officials with her judgement of what was best for her husband and her determination to ensure that they followed through on this. 'Ronald Reagan had sort of glided through life,' one aide close to both later remarked, 'and Nancy's role was to protect him.' With Nancy on board, Reagan wrote to two friends, 'I'm fairly certain I will run.'[4]

Shortly thereafter the Friends of Ronald Reagan, a newly established 42-member group composed of established backers, new business supporters, and some famous Hollywood names (including one-time liberal James Cagney, Walt Disney, Randolph Scott, and Robert Taylor), sent out a mailshot to GOP donors. It announced that Reagan, 'out of a deep sense of duty and dedication, is willing to serve his Republican Party as its candidate for governor providing a substantial cross-section of our Party will unite behind his candidacy'. An accompanying request for financial support raised most of the $135,000 spent on his campaign before its official launch. Though perfectly capable themselves of putting up the money, the Friends wanted a wider group of people to have a stake in their man.[5]

The core group of supporters hired California's slickest political consultancy firm, headed by Stuart Spencer and Bill Roberts, to run the campaign. '[O]ur toughest job', this duo told *Newsweek,* would be selling him as 'a sensible, reasonable guy who leans to the right' without being 'the darling of extremists'.[6] The client had no trouble accepting this was the only way to carry a state where registered Democrats had a three-to-two edge. George Murphy's winning strategy had attuned him to this reality. The internal schisms that undermined Richard Nixon's 1962 campaign further indicated that GOP unity was essential for victory. A front-line combatant in the feuding of 1964, Reagan now turned over a new leaf. 'I'll speak no evil (except about Democrats),' he promised Nixon, 'and I'll act like I hear no evil, but that will test my acting ability.'[7]

Reagan's status as a divorcee, still a black mark for politicians in those days, also worried Spencer–Roberts. To present Reagan as the ideal family man, the consultants took the hard-nosed decision to exclude Maureen and Michael from the campaign. The children from Reagan's first marriage found themselves expunged from publicity materials, which only referred to Nancy, Patti, and Ron. This was humiliating for Maureen, in particular, because she was active in Republican women's organizations. A party to the charade, Reagan passed the buck of responsibility by telling her, 'If you pay someone to manage a campaign, then you've got to give them the authority to do it as they see fit.'[8]

A ticket to Sacramento also required an understanding of issues facing California. Spencer–Roberts sent Reagan on the road to display this, but early results were mixed. Despite enthusing conservative audiences, he did not score well for detailed knowledge, especially during question-and-answer sessions.[9] Accordingly, Reagan's handlers interrupted the tour to get him tutored on how state government worked. They also hired behavioural psychologists Stanley Plog and Kenneth Holden to help him link practical issues into a broad philosophical framework. After intensive consultations with Reagan in a Malibu hideaway, this duo produced ring-binder notebooks that the candidate could use for easy-reference briefings back on tour.[10]

With the competence issue seemingly neutralized, a new danger arose. Press reports about Reagan's appearances on the same platform as John Birch Society (JBS) officials in the early 1960s threatened the strategy of positioning him as a responsible Republican. Embarrassed by its outlandish views, Nixon had repudiated the organization in his 1962 campaign. Unwilling to damn every Bircher, many of them pillars of their suburban communities in southern California, Reagan did not follow suit. Instead, with Stuart Spencer's assistance, he issued a statement denying JBS influence on his views: 'Any member of the society who supports me will be buying my philosophy. I won't be buying theirs.'[11] An unguarded quip that top JBS official John Rousselot was willing to come out for or against him, whichever did his candidacy more good, soon stirred the pot anew. The *Beverly Hills Courier* editorialized that being party to this cynical ploy made Reagan unfit for office. This compelled him to issue an unambiguous public statement denouncing JBS leader Robert Welch, denying rumours that he was himself a secret Bircher, and promising not to seek JBS support should he become a candidate for any office.[12] Though still short of a Nixon-style repudiation, this was sufficient to prevent damage to his campaign.

Reagan's formal candidacy announcement on 4 January 1966 embodied the television-age savvy of his campaign. The address was taped at his home, shown to reporters in advance of a press conference in downtown Los Angeles, and then broadcast state-wide on 15 television stations. It was light on specifics and syrupy in its fundamental message: 'Our problems are many, but our capacity for solving them is limitless.'[13] Wholly absent was any overt reference to ideology. Asked shortly afterwards on NBC's *Meet the Press* whether he was running as a Goldwaterite, Reagan responded that he was an un-hyphenated Republican. This had been his line for much of the previous year, even before Spencer–Roberts entered his life.[14] In private, however, conservative sentiments about the drift to socialism found frequent expression. 'I really have the feeling that time is running out,' Reagan told former WHO sparring partner and now ideological soulmate Representative H. R. Gross of Iowa, 'and the next few elections will really be the crossroads.'[15]

Reagan then set out to blitz the state on a two-month speaking tour that required conquest of his flying phobia to reach venues in northern California. The physical and emotional pressures of the gruelling schedule proved too great. 'There must be a vitamin shot for candidates,' he wrote to Barry Goldwater. 'I have only been one for six days, and I am already tired.'[16] A debilitating viral infection soon laid him low. Returning to the campaign before full recovery, Reagan made several gaffes when tiredness got the better of him. When repeatedly criticized at the National Negro Republican Assembly for opposing the 1964 Civil Rights Act, he stormed out, shouting, 'I resent the implication that there is any bigotry in my nature.' Addressing a lumber-industry group, he called for common-sense limits on conservation of redwoods that covered over 100,000 acres of the state, but scandalized environmentalists by ad-libbing: 'A tree is a tree – how many more do you need to look at.' This sentence was widely misquoted in the media as: 'If you've seen one [redwood], you've seen them all.'[17] Learning not to overschedule Reagan, his managers allowed more rest between appearances, including time for an afternoon nap. Once the new tempo was established, he found campaigning highly enjoyable: it stimulated his competitive juices, gave him a platform, and enabled him to connect with stump audiences. He never lost this sense of exhilaration in his five contests for state and national office. As press secretary Lyn Nofziger remarked, Reagan the campaigner was 'hell on wheels when the game begins'.[18]

The contest for the Republican gubernatorial nomination became a two-horse race with Mayor George Christopher of San Francisco. The champion of the moderate wing intended to attack Reagan as an unelectable extremist, but this strategy never got off the ground. To pre-empt the in-fighting that had damaged the party in recent campaigns, State Chairman Gaylord Parkinson invoked the so-called Eleventh Commandment, 'Thou shalt not speak ill of any fellow Republican.' This freed Reagan to concentrate his fire on Democratic misgovernment without having to damn fellow partisans. Romping home with 65 per cent of the vote, he asked Christopher supporters to join him in defeating the Democrats. There were some holdouts – Senator Thomas Kuchel withheld an endorsement over Reagan's refusal to repudiate the JBS – but California Republicans were now more united than they had been for a decade.[19] Only the far right was not invited into the big tent. Pleased with his coalition-building, Reagan confided to George Murphy, 'We do have the party glued together, if only we can keep some of the kooks quiet!'[20]

The election pitted the Republican greenhorn against a battle-hardened Democrat with big GOP scalps, including Richard Nixon's, already on his belt. A pragmatic liberal and deal-maker, Pat Brown could claim to be the builder of modern California since becoming governor in 1959. His highway, water, and higher-education programmes had assisted the Golden State's spectacular growth.[21] Now, however, there were thorn bushes in Eden in the form of racial unrest, rising street crime, campus disorder, and high taxes. With his popularity declining, Brown thought his best hope for re-election lay in making Reagan the big issue of the campaign. 'We [...] rubbed our hands in gleeful anticipation of beating this politically inexperienced, right-wing extremist and aging actor,' he recalled.[22]

Reagan was not an easy target for a negative campaign. He could whip up crowds with near demagogic appeals, but came across as the voice of reason on the evening news. Slick television commercials showcased his engaging personality as a way of underlining his lack of extremism. Democratic fundraiser, Manning Post, warned Brown: 'The sonofabitch is going to beat the shit out of you [...] You just can't make him a bad guy anymore.'[23] Making a virtue of inexperience, Reagan repeatedly told audiences: 'The man who has the job has more experience than anybody. That's why I'm running.' On the advice of Spencer–Roberts, he cast himself as a 'citizen politician' seeking to make Sacramento more accountable to the people. Instead of a Goldwater-style campaign against government, Reagan offered a positive vision of the 'Creative Society' under his stewardship. An idea recommended to him by Glendale pastor and radio talk-show host, W. S. McBirnie, this became a regular feature of his rhetoric after initial testing in the primary. Implicitly linking Lyndon Johnson's Great Society with cost, waste, and bureaucratic inefficiency, it embodied hope for bottom-up reform at state level. As defined by Reagan, the Creative Society envisioned the solution to California's problems coming from its 'incredibly rich human resources' that Sacramento should 'creatively discover, enlist, and mobilize'.[24]

In desperation, the opposition descended to attacking Reagan as a know-nothing actor. Brown could never resist making derogatory remarks against his old movies. The strategy hit rock bottom when his campaign team commissioned *Man v. Actor*, a half-hour attack documentary full of offensive remarks about Reagan. It climaxed in a scene of Brown telling an integrated class of schoolchildren, 'I'm running against an actor, and you know who shot Lincoln, don't cha?' The Democrats were so taken with this nasty line that they featured it in a television ad for the final days of the campaign.[25]

On Election Day Reagan won big with 58 per cent of votes cast, a lead of nearly 1 million, and carried all but three counties. In receiving 1 million votes from Democratic identifiers, he won the blue-collar suburbs, one-third of trade-union votes, and 40 per cent of Hispanic ballots – a record for a California Republican. African Americans constituted the only overwhelmingly anti-Reagan group. Moreover, Reagan's victory did not depend on his fat-cat backers. Foreshadowing Barack Obama's success some 40 years later, his campaign finance relied mainly on small donations from grassroots support-ers. Despite his outspending Brown by $2.6 million to $2 million, this was not a huge difference since the two-term incumbent did not need to build name recognition.[26] The victor's coat-tails carried Republicans into four of the other five state offices and boosted GOP strength in both chambers of the legislature, where the Democrats clung on to power with far smaller majorities. This vic-tory marked Reagan's first step in eschewing the Republican right's extremist image in order to broaden its appeal.

Popular disillusion with the Great Society helped the GOP make a nationwide comeback in 1966. It gained 47 seats in the House of Representatives, three in the Senate, and ten governorships. Reagan's victory stood out for beating an eminent Democrat in the nation's largest state. 'You're the best shot in the arm the Republican Party has received in many years,' declared Congressman John Ashbrook of Ohio. Though not yet fully understood, the California poll heralded the emergence of a new Republican coalition of blue-collar, middle-class, and high-income white voters united in opposition to big government, high taxes, and sociocultural change. Many of the habitual Democrats voting for Reagan were southerners drawn to California during the World War II defence boom and now living in suburban areas of Los Angeles, like Orange County, where they worshipped in evangelical churches. Reagan's intuitive understanding of the hopes and fears of this diverse electorate was the key to his victory.[27]

California was in the forefront of social, cultural, and political developments that undermined the national ascendancy of New Deal liberalism. After two postwar decades of prosperity and high employment, most white voters no longer regarded government as an economic saviour. Instead they wanted it to preserve societal order in the face of urban crime, student protest, counter-cultural lifestyles on University of California campuses, and ghetto unrest – the most serious occurring in the Watts area of Los Angeles, which left 34 dead, over 1,000 injured, and $40 million of damage from five days of violence in August 1965. An early indication that these developments had hurt Pat Brown was the unexpectedly strong showing of demagogic Los Angeles mayor Sam Yorty in winning 38 per cent of the Democratic primary vote. Yorty's consequent endorsement of Reagan made his supporters, almost exclusively blue-collar whites, prime targets for Republican overtures.[28]

As the incumbent, Brown found himself held responsible for every problem besetting California. Sensing growing popular anger about 'the mess in Berkeley', Reagan made it the symbol of everything that had gone wrong under his opponent. The 'leadership gap' in Sacramento, he declared, had enabled 'a small minority of beatniks, radicals and filthy speech advocates' to bring shame to 'a great university'.[29] Weaving white voters' concerns into a single theme, Reagan proclaimed that there was 'one overriding issue in the campaign [...] the issue of morality'.[30] As well as demonizing student radicals by associating them with an alien counterculture, this was a strategy that had a strong racial subtext without being openly racist. In essence, Reagan was one of the first Republicans to develop a message of colour-blind conservatism, something that became a staple of GOP national strategy in time.

Like Goldwater, Reagan had opposed the Civil Rights Act of 1964 and the Voting Rights Act of 1965. In his view, these federal initiatives to enforce legal and political equality for African Americans in the south violated individual and states' rights prescribed by the Constitution. Following their enactment, racial liberalism expanded to redress the discrimination that entrapped many

African Americans in economic and social inequality in the urban ghettoes of the north and west. This brought it into direct conflict with white blue-collar and middle-class interests as taxpayers and homeowners. Many Californians were resentful of rising state taxes that they saw as funding higher welfare payments for mainly black recipients. Using coded rather than overt racial symbols, Reagan exploited such concerns in repeatedly depicting public assistance as a boondoggle for benefit cheats. Hearing the 'animal roar of approval' from Hughes Aircraft assembly-line workers listening to his condemnation of handouts for able-bodied layabouts, veteran reporters Rowland Evans and William Novak commented that white Californians were 'somehow frustrated in the midst of affluence' and their rage was 'encapsulated in the welfare issue'.[31]

There was even greater agitation that ghetto dwellers might invade white suburbia. The Rumford Fair Housing Act of 1963 empowered state officials to combat housing discrimination, notably the use of restrictive covenants preventing homes in white neighbourhoods being sold to African Americans. It signalled that Sacramento no longer sanctioned the residential segregation that had kept the suburbs almost exclusively white. In reaction, realtor groups mounted the Proposition 14 ballot initiative to prevent the state from denying homeowners the right to dispose of their property as they wished. This won a sweeping two-to-one majority in a referendum held shortly before the 1964 presidential election. Fair housing resurfaced in the gubernatorial election after the California Supreme Court in *Mulkey v. Reitman* (1966) voided Proposition 14 for making the state a partner in the violation of federally guaranteed rights of equal protection.

Hitherto, the language of equal rights was the preserve of disadvantaged groups seeking change, but Reagan appropriated it in defence of homeowners. Railing against *Mulkey*, he declared in a San Diego address during the primary campaign:

> I have never believed that majority rule has the right to impose on an individual as to what he does with his property. This has nothing to do with discrimination. It has to do with our freedom, our basic freedom.[32]

Running against Brown, he went further: 'If an individual wants to discriminate against Negroes or others in selling or renting his home, he has a right to do so.'

To shield himself from charges of racism, he urged individual citizens to end 'the cancer of racial discrimination' through voluntary action, a pie-in-the-sky ideal. Commenting on blue-collar support for Reagan, Brown later acknowledged, 'Whether we like it or not, the people want separation of the races.'[33]

Another significant Republican winner in 1966 was Edward Brooke in Massachusetts, the first African American directly elected a US senator. In a letter of congratulation, Reagan declared that his victory 'does more than any other this year to re-establish the Republican Party in the minds of the people as a party of all the people'. Around the same time, he wrote Senator Carl Curtis of Nebraska, a veteran GOP conservative, 'I think we should start making a case that what happened was a turning away from the Great Society by the people.' Doing so would make it impossible for the GOP to live up to the vision that Reagan had outlined to Brooke, of course.[34]

The most important task facing Reagan was to show that he could run California as its 33rd governor. His inaugural address was short on specifics and strong on generalities. Reagan's core political idea featured early on: 'Freedom is a fragile thing and is never more than one generation away from extinction [...] it must be fought for and defended constantly by each generation, for it comes only once to a people.' In line with Creative Society ideals, the address then sermonized that government was not omnipotent, should lead but not lecture, and should have faith in the collective wisdom of the people. On California's problems: 'there are simple answers – there are just not easy ones'. Chief among them was the need to cut state spending. The best-remembered line was:

> We are going to squeeze and cut and trim until we reduce the cost of government. It won't be easy, nor will it be pleasant, and it will involve every department of government, starting with the Governor's office.[35]

In reality Reagan had not given much thought to the practicalities of government while campaigning. When a journalist asked what kind of governor he would make, his joking reply was close to the truth: 'I don't know. I've never played a governor.'[36] Those campaign aides who stayed on to help him in Sacramento underwent on-the-job training. 'We were not only amateurs, we were novice amateurs,' Lyn Nofziger later admitted. Even so, he was more in the loop than his boss. 'The days ahead are frightening at best but they'd be impossible without him,' the governor-elect admitted to Nofziger's wife.[37]

'Nothing went according to my plan,' Reagan recalled of his first year in office.

> We kept uncovering problems nobody had told me about before; there was continuing violence on our campuses; Democratic legislators rejected my proposals right and left; moderates and conservatives in my own party couldn't get along; and I made lots of mistakes because of inexperience.[38]

At times, he seemed out of his depth, once asking aides during a press conference, 'Can anyone tell me what's in my legislative program?' Democrats had no interest in making things easy for him. There was little prospect of getting anything done without support from assembly speaker Jesse Unruh, a man of excess in his personal life and immense skill in politics. Known in Sacramento as Big Daddy, this power-hungry, big-government liberal aspired to replace Reagan in the governor's chair when the next election came round.[39]

Also weighing on Reagan's mind was Nancy's evident displeasure in being California's first lady. She disliked socializing with other political wives, missed her rich Los Angeles friends, and insisted that the family spend their weekends in Pacific Palisades. In her eyes, the governor's mansion was a rundown firetrap on a busy street that was no place to bring up young Ron. The Reagans consequently rented a luxurious Tudor mansion that wealthy supporters eventually bought and leased back to them. The fiercely protective Nancy also resented the criticism of her husband that was part and parcel of Sacramento politics. 'I have to bar the door every once in a while,' Reagan joked, 'or she'll march forth and do battle.'[40] Even more difficult to take was becoming the target of unflattering media scrutiny herself. Especially hurtful was a *Saturday Evening Post* piece mocking her fixed smile and almost everything about her as an actress's carefully rehearsed performance. Reagan always gave her complaints a sympathetic ear, even taking calls during Cabinet meetings that created the mistaken impression among some aides that she was 'Governor Nancy'.[41]

Making matters worse, Reagan began showing ulcer-like symptoms that he attributed to the early cares of office. 'I was ashamed,' he recalled. 'I'd always regarded an ulcer as evidence of weakness.' More likely the virus that struck him in early 1966 had undermined his physical constitution. Medical diagnosis revealed prostate infection and bladder-stone constriction. In August 1967 Reagan entered hospital in Santa Monica for an operation to cure his ailments. In his memoirs, he made no mention of this surgery, attributing the disappearance of his 'ulcer' to the power of prayer – his own and that of supporters.[42]

Despite these problems, Reagan had plenty of solid achievements to his name during his first year as governor. To staff his administration with efficiency-oriented businessmen, a 'Kitchen Cabinet' of wealthy promoters was given the job of enlisting talented corporate managers, but those being headhunted were loath to quit lucrative private-sector positions. The real work of recruitment fell to temporary appointments secretary Thomas Reed, the northern California campaign chief. Wanting Reagan to run for president in 1968, Reed enlisted people who would give him a strong start in Sacramento. This meant putting ability above ideology as a criterion for appointment.

Reed's stellar pick was Norman 'Ike' Livermore, a progressive lumberman dedicated to conserving the state's wild rivers and redwood forests, as natural-resource administrator. Youthfulness and race were no obstacles to enlistment – among the top 100 appointees, the average age was 40, and 19 were non-white, including James Johnson as director of veterans' affairs, the first ever African American department head. However, the all-male line-up signified the limits of diversity in an administration that was slow to recognize the aspirations of women. As Nofziger remarked, 'It isn't that we were deliberately sexist, just that we were naturally sexist.'[43] The only Reed selection not to win favour was Caspar Weinberger for state finance director because of Kitchen Cabinet objections to a one-time Nelson Rockefeller supporter getting the most important Cabinet post. It went instead to management consultant Gordon Smith, who knew little about budgeting, underestimated the state's fiscal problems, and lacked political judgement. This gaffe-prone official lasted one year before giving way to the man who should have had the job in the first place.[44]

Uninterested in the minutiae of government, Reagan had to find a style of leadership that suited his strengths as political salesman while negating his weakness on detail. His approach became: 'Set clear goals and appoint good people to help you achieve them. As long as they are doing what you have in mind, don't interfere, but if somebody drops the ball, intervene and make a change.'[45] A competent team of administrators was essential for this to work. Chief of staff (CoS) Philip Battaglia, a dynamic young attorney who had chaired the election campaign, communications director Lyn Nofziger, and cabinet secretary William Clark, a rancher-attorney by background, were the key personnel in the governor's office. Clark took the lead in organizing the more than 40 state departments and agencies into three (later four) superagencies. The executive directors of these cluster groups plus the finance director joined the triad of top aides to form Reagan's inner cabinet. Despite initial problems, this advisory system generally worked well during his time in Sacramento.

Battaglia's tendency to assume too much power in interpreting Reagan's wishes caused early friction within the executive group until his dismissal in August 1967, a downfall involving the administration's most serious scandal. Suspicious of his disappearances in the company of a male co-worker, other aides conducted an investigation that found he was engaging in gay sex in violation of current law. Though not personally homophobic, Reagan felt it necessary to sack Battaglia because, he later reflected, 'if exposure comes, there would be a reflection on government'. To protect the former aide, a married man with a young family, he never publicly revealed the reason for the dismissal, allowing journalists to assume it resulted from an internal power struggle. However, Nofziger leaked the truth to pre-empt Battaglia returning to Sacramento as a lobbyist. His boss consequently found himself accused by columnist Drew Pearson of knowingly tolerating sexual deviants within the governor's office. Although Reagan steadfastly maintained that there had been no impropriety, the scandal became a distraction for several months. There was even scurrilous gossip that he himself was part of a Sacramento 'homosexual ring', a canard that resurfaced during the 1976 and 1980 presidential campaigns.[46]

Staff harmony improved significantly after William Clark became CoS. Edwin Meese III took over as cabinet secretary and later became Reagan's longest-serving gubernatorial CoS following Clark's appointment as California Superior Court judge in early 1969. Though not as well organized as Clark, Meese was skilled in helping translate the governor's sometimes half-formulated ideas into coherent policy. Both Clark and Meese were well served by their top aide Michael Deaver, also the first lady's closest ally in the administration. This trio later became key members of Reagan's first-term presidential staff.

Acting as honest brokers, Clark and Meese sought to ensure that Reagan had sufficient information and exposure to differing perspectives for efficient decision making. Once he reached a decision, they closed the debate and set about implementing his wishes. Accordingly, the administration was noted for its internal harmony, absence of turf wars, and lack of departmental leaks to the press. Aides learned that Reagan did not dally in making tough decisions if not overwhelmed by information about possible options. William Clark made the full Cabinet meeting the forum for final policy making. To prepare his boss, he wrote a one-page precis of key issues that outlined the pros and cons of alternative courses of action. Derided by some as evidence of Reagan's incapacity to grasp detail, the mini-memos greatly helped someone inexperienced in government become acquainted with myriad issues requiring action. They were especially valuable on matters that held little interest for Reagan. Foreshadowing his leadership style as president, his personal attention focused on a narrow range of subjects that really interested him. On these, he consulted more extensive briefing materials than the mini-memos.[47]

The most pressing problem in Reagan's in-tray was the big hole in California's public finances. The state had a larger budget than all but six countries in the world, but outlays now threatened to exceed revenues in violation of its constitution. The Brown administration had hidden the shortfall by accelerating tax collections and counting revenue not yet collected as already in the bank. Reagan's inheritance was a serious cash-flow shortage and a projected deficit of $1 billion (equivalent to 20 per cent of outlays) for the current fiscal year. The ill-judged advice from his new finance director was to plug the gap through across-the-board economies in departmental spending.[48]

The Reagan economy plan naively assumed that the state government could reduce outlays by 10 per cent without loss of service quality. Retrenchment of this dimension had no prospect of enactment by the Democrat-controlled legislature. Even if approved, the savings would not have delivered a balanced budget anyway. The proposal made Reagan look the amateur in government that he was. Political and fiscal reality soon compelled recognition that revenue enhancement was the only sure way to restore California's finances. This was the first and greatest of Reagan's departures from ideological principle in Sacramento.

On 8 March 1967, the new governor requested a $946 million increase in taxes, mainly on sales (excluding food and pharmaceuticals), personal income, banks and corporations, liquor, and cigarettes. The biggest tax hike hitherto sought by the governor of any state, it was four times larger than California's record tax increase obtained by Pat Brown in 1959. Add-ons in the legislature sent it over the billion-dollar mark. Democrats enthusiastically endorsed a measure that safeguarded their programmatic interests and promised to undermine Reagan's popularity, but they underestimated his skill in deflecting the blame. If tax increases were unavoidable, he told aides, better to enact them before 'everyone forgets that we did not cause the problem – we only inherited it'. Using television spots to get this message across, he told voters that the castor-oil cure was necessary because Brown had 'looted' the state treasury 'in a manner unique in our history'. To Democratic mystification, this public campaign helped to keep Reagan's approval ratings high.[49]

Reagan's revenue measure included a property-tax rebate that Unruh had long sought to enhance the progressivity of state taxation. This offered relief for non-affluent homeowners, particularly pensioners on fixed incomes, from the rising property assessments associated with California's buoyant house prices. Unruh also wanted income-tax withholding to speed up revenue collection from rich 'tax cheats' who intermittently left California when payments came due. The only conservative stamp that Reagan put on the bill was to insist instead on lump-sum payment in order that 'taxes should hurt'. In his calculation, regular deductions from pay packets would make it easier for politicians to raise future tax rates.[50] The state's need to take out bridging loans until one-time tax payments came due eventually forced a change of heart. In 1968 Reagan stubbornly insisted that his feet were 'set in concrete' against tax withholding. Announcing a U-turn two years later, he told reporters, 'that sound you hear is concrete cracking round my feet'.[51]

Determined that Democrats should not get blamed for the 1967 tax increase, Unruh withheld support for its enactment until GOP legislators backed it. Reagan became involved in carrot-and-stick negotiations to whip fellow Republicans into line behind a bill that most of them despised. Wheeler-dealer skills learned as a Hollywood union negotiator were put in service of a measure that had liberal hallmarks. Instead of starving the beast of government, the tax increase put state finances in good shape to support continued expansion of outlays. Under its terms, California's hitherto regressive tax structure acquired a progressive character as corporation taxes nearly doubled, bank-tax rates rose by half, the top personal tax rate underwent a similar increase, and tax brackets were narrowed to put more people into higher ones. Far from admitting this ideological deviation, Reagan denied that he was breaking faith. 'I'm the stingiest fiscal conservative you ever saw', he insisted when unveiling the measure. The tax bill 'does not represent my philosophy of government. I still think the government of California costs the people of California too much.'[52] Most Republicans were willing to accept this rationalization because Reagan remained their best hope for electoral success. Some right-wingers, like Senator John Schmitz, accused him of betrayal, but their barbs only served to underline his reasonableness and moderation in government.

Conservatives overlooked Reagan's gubernatorial record on taxes when he ran for president as a tax cutter. Other deviations from ideological purity would not be forgotten. In 1978, *Spotlight*, a far-right publication, accused him of signing a restrictive gun-control law that withdrew Californians' right to carry loaded weapons in public. The Mulford Act was actually intended to prevent the Black Panthers, a militant group founded in Oakland in October 1966, from carrying firearms as a means to protect African Americans from police harassment and brutality. On 2 May 1967, while the Assembly was debating the measure, 26 armed members of this group interrupted its session to protest against the legislation. Reagan forever more denied that the bill amounted to gun control, defending it as necessary to prevent further invasions of the legislature.[53]

Moreover, Reagan's signing of the Therapeutic Abortion Act of 1967 made him look anything but the paragon of traditional morality lauded by the likes of evangelist Billy Graham.[54] Another six years elapsed before the Supreme Court's *Roe v. Wade* decision decreed the partial decriminalization of abortion nationwide. California was in the forefront of states seeking to tackle this vexed issue on their own initiative. Enacted with bipartisan support, the abortion measure authorized pregnancy termination in cases of rape, incest, and when the mother's life or health was endangered. It aimed to reduce the 100,000 illegal, often barbaric, abortions carried out yearly in California. Reagan was in turmoil about putting 'an official stamp of approval on immorality'. As the parent of an adopted child, he also felt torn about a bill that could deny life to others like Michael. More than anything, he worried that lax interpretation of its 'mental health' provisions by physicians 'for the convenience – not the protection – of the mother' would open the floodgates to abortion. Looking back on the episode when preparing his presidential run, he wrote, 'I did more soul-searching and studying on the subject than anything else in my eight years [as governor].' Bearing out such misgivings, the number of legal terminations skyrocketed to exceed 100,000 by 1970, compared with just 517 in 1967. This outcome pushed Reagan into the anti-abortion camp for the rest of his life.[55]

After the steep learning curve of 1967, Reagan increasingly enjoyed a job he now felt equipped to handle, but his pragmatism endured. This was evident in his opposition to the first manifestation of California's anti-tax impulse that produced Proposition 13 a decade later. The Proposition 9 ballot initiative, devised by Los Angeles County assessor Phil Watson, would have restricted property tax and property assessment to 1 per cent of value and phased out property-tax support for education, welfare, and other 'people-related' services. Caspar Weinberger feared its enactment would be 'a complete disaster' that would necessitate either a $4.5 billion increase in other taxes to fund necessary programmes or massive retrenchment of services.[56] Needing little persuasion to head a public campaign against the initiative, Reagan helped bring about the landslide 68 to 32 per cent vote that buried it on 5 November 1968.

Meanwhile, despite his willingness to crack down on black militants, Reagan showed greater sensitivity to racial issues than he ever would as president. Fearing another Watts-style flare-up, he sought dialogue with African American community leaders, an engagement widely credited for helping to save California from the serious disorders that occurred elsewhere in the nation following Martin Luther King's murder in April 1968. Good minority citizens, he told the California Republican Assembly, are 'standing between us and those who have reached the end of the road and are turning to the club and the torch'.[57] The words of one such citizen – 'We would pull ourselves up by our own bootstraps, but we have no boots' – made a deep impression. Reagan highlighted black problems in a number of important commentaries, including a television address on 14 July 1968 about the need to ensure equal opportunity in California. Some saw this as an effort to position himself for a presidential run later that year, but he continued to speak out long after his prospective candidacy proved a damp squib. 'Jobs are the most important part of the race problem,' he declared in 1969. 'The walls of the ghetto are economic.'[58] Contrary to his campaign pledge, Reagan also promised to veto any repeal of the Rumford Act because of its important symbolism to minorities. Though still supportive of individual homeowner rights not to sell property to African Americans, he now deemed it unacceptable if done with the aid of a realtor, which implied organized discrimination.[59] However, the matter was taken out of state hands by congressional enactment of the Civil Rights Act of 1968 that made enforcement of fair housing a federal responsibility.

In further contrast to his performance as president, Reagan forged an environmental protection record that any liberal would have been proud of. He was not the gung-ho supporter of development that unguarded campaign remarks had made him appear. In fact, he had served a term as director of the Topanga–Las Virgenes Resource Conservation District in the early 1960s, his first post of any kind in government. Under Ike Livermore's guidance, Reagan used the gubernatorial podium to highlight the administration's commitment to cleaner air, purer water, and greater conservation. The plenary address delivered to the Governor's Conference on California's Changing Environment called for common effort to find creative solutions. 'The opportunity is ours,' Reagan asserted. 'The responsibility is ours. We messed it up to begin with – we can clean it up.'[60] Livermore was instrumental in persuading Reagan to oppose the Dos Rios dam development. A new stage in the California Water Plan developed by the Brown administration, this project would have flooded the Round Valley and done inestimable damage to northern California's remaining wild rivers. The fact that the Yuki tribe had been formally guaranteed settlement rights in the valley a century earlier was also important to Reagan. 'We've broken too many damn treaties,' he punned. Another indication of his support for wild river protection was the 1972 law incorporating five rivers into a California Wild and Scenic River System on which dam development was prohibited.[61]

The most significant second-term undertaking was to oppose construction of a federal trans-Sierra highway that threatened the John Muir and Minarets wildernesses. In June 1972 Reagan set off on horseback along the 250-mile John Muir Trail to conduct a two-day inspection of the threatened area with the media and 100 packhorses in tow. It culminated in a steep six-mile ride to a meadow below the 13,000-foot Minaret summit. To cap this publicity-generating event, Reagan delivered a powerful speech that detailed the environmental damage from a highway, urged a merger of the existing Minarets and John Muir wildernesses, and announced President Nixon's support for his stand against the highway project. Shortly afterwards, Congress legislated permanent closure of the Minarets Corridor, thereby killing the trans-Sierra highway project for good.[62]

The cresting of popular concern over environmental degradation in the late 1960s and early 1970s made support for green issues good politics as well as good ethics. This was a time when California initiated a major programme of parkland acquisition and beach shore preservation in addition to aforementioned conservation initiatives. Whether Reagan truly grasped the fragility of the environment must be a matter of doubt in light of his later record as president, but he was more exposed to people aware of it in the governor's office than in the Oval Office. There was only one issue on which he was unmovable. Livermore loathed highway billboards as a blot on rural beauty, but Reagan rather enjoyed these paeans to consumerism and would not support a ban on them.[63]

The conservative side of Reagan showed up intermittently, but not always to good effect. The early economies implemented to address the state's budget shortfall damaged California's mental-health-care programme, regarded as the best in the nation. The loss of 3,700 jobs in the Department of Mental Hygiene was a public-relations disaster that also made no fiscal sense because the state consequently received less federal funding for services still being provided.[64] Medi-Cal, the state version of the federal Medicaid programme for the indigent sick, also suffered retrenchment as part of the same economy drive. To Reagan's fury, a Superior Court judge invalidated cuts made through executive action as unconstitutional. The governor countered with a television spot claiming Medi-Cal extravagance was exhausting its funds and sacked highly respected public-health director Lester Brownlow for not supporting retrenchment. An inadvertent remark by the hapless Gordon Smith that there was no shortage of Medi-Cal funds cut the ground from under his boss's feet, a slip that cost the finance director his job. The entire imbroglio had made Reagan look heartless and incompetent.[65]

Reagan won greater plaudits as a conservative defender of the Vietnam War. In May 1967, 15 million Americans watched his appearance with Senator Robert Kennedy of New York on CBS's *Town Meeting of the World* to field questions from 18 students in London.[66] The print media billed it the first joust between conservative and liberal paladins likely one day to battle for the presidency. According to journalist David Halberstam, 'The general consensus was that Reagan [...] destroyed [Kennedy].' The pair faced questioning about the Vietnam War, much of it so hostile to America that CBS edited out 30 minutes of the taped programme. A leading critic of the war, the Democrat was unable to defend his country to good effect. A well-prepared Reagan, by contrast, rebutted criticisms with cogent and detailed responses, afterwards receiving thousands of letters of commendation for standing up for America.[67]

Rebellious students on University of California (UC) campuses offered even better targets for displays of conservative leadership. The new governor placed a plaque above his office door with a message aimed at this group: 'Observe the rules or get out.' Holding UC President Clark Kerr responsible for moral failure to safeguard order and decency, Reagan was determined to oust him from office. In a bid to safeguard his position, Kerr made the tactical misjudgement of asking the UC Board of Regents for a vote of confidence on 20 January 1967, but the 'mess at Berkeley' had undermined his support. Instead of backing him, the Regents voted for dismissal, thereby sparing Reagan a lengthy offensive to get rid of Kerr. The governor intended to convene an official inquiry into supposed communist influence and sexual misconduct at Berkeley as part of such a campaign. The sacking saved the university from having to undergo this because Reagan wanted to spare Kerr's successor the unrest it would likely have provoked.[68]

It was his early budget cuts that produced Reagan's first confrontation with campus protesters. On 11 February, some 7,500 students and professors – mainly from UC-Berkeley – staged a march on the Sacramento capitol. Relishing the opportunity to face them down in person, Reagan cancelled an out-of-town trip to do so. 'I wouldn't miss this for anything,' he told worried aides. The exchanges went out on evening television across the country, earning him a massive public-relations victory. Reagan never lost his sense of humour during these early encounters. When Fresno State College students hung his effigy, he told Governor James Rhodes of Ohio, 'I know that one hanging doesn't make an administration, but it's a beginning [...] [and] there is a certain prestige in being hung on some campus other than Berkeley.'[69]

Anger became uppermost in Reagan's response to growing campus disruption as his term progressed, however. The demands of black militants sparked mass protests, violent intimidation, and student strikes at San Francisco State College (SFSC) in 1968–9. There was continuing unrest at UC-Berkeley, where radicals and street people took possession of university-owned land they designated 'People's Park' in spring 1969. The following year UC-Santa Barbara activists engaged in prolonged protests that featured sporadic arson attacks and battles with police. Reagan was unyielding in his determination to preserve the rule of law on state campuses. Vowing to keep SFSC open by force if required, he declared, 'Those who want an education, those who want to teach, should be protected in that at the point of the bayonet if necessary.' With his support, new college president S. I. Hayakawa took a hard line with striking students and their faculty supporters. Fond of addressing his diminutive ally as 'Samurai', a grateful Reagan asked, 'Do you know where I can get another dozen like you?'[70] There was no reluctance on his own part to suppress campus disturbances through force. Called out by Reagan to quell the People's Park protests that heavy-handed police tactics had aggravated, the California National Guard occupied the city of Berkeley for 17 days and deployed helicopters to spray tear gas on a protest rally. It was also in action to bring the UC-Santa Barbara disturbances under control after the governor declared a state of emergency.

Concern that a revolutionary minority was intent on whipping up broader discontent shaped Reagan's hard line against campus disorder.[71] For him, this was another round in the battle with un-American subversives started 20 years earlier in Hollywood. To help win it, he enlisted the FBI to conduct a campaign of 'psychological warfare' against campus radicals. The tactics of exposé, innuendo, and intimidation that had undermined an earlier generation of leftists had no effect on the present one, however. Far from worrying about FBI smears hurting career prospects, student radicals treated them as a badge of honour.[72] Accordingly, the state government's coercive resources bore the burden for pacifying college campuses, something Reagan had no regrets about. 'We are still on the side of the angels,' he told a friend, 'but a little clout here and there is in order – after all, the Lord took a club to the money changers in the temple.'[73] Lasting peace would not return to California campuses until the early 1970s. Although Reagan's confrontational approach may have hindered its attainment, polls showed his stand was broadly popular with voters. One aide remarked, 'Campus unrest is an issue between Reagan and the people with nobody in between.'[74]

Reagan also conducted a war of words against student radicals that reached an inflammatory peak amid the Santa Barbara disturbances. Addressing the California Council of Growers on 7 April 1970, he seemingly advocated a no-holds-barred approach to end unrest: 'If it takes a bloodbath, let's get it over with. No more appeasement.' Careless at best and dangerously provocative at worst, these remarks caused a furore that Reagan unrepentantly blamed on his words being quoted out of context by unfriendly reporters.[75] A tragic event in another state put them in even worse light. Called out to maintain order at Kent State University on 4 May, the Ohio National Guard fired on a peaceful Vietnam War protest, killing four students. Henceforth, popular support for a hard line against campus demonstrations diminished markedly, causing Reagan to rein in his rhetoric rather than damage his imminent campaign for re-election.

With colleges refocused on learning by the time Reagan left office, S. I. Hayakawa declared that he had been 'a good friend to [higher] education' for rescuing it from the dreadful days of 1968–70.[76] In contrast, critics attributed Reagan's handling of campus unrest to his supposedly visceral anti-intellectualism, but this was unjustified. The first in his family to obtain a degree, Reagan took university education very seriously. This was one reason why he was so profoundly offended by the disruptions to student learning. His record of financial support for universities also belied charges of inherent hostility to them. The proposed budget cuts of 1967 were never fully implemented. Spending on higher education actually increased 136 per cent during Reagan's governorship, over a third more than state spending grew overall. Initial fears that Reagan posed a threat to UC academic standards also proved groundless. President Charles Hitch, Kerr's successor, had a number of fights with him, not least over the free-speech right of black militant Eldridge Cleaver to speak at Berkeley in 1968. Nevertheless, he was adamant that UC had retained its status as the best public university in the country under the 33rd governor.[77]

Despite the 'bloodbath' blunder, Reagan was set fair for re-election in 1970. His well-funded campaign mounted a blitz of television adverts that hyped his restoration of California's golden promise. At the same time, he ran as if he were still the citizen politician of 1966 going to clean up the mess in Sacramento. As Michael Deaver remarked, 'He campaigned as if he had not been part of [the state government] for four years.'[78] Nevertheless, his huge lead in early surveys shrank steadily amid a national recession from which California was not immune. Denunciations of him as 'the rich man's friend' by Democratic challenger Jesse Unruh began hitting home in these circumstances. Going on the counter-attack in the final weeks, Reagan did enough to stall his opponent's momentum. He eventually triumphed with nearly 53 per cent of the vote, but with a majority only half that of 1966 because his share of Democratic identifiers fell to 20 per cent. Despite chaotic campaign organization and inadequate funding, Unruh ran Reagan closer than any Democrat who ever came up against him. Nevertheless, the re-election victory was an impressive showing in a bad year for Republicans. George Murphy lost his Senate seat, the Democrats recaptured the California legislature that they had lost in 1968, and 11 Republican governors went down to defeat elsewhere in the nation.

Reagan's presidential ambition brought conservatism more to the fore in his second term. His principal goal was to reform a welfare system widely perceived as being in crisis because of the unsustainable expansion of Aid to Families with Dependent Children (AFDC), financed jointly by the federal government and the states since its creation under the New Deal in 1935. In California, AFDC recipients had increased in number from 375,000 in 1963 to 1,566,000 – nearly one in 13 of the population – by 1971. One reason for this was better identification of those needing assistance by welfare officials; another was the rise of welfare-rights organizations that mobilized the poor to claim their full legal entitlements. With caseloads increasing by 40,000 a month, welfare costs were set to increase by more than double what the state budget had anticipated. Reagan consequently adjudged California's fiscal position 'more desperate' than at any time since 1967.[79]

To Reagan, the 'heart of the problem' was that empire-building welfare officials felt no obligation to get the able-bodied off the rolls.[80] It was not until his first term neared its end that he got down to addressing reform, however. On 4 August 1970 a confidential memo drafted by Ed Meese was sent under Reagan's name to Cabinet members and senior staff. This announced the establishment of an expert panel to investigate solutions that would place 'heavy emphasis on the tax-payer as opposed to the tax taker; on the truly needy as opposed to the lazy unemployable'. It concluded in apocalyptic terms:

> This is our NUMBER ONE priority [...] I am asking you to make available your best employees including directors for this all-out war

on the tax taker. If we fail, no one ever again will be able to try. We must succeed.[81]

Once re-elected, Reagan conducted a public campaign to develop support for reform. In one press interview, he complained that liberalized welfare eligibility was 'a license to steal', created 'an endless and malignant' cycle of dependency because the poor had no incentive to uplift themselves, and provided 'a tax-financed incentive to immorality' because many unmarried teenage girls got pregnant to claim benefits. The unpalatable options facing California, he declared, were a massive tax increase or huge cuts in other programmes to 'feed this welfare monster' unless costs were brought under control.[82]

The Reagan reform proposal made four main recommendations: it increased assistance to the truly needy; required able-bodied welfare recipients to get a job or job training; placed Medi-Cal benefits on the same footing as other health-assistance programmes; and aimed to 'strengthen family responsibility as the basic element of our society'. Democratic leaders blundered in refusing the governor permission to unveil his proposals before a joint session of the legislature. Accordingly, Reagan arranged for a state-wide telecast of 'the speech the legislature wouldn't hear' when giving it instead at Los Angeles on 3 March 1971. He also called for a grassroots campaign to deluge new assembly speaker Bob Moretti with letters and cards demanding welfare reform.[83]

Sacramento remained deadlocked for months until Moretti, a deal-maker by inclination, suggested a one-to-one parley with Reagan. The meeting, held in late June, produced agreement to seek compromise through personal negotiations. The pair consequently engaged in five days of intense discussions that set the framework for their respective lieutenants to reach detailed agreement in six days of further talks. The master of policy arcana on this issue of personal significance, Reagan earned Moretti's respect for being a tough and crafty negotiator in meetings where shouting and swearing were frequent.[84] The outcome was the California Welfare Reform Act of 1971, arguably Reagan's greatest achievement as governor because it largely embodied his preferences over those of the Democrats. Honest welfare recipients received on average a 43 per cent improvement in benefits and an automatic cost-of-living increase – the latter a Reagan concession that would cost the state dear when inflation soared after he left office. In addition, eligibility rules were tightened, anti-fraud measures were expanded, and a uniform statewide standard on needs was established. Reagan also achieved his long-sought goal of a one-year state-residency qualification for welfare, only to have this invalidated in the Californian courts. Finally, a pilot Community Work Experience Program was established in some counties to place able-bodied welfare recipients without young children in public-service jobs.

Welfare rolls started to fall immediately on enactment of the bill, with the AFDC caseload declining by nearly 300,000 in three years. Although Reagan got the credit, circumstance may have been on his side. According to an Urban Institute report, California welfare demand had reached a natural peak by 1971 as baby-boom births tailed off and access to abortion grew. The author claimed that Reagan's reform only reduced welfare rolls by 6 per cent more than they would otherwise have fallen, but acknowledged its effectiveness in better safeguarding the truly needy.[85] Whatever its actual policy impact, the measure represented a philosophic victory for Reagan's oft-made claim that welfare could be better handled by the states than by Washington DC. This won him the admiration of conservatives nationwide and offered validation for his later calls to reorient social-programme responsibility away from Washington.

Reagan's other second-term crusade entailed an effort to control taxes through constitutional reform. Belying his constant assertions that California taxes were too high, he levied three significant tax increases during his governorship – in 1967 to repair state finances, and in both 1971 and 1972 to fund property-tax relief for homeowners through increasing levies on corporations, banks, and high earners. A frustrated Reagan wanted to deliver lower taxes for all but the continuous expansion of state spending on his watch seemingly prohibited this. Outlays had risen from $4.6 billion in 1967 to $10.2 billion in 1974, mainly due to inflation and uncontrollable entitlement costs. Convinced that this trend could not be reversed through the legislative process, Reagan decided to seek a constitutional solution through a ballot initiative to achieve spending control through tax control. The taxpayer, he warned, had 'become the pawn in a deadly game of government monopoly whose only purpose is to serve the confiscatory appetites of runaway government spending'.[86]

The Proposition 1 initiative was the brainchild of Lewis Uhler, a hardcore conservative who believed that the legislature's profligate tendencies would eventually destroy California 'unless we, the people [...] change the rules of the game'.[87] Ed Meese, a friend since college days, appointed him in September 1972 to lead the Tax Reduction Task Force, one of three committees created to devise an agenda for Reagan's last two years in office. Under Uhler, this body developed a proposed constitutional amendment to curb the state legislature's tax powers. This would have limited the percentage of total personal income within California that could be collected in revenue in any one year without a special vote of the people. The sliding-scale reduction from the current 8.3 per cent tax share to 7 per cent within 15 years would serve to lower taxes and tie subsequent expenditure increases to the growth in personal income.[88] In other words, the state would be forced into a fiscal straitjacket without regard to programmatic needs. 'A more thorough operational triumph of [conservative] ideology over pragmatism could scarcely be imagined,' one historian remarked.[89]

Ambitious for a permanent legacy of lower taxes, Reagan adopted Uhler's proposal as his own and campaigned wholeheartedly for its adoption by voters. No California governor had hitherto sponsored a ballot initiative, much less called for a special election to approve it. Reagan followed Meese and Uhler's advice that going for broke in 1973 when no other election was scheduled would focus voters' attention on Proposition 1, but this also enabled the underfunded opposition to concentrate its resources against the measure. With Reagan barnstorming the state in its support, the 'Yes' campaign benefited from a treasury of $1.5 billion, four times the 'No' campaign's budget. However, the opposition included the California Teachers Association, the California State Employees Association, the League of Women Voters, and other groups that called on supporters to reject the initiative. It put out scare stories that the limitation on state taxes would either mean higher local taxes or decimation of essential state services, but Reagan gave as good as he got. 'You can lecture your teenagers about spending too much until you're blue in the face,' he declared,

> or you can accomplish the same goal by cutting their allowance. We think it is time to limit government's allowance – to put a limit on the amount of money they can take from the people in taxes. This is the only way we will ever bring government spending under control.[90]

A week before the election, Reagan committed a significant gaffe. When asked during a television interview whether he thought the average voter understood the complex proposal that ran to 7,500 words in length, he replied light-heartedly: 'No, he shouldn't try. I don't either.' Proposition 1 opponents bombarded the electorate with full-page ads reproducing these careless words in large type. Reagan later made the nonsensical claim, 'We just didn't have the resources to counter their advertising blitz with the truth.'[91] Uhler had deliberately drafted a dense amendment in the belief that Reagan could sell it to uncomprehending voters, but not even he could make a silk purse out of this sow's ear. Voters ended up rejecting the initiative by 54 to 46 per cent. Many took the safe option of spurning a reform they did not understand; others feared a corollary rise in local taxes if it were approved; and Reagan's frontman role had a polarizing effect in mobilizing Democratic identifiers against Proposition 1.[92]

The outcome marked Reagan's first serious political defeat, but the Proposition 1 campaign ultimately did him more good than harm. Far from abandoning the cause, he told one supporter, 'We won't stop – this was only a first round.' In a *National Review* cover story, he defiantly declared:

> It was and is a daring idea and I do not regret the exercise […] People all over America have been alerted to the staggering burden which taxes impose on our economy and on every family in this country.[93]

The campaign had captured the conservative imagination nationwide. It spawned more successful imitations, most notably California's Proposition 13 that mandated rollback of property taxes in 1978. Reagan surfed the anti-tax wave engendered by Proposition 1 all the way to the White House. By the time he took the oath of office, 40 states had adopted some form of tax limitation. This facilitated his ultimate goal of reducing federal taxes as president. With the federal government collecting 65 cents of each tax dollar, he told a correspondent in the early 1970s, 'any real tax relief must come at the national level'.[94]

When Reagan's tenure in Sacramento ended, some commentators questioned the significance of his legacy. In their view he had merely provided a breathing space in California's relentlessly liberal march that had been in train since the early twentieth century.[95] Though not achieving all he wanted, his footprint was greater than such judgements allowed. He helped to make

California a safe Republican state in presidential elections from 1968 to 1988 and his pragmatic conservatism became a model for his Republican successors in Sacramento to follow during a new era of GOP gubernatorial ascendancy from 1983 to 2013. Reagan would have achieved far less had he not learned to temper his conservatism with a healthy dose of pragmatism. His major triumphs on tax policy and welfare reform testified to his willingness to negotiate and compromise. His impressive record as a conservationist showed a capacity to operate outside the shackles of ideology. His greatest defeat, over Proposition 1, occurred when he gave free rein to his conservative instincts.

Scholarly and journalistic opinions generally regard Reagan as a capable governor, but not a great one. This is a fair assessment provided allowance is made for the difficulties he faced as a Republican chief executive dealing with a Democrat-controlled legislature for all but two years (1969–70) of his tenure. It is reasonable to put him in the pantheon of California's best governors in the second half of the twentieth century, alongside Republican Earl Warren and Democrat Pat Brown. This trio for the most part showed pragmatic moderation in addressing the complex needs of a rapidly growing state. The programmatic and management reforms of the Reagan administration unquestionably made state government run better and deliver services more efficiently. The paradoxical legacy of this anti-statist governor was that, under him, 'government entrenched itself in many ways as a strong effective force in California society'.[96]

Ultimately, of course, Reagan's reputation in history was forged in Washington rather than Sacramento. Nevertheless, the governorship was a critical training ground for his presidency. In it he learned much about the art of politics, adapted his communication skills to meet the needs of governing, developed an administrative approach suited to his macro-level interests, and nurtured a political style that privileged pragmatism over polarization without ducking tough issues. When his time in Sacramento ended, the one-time actor was ready to test for the greatest starring role of all.

SIX

Right Man

I n 1966, Reagan wrote to Barry Goldwater, 'You set the pattern and perhaps it was your fate to be just a little too soon.'[1] In 1980, Reagan was elected president of the United States on a similar platform to the one that had earlier made Goldwater look extreme. Conservative ideas that had once been marginal were now mainstream. Reagan was critically important in bringing about this change, but his success was neither swift nor straightforward. It was third time lucky for his presidential ambitions. A desultory effort to become Republican nominee in 1968 only showed that he was not ready. A substantial but unsuccessful effort in 1976 indicated that the GOP was not quite ready for him. In 1980 Reagan was the right man at the right time. In one way his success was the triumph of ideas that he had consistently promoted since the late 1950s. It was also contingent on Democratic failure to resolve domestic and international problems that made the 1970s a miserable decade for America.

As soon as Reagan had trounced Pat Brown to become California governor, his wealthy backers began looking ahead to bigger things for their man. '[W]e don't have gubernatorial material here, we have presidential material,' one of them commented.[2] With Reagan not yet installed in Sacramento, the group funded an exploratory survey of his prospects were he to make a White House run in 1968. This found promising signs of support for him across the country. His backers consequently amassed some $500,000 in seed money for a nomination run to be managed by Clifton White, architect of Barry Goldwater's campaign to become the GOP standard-bearer. Sensing that the GOP would not want another right-winger so soon after the 1964 rout, Reagan resisted their entreaties. As a consequence, he stayed on the sidelines as the race for the GOP presidential nomination got going in 1968. This enabled Richard Nixon, risen Lazarus-like from his electoral defeats of 1960 and 1962, to rack up delegate support by uniting GOP centrists and right-wingers in his column.

Despite the former vice-president's advance, Reagan still harboured hopes of receiving the nomination. To avoid another bruising presidential primary in California, the state GOP made him its first-ballot 'Favourite Son' for the Republican National Convention in Miami Beach. This kept his own candidacy alive without having to enter the primaries and excused him from endorsing Nixon. Behind the scenes, Reagan was manoeuvring for an alliance with Nelson Rockefeller to block their mutual rival from gaining a first-ballot victory, thereby enabling the two of them to join battle when delegates were up for grabs on the later ballots. Well aware of what was going on, the frontrunner worried that Reagan's emotional power on the podium could stampede the convention in these circumstances. 'He reaches the heart,' Nixon told an aide. 'We reach the head.'[3] To pre-empt the danger, he engineered a series of backroom deals to ensure the loyalty of southern delegations, the most likely bolters to his putative rival.

Reagan finally yielded to conservative exhortations to declare himself a candidate when the convention met in early August, but it was too late to stop Nixon surging to a first-ballot nomination. 'I was the most relieved person in the world,' he later commented of this outcome. 'I knew I wasn't ready to be president.' Nancy thought this too but had not voiced her concerns. She would never again be reticent in speaking out, because, in Michael Deaver's words, 'it was always about protecting her husband, not about driving him on'.[4] However, there were plenty of positives that Reagan could take away from Miami Beach. A well-received podium speech had reaffirmed his power as an orator. As Governor Paul Laxalt of Nevada put it, the convention had enabled Americans to get 'a real look at you'. There was the added bonus that the California GOP had remained united, putting it in good shape for the upcoming elections. Finally, no one could doubt that Reagan was now a major figure in the national party. Sensing a shift in its centre of gravity on account of his rise, *National Review* publisher William Rusher dubbed him an inspiration for idealistic young conservatives who represented the Republican future. 'Your influence,' he remarked prophetically, 'will last as long as any of them are active in politics.'[5]

Although Nixon's consequent election as president closed off another White House bid until 1976, it gave Reagan plenty of time to lay the foundations for that. A collaborative relationship with the new occupant of the Oval Office was helpful in that cause. Reagan's initial opinion of Nixon when a vice-presidential candidate in 1952 was unflattering: 'Pray as I am praying,' he told a friend,

> for the health and long life of Eisenhower because the thought of Nixon in the White House is almost as bad as that of 'Uncle Joe' [Stalin] [...] [H]e is less than honest and highly undeserving of the high honor paid him.[6]

By 1960, as a Republican in all but name, Reagan's one-time disdain had turned into high regard for Nixon as a foe of liberalism and a forceful Cold Warrior. A year earlier, the vice-president's blunt talking on the evils of communism during a visit to Moscow had been music to his ears.[7] For his part, Nixon appreciated the boost that Reagan's 1966 victory had given Republicanism, but his esteem never extended to seeing him as a prospective presidential successor. In his eyes, the California governor was too conservative, had limited grasp of geopolitical realities, and was capable only of arousing audiences rather than informing them. Nevertheless, the pair cooperated to mutual benefit over the course of his presidency. Their only falling out was over the administration's Family Assistance Plan for welfare reform that Reagan considered 'contrary to Republican philosophy' for not incentivizing the poor to seek work. The public campaign that he conducted against the proposal was instrumental in Nixon's abandonment of it, but this did not cause a personal rift.[8]

As reward for Reagan's assistance in his presidential campaigns, Nixon sent him as special envoy on trips abroad that boosted his foreign-policy credentials. These featured visits to the Philippines in September 1969 (where he was a big hit with presidential spouse Imelda Marcos[9]), Taiwan, Japan, and South East Asia in October 1971, Western Europe in July 1972, and Australia, Indonesia, and Singapore in November–December 1973. The most important mission was a delicate one to explain the reasons for US recognition of the People's Republic of China to nationalist leader Chiang Kai-shek in Taiwan. It was Nixon's hope that this fervent anti-communist would be more receptive to a like-minded messenger. Meeting Chiang in his palace, Reagan departed from his official script to find the right words: 'Look, Generalissimo, I don't like this any more than you do. But it had to happen sooner or later, and we're a hell of a lot better having President Nixon do it [than a Democrat].'[10] The following year Reagan crossed the Atlantic to reassure NATO governments of America's commitment to European security. The trip not only generated valuable publicity but also made him unusually experienced for a governor in dealing with foreign leaders on international issues.

In a display of loyalty that could have been damaging, Reagan stuck with Nixon to the bitter end of his Watergate disgrace. 'I still have confidence,' he declared in the early days of the investigation into White House misdeeds, 'that when the smoke clears we will find the president was not involved.'[11] As the evidence piled up against Nixon, *National Review* founder William Buckley urged Reagan, a friend since the early 1960s, to begin 'a patient, cautious dissociation'. Having none of this, Reagan's wired response to a query whether *National Review* should advocate the president's resigna-tion was short and to the point: 'HELL NO.'[12] Reagan remained loyal until Nixon resigned to avoid almost certain impeachment for abuse of power and obstruction of justice in August 1974. Even then he refused to join the throng baying for the former president to be tried as a common criminal. 'The punishment of resignation,' Reagan told reporters, 'certainly is more than adequate for the crime.'[13]

Reagan's relationship with Nixon's successor rapidly deteriorated into mutual disrespect. Gerald Ford's accession changed the electoral calculus for 1976 by putting an incumbent into the equation. In Reagan's eyes, this traditional Midwestern Republican represented the past rather than the future of the GOP. For his part, Ford disdained Reagan's 'penchant for offering simplistic solutions for hideously complex problems'.[14] A longstanding Washington insider, the new president was suspicious of the conservative movement that operated outside the Beltway. The selection of Nelson Rockefeller, sworn enemy of the right, as his vice-president made plain his animus. Adding insult to injury, Ford tried to neutralize Reagan as the principal voice of conservatism with derisory offers of lowly Cabinet positions as either secretary of transportation or secretary of commerce.

These bungled efforts to get Reagan inside the tent simply ensured that he stayed outside. Once free of the governorship, he undertook a self-appointed mission to keep alight the flame of conservatism in national politics through speeches and media work. Former aides Michael Deaver and Peter Hannaford, now partners in their own public-relations firm, were hired to book engagements that would establish him, in their words, 'as a symbol of [conservative] hope'. Their client was soon giving ten speeches a month (at a $5,000 average fee); his bi-weekly column appeared in 226 newspapers, and his radio commentaries aired on 286 stations. Deaver also secured him a twice-weekly commentary spot on CBS evening news that would have placed him before the largest nationwide audience of any network newscast. Sensing that people would soon tire of him on television and wanting freedom to set his own agenda, Reagan turned this down in favour of the more intimate medium of radio.[15]

This public engagement, in the words of a Deaver–Hannaford memorandum, had three objectives: 'A. Maintain influence in the Republican Party; B. Strengthen and consolidate leadership as *the* national conservative spokesman; C. Enhance foreign affairs credibility.'[16] It also kept the door open for a presidential run if he decided to make one. There were other benefits, among them making money – his 1975 earnings exceeded $282,000, compared to $49,000 as governor. Furthermore, the new work did not consume his energies to the same extent as running California. As Nancy remarked:

> For Ronnie, this was the perfect job: He could earn a good living by doing what he enjoyed – communicating his beliefs about the direction in which the country ought to move. And best of all, his new schedule left him time to enjoy our new ranch near Santa Barbara.[17]

The funds for Rancho del Cielo came from a series of shrewd land deals that had the unwanted consequence of inviting media scrutiny for possible skulduggery. On entering politics, Reagan had worried about supporting his household on a governor's salary. As it had done before, MCA rode to the rescue of the man who had been so helpful in its rise to Hollywood conglomerate. Company boss Jules Stein created a trust for its former client, which sold 236 acres of the Yearling Row ranch in Malibu Canyon to 20th Century Fox at a price of more than $8,000 per acre in 1966, a huge increase over what Reagan had paid in

1952. Enriching the trust by $1.93 million, the sale made the governor-elect an instant millionaire. When Fox sold off the land in 1974 at a quarter of the price paid Reagan, the press scented a sweetheart deal in the earlier transaction, but prolonged investigation found no wrongdoing.[18] Meanwhile, the remaining Yearling Row land was used as a down payment on a 778-acre property in Riverside, south-east of Los Angeles in 1968. Unable to obtain water and power hook-ups to develop this into a working ranch, Reagan made another healthy profit in selling it off for $856,000 to a real-estate developer in 1976. The transaction remained secret for three years until revealed by a local newspaper vainly seeking evidence of financial impropriety. Unbeknown at the time, the Soviet KGB was also digging around without success for anything that might be used to embarrass Reagan.[19]

In November 1974, Reagan paid $527,000 from his trust for a 668-acre ranch in Refugio Canyon, north-west of Santa Barbara. To his disgust, reporters investigated 'whether we'd given "favors" as part of the purchase price [...] [but] there was no hanky-panky'.[20] Rancho del Cielo overlooked on one side the often misty Pacific Ocean from a 2,250-foot high mountaintop that was usually bathed in sunshine, and on the other side the majestic Santa Ynez Mountains. The property afforded Reagan plenty of opportunity for riding his stable of horses. Another benefit for the privacy-conscious owners was that access was via helicopter or a tortuous one-lane road that wound upwards for seven miles. Over the course of 1975–6, with help from two assistants, Reagan totally reconstructed the interior of the 1872-vintage adobe ranch house, put on a new roof, laid a rock patio, and built a fence of old telephone poles around the house. Employing skills learned on a summer job in Dixon 50 years earlier, he took immense pride at having worked with his hands to produce such a lovely home adjoining a lake that rounded off the beauty of the spot. 'No place before or since has ever given Nancy and me the joy and serenity it does,' he later remarked.[21]

As Reagan settled into his new life, conservatives fretted about his intentions for 1976. With less than a quarter of voters identifying with the Watergate-tarnished GOP, some on the right yearned to form a new party of conservative Republicans and Democrats to contest the presidential election.[22] Asked to head this, Reagan toyed with the idea but quickly recognized its impracticality. His wealthy backers, all GOP loyalists, left him in no doubt of their opposition.

'You're a Republican,' Holmes Tuttle remarked, 'and you're going to stay one.' The air remained thick with trial balloons until Reagan popped them in an address to the Conservative Political Action conference on 1 March 1975. Avowing commitment to 'Republican principle', he asked:

> Is it a third party we need, or is it a new and revitalized second party, raising a banner of no pale pastels but bold colors which make it unmistakably clear where we stand on all the issues troubling the people?[23]

These words hardly chimed with the mottled pattern of his gubernatorial palette, but Reagan was never one to let yesterday's reality shade the bright tomorrow. Conservative hopes that he would now challenge for the Republican presidential nomination turned to anger when no formal declaration was forthcoming. 'We're disgusted with him for not making the commitment,' remarked one right-winger after Ford announced his candidacy in July 1975. 'He's our man, but he just won't come in.'[24]

In fact, the object of this impatience was minded to run, but delayed announcing his candidacy until the middle of November. Staying out of the race, Reagan told a family powwow, would make him feel 'like the guy who always sat on the bench and never got into the game'.[25] Wresting the nomination from the incumbent posed formidable challenges, however. Ford controlled the party organization, enjoyed immense advantages in fundraising, and could sway primary voters with pork-barrel promises of federal grants for their states and communities. Accordingly, Reagan pursued a strategy of stealth to build up funds, organization, and support before formally putting his hat in the ring.

The first task was to build a campaign team around him. Old Sacramento hands Mike Deaver, Ed Meese, and Lyn Nofziger came on board straight away. Despite enjoying private life, Nancy gave her full support. Though Henry Salvatori's GOP loyalties bound him to Ford, others in the Kitchen Cabinet were supportive and Holmes Tuttle put his fundraising expertise at Reagan's service. A newcomer to the inner circle, former Nixon aide John Sears took the lead in devising campaign strategy. Unemotional, ruthlessly calculating, and relentlessly ambitious, he cared only about winning. For Sears, Reagan was a product, not a cause – in his words, 'a great piece of horseflesh [...] [if] properly trained'. Though suspicious of his philosophical emptiness, other aides valued his knowledge of national politics, excellent media contacts, and creative campaign management – one later called him 'the most brilliant political strategist I've ever known'.[26] In fact, Sears was not quite the maestro they imagined – his fingerprints would be on most of the blunders committed in the 1976 campaign.

Prior to entering the race, Reagan continued giving well-paid speeches that were essentially self-written, bromidic retreads of 'A time for choosing'. Conservatives clamoured for something more substantive as an indication that a declaration was coming. Aide Jeffrey Bell consequently drafted an address envisioning decentralization as the answer to many of America's problems. Top aides, including Sears, approved it as fundamentally in harmony with their boss's oft-expressed view that states and localities could better exercise government functions now controlled by Washington. However, the specificity of some of the proposals in the speech, intended to dispel charges that Reagan dealt only in clichés, ended up damaging his presidential prospects. The 'Let the people rule' address, delivered to the Executive Club of Chicago on 26 September 1975, proposed 'nothing less than a systematic transfer of authority to the states – a program of creative federalism for America's third century'. The idea was popular in principle but the devil was in the detail. Programmes targeted for devolution included welfare, education, housing, transportation, community development, and Medicaid. Reagan envisioned that the consequent savings of $90 billion for national government would make it possible to 'balance the federal budget, make an initial $5 billion payment on the national debt and cut the federal personal tax burden of every American by an average of 23 percent'.[27]

A big yawn for reporters, the speech received little media coverage but the rival campaign found it engrossing. The Ford organization pulled off the masterstroke of hiring Stuart Spencer to take charge of strategy. Piqued at not getting sufficient credit for managing the gubernatorial campaigns, he relished the chance to put one over on Reagan's team. The first challenge was persuading his new client not to underestimate the old one. Ford appeared to have taken to heart Richard Nixon's advice that Reagan was 'a lightweight and not someone to be considered seriously or feared in terms of the nomination'.[28] Spencer bluntly warned that the only way to beat the challenger was to discredit him. Tailor-made for this purpose, the '$90 billion' plan could be portrayed as a massive transfer of programme costs that states and municipalities could only fund through new taxes. In one biographer's judgement, 'Let the people rule' cost Reagan the 1976 nomination because it halted the early momentum that had given him a huge lead in opinion polls by the end of 1975.[29]

When the primary season opened in New Hampshire, Ford's strategy was to 'shine a light' on the '$90 billion plan' with a blitz of ads warning of its fiscal consequences for a state that presently had no income tax or sales tax.[30] Despite an energetic campaign featuring over 200 appearances in 17 days – a gruelling schedule for a 65-year-old – the challenger could not get off the back foot in the face of these attacks. Reagan's campaign pollster, Dick Wirthlin, found him holding just a 'whisper of a lead' going into the final days. In his assessment, winning now required 'a strong ground game' with Reagan leading the charge to get over the line. Instead, in a not untypical display of arrogance, Sears sent Reagan off to campaign in Illinois on the eve of the all-important primary without informing him of Wirthlin's concerns. After barnstorming the state on the weekend before polling, Ford eked out one of the narrowest wins in New Hampshire primary history. Arguably, it was Sears' misjudgement in sending Reagan to the Prairie State, not the '90 billion plan', that was the ultimate cause of defeat in the Granite State.[31]

The original Sears strategy was to 'pierce the incumbent's most credible political asset [...] [his] political leverage and pomp' in New Hampshire and build the momentum to finish him off in the next few primaries. Now Ford was the one looking likely to put his opponent down for the count. A vigorous campaign in the next primary in Florida hammered away at the '$90 billion' plan. It also recycled some old Reagan statements on the need to replenish Social Security finances by investing a portion of its trust fund in the stock market. This played very badly in a state where 38 per cent of registered Republicans were aged over 65. Only by shifting to foreign policy could Reagan start to turn things around. As well as hitting out against the strategy of détente with the Soviet Union, he made the Ford administration's negoti-ations to return the Panama Canal to Panamanian ownership into a symbol of America's post-Vietnam retreat from power. This change of focus was too late to stop the president winning Florida, albeit with a smaller majority than once looked likely.[32]

The next three primaries, in Illinois (a 59 to 40 per cent pummelling), Massachusetts, and Vermont, also went Ford's way. A host of eminent Republicans now called on Reagan to quit the race. Some conservatives like William Buckley were of the same mind in the interests of uniting the GOP in readiness for the general election. Without his boss's knowledge, Sears secretly met with Ford's representatives after the Illinois primary to discuss withdrawal terms. This encouraged the president to join the chorus urging his rival to quit. The challenger's position seemed hopeless: the succession of defeats had turned off the spigot of donations, the campaign was $2 million in debt, and top aides were working without pay. Manifesting the steely determination that underlay his genial exterior, Reagan still gave no thought to surrender. 'Tell him [Ford] to quit,' was his defiant response when urged by a group of Republican mayors to withdraw.[33]

This resiliency was a defining moment in Reagan's political career. Had he withdrawn, he would never have become president; instead, he created a platform for success in 1980 by staying in the 1976 race. Expecting to hear the last rites, senior aides met with Reagan on 23 March at the Stoddard Hotel in La Crosse, Wisconsin. However, John Sears brought news that a wealthy Texan anti-communist was willing to loan the campaign $100,000 on condition that the money was used to buy national television time for a speech attacking Ford's pursuit of détente with the Soviet Union. This seemed a riverboat gamble with no hope of success, but Reagan was determined to roll the dice. 'I am taking this all the way to the convention in Kansas City,' he declared, 'even if I lose every damn primary between now and then.' This was less a case of conservative conviction than competitive doggedness. As Sears remarked: '[Reagan] made some pretty bad movies [...] But he knows that if you make a bad movie, you don't stop making movies.'[34]

North Carolina went to the polls on the same day as the La Crosse meeting. Holding a seemingly unassailable opinion-poll lead, Ford had barely campaigned there. Reagan had little expectation of an upset because his attacks on détente in 12 days of campaigning had seemingly failed to draw blood. He flew out saying he would be satisfied with a 'strong showing', prompting the *New York Times* to headline a report: 'Reagan virtually concedes defeat in North Carolina'. However, Senator Jesse Helms' powerful organization pulled out all the stops to produce an unlikely triumph for his conservative soulmate.[35] That night, while flying back to California, Reagan received news of an astonishing victory by 52 to 46 per cent. This was the first occasion that any Republican president had ever suffered a primary defeat. The exuberant staff, with reporters as willing accomplices, enjoyed a boisterous party of heavy drinking on the campaign plane. The Reagans celebrated with a large bowl of vanilla ice cream and a small plastic cup of champagne.

Airing on NBC on 31 March, Reagan's television address enhanced the momentum gained from North Carolina. Warning that Soviet power had grown under cover of détente, he declared, 'The evidence mounts that we are Number Two in a world where it's dangerous, if not fatal, to be second best.' A punchy line on the Panama Canal, first deployed in Florida, was used to good effect: 'We bought it, we paid for it, we built it, and we intend to keep it.'[36] The address replicated the success of 'A time for choosing', with Reagan now the beneficiary of his own way with words. His headquarters received 40,000 letters of support and $1.5 million in contributions that put the campaign back on track in time to contest primaries in the west, his strongest region.

Now in the fight of its life, the Ford camp tried to paint Reagan as an unelectable extremist and got accused in return of lacking conservative fibre. In essence, the contest became one between state and local party functionaries beholden to the president and Reagan's grassroots support. The challenger carried Texas with a two-thirds ballot share on 1 May, helped by an intensive direct-mail campaign by conservative groups. 'We are in real danger,' a Ford aide warned, 'of being out-organized by a small number of highly motivated *right wing* nuts, who are using funds outside of the Reagan campaign expenditure limits.'[37] This assessment underplayed the breadth of Reagan's support that included 100,000 crossover votes from Democrats. Some were conservative supporters of former Alabama governor George Wallace, recently withdrawn from the Democratic nomination contest, and others were evangelicals enthused by hearing Reagan talk about his faith on Christian radio. Votes from Democrats further helped Reagan win Indiana, Alabama, and Georgia, and he overturned an opinion-poll deficit of 20 points to carry Nebraska, which forbade crossovers. Ford stemmed the tide with wins in West Virginia, Maryland, and his home state of Michigan. Neither man could now build a winning momentum in what remained a see-saw contest through to the final primaries, in which Reagan won California but lost Ohio and New Jersey.

Despite Reagan taking 50.7 per cent of the aggregate primary vote, Ford held a narrow lead of 1,091 to 1,030 in delegates, just short of the 1,130 needed for the nomination. Everything now hinged on who took the 136 unpledged delegates attending the Republican National Convention in Kansas City. Exploiting the advantages of incumbency, Ford's lieutenants wooed them with invitations to the White House, sympathetic hearings for their pet projects, and even favoured seating at the Washington bicentennial celebrations.[38] Knowing that a big play was needed, Sears urged Reagan to break with tradition by naming his running mate prior to the convention. The man he had in mind was Senator Richard Schweiker of Pennsylvania, a state with 47 uncommitted convention delegates. To sell his boss on someone with a relatively liberal voting record Sears arranged for the two to meet in secret at Reagan's Pacific Palisades home. The pair hit it off so well that Schweiker got the nod before the day was out. In Reagan's accurate assessment, Schweiker was in the early stages of a political journey rightward. 'I found,' he later remarked, 'I was talking to a man who […] reminded me of myself 20 years ago when, as a New Deal Democrat, I made my change.'[39] Contrary to what Sears hoped, the Schweiker selection did not sway unpledged moderates, but appalled many conservatives as a fundamental breach of ideological purity. Already wavering in the face of Ford's patronage promises, most of the Reagan-pledged Mississippi delegation used it as an excuse to jump ship. Christian crooner Pat Boone, a member of the California delegation, tried celebrity charm and religious conviction to get them back, but hard-nosed calculation proved too strong. The outcome of all the manoeuvring was that Ford ended up winning the nomination with a delegate count of 1,187 to 1,070.

In many regards Reagan was the real winner at Kansas City. Twelve years after Barry Goldwater's premature candidacy, it was evident that the grassroots insurgency of the GOP right was a rising tide. Ford's managers had no illusions that many of his delegates were itching to bolt. To pre-empt a pro-Reagan stampede if matters came to a floor vote, they accepted almost every conservative demand in platform committee deliberations, including a contentious 'Morality in Foreign Policy' plank that was an overt rebuke to détente. Other concessions included planks supporting constitutional amendments re-establishing prayer in school, protecting the right of the unborn, and prohibiting racial busing. As a consequence, Ford ran on a platform that was closer to Reagan's preferences than his own. With Nelson Rockefeller already dropped from the Ford ticket as a sop to the right, Reagan could have had the vice-presidential nomination for the asking, but he'd always ruled this out.[40]

The scenes on the evening of 19 August offered further confirmation that Reagan was, in Nancy's words, the GOP's 'emotional favourite'. In a unity gesture after delivering his acceptance speech, Ford called on his erstwhile opponent, watching from a skybox high above the arena, to join him onstage. This brought delegates to their feet and the chants of 'speech, speech' became deafening. Although Reagan had no idea what he would say as he made the walk down alongside Nancy, he found the inspiration for a six-minute address generally considered among the best of his career. He warned that the America of 1976 had the dual obligation to the America of 2076 to halt 'the erosion of freedom that has taken place under Democratic rule' and to make the world safe from nuclear destruction. 'This is our challenge,' he concluded. 'We must go forth from here united, determined that what a great general said a few years ago is true: "There is no substitute for victory."' The emotions in the auditorium finally spilled over into tumultuous applause that drowned out the last few words. Perfectly capturing what had happened, a journalist commented, 'Ford won the nomination, but Reagan won their hearts.'[41]

Earlier that same day Reagan had thanked campaign staff for their endeavours: 'The cause is there,' he avowed, 'and the cause will prevail because it is right [...] There are millions and millions of Americans out there who want what you want [...] Who want it to be a shining city on a hill.' This sounded like a clarion call for another tilt at the presidency. On the flight home to California, the mood among staff was one of hope rather than regret. Asked by aide Martin Anderson to sign his convention ticket as a souvenir, Reagan wrote: 'We dreamed – we fought & the dream is still with us.' The message was clear to Anderson: 'On August 20, 1976, Ronald Reagan in effect began his third drive for the presidency.'[42] Whether Reagan felt the same certainty is another matter. A believer in destiny, he was presently unsure what his future was to be. As he wrote to one supporter, 'We [Nancy and I] are at peace with ourselves and believe the Lord must have something else in mind for us.'[43]

The outcome of the 1976 presidential race determined Reagan's options. As a loyal Republican, he campaigned in 25 states for the GOP ticket, filmed commercials ranging from 30 seconds to five minutes in length, and put his signature to millions of direct-mail messages. The only occasion he shared a stage with Ford was at a Beverly Hills fundraiser where he praised the GOP platform rather than the president. [44] Ford blamed his eventual narrow defeat – by 297 to 240 votes in the Electoral College, the closest margin since 1916 – on intra-party disagreements engendered by Reagan's challenge.[45] In reality, the Ford–Reagan split was nowhere near as divisive as the Goldwater–Rockefeller chasm of 1964. Ford's clawback of Democratic presidential candidate Jimmy Carter's one-time poll lead of 33 per cent to lose by a popular-vote margin of just 2 per cent hardly testified to fatal GOP disunity.

Reagan's conviction that he would have defeated Carter was also ill-founded.[46] As the first southern presidential candidate since the Civil War, the Democrat's support among African Americans and his fellow white Baptists would have turned back any Republican challenger in Dixie. Having established a reputation for fiscal prudence as Georgia governor from 1971 to 1975, he was less vulnerable than in 1980 to charges of being a big-government Washington man. Finally, the critically important independent vote was not yet ready to swallow a conservative Republican. On balance, Reagan was fortunate not to have been the GOP nominee in 1976 because a probable loss to Carter would have forestalled success four years later.

As it was, the Democrat's victory cleared the way for Reagan to embark on a four-year journey to the White House. The first stage saw him resume the public communication campaign interrupted by entry into the presidential race. His message constantly reiterated the need to restore the free market at home and defend the free world abroad. In delivering it, Reagan followed a hectic schedule of speaking engagements (some 150 in 1977–8), wrote bi-weekly newspaper commentaries, and delivered radio spots five days a week. With the potential to reach over 20 million people, the radio broadcasts provided a regular channel of communication that was uniquely Reagan's – no other politician of note exploited the medium in a comparable way. With federal rules requiring equal time for other presidential candidates, he would leave his own declaration as late as possible to reap maximum benefit from the radio spots.[47]

The 1980 election took place amid a political landscape profoundly different from 1976. After Ford's defeat, a string of media commentaries portrayed the GOP as a moribund force lacking a future. The strongest voice to the contrary was Reagan's. Avowing that 'most Americans are basically conservative', he electrified the American Conservative Union in early 1977 in calling for a 'New Republican Party' that embraced both economic and sociocultural conservatism in pursuit of becoming a mass party rather than an elitist one 'limited to the country-club big business image [...] it is burdened with today'.[48] This vision appeared far-fetched to all but the faithful but it bore more than a semblance of reality by 1980. Openness to new conservative forces would restore Republican dynamism. A leading Democrat, Senator Daniel Patrick Moynihan of New York, acknowledged that the GOP had 'all of a sudden become a party of ideas'. Fearing a 'terrifying' transformation of American politics, he warned that 'there is a movement to turn the Republicans into Populists, a party of the People against a Democratic Party of the State'.[49]

The opportunity for this flowed from the travails of liberalism in the troubled 1970s. First and foremost, Keynesian prescriptions that had underwritten the long postwar boom could not cure the novel phenomenon of stagflation (high inflation and stagnant growth) that increasingly plagued the economy as the decade progressed. In 1980 the inflation rate reached 13 per cent – as well as staggering increases in consumer and energy prices, another consequence of this was a prime interest rate of 20 per cent – and unemployment stood at 7 per cent. Concern was also growing that America was losing the Cold War as a result of détente, a strategy initiated by Republican presidents Richard Nixon and Gerald Ford but associated with the Democrats when pursued by Jimmy Carter. On Ford's watch, South Vietnam, Cambodia, and Laos had fallen to communism and Angola and Mozambique came under the control of Soviet-backed Marxist regimes. Things went from bad to worse under Carter as Moscow expanded its influence in Central America, the Horn of Africa, and south-west Asia and forged ahead in the arms race. As a senior CIA official noted, '[T]he sense that the Soviets and their surrogates were on the march around the world was palpable in Washington and elsewhere.'[50] Meanwhile, the culture wars had broken out at home as moral conservatives mobilized in defence of traditional values against feminism, gay rights, and pro-choice support for abortion, all associated in their eyes with the legacy of 1960s liberalism.

In reaction to this state of affairs, a number of groups came together under the banner of a loosely knit conservative movement that was far more diverse, powerful, and better-funded than the fledgling version that supported Barry Goldwater in the early 1960s. Critical in this was the revitalization of corporate conservatism, which was a relatively dormant force while prosperity benefited balance sheets in the 1960s. In the era of stagflation, however, big business blamed its woes on overtaxation, over-regulation, and overspending by big government.[51] As a consequence, it vastly expanded lobbying activities, channelled ever-larger political contributions to pro-market Republicans, and funded an intellectual renaissance on the right. Corporate money poured into conservative think-tanks to develop policy ideas for freeing private enterprise from statism. Business-funded grants also helped to transform the academic discipline of economics, once a Keynesian bailiwick, into one that starred monetarists, supply-siders, and free-marketeers.[52] Meanwhile, neoconservatives (many of them one-time Cold War liberals) and traditional anti-communists joined forces to condemn détente for preferring peace to resistance. Operating through bodies like the Committee on the Present Danger, they called for military rearmament to meet the rising Soviet challenge.[53] Finally, moral conservatives formed a loose affiliation of New Right organizations that used direct-mail techniques to mobilize grassroots support for family values. A related movement, the Christian Right, summoned evangelicals into battle to defend the family, the community, and the church against the secular interference of the state.[54]

Assessing these developments, Reagan aide Martin Anderson commented:

> [W]hat has been called the Reagan revolution is not completely, or
> even mostly, due to Ronald Reagan. He was an extremely important
> contributor to the intellectual and political movement that swept him to
> the presidency in 1980. He gave that movement focus and leadership.
> But Reagan did not give it life.[55]

Though fundamentally accurate, this judgement rather downplays Reagan's indispensability to conservatism's political success. First, he was the right's only electable candidate for president in 1980; second, he had spent years staking out the broad terrain on different parts of which the various conservative groups now planted their flags; and, finally, he was the only political figure capable of appealing across the broad spectrum of the not-always-harmonious elite and grassroots organizations that made up the conservative movement. It was also significant that Reagan's adaptability enabled him to reach those parts of the right that did not consider him their natural champion.

Of all the conservative groups, Reagan was most in tune with the anti-détente Cold Warriors. Like them, he regarded the struggle with the Soviets as an ideological battle between Western freedom and communist enslavement that could not be resolved through superpower détente. They were also like-minded in the conviction that the Soviet Union was exploiting America's post-Vietnam loss of resolve to build up its power for an ultimate showdown. As protégés of Democratic Senator Henry Jackson of Washington, some of the most influential neoconservatives were moderately liberal on domestic issues, but this outlook was subordinate to their regard for Reagan's foreign-policy ideas. One of their number was Georgetown professor Jeane Kirkpatrick, author of an influential article berating Jimmy Carter for abandoning anti-communist autocracies in Latin America in the name of human rights. In her view, authoritarian regimes were capable of self-reform, making them suitable allies for the United States. This accorded with Reagan's own conviction that Cold War priorities overrode any concern about the failure of military dictatorships to operate 'as we might wish in their internal priorities'.[56] Though a registered Democrat, Kirkpatrick would join his campaign team as a foreign-policy advisor and later serve in his administration.

The Soviet Union's invasion of Afghanistan in late 1979 was grist to the mill of détente's critics. Precipitating a renewal of Cold War confrontation, this first resort to military intervention outside Eastern Europe may well have been a defensive manoeuvre against the spread of Islamic fundamentalism from Iran. Nevertheless, it also reflected the Kremlin's confidence that the Soviet Union had established a preponderance of power over America.[57] Although Jimmy Carter responded with a raft of hawkish measures to deter further Soviet adventurism, Reagan had little confidence in their efficacy. In his estimate, the United States might face a 'surrender or perish' ultimatum unless it quickly regained Cold War ascendancy through massive expansion of its military power and rollback of recent Soviet gains in the third world. An arms race in which America would have the advantage of vastly superior economic resources, he declared, is 'the last thing they want from us [...] because they are running as fast as they can and we haven't started running'.[58]

Reagan's rapport with neoconservatives obscured a fundamental difference between them. For Kirkpatrick and others, once established anywhere, communism was reversible only through force, and the Cold War was permanent.

In contrast, Reagan anticipated America's peaceful triumph provided its people rediscovered the national will to prevail. In his credo, moral rearmament was as important as the military kind to sustain what he regarded as America's God-given mission to overcome the Soviet threat to freedom. 'Only by mustering a superiority, beginning with a superiority of the spirit,' he declared in one radio address, 'can we stop the thunder of the hobnailed boots on the march to world empire.'[59] Though never thinking himself the chosen instrument of a 'Divine Plan', Reagan believed that freedom's victory over communism would occur within his lifetime. In 1977, he told long-time foreign-policy advisor Richard Allen, 'my idea of American policy towards the Soviet Union is simple. It is this: "we win and they lose."'[60]

Communism's violation of the basic human desire for freedom doomed it to eventual collapse in Reagan's estimation. Faced with America's military and moral superiority, the Soviet Union would have no option but to rein in its aggression and enter meaningful peace negotiations, both of which were impossible under the sham of détente. The United States would thereby stand as the beacon of liberty that inspired those living under oppression in Eastern Europe and elsewhere to demand freedom. This is what Reagan meant when remarking to aides on a brief 1978 visit to East Berlin, his first foray behind the Iron Curtain, 'we must free these people'.[61] The vision of peaceful victory got overshadowed in Reagan's bellicose-sounding rhetoric amid escalating Cold War tensions in 1980. As a consequence, the image of being a sabre-rattling warmonger dogged him throughout the presidential campaign.

The natural partnership that Reagan formed with the critics of détente was not immediately paralleled in his relationship with corporate conservatives. A *Fortune* journalist reported in May 1980 that business leaders were 'lukewarm' about Reagan, regarding his economic proposals as simplistic solutions to America's current problems. The same article quoted the candidate as being more interested in gaining support from people with 'calluses on their hands'.[62] The populist image that Reagan projected was a turn-off to big business, particularly in regard to tax reduction. Fearing that his plan for across-the-board personal income-tax cuts would fuel inflation, it regarded capital-tax reduction as a better guarantee of economic renewal. Reagan was more intent on tapping into what he regarded as a visceral anti-tax sentiment beating in the hearts of ordinary people as inflation pushed them into high income-tax brackets and forced up property-tax assessments on their home. Popular approval of various tax-limitation referenda at state level in the late 1970s convinced him that a Second American Revolution was afoot. He had hailed the Proposition 13 victory in California, which sparked similar initiatives elsewhere, 'as a little bit like dumping those cases of tea off the boat in Boston harbor'.[63]

Slowly but surely Reagan and big business grew closer together as the election drew near – a recognition of reality on both their parts. He needed financial contributions and the legitimizing endorsement of his economic plan from the corporate community. Once the nomination was sewn up, business had to get behind him in order to pre-empt its worst nightmare – the re-election of Jimmy Carter. One manifestation of this closer relationship was the formation of conduits like the Business Advisory Panel and the Executive Advisory Council to feed business views into the Reagan campaign. Reagan also appeared before groups of corporate leaders to solicit their opinions. Most significantly, Charls Walker, chair of the American Council of Capital Formation, was enlisted to serve in the small group advising Reagan on economic policy. This insider's insider was influential in getting a 10–5–3 business depreciation allowance on buildings, vehicles, and machinery included in the GOP platform.[64]

Meanwhile, Reagan cherry-picked ideas from the conservative economic doctrines that had arisen to challenge Keynesianism. One-time Goldwater advisor Milton Friedman had gravitated into his orbit as a member of the gubernatorial task force that drafted California's Proposition 1 in 1973. Seizing on this monetarist guru's theory that inflation resulted from excessive money-supply expansion, Reagan adapted it in support of his conviction that the federal government was monetizing the public debt. In the single 1980 presidential debate, he declared, 'We have inflation because government is living too well.' The solution was balanced budgets so '[we] are no longer grinding out printing press money, flooding the market with it because Government is spending more than it takes in'. The 1970s deficits (like those of the 1980s) were actually financed from public borrowing rather than what Reagan called 'the roller-coasting of money', but his words were in tune with the popular instinct that deficit spending was the source of inflation.[65]

Reagan also found much to like in new supply-side thinking on how to restore economic wellbeing. Contrary to Keynesian management of aggregate demand, this doctrine posited the motivations of entrepreneurs, workers, and consumers as the keystone of economic behaviour. In its credo, tax cuts that enabled individuals to keep a greater portion of their income constituted the surest way to incentivize productivity growth.[66] Championing this approach, Congressman Jack Kemp of New York and Senator William Roth of Delaware co-sponsored a measure providing for a 30 per cent reduction in income taxes spread over three years. Though rejected by the Democratic majority, this gained widespread support from congressional Republicans. A one-time star quarterback for the Buffalo Bills, Kemp now eyed a drive for the White House, a quixotic undertaking because he lacked funds and organization, but a threat to Reagan because it could draw support from his conservative base. To pre-empt this danger, John Sears got his boss to endorse Kemp–Roth in late 1979 in return for Kemp's agreement not to run for president himself.[67]

Reagan's approval of Kemp–Roth did not equate to embracing its doctrinal credo. In Ed Meese's opinion, he had been 'a "supply-sider" long before the term was invented'.[68] Instead of being theory-driven, however, his economic ideas were drawn from his political philosophy and his personal experience – or at least his remembrance of it. According to Reagan's memoirs, he came face-to-face with the disincentive of huge taxes in postwar Hollywood when '[Uncle Sam] took such a big chunk of my earnings that after a while I began asking myself whether it was worth it to keep on taking work.'[69] This hardly squared with the fact that he had been desperate to make more movies at a time when his film career was in decline. Whatever the imperfections of memory, supply-side theory still offered intellectual legitimacy for his conviction that high taxes hurt the economy.

One idea that Reagan swallowed hook, line, and sinker offered reassurance that taxes could be cut without enlarging the budget deficit. Laffer Curve theory, promulgated by supply-side pioneer Arthur Laffer of the University of Southern California, decreed that revenue would 'reflow' to government from the economic growth generated by tax reduction. This beguiling idea was bereft of empirical guidance regarding the point between 100 per cent and 0 per cent taxation of income at which reflow would occur and the proportion of revenue that might be recouped. Nevertheless, Reagan avowed in one radio broadcast that Kemp–Roth 'would reduce the deficit which causes inflation because the tax base would be *broadened* by increased prosperity'. Within weeks of becoming president, he voiced the same belief: 'A cut in tax rates can very often be reflected in an increase in government revenues because of the broadening of the base of the economy.'[70] On the other hand, Reagan found unpalatable the disinclination of many supply-siders to cut spending because they expected the budget deficit to disappear as a consequence of economic expansion. According to Jack Kemp: 'A prosperous private economy can afford a strong safety net of public services. A stifled, smothering economy can't.' For Reagan, however, Kemp–Roth was both an agency of economic growth and a continuation of his Proposition 1 strategy of constraining government through limitation of its tax revenue. As such, he always prefaced advocacy of it 'with the declaration that we must immediately start to reduce the size and cost of our federal government to bring it down to a lesser percentage of our gross national product'.[71]

Far more important, of course, than the differences of detail between Reagan and other economic conservatives, whether of the business or intellectual variety, was their agreement on fundamental principle. Liberation of the market from the dead hand of big government was the bedrock of his philosophy. Appearing on William Buckley's *Firing Line* television programme, Reagan avowed, 'I just have faith in the *marketplace*, and I believe that this is the way we must go to curb inflation [...] to put us back where we were as an industrial giant.'[72] There was also something for every brand of conservative in the blueprint that shaped his economic policy in office. In August 1979 Martin Anderson drew up a summary of the ideas Reagan had promulgated for restoring prosperity under the title 'Policy memorandum No 1'. The formula for economic renewal outlined in this featured tax reduction, tax-bracket indexation to end 'bracket creep', substantial deregulation, control of federal spending through elimination of waste and the transfer of some social programmes to the states, and balanced budgets mandated if necessary by constitutional amendment.[73]

The conservatives that Reagan found hardest to bring into his tent were the moral traditionalists of the New Right and Christian Right. Aides worried that a close association with these groups would cost the support of moderate Republicans nationwide. The battle over California Proposition 6, better known as the Briggs Initiative (after State Senator John Briggs), showed the difficulty of satisfying both constituencies. Reagan made common cause with a broad coalition of liberals, middle-of-the-roaders, and mainstream conservatives against this ballot proposal to ban homosexuals from teaching in public

schools. Doubtless there was advantage in demonstrating his lack of extremism, but principle also drove him to take a high-profile stand against anti-gay
discrimination as an unconstitutional infringement on the rights of privacy.[74]
A leading gay-rights magazine later praised Reagan's contribution as critically
important in the landslide defeat of the proposal by more than a million votes.
In contrast, Moral Majority founder Jerry Falwell warned that Reagan would
'face the music from Christian voters two years from now', but this would
actually prove to be a hymn of praise.[75]

If Reagan was to become president, he needed to be a credible candidate
in the south, both to capture convention delegates, and, more particularly, to
challenge Jimmy Carter in his home region thereafter. To this end, he undertook
a patient courting of the Christian Right leadership once the dust from Briggs
had settled. This opened with an impressive avowal of his faith at a meeting
with evangelical leaders sponsored by the National Religious Broadcasters in
August 1979. In regular election-year appearances before true believers, Reagan
created a favourable impression with his avowals of belief in America's divine
mission to defend freedom, of the need to stand up to godless communism
(his toughest anti-Soviet rhetoric in 1980 was before evangelical audiences),
and of the necessity for a moral crusade to redeem America against the threat
of humanism.[76]

The most important factor in swinging the Christian Right to Reagan,
however, was its growing revulsion against Jimmy Carter. The most pietistic
president of the twentieth century came under evangelical attack for being on
the wrong side of every issue they cared deeply about – notably abortion, gay
rights, school prayer, and the Equal Rights Amendment. For them, his most
abominable shortcoming was failing to overrule the Internal Revenue Service's
decision to revoke the tax-exempt status of private schools with an 'insignificant
number of minority students'. This struck at the virtually all-white evangelical
schools that had proliferated since the 1960s, notably in the south, to provide
a Christian education not offered in desegregated public schools. Following a
prayer meeting with Carter, evangelical pastor Tim LaHaye issued a prayer of
his own: 'God, we have to get this man out of the White House and get someone
in here who will be aggressive about bringing back traditional moral values.'[77]
Reagan met this need with his promise to 'keep government out of the school
and the neighborhood; and above all – the home'. An appearance at a Religious

Roundtable meeting in Dallas on 22 August 1980 resulted in Reagan's virtual anointment as God's chosen candidate. A crescendo of applause from the audience of local Christians greeted his avowal: 'I know you can't endorse me. But I want you to know that I endorse you and what you are doing.' This line, inserted into the speech on the advice of televangelist James Robison, signalled where his heart and soul lay. A once sceptical Jerry Falwell now declared him 'the president He wants us to have'.[78]

Reagan had found the right pitch for his voice that had been off-key early in the campaign owing to the distractions of staff in-fighting instigated by the power hungry John Sears. The first casualty was Lyn Nofziger, ousted for advocating a conservative Sunbelt-suburban strategy rather than a catch-all approach that would net moderate support from other regions. Shortly afterwards, longstanding insider Martin Anderson quit after being repeatedly undermined in his policy-development role. Mike Deaver then resigned to save Reagan from having to make a decision on a 'him or me' ultimatum from Sears. After this confrontation, Reagan would never talk warmly of his campaign manager again, but would sarcastically remark of his untrustworthiness, 'I look him in the eye, and he looks me in the tie.' The next target for the Sears hatchet was to be Ed Meese, but his own head would be the one to roll.[79]

Reagan's strongest rival for the nomination was former CIA director and United Nations ambassador George H. W. Bush. Overturning a huge poll deficit, he sprang a surprise to win the Iowa caucuses that launched the presidential race. Whereas Bush worked the state hard, Reagan adopted an above-the-fray strategy advocated by Sears. Calling the plays himself henceforth, he campaigned intensively in the New Hampshire primary, where Bush initially held a 9 per cent poll lead. The best remembered moment came at the Nashua debate, billed as a one-to-one with Bush until Reagan brought the other candidates into the venue after they demanded equal time. When Bush objected to the change of format, moderator Jon Breen called for Reagan's microphone to be switched off unless the original rules were observed. The angry response – 'I paid for this microphone Mr Green [*sic*]' – had the crowd stomping approval for one of the most iconic lines of the entire campaign. Reagan had by now swung ahead in the polls, so this was not the deciding factor in his victory. What the moment had created, however, was an image of decisiveness conveyed nationwide through television replays of the clip. As

Reagan pollster Dick Wirthlin observed, it provided something that candidates and strategists dream about but rarely achieve – 'the chance to bottle strength and command in a seven-second sound bite'.[80]

What finally did for Sears was Nancy Reagan's discovery that expenditures he had sanctioned had already gobbled up two-thirds of the legal spending limit for the entire nomination campaign. She engineered a coup that brought in tough-minded securities lawyer William Casey to run the show in place of the man who had become error-prone and divisive. Within a short time, all the old hands purged by Sears were back on board, the campaign gained unity of purpose, and Reagan recovered his verve. '[T]he organization had begun to come apart,' the candidate reported to a friend. 'We have a happy ship now.'[81] Casey got rid of the expensive campaign plane, fired pro-Sears aides by the dozen, and squeezed every dollar in anticipation of a prolonged race to the nomination. However, a string of primary victories quickly saw off every Republican rival except Bush. On 18 March a big win in Illinois effectively turned the race into a coronation procession. A week later Reagan swept to victory in New York, once the bedrock state of Rockefeller Republicanism.

Bush hung on to win the Pennsylvania primary, in which he famously derided Reagan's planned tax cuts without corollary expenditure savings as 'voodoo economics' that would send the fiscal deficit into the stratosphere. Overall, his increasingly hopeless campaign garnered nearly a quarter of the aggregate votes cast in the GOP primaries. Despite this, both Reagans disdained their blue-blooded opponent as an Establishment wimp because of his conduct in the Nashua debate. Neither was keen on him being the running mate when the vice-presidential selection had to be made for the GOP national convention in Detroit. 'I'll never choose that man; he lied about my record,' Reagan told aides.[82] Instead he flirted with the idea of recruiting Gerald Ford onto an unprecedented and seemingly unbeatable dream ticket. Their earlier differences forgotten, the two were now reconciled in disdain for Jimmy Carter. Initial overtures found the former president responsive but it proved impossible to work out mutually satisfactory details. Ford talked himself out of a job, perhaps intentionally, with demands that effectively amounted to becoming co-president rather than vice-president.[83]

The dream-ticket idea was conceived with a view to broadening Reagan's support among moderates, but it could have become a nightmare by handing the Democrats a constitutional issue to exploit. 'I can't tell you with what anticipation we began to look forward to the idea that this was really going to happen,' recalled Carter pollster Pat Caddell.[84] With Ford eliminated, Reagan immediately asked Bush to take the job, an offer that was enthusiastically accepted. An asset to the ticket, Bush strengthened GOP hopes of carrying his home state of Texas (narrowly won by Carter in 1976), brought foreign-policy experience to the campaign, and his establishment credentials complemented Reagan's populism. Despite the 'voodoo economics' remark, he was solidly conservative on economic issues. Above all, he knew the foremost requirement of a running mate was loyalty to the boss. Drawing on his oil-industry experience, Bush told aides, 'We're now a wholly owned subsidiary and we're going to behave as one.' In line with this, he agreed to change his pro-choice position on abortion, thereby enabling Reagan to reassure conservative supporters that 'I am not about to be taken over' by the Eastern establishment.[85]

The most watched speech he had given hitherto, Reagan used his nomination acceptance address to establish the core themes of the campaign against Carter in accordance with the recommendations of Dick Wirthlin. Appointed chief strategist following the Sears ouster, Wirthlin relied on a massive computerized information system developed by his polling organization to 'war game' how rhetoric could carry his client to victory. It was evident to him that the Republican base was 'simply not large enough to win the presidency'. Through the new technology, he found a majority of voters yearned for a 'leader who can take charge with authority; return a sense of discipline to our government; and manifest the will power needed to get his country back on track'. This called for a campaign that emphasized leadership, not ideology, in appealing to the group that would become known as the 'Reagan Democrats'. The election could be won through building popular expectation that a Reagan presidency 'will take courageous stands on pressing national issues […] and reaffirm the nation's highest purposes'. The campaign had to reduce 'uncertainty about what the future portends. Leadership is the ability to enlarge men's vision about the future and give them expectations of a less uncertain and more gratifying future.'[86]

In words crafted by Peter Hannaford with input from Wirthlin, Reagan declared that the major issue of the campaign was 'the direct political, personal, and moral responsibility of the Democratic Party leadership – in the White House and in Congress – for this unprecedented calamity that has befallen us'. Drawing a sharp contrast with his opponents, he avowed:

> They say the United States has had its day in the sun; that our nation has passed its zenith [...] I will not stand by and watch this great country destroy itself under mediocre leadership that drifts from one crisis to the next, eroding our national will and purpose.

The invocation that 'Divine Providence' intended America to be an 'island of freedom' led to the climax that asked: 'Can we begin our crusade joined together in a moment of silent prayer?' As one of the listening reporters remarked, 'It is hard to think of another politician who could pull this off – or would try to.'[87]

While Republicans left Detroit in good heart, Democrats were divided, dispirited, and defeatist at their national convention in New York City. The liberal insurgency that Senator Edward Kennedy of Massachusetts had mounted for the presidential nomination had left Carter badly wounded in victory. There was little enthusiasm in the nation for his candidacy in light of the intractable problems that had overtaken America on his watch. More than anything else, the long-running Iranian hostage crisis, precipitated when militants had seized US embassy personnel in Tehran on 4 November 1979, had come to symbolize national decline. An unsuccessful attempt at military rescue in April 1980 only made Carter look weak, inept, and unsuited to be president at a time of crisis. On the other hand, Reagan did his unintended utmost to turn the election into a close race with early gaffes that made him look anything but the right man to get America out of its present mess.

Despite Wirthlin's frantic imploring, a stubborn Reagan went ahead to address the Neshoba County Fair, Mississippi, just a few miles from where three civil rights workers were murdered by white racists in the 'Freedom Summer' of 1964. His insensitive defence of states' rights whipped up a press furor that was typified by a *Washington Post* editorial on 11 August headlined 'Chilling words in Neshoba County: is Reagan saying that he intends to do everything he can to turn the clock back to Mississippi justice of 1964?' Another outcry greeted remarks of approval for the Vietnam War that he insisted on inserting into an address to the Veterans of Foreign Wars in Chicago on 18

August. 'It is time,' Reagan declared, 'we recognized that ours, in truth, was a noble cause.' To many Americans, these words suggested that Reagan would have no qualms about taking them into another conflict in a far-off country. These were the worst of the numerous oratorical stumbles littering the early campaign. Taken together, they called into question Reagan's steadiness, intelligence, and competence on the key issue of leadership. 'We were close,' one aide told reporter Lou Cannon, '[...] to making Reagan rather than Carter the chief issue of the campaign.' To get him back on track, Nancy called for Stu Spencer to be drafted into the campaign, setting aside grudges about his role in 1976 in recognition that 'he had the greatest political instincts of anybody I've ever met'. Only too pleased to be back in the fold, Spencer made it his business to ensure that Reagan stuck to the agreed script and did not engage too much with the press.[88]

The White House had once been confident that Reagan would be a pushover in the general election, which it expected to be a replay of the Johnson–Goldwater race of 1964. One senior aide presciently warned that this outlook was 'both wrong and dangerous' because their opponent was in tune with the mood of the country, but others took a long time to recognize this reality.[89] As the election neared, the Carter organization decided that a major effort to discredit Reagan as a vacuous extremist represented its only hope of victory. In order to maintain a presidential image, incumbents usually delegated the dirty work of negative campaigning to subordinates. Worried that the media was giving his opponent an easy ride, Carter decided that he alone could get the message over to voters. Three addresses were especially noteworthy for their nastiness: on 16 September he came close to decrying Reagan as a racial bigot before a black audience at Martin Luther King Sr's Ebenezer Baptist Church in Atlanta; on 23 September he told a California labour convention that the election would decide whether 'we have peace or war'; and on 6 October he told a Democratic fundraiser in Chicago that a Reagan presidency would divide 'black from white, Jew from Christian, North from South, rural from urban'. These attacks, in combination with negative Democratic television ads, sparked doubt among the large body of still-undecided voters about Reagan's trustworthiness to lead the country.[90]

There were also rumours circulating in Washington that the president might spring an 'October surprise' by announcing the release of the Iranian hostages. The crisis had long posed a political dilemma for Reagan. In private he fulminated that Carter's foreign-policy weakness had encouraged Iranian belief that the captives could be held with impunity. In public he guarded his words because, he told Caspar Weinberger, 'I don't want to say anything to endanger those people.'[91] Accordingly, the Reagan campaign largely maintained silence on the issue, but stood ready to question the nature of any deal that brought the hostages home on election eve. Carter National Security Council staffer Gary Sick later claimed that key Reagan aides, including William Casey, had conducted secret negotiations with Iranian officials to postpone the hostages' release until after the election. Two congressional investigations found no evidence of wrongdoing – the 968-page 1993 report of a House committee investigation stands as the definitive statement on this score.[92]

With just weeks to go, several polls put Carter ahead before the advantage swung back to his opponent. Worried by this volatility, Stuart Spencer advised Reagan that the best means of protecting his lead was to demonstrate presidential calibre by debating Carter, a ploy that also carried risks of a gaffe in front of the nationwide audience. The terms of engagement for this encounter held in Cleveland, Ohio, on 28 October constituted a triumph for Reagan negotiators because the president was so anxious to have the chance to expose his rival as ignorant and dangerous. There was only one debate – the White House had wanted three in order to better expose Reagan's supposed lack of policy knowledge; it was held near the election to reduce the impact of any gaffe by the challenger; and Reagan was allowed to make the closing statement in return for agreeing to take the first question that Carter aides thought most likely to generate a nerves-induced error. To the relief of both camps, the once-healthy poll numbers of independent candidate John Anderson had nosedived below the 15 per cent threshold required for participation – but Reagan had got valuable practice through debating him one-on-one (the president refused to participate) in Baltimore on 21 September.

With every poll making Reagan the winner by clear margins, the debate with Carter proved a turning point in the campaign. Unable to accept being bested by someone he considered inferior, the president confided to his diary:

> He has his memorized tapes. He pushes a button and they come out.
> He apparently made a better impression on the TV audience than I

did, but I made all our points to the constituency groups – which we
believe will become preeminent in the public's mind as they approach
the point a week from now of actually going to the polls.[93]

This self-delusion overlooked what was supposedly Carter's main goal. He
never landed a serious blow because he was neither the first nor the last to fall
into the trap of underestimating Reagan. As a seasoned debater, the challenger
had prepared assiduously in mock debates with aides (helped by possession of
Carter's debate-briefing books, courtesy of a mole in the president's campaign
staff). There was no way he was going to cooperate in the opposition plan to
put him in the 'stupid-and-dangerous' box.

  Reagan pre-empted hopes of depicting him as trigger-happy in answering
the opening question:

  I believe with all of my heart that our first priority must be world peace
  [...] America has never gotten into a war because we were too strong.
  We can get into a war by letting events get out of hand, as they have
  in the last three and a half years.

He held his cool when Carter tried to present him as a threat to environmental
regulation, Social Security, and Medicare, gaining a laugh from the invited
audience when he responded to one final barb, 'There you go again.' If there
was a knock-down blow, Reagan delivered it through posing a series of questions to Americans in his closing statement, when Carter had no comeback:
'Are you better off than you were four years ago [...] Do you feel that our
security is as safe, that we're as strong as we were four years ago?'[94] In this way
Reagan stopped Carter claiming the benefits of incumbency without bearing
responsibility for the nation's current problems. He had made the election a
retrospective one on his opponent's record rather than a prospective one on
his own presidency.

  Reagan's poll lead grew incrementally but not dramatically after the debate,
but there was one last drama to play out. On the Sunday before the election,
Carter got word on the campaign trail that Tehran was offering fresh terms
for the hostages' release. What he discovered on rushing back to the White
House was that the 'new' conditions were no different from previous ones. The

president had to go on national television to break the bad news. Two days later Americans cast their ballots on the first anniversary of the hostages being taken. Most polls were still predicting a close race but both candidates' private surveys were in agreement that hitherto undecided voters had swung heavily to the challenger. The final dashing of hopes for the hostages' release had seemingly crystallized doubts about the president's leadership on the entire panoply of peace and prosperity issues. Carter knew his fate before the count started.[95]

In the Electoral College, Reagan's 489 to 49 margin was bettered only by FDR in 1936 and Nixon in 1972 – only Georgia, Hawaii, Maryland, Minnesota, Rhode Island, West Virginia, and the District of Columbia went to Carter. The race was much closer in popular-vote terms, with Reagan taking 50.7 per cent, Carter 41 per cent, and Anderson 6.6 per cent. In regional terms, Reagan ran strongest in the west, carried all but one southern state, and performed solidly in the north-east/upper Midwest where Anderson's ballot share prevented Carter winning Massachusetts, Michigan, New York, and Wisconsin. The battle in the south was closer than the Electoral College scorecard suggested. Reagan carried Alabama, Arkansas, Mississippi, North Carolina, South Carolina, and Tennessee with less than 50 per cent of votes cast because Anderson took support away from Carter. Nevertheless, his achievement in Dixie was still significant because he had targeted winning only five states from a southern candidate. In terms of group support, Reagan's victory was remarkably broad-based: he won every demographic other than African Americans, Latinos, those aged under 30, low-income voters, and the least educated. He even turned round Carter's initial lead among women to take a 46 per cent plurality of their vote, a stunning reversal for a president who backed the proposed Equal Rights Amendment to the Constitution that would prohibit abridgement of equal rights on grounds of gender.

At one level, the election was nothing more than an expression of an anti-incumbent mood. A *Time* poll found that 63 per cent of voters agreed that the election was 'mostly a rejection of President Carter', whereas only 25 per cent deemed it a 'mandate for more conservative policies'. Exit polls confirmed that economic problems principally influenced voter choices.[96] Accordingly, Carter's defeat was hardly surprising since his record featured the worst economic indicators for any incumbent since Herbert Hoover. Despite the hostage crisis, barely one in three voters rated foreign policy more important than the economy. Further casting doubt on the transformative significance of the 1980 vote, almost half the electorate did not bother to cast a ballot. Reagan was in reality the choice of barely one in four eligible voters.

At another level, however, the election could be viewed as marking a right turn in the nation's political history. Although Reagan had framed it as one about leadership rather than ideology, Americans could have had little doubt about the direction in which he intended to lead the nation. The New Deal coalition of voters that had sustained the Democrats since the 1930s looked to have finally disintegrated. Nixon had won a landslide in 1972 without benefit to the rest of the GOP ticket. Reagan's 1980 coat-tails were an important factor in the Republicans gaining a Senate majority for the first time since 1954, with a net gain of 12 seats and picking up 33 seats in the House, their biggest increase since 1966. Opinion surveys also pointed to a broader change in the national mood. Popular confidence in government to manage the economy, one of the staples of the liberal ascendancy, was at its lowest ebb since World War II. More broadly, Harris polls found that three-fifths of respondents now agreed that 'the best government is the government that governs least', compared with a third in 1974.[97]

The election furthermore signalled the emergence of 'Reagan country', the fast-growing Sunbelt region that nurtured conservative Republicanism. The factors that had turned California into an economic powerhouse in the 1940s – notably federal defence contracts, the development of high-tech enterprises tied into the military-industrial complex – like aerospace and electronics, cheap energy, and the business opportunities offered by suburban growth – had steadily extended into the rest of the south-west and parts of the south in the following decades. This underwrote the emergence of a conservative constituency that was broadly anti-statist, anti-communist, and super-patriotic. In terms of national politics, the south-west had been fertile GOP terrain since the mid-1960s. The 1980 vote indicated that a parallel Republicanization of Dixie was in progress. Helped by economics and evangelicals, Reagan carried 61 per cent of white voters in the south, while the GOP gained four Senate seats and increased its House representation in five states in the region. As this process gathered pace in the final decades of the twentieth century, a new southern leadership would emerge in the national Republican Party to build on the conservative foundations laid by Reagan.[98]

The election winner emerged from the shower at his Pacific Palisades home to take Jimmy Carter's phone call conceding defeat. It was 5.15 p.m. Pacific time. The polls were still open in California, but the networks were calling the outcome a sure thing. A night of quiet celebration followed with dinner at the Bel Air home of steel magnate Earle Jorgensen, a longstanding wealthy backer, and later a party at campaign headquarters in the Los Angeles Century Plaza Hotel. Late in the evening Neil Reagan dropped by to offer his congratulations. The two brothers wondered how the news was being greeted in their home town. 'I bet there's a hot time in Dixon tonight,' said Moon. 'I'd like to be there off in a corner just listening,' replied Dutch.[99] Ronald Reagan was now ready to complete his journey from the early twentieth-century small-town Midwest to the late twentieth-century White House.

SEVEN

Mr President

S oon after receiving Jimmy Carter's personal concession, Ronald Reagan got another telephone call. Pat Boone was ringing to ask if he could be one of the first to call him 'Mr President'.[1] This would be Reagan's mode of address for the next eight years and beyond from virtually everyone but close family and a small circle of friends and foreign leaders. In 1964, United Artists had rejected him for the starring role in *The Best Man*, a movie about a White House aspirant, on the grounds that he did not look sufficiently presidential. In office, however, Reagan succeeded in projecting an image of strength, decisiveness, and optimism that made him appear uber-presidential. He would enjoy being president – not something that could be said of his recent predecessors – and would be remarkably unchanged by the experience of holding the world's most important job. An average Gallup approval rating of just 53 per cent attested that Americans were far from being in agreement about whether they enjoyed his presidency, but no one could doubt that the United States and indeed the world had changed significantly as a result of it.

Reagan operated a presidency that lived up to the leadership ideal that FDR had implanted in his mind in the 1930s. As dean of presidential scholars Richard Neustadt put it:

> [H]is Presidency restored the public image of the office to a fair (if perhaps rickety) approximation of its Rooseveltian mold: a place of

popularity, influence and initiative, a source of programmatic and symbolic leadership, both pacesetter and tonesetter, the nation's voice both to the world and us, and – like or hate the policies – a presence many of us loved to see as Chief of State.[2]

Reagan's success in this regard owed much to his powerful use of the presidential podium to chart the course he set for the nation and to his restoration of the presidency's spectacle following its parsimonious de-pomping under Carter. Both elements were on show on the 40th president's very first day in office.

Composed with the help of speechwriter Ken Khachigian, Reagan's inaugural address set the tone for his presidency. Most of these oratorical efforts quickly faded from history – the few exceptions included Abraham Lincoln's in 1861, FDR's in 1933, JFK's in 1961, and Reagan's in 1981. What the memorable ones have in common is strength of vision, moral uplift, and identification of the president with the nation's values. They also have at least one line that forever more defines his image. The 40th president's 2,452-word inaugural address was delivered on 20 January, a spring-like day that followed two weeks of bitter cold. It was classic Reagan: simple, radical, optimistic. Offering a philosophy of government rather than a programmatic agenda, it unambiguously established economic renewal as the overriding priority – only four short paragraphs comprising 224 words towards the end dealt with foreign policy. It was the first inaugural since Calvin Coolidge's in 1924 to idealize a smaller state – specifically through linkage of America's economic woes to the 'unnecessary and excessive growth of government'. Finally, it evinced absolute belief in the capacity of Americans to prove as so often before that they could overcome present difficulties: '[W]e're too great a nation,' Reagan declared, 'to limit ourselves to small dreams. We're not, as some would have us believe, doomed to an inevitable decline.' The most memorable line was: 'In the present crisis, government is not the solution to our problem; government is the problem.' With these words, Reagan declared his intent to free the creativity, ingenuity, and enterprise of the American people from unconscionable federal spending, taxation, and regulation.

The inaugural address was also noteworthy for being the first delivered from the West Front rather than the East Front of the Capitol. As a consequence, Reagan faced The Mall and looked out on the monuments of George

Washington, Thomas Jefferson, and Abraham Lincoln. With an actor's under-standing of his stage, he praised 'the giants on whose shoulders we stand' to reaffirm the constitutional order they created and defended. He then drew attention to another set of monuments, the headstones of Arlington National Cemetery, visible in the far distance, where lay buried those who had fought and died for American freedom. Among them, Reagan declared, was Martin Treptow, a young soldier who died a hero in France in 1917. The diary found on his body contained the pledge that he would do everything possible to help America win the Great War. It turned out that Treptow was actually buried in Wisconsin. Though aides had alerted him to this, Reagan decided not to let factual accuracy complicate the dramatic significance of a story linking Arlington with the other national monuments. In his mind, Treptow's real place of burial was irrelevant to the broader truth that the virtues of its ordinary citizens constituted the real source of the nation's greatness in times of crisis.

It became part of Washington lore that Reagan had arranged for the inau-gural to be moved so that he could link himself to the heroic past. The truth was more prosaic – the congressional Joint Committee on the Inauguration had decided on the change in June 1980 to save money (the West Front terraces could be used as a platform, avoiding the need to build one from scratch) and to accommodate more spectators on The Mall. Reagan's cleverness lay in understanding how he could use the new venue to best advantage. Ironically, it was the location of his second inauguration on 21 January 1985 that he actu-ally changed. With freezing temperatures anticipated, his aides asked for the ceremony to be held indoors, so Reagan became the only president to take the oath of office in the Capitol Rotunda.[3]

Within minutes of being sworn in, Reagan's presidency got off to the perfect start when word arrived that the American hostages held in Iran were coming home. Knowing this was imminent, he was graciously ready to interrupt his address for Jimmy Carter to announce the news from the inaugural dais if required. The Tehran regime inflicted one last humiliation on the outgoing president by refusing to free the hostages until the ceremony was over. Carter's patient diplomacy had finally paid off, but his successor was widely credited with having frightened the Iranians into ending the imbroglio by condemning them as 'criminals' and 'barbarians' in the transition period.

Caught up in the euphoria that the national nightmare was over, some pundits commented that America appeared to have rediscovered its optimism on Inauguration Day.[4]

That evening the other side of the Reagan presidency was on display in the most lavish inaugural celebrations hitherto seen. Out went republican restraint; in came the Republican rich. Tickets to the various events were priced up to $500, in contrast to $25 four years previously. Whereas the slogan for the Carter inaugural had been 'Y'all come', the Reagan gala – in the words of one commentator – 'was a celebration of wealth, by the wealthy, for those who wanted to be wealthy (the rest of us)'.[5] The bash attracted considerable criticism as an insensitive exhibition of opulence at a time when many citizens were suffering the effects of stagflation. In putting the president at the centre of the wealthy, the successful, and the powerful, however, the purpose had been to tie him to America's still vast possibilities in rebuttal of declinist jeremiads. The celebrations bespoke a promise that a rising tide would lift all boats if the obstructive dyke of government could be got out of the way of wealth-makers – but the pageant overlooked a different truth: that a mink coat doesn't have any tails.

Within weeks of the inauguration pomp, it was the unmanaged spectacle of Reagan's courage in the wake of attempted assassination that gripped the nation.[6] On 30 March, he delivered a luncheon address to labour chiefs at the Washington Hilton Hotel, considered the safest private venue in Washington because of its secure entrance/exit passageway. Accordingly, the Secret Service excused the president from wearing a bulletproof vest, but inexplicably allowed an unscreened group of admirers to stand within 15 feet of him when exiting the hotel at 2.27 p.m. eastern time.[7] Among them was John Hinckley Jr, a deranged young man with an erotomanic fixation on actress Jodie Foster for her starring role in Martin Scorsese's 1976 movie *Taxi Driver*. In the film, the main character, played by Robert De Niro, planned to assassinate a nationally prominent politician. Inspired by this, Hinckley thought he could capture Foster's attention by killing Reagan.[8]

As the president passed near, Hinckley fired off in less than two seconds six 'Devastator' rounds, intended to explode inside the target, from a Röhm RG-14 revolver before being overpowered and disarmed. The first bullet, the only one to explode, hit White House press secretary James Brady in the head, causing permanent brain damage. The second wounded police officer Thomas

Delahanty in the neck as he turned to protect Reagan. Now with a clear sight of the president, Hinckley fired directly at him but missed. At that juncture, detail head Jerry Parr, the one-time fan of Brass Bancroft, bundled Reagan into the waiting presidential limousine and threw himself over him. The fourth shot wounded Secret Service Agent Timothy McCarthy as he spread his body to make a target. The fifth hit the bullet-resistant glass of the window on the open door of the limousine. The final bullet ricocheted off the armoured side of the limousine to hit Reagan in his left underarm, grazing a rib and lodging in his lung less than an inch from his heart.

At first, no one knew that the president had been shot, and Parr radioed that 'Rawhide [Reagan's Secret Service codename] is OK [...] we're going to Crown [the White House].'[9] In great pain, Reagan thought that he had cracked a rib when shoved into the limousine. When he began coughing blood, Parr ordered the motorcade to nearby George Washington University Hospital out of concern that the broken rib had punctured a lung. The entire journey took less than four minutes. Reagan walked unassisted into the hospital emergency room but once inside he complained of breathing difficulty and collapsed onto one knee. To his annoyance the surgical team that finally discovered the bullet wound cut away his expensive new suit to conduct its investigation. Newly arrived FBI agents then confiscated the suit as evidence and waited 48 hours to release Reagan's wallet that contained the Gold Codes card used to trigger the nuclear 'football' in case of foreign missile attack.

Displaying grace and courage, Reagan joked with the trauma-team doctors and nurses before they operated on him, 'I hope you're all Republicans' – eliciting the classy response from the chief surgeon, 'Today, Mr President, we're all Republicans.' Nevertheless, he had been very close to death in the emergency room when his systolic blood pressure had fallen from the normal 140 to 60, enough to kill most 70-year-olds. Fortunately, he was in excellent physical shape and had been shot by a .22 calibre pistol, rather than the more deadly .38. Parr's decision to take him to hospital and the quick action of the trauma team in getting his blood pressure back to normal in 30 minutes probably saved his life. Even so, he lost over half his blood volume while being treated in ER and then being operated on to remove the bullet. The surgery went sufficiently well for doctors to predict that he could leave hospital within two weeks and return to work in the Oval Office within a month.

The Twenty-Fifth Amendment providing for the vice-president to become acting president in the event of presidential incapacity was never invoked. On a speechmaking visit to Texas, George Bush was initially informed that Reagan was unharmed. He was flown back to Washington DC on Air Force Two when the gravity of the situation became known but did not reach the White House until 7 p.m. His decision to take the Marine helicopter from Andrews Air Force base to the vice-presidential residence in Massachusetts Avenue and go by limousine to the White House added 15 minutes to his arrival time. Bush was concerned about sending the wrong signal to the television cameras if he landed on the south lawn that was exclusively reserved for the president. Reagan regained post-operative consciousness shortly after the vice-president got to the situation room. Accordingly, Bush could go on television at 8.20 p.m. to reassure the nation and the world that America's government 'is functioning fully and effectively'.[10]

Reagan had behaved with the insouciant bravery shown by wounded heroes in old Hollywood movies. For Americans he was the Gipper come to real life in the face of death, but now playing the only president ever to survive being shot. The palpable outburst of pride in their leader inspired a wave of patriotic emotion not seen for many years. Through his bravery, Reagan had become the living embodiment of the resilience of the American spirit invoked in his inaugural address. His conduct also did much to revive popular respect for the presidency after Vietnam and Watergate had tarnished its image.

Restoring national pride in the presidency as the symbol of America's best values was very important to Reagan, who managed to combine personal reverence for his office with lack of airs about his occupancy of it. After addressing Congress for the first time, he remarked in his diary: 'I've seen Presidents over the years enter the House chamber without ever thinking I would one day be doing it [...] it was a thrill and something I'll long remember.' Hearing 'Hail to the Chief' was long a source of wonderment. 'I don't think I'm ever going to get used to the fact that they're playing that song for me,' Reagan told an aide.[11]

Such modesty did not limit his understanding of the importance of spectacle as a means to link the presidency to ordinary Americans. At times of national triumph, he became celebrant-in-chief, as when opening the 1984 Los Angeles Olympic Games. The event featured a 1,000-voice choir and a 750-strong marching band performing 'America the Beautiful' in front of a flag-waving audience of 90,000 thronged in the Coliseum stadium. In times of tragedy there was no shrinking from being the nation's mourner-in-chief. The memorial service that Reagan attended with Nancy in Camp Lejeune, North Carolina, for the 241 servicemen killed in the Beirut bombing of 23 October 1983 was 'as hard as anything we've ever done'. Reflecting on intimate remarks to families of the deceased, he wrote, 'That was ad-lib & the Lord was with me – the right words came.'[12]

Words of a more formal nature to project his values and vision had even greater significance than spectacle for Reagan's presidential leadership. While recognizing the need to bargain with other political elites in Washington to secure his ends, he engaged far more than any predecessor in a strategy that political scientists dubbed 'going public' to mould popular support.[13] Commenting on how this approach had earned him journalistic accolades for being the Great Communicator, he remarked in his farewell address:

> I wasn't a great communicator, but I communicated great things, and
> they didn't spring full bloom from my brow, they came from the heart
> of a great nation – from our experience, our wisdom, and our belief in
> the principles that have guided us for two centuries.[14]

Reagan 'did not sound like a politician', widely syndicated columnist Richard Reeves commented of his rhetorical style, 'which made him a great politician'. His speeches were rarely grandiose and never bombastic. 'I try to remember,' he reminisced, 'that audiences are made up of individuals and I try to speak as if I am talking to a group of friends [...] not to millions.'[15] The language was kept simple, spiced with humour when appropriate, and eschewed sermonizing. Rhythm, repetition, and alliteration found their place in well-structured addresses that contained a rational component to appeal to listeners' sense of logic, a framing of the issue at hand as a twofold choice, and an emotional element that connected to people's deeply held beliefs. According to Reagan's personal pollster, Dick Wirthlin, he aimed for the heart, not the head, because he wanted listeners to react 'Damn right' rather than 'That's interesting'.[16]

It was impossible, of course, for Reagan to continue writing his speeches as president. This became the job of a team of speechwriters. One of the best known, Peggy Noonan, recalled: 'Speechwriting was where the administration got invented every day. And so speechwriting was, for some, the center of gravity in that administration, the point where ideas and principles still counted.'[17] To capture Reagan's authentic voice, speechwriters studied his earlier rhetoric as a guide to what he wanted. According to Anthony Dolan, formerly a Pulitzer Prize-winning conservative journalist, his main function was 'to plagiarize the president's old speeches and give them back to him to say'. Reagan reviewed speech drafts a few days before scheduled delivery, occasionally requiring substantive changes but more often amending the text to improve its flow or inject a personal touch. He was, in speechwriter Mari Maseng's assessment, 'the best editor I ever had'.[18]

Within the broad strategic purpose of promoting his ideas, Reagan's speeches had three fundamental aims. One was to mobilize public opinion in support of his philosophy, but he understood that this required long-haul effort. As speechwriter Landon Parvin recalled, 'Reagan used to say that it took twenty years of saying something before it got into the nation's consciousness.'[19] Replicating the practice of his governorship, his speeches also articulated constancy of purpose whenever his policy diverged from his philosophy, as it often did. Finally, Reagan's public remarks established the framework for policy development by White House staff and Cabinet department chiefs. This facilitated his preference to delegate considerable authority to subordinates rather than micromanage decisions.

The appointment of personnel dedicated to converting Reagan's philosophy into policy was essential to the success of this chairman-of-the-board approach. One of the most well managed presidential transitions of modern times laid the foundations for doing so. Presidential candidates are usually too wrapped up in winning office to plan their prospective administration, but Reagan's team showed greater foresight. Veteran headhunter Pendleton James was commissioned to head a personnel operation that prepared a huge file of curricula vitae and matched individuals with government posts in the pre-election months. With Reagan's victory, prospective cabinet secretaries and the 700 or so political appointments usually decided by departmental heads were screened, first by longstanding Reagan associates Lyn Nofziger, Martin Anderson, and Richard Allen, and then by members of the old 'Kitchen Cabinet' – renamed the Executive Advisory Council. In contrast to the equivalent process for the governorship, loyalty was as important as ability for selection. The nominees received final vetting from the so-called 'troika' of top presidential aides, chief of staff (CoS) James Baker, counsellor to the president Ed Meese, and deputy CoS Michael Deaver.[20]

To exercise ultimate approval of those chosen to lead departments vital to his core agenda, Reagan required a list of three names for each post, but mostly went along with his advisors' preference. The main exception was his selection of former NATO chief General Alexander Haig as secretary of state over George Shultz, largely because of Richard Nixon's lobbying on behalf of his one-time top aide. Though not the transition team's first choice, Merrill Lynch chairman Donald Regan got the key post of Treasury secretary. In this instance, two preferred nominees turned Reagan down, a rare occurrence because he was generally very persuasive in getting those he wanted.[21] The president played virtually no part in deciding choices for lesser Cabinet departments like Agriculture, Commerce, and Housing and Urban Development (HUD). The last of these went to New York attorney and business executive Samuel Pierce, a selection that fulfilled the political need for an African American appointee. Such was Reagan's lack of interest in HUD that he failed to recognize Pierce – greeting him 'Hello Mr Mayor' – when hosting a White House luncheon for the United States Conference of Mayors in June 1981. Most appointees would not have looked out of place in the Nixon–Ford administrations. Accordingly, their selection provoked dismay on the right, but Reagan's team largely held firm in choosing competent people who had pledged support for his agenda. The outcome was an administration that was unusually like-minded with regard to philosophy. Whereas his predecessors had made Cabinet appointments with an eye to pleasing different party factions and interest groups, Reagan headed a team dedicated to his broad objectives.[22]

The troika had ultimate responsibility for ensuring that the administration's economic programme, its first priority, made it into law. Breaking with tradition, Reagan announced these appointments prior to any Cabinet selections in recognition of their pivotal significance for his chief-executive style. Houston attorney James Baker got the job that Ed Meese had held in Sacramento and wanted in the White House. A late recruit to the Reagan team, he had been a Ford man in 1976 and ran George Bush's 1980 presidential campaign. Baker got the nod for being a tough, disciplined, and wily operator well versed in the ways of Washington, whereas Meese was known for being disorganized and lacked inside-the-Beltway experience.[23] In their division of labour, agreed in a co-signed memorandum of 17 November 1980, Baker managed political affairs and organized the White House, while Meese oversaw policy development in a kind of minister-without-portfolio role that carried Cabinet rank as a sop for not becoming CoS. Deaver had responsibility for presidential scheduling, public relations, and ensuring that Nancy Reagan's voice was heard on matters of concern to her – usually when she felt an administration official was not serving her husband's best interests. A political fixer rather than an ideologue, Baker proved the craftier combatant – usually with the pragmatic Deaver's support – in turf wars with Meese. This conservative true believer established five (later six) Cabinet Councils to devise policy in specific areas. The Legislative Strategy Group, Baker's fiefdom, shepherded proposals from these bodies into law and often made unilateral adjustments in order to gain congressional support. As such, the Texan demonstrated better understanding than Meese that policy making was as much about implementation as conception. A master of the well-timed leak, Baker's skill in getting the press on his side further undercut his rival.[24]

Despite the inherent tensions of power sharing, the troika generally worked well in driving the administration forward on domestic issues. It was less successful in the national-security domain in which a phalanx of powerful department and agency heads with fluid jurisdictions competed for ascendancy. Their in-fighting made the administration appear disjointed, discordant, and disorganized in the international sphere. Al Haig had accepted appointment as secretary of state on condition of being what he called the 'vicar' of foreign policy, namely its formulator, executor, and articulator. His take-charge approach soon looked more like a takeover to recreate Henry Kissinger's control of foreign policy in the Nixon–Ford administrations. Just hours after the inauguration, Haig despatched for presidential signature a draft National Security Decision Directive (NSDD) putting him in charge of crisis management. Unwilling to be railroaded, Baker and Meese insisted on its prior review by the Senior Interagency Group, the consultation forum for top national-security officials. Thereafter, they collaborated to ensure that George Bush was named chair of the Special Situations Group when eventually established. Haig submitted a resignation letter over this snub, the first of several during his 17-month tenure, but an emollient president talked him out of leaving. Nevertheless, the high-maintenance secretary of state was living on borrowed time. 'It's amazing how sound he can be on complex international matters,' Reagan later remarked, 'but how utterly paranoid with regard to the people he must work with.'[25]

Still fixated on monopolizing the president's ear, Haig behaved like a jealous courtier when others received a hearing. In any administration, the secretaries of state and defence are natural rivals but their competition reached a new pitch in Reagan's. Barely a day went by, James Baker recalled, when Haig and Caspar Weinberger 'weren't at each other's throats'.[26] Haig also resented Jeane Kirkpatrick having direct access to Reagan through her post as United Nations ambassador being endowed with Cabinet status. Her high-profile confrontational speeches in the UN made her a menace in the diplomacy-oriented State Department's eyes. Another rival, CIA director William Casey, who had hoped to become secretary of state himself, disdained Haig as a mere blusterer while his reinvigorated agency's clandestine operations confronted the Soviet Union in many parts of the globe.

As CIA deputy director Robert Gates recognized, Reagan needed a strong National Security Advisor (NSA) to 'bring the national security mandarins together, develop agreement and compromises when possible, and crystallize disputes into manageable alternatives for presidential decision'.[27] Richard Allen was hamstrung by having his post downgraded to prevent its usurpation of the secretary of state's authority as in the Nixon and Carter administrations. His office was relocated from the main floor to the basement of the West Wing, the National Security Council (NSC) staff was reduced to half its previous complement, and – worst of all – he had to report to Reagan indirectly through the administratively chaotic Ed Meese rather than face-to-face.[28] Brought down by embarrassing revelations of his ties to Japanese business, Allen gave way to William Clark in early 1982. A friend of the president since Sacramento days, Clark could insist on having the authority of his post upgraded, enabling him to establish a more orderly process for the formulation and implementation of foreign policy.[29] Lacking the foreign policy expertise to act as honest broker, Clark sided with the hawks – Weinberger, Casey, and Kirkpatrick – against the advocates of negotiations with the Soviets, notably George Shultz, Haig's successor as secretary of state.

Worn down by the constant in-fighting and Nancy Reagan's growing suspicion that he was claiming too much credit with the media for directing foreign policy, Clark transferred to the Department of the Interior in late 1983. James Baker, someone tough enough to deal with the foreign-policy principals, now lobbied to get the NSA job, with support from George Shultz. Although the president had effectively agreed his appointment, Clark enlisted Meese, Weinberger, and Casey to block it on grounds that Baker was manipulative, insufficiently conservative, and too prone to leak. Their candidate for the post was Jeane Kirkpatrick, but Shultz's veto ruled her out. Accordingly, Reagan opted for Clark's deputy, Marine lieutenant colonel Robert 'Bud' McFarlane, as the best hope for ending the 'bad chemistry' within his national-security team.[30] The compromise candidate lacked the strength of personality to impose a unifying influence on the fractious principals in his two-year tenure. Even worse, he facilitated presidential engagement in the illegal operations that became known as Iran–Contra and had near disastrous consequences for Reagan when they finally came to light. The same was true of his successor, Admiral John Poindexter, who resigned in disgrace over the scandal. A stickler for legalism, James Baker might have saved the president from Iran–Contra had he been in post. Thereafter, Frank Carlucci and Colin Powell did much to establish unity in the foreign-policy process during their brief clean-up tenures as NSA in 1987–8. In total, therefore, there were six post-holders over eight years, a discontinuity that perpetuated bureaucratic competition over foreign policy for most of Reagan's presidency.

If effective management requires information gathering, making decisions on its basis, and then ensuring their implementation, Reagan was a hands-off chief executive. As Donald Regan remarked, 'The President seemed to believe that his public statements were all the guidance his private advisors required.'[31] Instead of riding herd on feuding subordinates, too often he left them unclear as to whether he agreed with them or not. At the same time, Reagan's emotional reserve inhibited him from letting appointees know whether they were doing a good or bad job. Put in charge of the CIA after William Casey's death in 1987, William Webster remarked in frustration to Colin Powell: 'I'm pretty good at reading people, but I like to get a report card. I can't tell whether I'm helping him or not.' The NSA told him not to worry because 'I'm with him a dozen times a day, and I'm in the same boat'.[32] This trait was especially hurtful to aides who had served Reagan loyally for years. James Baker was philosophical about not becoming NSA, but Michael Deaver regarded his consequent non-promotion to CoS as a personal slap.[33] Another of Reagan's traits was an inclination to believe anything that crossed his desk as gospel instead of acting as his own political intelligence officer to check its veracity. In essence, his sunny tendency to believe the best of people made it difficult for him to suspect anyone of not telling the truth. Deaver cautioned members of the new administration that anything they gave him 'would be entered into his mental computer and could be spit back any time in the future'. Aides were particularly keen to keep him away from *Human Events*, a right-wing weekly from which he liked to clip articles that did not always live up to the finest standards of journalistic truth.[34]

These negatives were just one side of Reagan's management style. As Frank Carlucci remarked, 'He had a facility for charming people while he was not budging an inch.'[35] On the core issues of his agenda, Reagan was his own man. He was resilient in defence of personal-tax cuts when faced with calls that the deficit should receive priority in 1982–3. He promoted the Strategic Defense Initiative (SDI) over initial State Department opposition to its violation of conventional deterrence theory. In his second term, he stopped seeing the Soviet Union as a threat whereas the Pentagon clung to the realist orthodoxy that its nuclear capabilities still made it dangerous. Nor was Reagan the 'amiable dunce' that Democratic grandee Clark Clifford once labelled him. Guided more by emotional intuition than cognitive intelligence in his decision making, this had its downside in Iran–Contra but its upside was his understanding that Mikhail Gorbachev was a different kind of Soviet leader to his Kremlin predecessors. As Soviet ambassador Anatoly Dobrynin would observe, the president 'grasped matters in an instinctive way but not necessarily a simple one'.[36]

Reagan should have put a stop to the bickering that went on in his administration, but its existence at least signified that no one dominated him. Haig would describe the White House as a 'ghost ship' wherein it was unclear 'which of the crew had the helm', a remark that testified to his desire to be the captain. In June 1982, their disagreement, in Reagan's words, 'over whether I made policy or the Sec. of State did' finally got him sacked.[37] Shultz became a much closer confidant but only with time. The new man had seen active service as a Marine officer in World War II, held a PhD in industrial economics, and had forged successful careers in academia, business, and government. This impressive curriculum vitae endowed self-confidence in his capacity to run foreign policy but did not ensure his authority to do so. A one-time labour negotiator inclined to pragmatism, persuasion, and dialogue, Shultz soon fell afoul of hard-line rivals. Feeling undermined by William Clark in particular, he bluntly warned of his intent to quit unless things changed at an Oval Office showdown in July 1983, but Reagan did not step in to put matters right until late 1984. A sense that Shultz was finally about to resign prompted this diary entry: 'I can't let that happen. Actually George is carrying out my policy. I'm going to have to meet with Cap [Weinberger] & Bill [Casey] & lay it out to them. Won't be fun but has to be done.'[38] At this juncture Reagan's initial hawkishness was giving way to desire for dialogue with the Soviet Union. Shultz's perceptive counsel, nuanced view of the world, and diplomatic skill made him critical to the success of the new approach. Like other subordinates, however, his significance was in being an agent for Reagan's ends rather than the catalyst for changing them.

One man thought to have had ambitions of dominating Reagan was his second-term CoS. Wanting to be closer to the centre of power, Donald Regan proposed a job swap with James Baker, now keen to remove himself from the hot seat after four exhausting years. In line with his laid-back managerial approach, the president played no part in an arrangement of crucial significance to the White House – other than to agree it. Regardless of his organizational skills, the abrasive Regan was not the right man for a job that required the political antennae of a Machiavelli. In Edmund Morris' words, 'Here was no Beltway bureaucrat but a Boston Irish slugger, not entirely smoothed by Harvard.' Although the new CoS got on well with his boss, others in the White House regarded him as power hungry in the extreme – he combined in himself all the functions hitherto performed by the troika – and behaving as though he were the president in allowing only proposals that gained his approval through to the Oval Office. In Nancy Reagan's biting commentary, 'He liked the word "chief," but he never really understood that his title also included the words "of staff."' Instead of someone trying to run the show, Regan aides (known derisively to his critics as 'the Mice') remembered the CoS taking pains to ensure that he was carrying out his boss's wishes. In Peter Wallison's view, 'he was loyal to the presidency as well as the President'. This did not save Regan from becoming the fall guy for Iran–Contra despite being less responsible than the president for the descent into illegality.[39]

The member of the administration whom Reagan could count on for consistent support was vice-president George H. W. Bush. The hard feelings of the 1980 primary campaign were soon forgotten. Reagan's appreciation of Bush's loyalty was evident in the satisfaction he took in seeing his number two win the presidency in his own right in 1988.[40] This made him the first vice-president elected successor to the president he served since Martin Van Buren followed Andrew Jackson into the White House in 1837. As a foreign-policy specialist, Bush carried out important tasks in this field for the administration, but he should have done more to warn Reagan about the risks involved in Iran–Contra operations. The trouble was that the vice-president was reluctant to be the bearer of bad tidings for fear of appearing disloyal. Significantly, when sceptical foreign-policy principals made their greatest effort to persuade Reagan to abandon the arms-for-hostages initiative to Iran at a White House meeting on 7 December 1985, Bush absented himself on grounds of prior commitment to attend that day's Army versus Navy football game. When the White House was in crisis over revelations of Iran–Contra operations a year or so later, Bush privately recommended to Nancy Reagan that Don Regan should be made to resign, but was unwilling to be the one to tell the president this on the grounds that it was not part of his job description to do so.[41]

If the Reagan White House was not a place of serenity, at least the president himself remained serene. A 75th birthday greeting from 82-year-old Hollywood friend Cary Grant opened: 'Mr President: Young Man.' The presidential response to that salutation of youthfulness was: 'Frankly, that's just how I feel.'[42] Relaxed work habits were one reason why the job did not wear him down. He did not quite live up to his oft-quoted quip, 'They say hard work never killed anyone, but I say why take the risk?' Nevertheless, his working day usually started at 9.30 a.m. and declined in intensity after 5.30 p.m. – evenings were for reading briefing materials, catching up with correspondence, and hosting White House formal dinners and social events (for informal dinners his favourite dishes were macaroni cheese or meatloaf). Nearly 200 weekends were spent at Camp David, the presidential retreat in the Maryland hills, where there was time for horse-riding and general relaxation amid ongoing presidential duties.

Wherever he might be, Reagan's preferred form of indoor recreation was watching movies. As his diary reveals, his favourites were Hollywood golden oldies – even *Bedtime for Bonzo* once got a showing for Camp David guests.

To James Baker's annoyance, he watched *The Sound of Music* (1965) instead of reading briefing books prepared for the next day's international economic summit in Virginia. Some on the right were shocked that he hosted a White House screening of *Reds* (1981) in the company of director–star Warren Beatty. A 'most imaginative job' was his verdict on this sympathetic account of American socialist John Reed that would never have got made in the Hollywood of his day. In general, however, many contemporary films were distasteful to him. His judgement on the steamy Richard Gere–Debra Winger movie *An Officer and a Gentleman* (1982) was typical – 'good story spoiled by nudity, language & sex'.[43] If not watching films, Reagan loved to talk over old times with movie-star friends such as James Stewart, Cary Grant, and Claudette Colbert. Rarely was a request turned down to tape some salutation for a ceremony honouring those belonging to what he had once called 'the greatest collection of exciting personalities ever assembled any place in the theatrical world'.[44] The death of fellow stars saddened him – notably Pat O'Brien in 1983 (the day after speaking to Reagan on the phone), James Cagney and Cary Grant in 1986, and Fred Astaire in 1987.

The place where Reagan could best relax when president was back in southern California, where he passed the equivalent of one year of his tenure. Every Christmas was spent at the White House in order that Secret Service agents could pass the day with their families, but the Reagans headed westward on 26 or 27 December – often to vacation in Palm Springs for golf and socializing with friends. Other trips were mostly to Rancho del Cielo, a place that Reagan could not get enough of. In June 1985 the TWA hostage crisis in Beirut forced the cancellation of a trip to the ranch, even though it could just as easily have been managed from southern California as from the White House. 'Well my heart is broken,' Reagan plaintively wrote in his diary. '[T]he perception of me vacationing while our citizens are held in durance vile is something I can't afford.' The regret was still palpable in his wistful comment a week later: 'We would be riding at the ranch if it were not for the hostage situation.' Borrowing Lord Palmerston's adage, Reagan often remarked: 'There is nothing so good for the inside of a man as the outside of a horse.' Nevertheless, he did stop horse-jumping on becoming president because the possibility of an accident made this much-loved activity '[un]fair to the job I now have'.[45] As well as riding, he spent hours on the ranch clearing brush, chopping wood, and performing other vigorous activities that few people his age could have countenanced. Casting him as a frontiersman of old, images of a cowboy-hatted Reagan in denim shirt and jeans helped to reinforce his political message that America could be renewed through the traditional values of hard work and individualism.

Whatever the means of doing so, it was essential for Reagan to recharge his batteries – otherwise he might not have survived two terms in office. The stage-managed image of a president swiftly restored to vigour following attempted assassination belied a reality kept hidden from the public. After leaving hospital, Reagan had to undertake a regime of regular workouts in the White House gymnasium to improve his lung function. Sustaining this for the remainder of his presidency, he expanded his chest and biceps so much that he eventually needed a larger suit size. Even so, it took nearly six months to achieve real recovery. 'What I saw,' Martin Anderson recalled, 'was that for a period of months, he was sick. I mean, he got a tremendous shock.'[46] Furthermore, no amount of vigorous exercise could hold back the illnesses that creep up on people in their seventies. The missteps into the arms-for-hostages trade with Iran were taken while Reagan was still weak from surgery to remove a five-centimetre cancerous growth in his colon as well as a large section of the intestine itself. As Iran–Contra threatened to engulf him in early 1987, the president underwent a transurethral resection of the prostate. There were also three occasions in the second term when he underwent local anaesthetic to have cancer spots removed from his nose skin that he ascribed to 'too much suntan all my life'.[47] Meanwhile, Reagan needed special hearing aids because he found it increasingly difficult to deal with background noise on occasions like state dinners, while continuing to use smaller ones fitted early in his presidency at other times.[48]

Religious faith did much to sustain Reagan through the political trials and health tribulations of his presidency. While recovering in hospital from being shot, he told daughter Maureen that God had spared him to steer America 'into a bold new era'. He wrote in his diary on the first evening back in the White House, 'Whatever happens now I owe my life to God and will try to serve him in every way I can.'[49] Sometime later he responded via an aide to a congressman's query about how he handled stress: 'I look up instead of back. I couldn't face one day in this office if I didn't know I could ask God's help and it would be given.'[50] Prayer, usually private and silent, was therefore an almost daily part of White House life for the 40th president. Sharing his faith with like-minded people was also something he enjoyed. A proud moment but one that also made him feel 'very humble' was being told by Billy Graham that his address to the Annual Convention of Religious Broadcasters in early 1983 was 'the greatest declaration for the Lord any Pres. has ever made'.[51]

Even with God on his side, Reagan would never have got through the presidency without Nancy. If anything, the emotional dependency on her that he brought into office became even stronger. 'I pray I'll never face a day when she isn't there,' he recorded in his diary after the Hinckley shooting. 'Of all the ways God has blessed me giving her to me is the greatest and beyond anything I can ever hope to deserve.' Over the years many entries attested to his sense of desolation when she was away from him for any length of time. Unable on medical advice to attend the royal wedding of Prince Charles to Lady Diana Spencer, he dreaded Nancy making the trip to London alone. 'I worry when she's out of sight for 6 minutes,' he wrote. 'How am I going to hold out for 6 days?' Two years later, a diary entry read: 'Nancy's Birthday! Life would be miserable if there wasn't a Nancy's Birthday. What if she'd never been born? I don't want to think about it.'[52] One of the greatest blows he suffered as president was being told in October 1987 that Nancy would require surgery if a tumour found in her left breast was malignant – as it turned out to be. The doctor bearing the news later told the first lady that he would never forget the stricken expression on her husband's face. 'I think the president,' he declared, 'has always believed that nothing would ever happen to you.'[53]

In her own way, Nancy was as dependent on Reagan as he was on her. Seeking the comfort of his scent while he was in hospital after being shot, she slept in one of his shirts. As she herself admitted, 'I continued to be haunted by what had happened, as well as by what had almost happened.'[54] The possibility of another attempt on his life preyed on her mind – and with good reason. In late 1981 word reached Washington that Libyan leader Colonel Muammar al-Gaddafi had despatched hit squads to kill Reagan, Bush, Weinberger, and Haig in revenge for US aircraft downing two of his planes during a dispute over territorial waters. The enhanced security meant Reagan having to wear an 'iron vest' in every public appearance and presidential helicopter routes being selected at the very last minute for fear of attack by Libyans armed with hand-fired, heat-seeking missiles. The hit-squad scare was ultimately revealed to be a hoax concocted by Manucher Ghorbanifar, an agent of the Israeli Mossad and one of the shadowy figures later involved in the arms-for-hostages affair.[55]

Unwilling to rely on conventional security to protect her husband, Nancy Reagan began regular consultations with San Francisco astrologer Joan Quigley, who had previously volunteered advice during the 1980 campaign. Now, however, Quigley claimed that she could have warned about the 30 March shooting because the president's charts signified it was a dangerous day for him. Most people would have dismissed this as quackery, but a vulnerable Nancy did not. 'My relationship with Joan Quigley,' she later declared, 'began as a crutch, one of several ways I tried to alleviate my anxiety about Ronnie.' Nancy began paying substantial fees for consultations on whether the president's chart portended further danger in his schedule. A party to this, Mike Deaver had to adjust presidential plans, often at such short notice that many in the White House came to see him as high-handed for refusing to explain why the change was necessary. The president found out about Nancy's arrangement some months after it started. A casually superstitious person, who believed in psychic forces and carried a good-luck penny, Reagan was not shocked at the revelation. Seeing that the consultations helped reassure Nancy, he allowed their continuation if kept hidden from the media. When the truth finally came out, it would cause maximum embarrassment to both Reagans. Holding her responsible for his dismissal, Don Regan spilled the beans in memoirs that gave chapter and verse about how Nancy's astrologer had influenced, among other things, the scheduling of summit meetings and the president's various medical operations.[56]

This was not Nancy Reagan's sole brush with unfavourable publicity. On learning that her inaugural wardrobe had cost $25,000, the press began reporting her practice of accepting gifts of costumes and jewellery with a total estimated value of $1 million over eight years. She claimed that designers got valuable publicity from her being seen in their clothes – appearances in Oscar de la Renta's tomato-red outfits certainly raised his profile. Nevertheless, it was unclear how far she followed through on her promise to return the clothes or donate them to a museum. Reports that she had expensively redecorated the White House family quarters and purchased a new set of White House china (it was actually donated by the Knapp Foundation, a non-profit organization interested in widening educational opportunity) got her more bad press. In Reagan's assessment, Nancy was being subjected to 'a concerted effort to build a false image of both of us, but using her as a means to bring that about'.[57] Showing a sense of humour rarely accredited to her, the first lady wowed some critics with a satiric rendition, dressed as a down-and-out, of a specially composed ditty sung to the tune of 'Second hand Rose' at the 1982 Gridiron Club Dinner. She needed to do something more substantial to improve her public standing. Accordingly, from early 1982 onwards Nancy worked to promote various good causes, most notably discouraging drug use in schools with her 'Just Say No' campaign. Another of her interests was the Foster Grandparents programme that she had initiated as California's first lady and was instrumental in expanding into a multi-state programme as America's first lady. This enlisted senior citizens to help mentally retarded and institutionalized children. With Nancy as the driving force, approximately 19,000 foster grandparents served 65,000 youngsters in 245 projects across all 50 states in 1985.[58]

Much more important for the president was Nancy's determination to protect and guide him. Initially, she kept tabs on what was happening and gave her views about what needed to be done via Michael Deaver, but her ally departed to run his own public-relations firm in May 1985. Lacking such a close confidant thereafter, she became more directly involved in helping Reagan navigate the choppy waters of the second term. Belying a conservative reputation, she had no truck with right-wingers who put the cause above her man. 'From the very first,' NSC Soviet specialist Jack Matlock commented, 'she wanted him to be the "president of peace."'[59]

In the first term, Nancy was a consistent supporter of George Shultz, an advisor she admired and trusted. A skilful bureaucratic operator, Shultz in turn was always attentive to her preferences. In contrast, the first lady thought William Clark was getting too big for his cowboy boots as the administration's anti-Soviet hard man. The last straw was the *Time* issue of 8 August 1983 featuring the NSA's face on the cover and containing a report headlined 'The man with the president's ear', which asserted that Clark was responsible for getting Reagan 'to follow his raw, conservative instincts' in foreign policy with consequences that were often problematic. Nancy phoned Shultz to tell him that his rival 'ought to be fired' because he did not have her husband's 'best interests at heart'. Washington was stunned when Clark resigned as NSA two months later on 13 October, apparently at the height of his influence but in reality undermined by the collusion of the first lady and secretary of state.[60] On another occasion, Nancy Reagan put Andrei Gromyko in his place. In a one-to-one conversation at a pre-luncheon reception on the occasion of his visit to the White House in September 1984, the Soviet foreign minister toasted her with the words, 'Whisper "peace" in your husband's ear every night.' The response was, 'I will and I'll also whisper it in *your* ear.'[61] In the second term Nancy was enthusiastic about Reagan and Mikhail Gorbachev getting together in summit meetings – even if she never enjoyed the company of her opposite number, Raisa Gorbachev, on these occasions.

The Reagans looked to their children for emotional sustenance in the presidential years, but it was not always forthcoming. The most supportive, Maureen spent a good deal of time in the White House on trips to attend Republican National Committee meetings. Growing close to Nancy, she began calling her 'Mom' for the first time. They were united in wanting to get more women to support Reagan and shared a mutual disdain for Don Regan. Maureen was disappointed that her father did not support her run for the GOP senatorial nomination in California in 1982, but accepted that he never endorsed primary candidates in the interests of party unity – she took some comfort that he did at least vote for her. She never forgave Neil Reagan, who felt she was exploiting the family name, for taping ads against her, however.[62]

In contrast, the Reagans had a troubled relationship with Michael. At the end of a long day of meetings in November 1984, Reagan telephoned his son to explain Nancy's comments in a newspaper interview about being estranged from him, but Michael finally hung up saying, 'I wish I had never been adopted by you.' This elicited a sorrowful diary comment: 'I'm more than ever convinced that he has a real emotional problem that is making him paranoid.' A few years later Michael was offered a large sum to write what he planned to be a negative book about his father, but it ended up a different one. On a visit to Rancho del Cielo in April 1987, he was able to tell the Reagans the truth of what was troubling him for the first time. Therapy had helped him to understand that his emotional problems stemmed from being sexually abused as an eight-year-old. The presidential diary entry this day read: 'It was a new Mike [...] he now saw himself as he had been & what he wanted to be.'[63]

Relations with Patti were also difficult – and without a happy ending during the White House years. It is possible that she had inherited her grandfather's addictive tendency, but in her case to drugs. By 15 she was hooked on pharmaceutical amphetamines and speed, a dependency that evolved into a cocaine habit in her early twenties. Convinced that the addiction flowed from her genes, she had a tubal ligation at age 24 (reversed ten years later) to prevent a pregnancy that would pass it on to a child. Getting off cocaine by the time of her father's presidency, she became active in the nuclear-freeze movement. At Patti's behest, Reagan met with prominent fellow campaigner Dr Helen Caldicott on condition that the meeting was kept private so the press could not play up family disagreements. Unsurprisingly, there was no meeting of minds – a disappointed president wrote in his diary, 'I'm afraid our daughter has been taken over by that whole d—n gang.' Worse was to follow – Caldicott caused a media stir with claims that Reagan had told her a nuclear war was winnable, a comment he denied making.[64] There was something of a family reconciliation when Patti got married to her yoga teacher in August 1984 but this did not last long. In 1986 she published a novel about a young woman with left-wing politics having to deal with a conservative president for a father. The story trashed the central character's entire family. A shocked Nancy would spend the morning of her 34th wedding anniversary seeing her daughter hype the hurtful book on various talk shows.[65]

Usually a reliable defender of his parents, even Ron Jr broke ranks on occasions. 'Darn good,' Reagan commented on seeing him perform in a Joffrey Ballet benefit performance, but limited opportunity for advancement induced Ron to find a new career as a political journalist. This gave Nancy the opportunity to see him quite regularly but it also put him on different sides to his parents on some issues. Most notably, he became a severe critic of the White House response to the Aids epidemic as being overly concerned about the views of moral traditionalists. 'Ron gave [...] us hell,' a dismayed Reagan remarked on one of his pieces. 'He can be stubborn on a couple of issues & won't listen to anyone's argument.'[66]

With Patti's exception, the Reagan siblings coped as well as might be expected with the challenges of being part of the first family. Presidents or prime ministers having less than perfect offspring are not unusual – as both FDR and Winston Churchill could have attested. On balance, there were more pluses than minuses in the togetherness of the Reagans. Nancy could write in her memoirs that she had forged a better relationship with three of the siblings during her time in the White House. Of Patti, she still hoped that someday they could put past difficulties behind them. 'Nothing,' she declared, 'would make me happier than to work that out.'[67]

Ups and downs also marked Reagan's relationship with foreign leaders. When he became president, a number of NATO heads of government held him in low esteem as a trigger-happy simpleton ill-suited to lead the Western alliance. Sharing this disdain at first, Helmut Schmidt mellowed on hearing of Reagan's early efforts to enter into personal correspondence with Kremlin boss Leonid Brezhnev. Meeting the president in the White House, the West German chancellor urged him to visit Western European capitals to dispel his image as 'a cowboy or one who appears only in cowboy films'. Reagan was too polite to point out that he had only made six westerns in his entire movie career. There was nothing polite about Canadian prime minister Pierre Trudeau's contemptuous criticism of his new economic programme at the economic summit in Ottawa in July 1981. Still weak from the near-fatal shooting, Reagan did not make a good impression at his first international gathering and struggled to keep pace with the constant meetings. 'The schedule was heavy,' he recorded in his diary. Both before and after this meeting, top officials of the French Foreign Ministry were openly dismissive of him in their public comments. Things got so bad that William Clark was despatched to Paris in October 1982 to warn President François Mitterrand that the administration found such remarks offensive.[68]

Fortunately for Reagan, one Western leader was in his corner – at least most of the time. Margaret Thatcher had first met him in April 1975 when he was on a European tour to boost his foreign policy credentials before running for president. Unwilling to spend time with someone he regarded as an obscure ex-governor, foreign secretary James Callaghan delegated junior minister Roy Hattersley to deal with him. Treated to a run-through of Reagan's economic ideas, Hattersley and his officials thought him something of a joke. The reception was entirely different when he met with Margaret Thatcher, then the newly elected Conservative Party leader, at the House of Commons for a courtesy visit arranged by Justin Dart, one of his wealthy backers with strong connections to the UK Tories. Instead of a brief exchange, the pair 'fell into conversation as if they'd been friends for years', recalled aide Peter Hannaford. Having researched Reagan's economic speeches, Thatcher found herself in agreement with every word he spoke. Regular correspondence and another meeting in London in

1978 consolidated the strong bond between them. Thatcher's election as prime minister in May 1979 delighted Reagan, and she saw his election as president as the opportunity to strengthen the Anglo-American special relationship as the core of British foreign policy.[69]

Thatcher was the first foreign leader invited for official talks in Washington barely a month after Reagan assumed office. She was unimpressed with her ideological soulmate's intellectual engagement with policy issues in their private exchanges, but resisted her normal impulse to show impatience with lesser mortals in the interests of the charm offensive that was the main purpose of the visit.[70] The high point was the dinner she hosted at the British embassy on the evening of 27 February, an event the president described as 'truly a warm and beautiful occasion'. In a flattering address, much appreciated by Reagan, she avowed full confidence in his 'two o'clock in the morning courage' to make the right decision 'for protecting the liberty of common humanity in the future'.[71] Afterwards, he wrote in his diary, 'I believe a real friendship exists between the P.M. her family & us.' As a demonstration of this, the prime minister handbagged other leaders who treated Reagan with disrespect at the Ottawa summit. 'Pierre, you're being obnoxious,' she snapped at Trudeau. 'Stop behaving like a naughty schoolboy.' This only strengthened Reagan's admiration – another diary entry opined, 'Margaret Thatcher is a tower of strength and a solid friend of the US.'[72]

The Reagan–Thatcher relationship was not always harmonious – they did not see eye-to-eye over economic sanctions against the Soviet Union, the Falklands War, the invasion of Grenada, and the SDI. Nevertheless, the positives far outweighed the negatives. In 1983, Reagan told Peter Hannaford that Thatcher was his 'favourite head of state' [*sic*], an opinion that held good throughout his presidency. The prime minister received the honour of being the last 'official visitor' at the Reagan White House on 16 November 1988. 'Her speech [at the welcoming ceremony] was a eulogy to me and my administration,' a grateful president recorded in his diary. 'She praised me as having changed the whole world.' Adding his appreciation of her, he commented, 'She really is a great stateswoman.'[73]

Another Western leader whom Reagan held in high esteem was Helmut Schmidt's successor, Helmut Kohl. Their friendship was solidified by their willingness to take political risks on each other's behalf. Reagan also got on well with Trudeau's successor, Brian Mulroney (another great storyteller), prime minister Yasuhiro Nakasone of Japan (a particularly warm friendship), and eventually, François Mitterrand.[74] Once disdainful of Reagan's lack of intellectual sophistication, the French president came to see him as 'primal: like a rock in the Morvan desert, like plain truth, like the wilderness of Nevada'. For his part, the American president was pleased to tell 'François' that British genealogists had discovered they were distant cousins descended from early eleventh-century Irish king Brian Boru.[75] To the chagrin of America's most pro-Israeli president, the allied leader whom he most distrusted was prime minister Menachem Begin, a feeling that was mutual. Their relationship deteriorated into personal hostility over Reagan's efforts to be even-handed in Middle Eastern affairs. Desperate to connect with Begin's successor, he told Yitzhak Shamir in a November 1983 White House meeting that his determination to ensure the survival of Israel stemmed from experience of filming the Nazi death camps at the end of World War II, a case of speaking an emotional rather than literal truth.[76]

Two heads of state also proved significant to Reagan's presidency. Queen Elizabeth II played an important part in British efforts to bring Reagan's Anglophilia into full bloom. On 8 June 1982, one of the greatest photo ops of his presidency was the horseback ride he took with the sovereign, an accomplished horsewoman, in the grounds of Windsor Castle with over 600 members of the media looking on. The public-relations success of this first visit to the UK as president delighted the American entourage. 'Buckingham Palace really went out of their way for the Reagans,' aide Jim Kuhn commented. This was quite a moment for the one-time small-town boy, but the Dixon years came in handy when the royals hosted a dinner at Buckingham Palace for leaders attending the London economic summit in 1984. To the delight of the Queen Mother in particular, Reagan was prevailed on to recite for the gathering 'The shooting of Dan McGrew', a narrative poem he had learned in youth. Between these occasions, the Reagans' hosting of the Queen and Prince Philip at Rancho del Cielo on 1 March 1983 was not such a success. Bounced around on the ride up its narrow access road, the royal couple were unable to go riding as planned because of heavy rain, could not see the magnificent views that were enshrouded in fog, and found the Tex-Mex cuisine not to their liking. At one point, a British reporter commented, the Queen looked like 'she had backed a loser at the Newmarket races'. The small party that she hosted on the royal yacht *Britannia* to celebrate the Reagans' 31st wedding anniversary three days later went much better, and all parted good friends. The bond would even survive the humiliation of Reagan's failure to consult the UK government before the invasion of Grenada, a Commonwealth nation.[77]

The day before his ride with the Queen, Reagan had his first meeting in the Vatican with Pope John Paul II. In many ways, one historian commented, they were 'a perfect match'. Both had survived assassination attempts, had prayed in forgiveness of their attempted murderer, and believed that God had spared them to assist in the overthrow of communism in the Soviet bloc. While Reagan was president, the pontiff resisted calls from co-religionists to condemn America's military build-up, the interventions in Central America, the SDI, and the impact of his economic programme on the poor. As a sign of his esteem in return, Reagan extended diplomatic recognition to the Vatican in 1984, something every president since Harry S. Truman had resisted. The two would collaborate in their efforts to undermine the military regime established in 1981 to crush democratic dissent in Poland, the Pope's homeland.[78]

To his embarrassment, Reagan nodded off briefly during the audience with the Pope that came at the end of a long day. Thereafter, Nancy insisted that he have plenty of time for rest on overseas visits. This did not prevent the same thing happening on a visit to the Vatican in 1987 – aides attributed it on this occasion to the hypnotic effect of the pontiff's voice. Other than these slips, Reagan held up well to the physical challenges of foreign travel that was an essential part of being president. Western Europe, visited eight times – mostly on extended multi-state trips – was the most frequent destination. There were five trips to Canada, the destination of his first state visit as president, and four to Mexico. In the Caribbean, Jamaica and Barbados received visits in 1982, as did Grenada in 1986. A tour of South and Central America took in Brazil, Colombia, and Costa Rica (plus a brief stop in Honduras) in late 1982. Asian destinations featured Japan and South Korea in 1983, China in 1984 (in line with Richard Nixon's advice, the Reagans 'didn't ask what things were – we just swallowed' at a 12-course state dinner), Japan again and Indonesia in 1986. Reagan never went to Israel, because even-handedness required a detour to an Arab state, a compromise that would have pleased neither party. In his final year, aides were keen for him to visit the Antipodes. Already winding down in body and spirit from the cares of office, Reagan's response was: 'Well, you guys are all free to go to Australia – but you ain't taking me.'[79]

Foreign trips became the occasion for some of Reagan's best oratorical efforts, notably the speeches in the British Parliament in 1982, the Irish Dáil in 1984, and West Berlin in 1987. Paradoxically, commemorations on foreign soil of World War II were among the most uplifting and most embarrassing moments of his presidency. In a speech superbly crafted by Peggy Noonan, Reagan celebrated how US Army Rangers on D-Day had scaled the 130-foot Pointe du Hoc with grappling hooks and ladders despite taking huge losses from German fire above. Speaking to surviving veterans on this spot 40 years later, he declared: 'These are the boys of Pointe du Hoc. These are the men who took the cliffs. These are the champions who helped free a continent. These are the heroes who helped end a war.' By the time he finished, many of those present, including journalists and Secret Service agents, were in tears. The president himself nearly broke down when later visiting Omaha Beach, scene of the bloodiest D-Day fighting. According to biographer Lou Cannon, Reagan was pitch perfect because he was returning to a Normandy that he had often visited in his mind as a result of watching old war movies. Perhaps so, but his words also bespoke a visceral hatred of war. His Pointe du Hoc address commemorated the losses of all the allied nations in World War II, including 20 million Russians – 'a terrible price that testifies to all the world the necessity of avoiding war'.[80]

There was another great speech of commemoration at Bergen-Belsen on 5 May 1985, but this was in compensation for participation earlier that day in a brief wreath-laying ceremony at the German military cemetery near Bitburg, where 49 members of the SS were belatedly discovered to lie buried amid some 2,000 soldiers. The Bitburg visit was intended both to observe the end of World War II and to commemorate the ensuing 40 years of friendship between West Germany and America. Once the presence of the SS graves became known, Reagan came under huge pressure to cancel the trip. Public opinion, veterans groups, and Jewish organizations were united in protest. When being presented with the Congressional Medal of Honor at the White House, Holocaust survivor Elie Wiesel departed from scripted remarks to declare: 'That place, Mr President, is not your place. Your place is with the victims of the SS.' Top aides and Nancy implored him to back out, but Reagan held fast in the wake of Helmut Kohl's emotional plea that cancellation would be regarded as an insult by West Germans. His diary testified to the mounting anger he felt at being pressured to change his mind – on 22 April, he wrote, 'I'm not going to cancel anything no matter how much the bastards scream.' The Soviets took every opportunity for propaganda profit from the visit and the Ramones punk-rock band satirized it in 'Bonzo goes to Bitburg', but Reagan's steadfastness eventually produced a ten-point gain in his approval rating. 'I always felt it was the morally right thing to do,' he remarked. The supportive letters he received from veterans and their relatives – notably the daughter of a private whom he had celebrated when visiting Omaha Beach a year earlier – were especially gratifying.[81]

As the Bitburg episode indicated, Reagan valued reading the views of ordinary Americans. Of course, only a small volume of the thousands of letters received by the White House made it to his desk. Early in his presidency, he had instructed aides to keep him supplied with samples of mail addressed to him, including critical ones. When time allowed, he would reply to these, drafting his response on a yellow legal pad (always writing on both sides to save paper). Gathered together in the Presidential Handwriting File in his library, this correspondence is one of the key sources for understanding Reagan the president. Anyone reading these letters cannot help but get the sense that he cared deeply about his fellow citizens and their thoughts. They also provide evidence of the many individual kindnesses that he performed for people, especially young Americans, who had written to him. Two examples suffice to convey this side of him – though there are many that could have been chosen. In early 1985, he heard from a non-vocal, disabled 25-year-old young man from Caldwell, Idaho, a history buff whose dream was to meet a president. Reagan's heartwarming response promised a handshake once his schedule allowed – their meeting took place in the White House on 30 May following his return from Bitburg. Around this time, he also granted the dying wish of 13-year-old Californian John Zimmerman, who wanted his ashes interred alongside his Marine Corps heroes. Although the Veterans' Administration ruled this was impossible, Reagan ordered it done after reading about the case two years after the boy died.[82]

The political, philosophical, and personal sides are all important to understanding Ronald Reagan's presidency. In contrast to most modern presidents, he never appears to have thought deeply about his place in history. Nancy was always more overtly concerned about his legacy. Reagan's insouciance was likely a product of his advanced years – he had a self-sufficient sense of his own achievement without caring too much what scholars would think about him in the future. '[T]he history will probably get distorted when it's written,' he told political aide Ed Rollins in 1985. 'And I won't be around to read it.'[83] No Oval Office occupant achieves everything he sets out to do and Reagan was no exception – but his domestic and foreign policies made his presidency a momentous one.

EIGHT

Pragmatic Conservative

A ddressing the Conservative Political Action Conference shortly after his inauguration, Reagan proclaimed that his election 'was not so much a victory of politics as it was a victory of ideas'.[1] The domestic changes that he instituted during his first year in office prompted some political commentators to speak of a 'Reagan Revolution' that had rolled back the New Deal–Great Society tradition.[2] If measured in terms of eliminating key programmes put in place during the liberal ascendancy, this catchy alliteration was wide of the mark. From another perspective, however, a transformation in the ethos of government was in process. Reagan was part of a small band of presidents whose names became labels for political creeds. The New Deal-inspired political order that stretched from the 1930s to the 1970s had aimed, however imperfectly, to correct the flaws of the free market, safeguard workers' rights, and improve the lives of the disadvantaged. In its domestic aspects, Reaganism as a governing ideology promoted unfettered capitalism as a social good, rewarded individualism, and limited the state's role in mitigating inequality in American society. If Reagan's supporters were mainly responsible for operationalizing this credo, he was essential to its emergence as the new orthodoxy. Adapting to the reality that a full frontal assault on the liberal state would doom his presidency, Reagan combined ideological conviction and pragmatism to embed a conservative philosophy in government.

In the estimation of conservative economist Milton Friedman: 'You want a principled man, which Reagan is. But he is not rigidly principled, which you don't want.'[3] Reagan had no sympathy for what he often called the 'off the cliff with all flags flying' approach of hard-shell conservatives. As he commented in his diary, 'A compromise is never to anyone's liking – it's just the best you can get and contains enough of what you want to justify what you give up.'[4] In fact, Reagan never thought of himself as giving up anything for keeps. He might have taken take the proverbial half a loaf as being better than none, but still saw himself as opening the way for conservatives to come back later for the rest. When Representative Newt Gingrich of Georgia launched into a litany of what was left undone at a White House meeting in 1987, Reagan's soothing response to the conservative firebrand was: 'Well, some things you're just going to have to do after I'm gone.'[5]

Reagan was more interested in redirecting the nation's future course through promoting a tightly focused agenda than in advancing on a broad front in pursuit of myriad incremental goals. As pollster Dick Wirthlin observed: 'He is gambling very much on his ability to induce structural change in the long run. His poker chips on the table are what happens in the short run.' From the outset, Reagan's holy trinity consisted of cutting taxes, reducing government, and restoring America's defences. Presidential unwillingness to invest political capital in other policy areas disappointed moral conservatives. From Reagan's perspective, issues of particular concern to this constituency were 'very vital and very important, but they're a periphery to a philosophy'.[6] His approach to governance followed the recommendations of the Initial Actions Project, a White House staff report written mainly by Dick Wirthlin in the transition period, discussed in draft form by the president-elect and key advisors in mid-December, and formally approved on 29 January 1981. This blueprint called for a strong start in the first 180 days in office when the opportunity to effect change was at its peak. 'The public sense of urgency,' it warned,

> requires that the new President immediately undertake to steer a new course, to advance policies designed to support that new direction, and to follow those policies with firmness and consistency [...] How we begin will significantly determine how we govern.[7]

Restoration of prosperity was the immediate measure of success. 'In 1981,' Reagan later stated, no problem the country faced was more serious than the economic crisis [...] because without a recovery, we couldn't afford to do the things necessary to make the country strong again [...] Nor could America regain confidence in itself and stand tall once again. Nothing was possible until we made the economy sound again.[8]

His presidency began with symbolic and substantive initiatives to signify this priority. Immediately the oath of office was taken, White House officials executed instructions to move the portrait of Calvin Coolidge, patron saint of small government, tax cuts, and 1920s prosperity, from the Grand Hall into the Cabinet Room in place of Harry S. Truman's.[9] More significantly, the 40th president's first executive order, issued on 28 January, decreed immediate removal of remaining oil- and gas-price controls with the aim of boosting domestic production. Horrified Democrats feared that this would encourage oil corporations to raise the price of a gallon of gasoline, currently around $1.40, to $2 or even $3. Instead, the reverse happened, as increased production almost immediately led to lower prices and diminishing oil imports.[10] This was the hors d'oeuvre to the main course of economic renewal.

In a televised address to the nation on 5 February, Reagan blamed big government for inflation and slow growth, economic ailments that he proposed to cure through simultaneous cuts in spending and taxes – in defiance of the orthodoxy that the former should precede the latter to constrain budget-deficit expansion. 'It's time to recognize that we've come to a turning point,' he declared. 'We're threatened with an economic calamity of tremendous proportions, and the old business-as-usual treatment can't save us.'[11] His first address to Congress followed two weeks later in support of the newly unveiled plan, *America's New Beginning: A Program for Economic Recovery.* Peppered with statistics, this was by no means his best speech, but public reaction was overwhelmingly favourable. The new programme put the flesh of detail on the bones of principle embodied in 'Policy memorandum No 1' that aide Martin Anderson had drafted in August 1979. It projected a 30 per cent three-year cut in income taxes, the most significant domestic spending retrenchment since World War II, and the achievement of a balanced budget by the end of Reagan's first term. This ambitious agenda was hailed as 'a rare opportunity [...] to stimulate growth, productivity and employment at the same time as we move toward the elimination of inflation'.[12]

The principal agency for converting these aspirations into reality was the budget plan for Fiscal Year (FY)1982 (running from 1 October 1981 to 30 September 1982). Conventional Washington wisdom deemed it impossible to transform within weeks of taking office a blueprint that had taken a year to prepare. New presidents usually made incremental adjustments to proposals inherited from their predecessor before putting their mark on the following year's plan (for FY1983 in Reagan's case). However, Reagan delivered what was effectively a new budget to Congress on 10 March 1981 – just 49 days after his inauguration. The individual most responsible for this was Office of Management and Budget (OMB) director David Stockman.

The youngest Cabinet appointee in 160 years, the 34-year-old Stockman owed his appointment to having played Jimmy Carter in mock exchanges to prepare Reagan for the 1980 presidential debate. A strong supporter of the Kemp–Roth tax-reduction plan, he developed prodigious knowledge of the budget process during two terms as a Michigan GOP congressman (1977–81). Mastery of fiscal intricacies little understood by other key administration personnel enabled Stockman to dominate the Economic Policy Coordinating Committee charged with producing *America's New Beginning.* The OMB director also worked a punishing schedule and drove his staff hard to produce a new budget that embodied Reagan's vision of economic renewal.[13]

Development of the budget plan was a presidential responsibility, but Congress alone could enact its proposals into law. In contrast to the aloof Jimmy Carter, Reagan courted legislators assiduously to seek their support for his economic plan – launching his campaign with three visits to Washington during the transition period. Senate Republicans were united in support of a presidential Moses who had led them to the promised land of majority status for the first time since the 1953–4 Congress. As their leader, Howard Baker of Tennessee, commented, 'We are a team, the president is the quarterback and we are his blockers and we can't say now we don't like the plays.'[14] In the Democrat-led House of Representatives, however, Reagan faced speaker Thomas P. 'Tip' O'Neill of Massachusetts, who would eventually prove a formidable adversary.

At their first White House meeting, O'Neill told a president inexperienced in the ways of Washington, 'You're in the big leagues now' – gratuitously offensive words that he would soon choke on. The representative of a working-class Boston district since 1953, this Irish American Democrat was an unreconstructed New Deal–Great Society liberal. In his biographer's words, he believed that 'government was the means by which a people came together to address their community's ills, to right wrongs, and craft a just society'. In O'Neill's eyes, Reagan 'forgot where he came from' by abandoning his one-time liberalism. The speaker considered it his duty to look out for working people and the poor when this friend of the rich became president.[15] During social occasions together, the two men could be full of bonhomie in swapping Irish jokes but they often exchanged harsh words behind closed doors. As Reagan recalled of O'Neill:

> When it came to the things he believed in, he could turn off his charm and friendship like a light switch and become as bloodthirsty as a piranha [...] Until six o'clock, I was the enemy and he never let me forget it.

The hard-nosed, overweight, and un-telegenic speaker initially found himself outmanoeuvred by a media-savvy president. 'I'm getting the shit whaled out of me,' he admitted at one point. Upping his game over time, O'Neill made himself more accessible to journalists and improved his television image by shedding some weight and updating his wardrobe. He also discovered a capacity to needle Reagan by accusing him of lack of compassion for the poor.[16]

For the time being, however, O'Neill's ranks were less than united in resisting Reagan. Conservative Southern Democrats, nicknamed 'Boll Weevils', were wary of his popularity in their region, particularly as the White House framed the budget vote as a test of whether legislators were for or against the president. Reagan's high approval ratings following the attempted assassination further swung the political momentum in his favour. White House aides shrewdly intertwined the battle for the budget with the president's return to duty by getting him to address Congress on 28 April. A still weak Reagan received a tumultuous ovation when he entered the chamber. Although few Democrats joined in the applause for the actual speech, television networks denied O'Neill the right to reply – almost as if the wounded commander-in-chief's words had become sacrosanct. Unsurprisingly, therefore, the president's message received widespread popular approval. 'We've been outflanked and outgunned,' majority leader Jim Wright of Texas recorded in his diary. Tip O'Neill's forces were now 'embattled, trying to stem the flow of conservative sands through the sieve'. Nine days later, 63 Southern Democrats joined with Republicans to approve an administration-backed budget resolution by 253 to 176 votes. 'We never anticipated such a landslide,' a jubilant president wrote in his diary. 'It's been a long time since Repubs. have had a victory like this.'[17]

Important as this vote was, it merely established a framework for the deliberations of the various standing committees that vetted outlays on the numerous domestic programmes. To pre-empt these bodies from marking up expenditure, the Legislative Strategy Group (LSG) that White House CoS James Baker had established to promote enactment of the Reagan programme advocated a parliamentary manoeuvre to substitute all committee allocations with one omnibus reconciliation measure. This high-risk tactic could not count on the same level of Boll Weevil support because it threatened the sovereignty of the standing committees. If successful, LSG coordinator Richard Darman informed Reagan, the 'perception of your leadership and commitment will be strengthened, the traditional House Democratic leadership will be weakened, and the prospect of building upon the new bipartisan coalition will be enhanced'. But, the aide continued, the president would have to work hard to win votes that 'are not there now'. The speaker, for his part, would pull out all the stops to inflict 'a major Administration loss' that could halt the momentum of its economic programme.[18]

Convinced he was on a winning streak, Reagan never entertained doubts about challenging O'Neill in his own domain. He personally lobbied individual Democrats, promised not to campaign in the 1982 midterms against those supporting his budget, and authorized administration negotiators to agree constituency-interest concessions to win over waverers.[19] Among the latter, Representative John Breaux of Louisiana memorably remarked on securing renewed support for sugar producers in his district, 'They're not buying my vote, only renting it.'[20] O'Neill appeared to have staunched the flow of defectors by the time Reagan headed off for a scheduled visit to California the day before the vote, so the presidential lobbying effort continued in mid-air and then by long-distance telephone. The speech to be given in Los Angeles on 24 June originally anticipated defeat, but had to be rewritten minutes before delivery to celebrate 'a great victory [...] the greatest reduction in government spending that has ever been attempted'. News had come through that the Democratic leadership had lost its procedural motion against reconciliation by seven votes, with every Republican and 29 Democrats supporting the administration. Next day, House approval of the omnibus budget sealed the presidential triumph.[21]

As finally enacted, the Omnibus Budget and Reconciliation Act (OBRA) of 1981 retrenched over 200 domestic programmes at projected savings of $35.2 billion in FY1982 and $140 billion over three years. The axe mainly fell on programmes that benefited low-income Americans – starting 1 October, at least 400,000 families of the working poor would lose all welfare assistance, another 300,000 would forfeit some benefits, a million people would lose food stamps, 3 million pupils would be taken off the school lunch programme, 700,000 students would be denied guaranteed federal loans, and $1 billion in aid to state government to cover Medicaid costs would vanish. Since most of the economies were achieved by tightening eligibility for assistance, their scale could never be precisely computed. Even so, OBRA undoubtedly constituted the largest retrenchment of non-military spending hitherto in American history. Over time, non-entitlement domestic budget appropriations declined from 4.5 per cent GDP in Jimmy Carter's last budget to 3.1 per cent GDP in Reagan's final one. In the short-term, however, the savings nowhere near kept pace with the corollary expansion of defence outlays. When it came to retrenchment, Jim Wright complained, Reagan's 'definition of spending is purely domestic'.[22]

Far from undertaking a thoroughgoing assessment of America's military needs, the new administration built its long-term defence strategy on the assumption that the sheer size of the Pentagon budget was the primary index of American power. Reagan had pledged to spend at least 5 per cent more a year than Carter on defence. In fact his predecessor's lame-duck budget, drawn up amid the worsening Cold War situation of 1980, already provided for an increase of this magnitude. Overlooking this in the scramble to revise military spending estimates within the tight budget deadline, Stockman and secretary of defense Caspar Weinberger agreed a five-year programme of 7 per cent real increases over the inherited FY1982 baseline. This error would make it impossible to balance the budget in accordance with the administration's timetable. The OMB director's frantic efforts to redress it, once discovered, ran into the immovable wall of military resistance. The Pentagon had acted quickly to produce a long-term plan committing every cent of its unanticipated $1.46 trillion bounty. Weinberger's insistence that any retreat on these allocations would send the

Soviets the wrong signal struck a chord with Reagan. In a choice between deficits and defence, the president avowed, national security had to come first. As a consequence, there was a total disjunction between military outlays and fiscal control. Defence spending, which amounted to 4.9 per cent of GDP in FY1980, averaged 6.0 per cent of GDP annually in FY1982–9. Aggregate outlays of $2.7 trillion under Reagan paid for nuclear-weaponry expansion (notably the B-1 and B-2 bombers, MX missiles, and cruise missiles), significantly higher force levels – including a 600-ship Navy, and much greater investment in weapons procurement, research, and development.[23]

Once his spending legislation was safely through Congress, Reagan turned his attention to enacting what would prove to be the largest tax cut in American history. The Economic Recovery Tax Act (ERTA) of 1981 drew its lineage from the Kemp–Roth supply-side measure that congressional Republicans had promoted in vain in the late 1970s but included massive add-ons that had little to do with economic doctrine. Having failed to prevent Reagan's domestic retrenchment, the Democratic House leadership tried a different ploy to stall his momentum over tax reduction. The plan was to wrest the initiative from the president by outbidding what the administration measure proffered, but the outcome was a near complete loss of political control over ERTA revenue costs.

An alternative Democratic bill contained allowances for oil and gas industries and other corporate benefits to corral Boll Weevil support. Ways and Means Committee chair Dan Rostenkowski of Illinois also reinserted an immediate cut in the top marginal tax rate of 70 per cent (applied only to investment income) to 50 per cent, something Reagan had reluctantly given up during administration planning of the legislation for fear it would be attacked as a giveaway to the rich. Tax lobbyists then jumped on the bandwagon to secure further relief for business interests, notably a reduction in the capital-gains tax and a tripling of the wealth threshold on estate taxes. The most significant addition, at least in terms of revenue costs, was the indexation of personal income tax rates to inflation from FY1985 onwards. Its sponsor, Senator William Armstrong of Colorado, a Republican freshman, wanted to control spending through eliminating the automatic increase in revenues generated by bracket creep. The extra provisions resulted in revenue loss about twice that of the original Reagan bill. The cost amounted to just over $750 billion in the first five years ($557 billion for individual income-tax cuts, $151 billion for business-tax cuts, and

$47 billion for other adornments), but would nearly double over the entirety of the Reagan budgets as inflation indexation came into play.[24]

Reagan accepted all these changes because they accorded with his goal of reducing the tax burden. He rejected a Democratic proposal to shrink the personal-income-tax cut into two annual instalments of 5 per cent and 10 per cent that were skewed towards those earning less than $50,000 – with a third instalment of 10 per cent contingent on whether the initial reduction inflated the deficit or not. His only concession, a reluctant one intended to appease deficit-conscious Boll Weevils, was to reduce the first instalment to 5 per cent and delay its implementation until October 1981 (instead of backdating it to 1 January). With his competitive juices in free flow, Reagan told economic advisor Murray Weidenbaum, 'I can win this.' Lacking the same degree of confidence, some aides urged him in vain to consider a two-stage tax cut instead.[25]

The president requested network prime-time to take his case to the nation on 27 July. With Nancy away for the royal wedding in London, he spent the weekend at Camp David composing the address himself. Friend and foe agreed that this was his best rhetorical effort to date. He was confident, in command of his material, and framed the issue crisply before the cameras. 'If the tax cut goes to you, the American people, in the third year,' he declared, 'that money [...] won't be available to the Congress to spend, and that, in my view, is what this whole controversy comes down to.' The next day the White House got more telephone calls than for any previous appearance, running six-to-one in favour of the president. Congressmen of both parties reported that their phones were ringing off the hook, with calls estimated to total 40,000. Taking nothing for granted, Reagan mounted an intensive personal lobbying effort, hosting 58 wavering legislators of both parties for beer and hamburgers at Camp David (39 backed him) and telephoning another 26 (winning 17). In the late afternoon of 29 July he got his reward with a lopsided victory in the Senate, where 17 of the 18 Democrats up for re-election in 1982 backed him, and a solid one in the House, where 40 Democrats crossed the aisle. In combination with the budget vote, he considered this 'the greatest pol. win in half a century'.[26]

That night a disbelieving Jim Wright wrote in his diary:

> We haven't really laid a glove on [Reagan] [...] His philosophical approach is superficial, overly simplistic, one dimensional. What he

preaches is pure economic pap glossed with uplifting homilies and inspirational chatter. Yet so far the guy is making it work. Appalled by what seems to me a lack of depth, I stand in awe nevertheless of his political skill. I am not sure that I have seen its equal.

More pithily (and profanely), fellow Texan Charlie Wilson (later celebrated for his covert role in getting US aid to Afghanistan in the 2007 Tom Hanks movie *Charlie Wilson's War*) remarked, 'I sure as hell hope that sonofabitch doesn't come out against fucking.' This conservative Democrat had kept a promise to support his party's alternative bill provided tax breaks for oil interests were included. Cheerfully admitting that his vote had been bought, he deemed it essential to stay bought. 'You're not worth a damn round this place,' Wilson declared, 'if you don't keep commitments like that.'[27]

There was one last conservative thrust left in Reagan's first-year blitzkrieg. On 3 August the Professional Air Traffic Controllers Organization (PATCO) struck for a new contract featuring an unprecedented $10,000 across-the-board immediate pay increase for members, another 10 per cent pay rise in the second year, a four-day working week, and generous cost-of-living provisions. In response the president ordered the strikers back to work within two days or be fired, a threat that union leaders considered a bluff because of the damaging effect on air travel and flight safety. Within two weeks, however, 11,000 controllers – half the PATCO membership – had lost their jobs, but 80 per cent of all flights had returned to normal service after military air personnel were reassigned to assist controllers who had returned to work. Reagan had taken a huge gamble because he would have been blamed had there been an air disaster. As it was, most Americans praised their president for standing up to a group of well-paid professionals with secure jobs if they obeyed the rules – telephone calls to the White House ran 13-to-one in favour of his action. Within a month, the Federal Aviation Authority received more than 100,000 applications for air-traffic-controller posts. PATCO's decertification meant that new recruits could no longer join the union, but this was a price they were happy to pay.[28]

The only president to have been a union leader had crushed a strike more effectively than any predecessor since Grover Cleveland sent troops against Pullman workers in 1894 – and in the process had defeated a labour organization that endorsed him in 1980. Reagan saw himself emulating Calvin Coolidge, breaker of the Boston police strike of 1919 when Massachusetts governor. The reality was somewhat more complex. John F. Kennedy's Executive Order 10988 of 1962 allowed government workers to organize in order to voice grievances but not to negotiate pay and conditions, let alone strike. Instead of being the tough-minded enforcer of this rule, Reagan had authorized a counter-offer that included an 11.4 per cent pay increase in an effort to avoid a disruptive stoppage. No president had previously put such generous terms before public-sector workers threatening a strike, but PATCO leaders rejected them. Reagan took no pleasure in ordering the dismissal of strikers, many of whom had served as military air controllers before entering civilian employment. Writing to the mother of one, he lamented, 'I do feel a very real sorrow for those who followed the union leadership at such sacrifice.'[29]

Reagan's defeat of PATCO not only discouraged other public-sector unions from striking but also inhibited private-sector unions from utilizing the most powerful tool at their disposal. In the estimate of Federal Reserve chairman Paul Volcker, standing up to an aggressive and well-organized union was 'the most important single action he [Reagan] took as president to control inflation'.[30] Though Reagan was by no means anti-union, the unintended outcome of his actions against PATCO was the weakening of the entire labour movement. Encouraged by his example, historian Joseph McCartin noted, 'prominent employers saw strikes not as conflicts to be avoided, but as opportunities to break or tame unions'. Within a few years, corporations like Phelps Dodge, Greyhound, International Paper, and Hormel Foods had fired strikers rather than bargain with them, a strategy that took advantage of weak labour-market conditions, automation, and computer-generated flexibility in supply and production networks. As a consequence, the number of major work stoppages in the United States fell to one-third of pre-PATCO levels.[31]

Shortly after breaking the air controllers' strike, Reagan signed OBRA and ERTA into law at Rancho del Cielo on 13 August just as the mist rolled in from the ocean. There was nothing foggy about his achievement, however. Taken together, the three successes constituted the most significant reversal of the New Deal political order since its establishment in the 1930s. Seeking to capture the importance of the moment, journalist Martin Tolchin commented that Reagan 'had engineered a revolutionary change in the direction of Government, reducing its size, powers, and appetites'.[32] The actual transformation that he wrought was somewhat different to the one this reporter envisaged. It was soon evident that what Reagan had done was to replace tax-and-spend government with spend-and-borrow government.

The fiscal costs of the president's political successes were about to become evident. The man who thought himself the chief accountant of Reaganomics now worried about being its chief miscalculator. The budget plan that David Stockman had compiled in such haste contained a so-called 'magic asterisk' requiring additional but unidentified savings of $44 billion in FY1982 to keep the budget on track to being balanced in 1984. Without these, the Reagan economic plan's rosy scenario would acquire deep-red hues. While ERTA progressed to triumphal enactment, Stockman manoeuvred for a 'fall offensive' to head off massive deficits. His hopes of scaling back the defence expansion encountered predictable Pentagon resistance. At a White House meeting on 9 September, Weinberger trumped Stockman's numbers with the military-strength-is-paramount card. Thereafter, in Richard Darman's words, 'the struggle for the president's mind was over' insofar as significant defence cuts were concerned.[33]

Stockman's next target was Social Security, the 'third rail' of American politics (touch it and you die) because of its status as the cornerstone of the middle-class welfare state. The hubristic OMB director had already blown the administration's best chance of pension economies by advising Reagan back in February to reject a bipartisan Senate Budget Committee proposal to freeze cost-of-living adjustments to Social Security benefits. Convinced that greater retrenchment was possible, he played a key role in an administration task force that produced a wide-ranging Social Security reform plan with projected multi-year savings of $110 billion, derived in part from a controversial proposal to penalize early retiree benefits from 1982 onwards. Seeing an opportunity to make progress on an issue of longstanding interest to him, Reagan quickly gave the go-ahead for the initiative. Angered at not being consulted, Senate Republicans immediately joined with Democrats in a 96–0 vote against the administration plan on 20 May. When Stockman called for a new offensive on pensions in the fall, CoS James Baker enlisted GOP congressional leaders to inform Reagan that lack of bipartisan support would doom this to failure. Forced to find savings elsewhere, the OMB director then advocated deferral of the second and third instalments of ERTA's income-tax cuts at an Oval Office meeting on 22 September. Reagan needed no one's advice in deciding his response: 'Delay would be total retreat. We would be admitting we were wrong.'[34]

In his memoirs Stockman bemoaned Reagan's refusal to take unpopular actions to control the deficit: 'He was a consensus politician. Not an ideologue. He had no business trying to make a revolution because it wasn't in his bones.'[35] This assessment belied the reality that Reagan achieved most of what he set out to do. It also manifested supreme misunderstanding of what the Reagan Revolution entailed in its creator's eyes. Stockman was prepared to scale down the defence expansion to control the deficit in violation of Reagan's belief that the dollar size of the budget was critical to persuading the Soviets of their incapacity to win an arms race. Furthermore, his willingness to delay ERTA's second and third personal-tax-cut instalments signified that the one-step top-band reduction and the business-tax cuts were his personal priorities. Stockman admitted as much in telling journalist William Greider: 'Kemp–Roth was always a Trojan horse to bring down the top rate [...] The supply-side formula was the only way to get a tax policy that was really trickledown.'[36] For Reagan, by contrast, universal and broad-based tax cuts were fundamental to his vision of individual freedom and economic growth. He wanted to balance the budget but not at the expense of these core goals. Furthermore, once aware of the political stakes on Social Security reform, he had no interest in a kamikaze assault on middle-class entitlements that could have made him a one-term president, thereby putting his entire legacy at risk.

Reagan could resist pressure from the likes of Stockman to change course but the worst recession to hit the economy since the 1930s posed a far greater threat. During a downturn lasting from mid-1981 to late 1982, GDP fell 2.9 per cent and some 3 million payroll jobs were lost. The independent Federal Reserve's decision to shake inflation out of the economy with a shock dose of monetarism precipitated the decline. Conventionally, the central bank had raised interest rates to combat price instability. Under Paul Volcker's leadership, however, it now adopted a more radical monetarist approach of money-supply control as the last hope of stifling America's hyperinflation.[37] Virtually every sector of the economy felt the effects of tighter money quantity that compelled banks to levy ever-higher interest charges on borrowers. Reagan's economists had alerted him to the onset of recession in mid-year but wrongly anticipated that it would only last two quarters before the ERTA tax cuts revived economic growth.[38]

Volcker's monetarist typhoon threatened to sink the administration's economic plan. *America's New Beginning* anticipated a stable and predictable reduction of 50 per cent in money-stock growth spread over six years to avoid substantial output loss and allow the tax cuts time to boost the economy, but the Fed delivered the entirety of this in 1981–2. Reagan's promise of renewed prosperity appeared increasingly empty in the face of growing joblessness. Meanwhile, the depressing effect of economic decline on tax revenues sent the budget deficit skyrocketing. The federal government ran unprecedented dollar-size imbalances of $128 billion (4.0 per cent GDP) in FY1982 and $207 billion (6.0 per cent GDP) in FY 1983, the first ever breaches of the symbolically significant $100 billion and $200 billion thresholds. Reagan's accusations that Jimmy Carter's much smaller deficits had caused price instability now came back to bite him.

Despite its harsh consequences, the president was publicly steadfast in support of the Fed's stand, something Volcker attributed to his 'strong visceral aversion to inflation'. In reality, Reagan had little alternative. As an OMB official noted, 'Scapegoating the Fed while we struggle with triple-digit deficits will do the administration a lot of harm.' The average voter blamed deficits for the inflation that the central bank was seeking to eradicate. Moreover, the financial markets considered Volcker their last hope of preserving investment values. Public criticism of the Fed chair would also risk his condemnation of the administration's loose fiscal policy.[39] In private the White House lobbied for a change of course in the spring of 1982 through the person of Donald Regan. Following a series of meetings, the Treasury secretary reported that Volcker was ready to ease monetary policy 'if he could see some movement by us on the deficits'. A disappointed Reagan confided to a friend, 'There's no real reason why interest rates shouldn't be coming down.' By mid-year presidential frustration with monetary policy was increasingly palpable. 'This is becoming an obsession with me,' Reagan wrote to a supporter, 'but I'll try not to picket a bank.'[40]

Regardless of Volcker's implicit warning that there would be no change of monetary policy unless the deficit was brought under control, Reagan's FY1983 budget plan still attempted to steer the same course as its FY1982 predecessor in requesting an extra $33 billion for defence. The deficit projection of $91 billion was a fiscal hoax concocted by Stockman. The OMB director should have been sacked for his embarrassing revelations to William Greider but his budgeting skill saved him. Proving his wizardry, Stockman by his own later admission had 'out-and-out cooked the books' to keep the deficit forecast beneath $100 billion through inventing phony domestic spending cuts and overestimating revenue by 10 per cent.[41] Even this did not save the Reagan plan from being declared dead on arrival in Congress. Democrats attacked it as a giveaway to defence corporations and the wealthy. Hammering on the fairness issue, they ran a television ad in response to the State of the Union Address charging that Reaganomics gave the rich tax breaks and deprived ordinary Americans of their jobs.[42] Meanwhile, many Senate Republicans were unwilling to follow Reagan into the uncharted territory of out-of-control deficits that violated GOP balanced-budget orthodoxy. Emerging as their spokesman, Senate Finance Committee chair Bob Dole of Kansas led the drive to harmonize Reaganomics with fiscal responsibility, a circle ultimately impossible to square. A Midwestern conservative rather than a Sunbelt one, Dole had a prairie Republican's compassion for the poor and was suspicious of market forces. Becoming almost as much a thorn in Reagan's side as O'Neill, he had no compunction about preserving welfare programmes from further retrenchment and sacrificing ERTA's tax breaks for corporations and the wealthy.[43]

The White House now had little option but to negotiate with House Democrats and Senate Republicans to produce a fiscal compromise. An acceptable budget resolution took months to secure, but there was devil in its detail. It projected a $375 billion three-year deficit reduction package made up of spending cuts and revenue increases on a three-to-one ratio. Most of the expenditure savings flowed from lower interest costs produced by deficit reduction, soft economies of management efficiencies, and domestic cuts that were notoriously difficult to achieve in practice. Unsurprisingly, little of this retrenchment made it from blueprint to reality. Meanwhile Dole produced a substantive revenue-enhancement measure to raise $98 billion over three years, mainly by rescinding some of ERTA's business-tax breaks. This was the largest tax increase in peacetime history when enacted as the Tax Equity and Fiscal Responsibility Act (TEFRA) on 19 August.

As the vote drew near, Reagan intensively lobbied anti-tax Republicans in support of the measure. One indication of its importance to him was that he stayed in Washington to do so rather than accompany Nancy to Phoenix to be with her stepfather, Loyal Davis, who was dying of congestive heart failure.

O'Neill acted in bipartisan spirit to get the bill through but – like Jesse Unruh in a similar Sacramento scenario in 1967 – took pleasure that Reagan had to 'use his smiley countenance and sweet-sounding voice and hard knuckles with his Republicans'. The speaker had his own difficulties because many liberal Democrats objected to entitlement economies in the measure. The intra-party splits resulted in only narrow majorities for TEFRA in both chambers. Reagan expressed anger that 'some of our ultra-pure conservatives deserted' – but only to his diary.[44]

Howsoever they voted, Democrats celebrated TEFRA as a momentous victory. Not only had the president raised taxes but also tax-cut pioneers Jack Kemp (against) and William Roth (for) were symbolically divided on the measure. Congressman Henry Reuss of Wisconsin crowed: 'Reaganomics […] is no more. Supply-side economics is un-Kempt.'[45] Fearing that this was so, prominent supply-siders Paul Craig Roberts and Norman Ture had earlier resigned their Treasury under-secretary posts in disillusion. A large group of House Republicans lamented that their party was 'in danger of making a U-turn back to its familiar role of tax collector for Democratic spending programmes'.[46] When the expected three-to-one spending cuts failed to materialize, Reagan himself came to believe that the Democrats had deceived him into agreeing the TEFRA compromise, characterized by Ed Meese as the administration's 'greatest domestic error'.[47] Of course, the existence of the deal was a case of wishful thinking because of the spurious nature of the savings in the gim-mick-laden budget resolution that Senate Republicans had connived in as much as House Democrats.

Even absent the spending retrenchment, Reagan in reality gained far more than he lost from TEFRA. Instead of marking a counter-revolution, the measure preserved the most important elements of what he had already achieved. During the initial FY1983 budget negotiations, he had recorded in his diary: 'The D's are playing games – they want me to rescind the 3d year of the tax cut – Not in a million years!' Nevertheless, he anticipated coming under growing pressure to do so unless revenues were enhanced in other ways. Since TEFRA addressed this problem, Reagan made his support for it conditional on preservation of the remaining ERTA instalments.[48] As was his habit in Sacramento when practice and principle seemingly diverged, Reagan told Americans that the measure 'absolutely does not represent any reversal of policy or philosophy on the part of this administration or this President'.[49] On this occasion there was some truth in his claim that it primarily ensured tougher compliance 'from those not now paying their fair share' of existing taxes, instead of being a wholly a new tax. TEFRA's defence on fairness grounds marked the genesis of Reagan's evolution from tax cutter to tax reformer that reached its culmination in 1986. Its enactment coincided with Federal Reserve abandonment of monetarism. Now that the castor-oil cure had effectively broken the hold of inflation, Volcker had yielded to pressure from his Board of Governors to ease monetary policy in order to combat the recession. There is no evidence that TEFRA influenced this decision but Reagan considered it critical to the central bank's change of course.[50]

Regardless of TEFRA's enactment, Reagan's Gallup approval ratings hovered round 40 per cent over the second half of 1982 compared with his 1981 average of 57 per cent. With the deficit a factor in this slide, he looked to recast himself as the paragon of fiscal virtue by promoting a constitutional amendment requiring annually balanced budgets with a tax-limitation rider. Addressing a rally on the Capitol steps on 19 July, Reagan commended this reform as the means to bring 'to heel a federal establishment that has taken too much power from the States, too much liberty with the Constitution, and too much money from the people'. Not a word was said about administration budget busting. *Time* magazine commented that Reagan's stance was akin to the nation's largest distiller coming out in support of Prohibition, but his purpose was political rather than principled.[51] Thanks to presidential lobbying, the amendment proposal secured the necessary two-thirds supermajority in the GOP-controlled Senate, but there was only a plurality of 'ayes' in the House, where most Democrats opposed the measure as a dire threat to domestic programmes. This predictable outcome enabled Reagan to blame them for perpetuation of the deficit problem. Even if approved by Congress, however, a balanced-budget amendment was no answer to immediate fiscal needs. It required ratification by three-quarters of the 50 state legislatures, a process likely to take years. A constitutional fix for America's deficit habit might also have created more problems than it solved by denying fiscal flexibility amid changing economic and international conditions.

With the economy still in the doldrums and joblessness rising, Reagan was powerless to shield the GOP from a beating at the 1982 midterm polls.

The Republicans lost 26 House seats, the worst result for an elected first-term president's party since 1930, and seven governorships, but suffered no losses in the Senate where they were defending safe seats. The GOP had long since abandoned hope of capturing the House, something that had once seemed possible in the immediate aftermath of the 1980 vote. It was now evident that there would be no Reagan realignment capable of producing a new Republican majority any time soon. The outcome strengthened O'Neill's hand – it not only brought more Democrats to the House but also forced Boll Weevils to reassess the advantages of supporting a president who was patently not the all-conquering political force they once imagined. Indeed, Reagan's own re-election two years hence no longer looked the sure thing that it once had.

One thing the midterms made plain was that Reagan would be in trouble in 1984 if he did not fix Social Security. On the eve of the vote the Democrats had got hold of a Republican fundraising letter asking donors if they supported making the programme a voluntary contribution system. This contrasted with a GOP campaign ad that showed a beaming mailman delivering Social Security cheques 'with the 7.4 per cent cost-of-living adjustment that President Reagan promised'. The Democrats had been claiming for months that the White House was scheming to undermine Social Security, something Reagan dismissed as a 'dishonest canard'. Now, GOP candidates across the nation faced a blitz of last-minute ads that used the fundraising letter to publicize the danger to pensions. '"They used it against us and killed us with it," James Baker acknowledged.'[52]

The real threat to Social Security was the imminent insolvency of its trust fund. Realizing the dangers of seeking a fix through the political process, Reagan had appointed a bipartisan blue-ribbon commission to devise a long-term solution. Established under Alan Greenspan's chairmanship in December 1981, this body was mandated to report within a year, but became deadlocked between members wanting benefit cuts and those preferring tax increases to sustain pensions. Following the midterms, Greenspan convened secret meetings with O'Neill's lieutenants and top Reagan aides to hammer out a 50/50 compromise on the contentious issues. Among other things, the White House got a suspension of automatic cost-of-living increases in payouts, while the Democrats won the argument that the benefits of wealthier recipients should be subject to income tax. Both sides also accepted an accelerated introduction of previously scheduled payroll tax increases, a gradual increase in the retirement age, and other cost-saving measures.[53]

Signed into law in April 1983, the reforms placed Social Security on a sound footing for more than 30 years on a cash-flow basis and about 60 years on trust-fund solvency terms. At the bill-signing ceremony, held 48 years to the day when FDR approved the original, Reagan paid tribute to his hero and expressed pride in perpetuating his creation. 'We have shared an historic moment,' he declared. '[W]e've restored some much needed security to an uncertain world.'[54] The ideological Reagan had advocated privatization of Social Security when an ultra-conservative in the early 1960s. The pragmatic one helped to ensure the survival of the New Deal-established system as president. His reward was to neutralize the issue for the 1984 election.

A second term now largely hinged on the state of the economy. Although the recession was officially over, unemployment peaked at 10.8 per cent in November–December 1982, with the consequence that Reagan's Gallup approval sank to its lowest ever level of 38 per cent in January 1983. The White House was simultaneously staring at multi-year deficit projections of $200 billion plus. A horrified Reagan reportedly exclaimed at the Budget Review Meeting of 3 January: 'We can't live with the out-year deficits [...] How can we come out with that string of figures without driving interest rates right back up? How can we put this out without creating a panic?'[55] Given his conviction that the Fed had eased monetary policy because of TEFRA, he feared its response to the new fiscal data would be an even harsher dose of monetarism that would plunge the economy into another tailspin. A group of 500 business, political, and academic leaders signed a public letter warning of this likelihood. A *New York Times*/CBS opinion poll also showed that 63 per cent of respondents favoured reducing the defence expansion and 62 per cent were willing to forgo the final ERTA instalment due in July in order to improve the budget numbers.[56]

It was at this juncture that Reagan came closest to retreating from his core goals. The 1983 State of the Union Address outlined a deficit-reduction plan, crafted by David Stockman and Richard Darman, that featured a domestic spending freeze, unspecified entitlement cuts, defence savings, and new taxes – including a standby surcharge of 1 per cent on corporate and personal income to come into effect if the deficit exceeded 2.5 per cent of GDP in FY1986. In substantive terms, these proposals were hardly counter-revolutionary, but

Darman firmly believed that Reagan was sufficiently worried about the deficit to go much further in an effort to control it.[57] However, the plan was never put into operation because the rapidity of economy recovery produced a parallel recovery of presidential nerve.

The recovery that started in the second half of 1982 would prove remarkably durable. Its 92-month duration was more than twice the average length of post-1945 expansionary cycles. From 1983 until 1988 economic growth annually averaged 4.2 per cent, gross private investment increased in real terms by 58 per cent, and Standard & Poor's index of 500 stocks went up 300 per cent. Allowing for the jobs lost in the recession, aggregate civilian employment grew from 99 million to 117 million under Reagan. Meanwhile, consumer price inflation averaged just 3.5 per cent annually. Liking what it saw, the Federal Reserve pursued a moderately expansionary monetary policy until mid-1987 despite still huge fiscal deficits.[58]

Reagan's toleration of unprecedented peacetime imbalances averaging $209 billion yearly (5 per cent of GDP) in FY1983–6 aroused Democratic suspicions that they were intended to defund the welfare state. The likes of Senator Daniel Patrick Moynihan, Representative Jim Wright, and Senator Ernest Hollings of South Carolina subscribed to this 'starve-the-beast' theory. As Hollings remarked: '[Reagan] knows what he is doing. He's not amnesiac. He's intentional. He not only cuts the programs but he likes the fact that those deficits keep us Democrats from ever even discussing new programs.'[59] Those charges were groundless. As Richard Darman observed, the notion that big imbalances 'were a matter of conscious, conspiratorial design, back in 1981, gives too much credit (and blame) to the alleged conspirators'.[60] Reagan wanted the threat, rather than the reality, of huge deficits to force domestic retrenchment. Their arrival was an unpleasant shock to him. Far from advancing his goals, they made it more difficult to achieve them.

One casualty of the exploding deficit was the New Federalism plan embodying Reagan's longstanding interest in devolution of federal programmes. This envisaged states taking full responsibility for funding public assistance (mainly Aid to Families with Dependent Children and food stamps) and 40 grant-in-aid programmes over a ten-year phase-in process. In return, Washington would transfer various excise taxes to the states to help finance their enhanced responsibility and assume the entire funding of Medicaid (medical assistance for the poor). According to Reagan, the New Federalism projected the 'biggest turn-around in govt. since Wash. started usurping local & state rights'.[61] Congressional Democrats, in contrast, called it a backdoor ploy to resolve the deficit problem by transferring long-term social programme costs to the states, a concern shared by state and local officials of both parties. Governor Richard Snelling of Vermont, the Republican chair of the National Governors Association, urged Reagan to reduce the deficit through military retrenchment and scaling back of ERTA as a precondition to a programme swap. Failure to negotiate an agreement with this group impelled the White House to abandon its plan in April 1982.[62] The real losers were the states, however. The deal would have spared them the huge burden that Medicaid would become on their twenty-first-century treasuries.

The most persuasive evidence against the fiscal-conspiracy theory is that Reagan's toleration of huge deficits, far from being an offensive strategy against domestic spending, was a defensive response against continuous pressure from his own advisors, Democrats, and congressional Republicans to sacrifice his core priorities. After a White House meeting with House GOP leaders on 11 January 1982, he wrote in his diary: 'Except for Jack Kemp they are h—l bent on new taxes and cutting the defense budget. Looks like a heavy year ahead.' A year later, the entry for 3 January 1983 read:

> A tough budget meeting & how to announce the deficits we'll have – they are horrendous [...] Met with a group of young Repub. Congressmen. Newt Gingrich has a proposal for freezing the budget at the [FY] 1983 level. It's a tempting idea except that it would cripple our defense program.[63]

While Reagan was utterly resilient in protecting personal-tax cuts from reversal, budget pressures compelled his approval of TEFRA and the Deficit Reduction Act of 1984, a smaller measure that yielded $50 billion over three years from tax loophole closures and excise-tax increases. He could hardly have anticipated in his early pomp having to sign these tax hikes that together recouped about a third of ERTA's revenue loss.

A final argument against the intentional-deficits claim is that the imbalances were a matter of grave concern for the American public throughout 1982 and most of 1983. In August 1983, Dick Wirthlin's private polls found that 47 per cent of respondents agreed that large deficits affected the economy 'a great deal' and 32 per cent thought they did 'somewhat'. Over three-quarters of those surveyed considered deficit control an important presidential responsibility, and only one-third approved Reagan's performance in this regard. As confidence in the recovery grew, however, popular concern about unbalanced budgets receded. In January 1984 the *New York Times*/CBS survey found 72 per cent of respondents now unwilling to pay higher taxes for the sake of deficit reduction.[64]

Buoyed by this change, Reagan grew more stubborn in defence of his priorities. In January 1984 Council of Economic Advisers chair Martin Feldstein, supported by David Stockman, advocated timely enactment of the standby tax mooted a year earlier in order to reassure business about administration commitment to tackle the deficit. The president responded by lecturing his errant aides that no tax hike in American history had ever actually raised revenue. When Feldstein produced a memo demonstrating that every increase in tax rates from 1917 to 1969 had done so, the president still considered him 'wrong as h—l'. This eminent scholar, the pride of the Harvard Economics department, was unused to having his wisdom contested by a mere layman. Feldstein's increasingly intemperate private and public remarks urging deficit reduction ensured that his White House days were numbered.[65]

Reagan's refusal to sacrifice the ERTA personal tax cuts and the defence expansion in the cause of deficit reduction contrasted with pragmatism on issues outside his core agenda. In contrast to his record as California governor, he gave free rein to anti-environmental and pro-development interests at the outset of his presidency. Guided by Senator Paul Laxalt of Nevada, a longstanding ally, he selected James Watt, president of the Mountain States Legal Foundation – a conservative Denver organization supported by the Coors brewing family, as secretary of the interior. The most right-wing member of the Cabinet, this evangelical free-marketeer proclaimed, 'We will mine more, drill more, cut more timber,' and infamously likened environmentalists to Nazis on one occasion. To encourage exploitation of natural resources, he opened previously sequestered land to development, imposed a moratorium on national-park creation, and closed down the office that regulated strip mining. Put in charge of the Environmental Protection Agency (EPA), fellow free-marketeer Anne Gorsuch Burford reduced its staff by nearly one-third and oversaw a decline in pollution prosecutions from 230 in 1980 to 42 in 1981. Meanwhile Rita Lavelle, the official in charge of the EPA Superfund for toxic-waste clean-up, delayed taking action on the worst dumps.[66]

The trio of environmental non-regulators ultimately had the effect of galvanizing support for environmental causes, discrediting the cause of deregulation, and embarrassing the White House. With a combination of congressional Democrats and Republicans clamouring for their heads, the axe fell on each of them in 1983. Watt's inability to open his mouth without putting his foot in it ultimately did for him. The 'Sewergate' scandal – favoured companies were being allowed to avoid compliance with environmental laws and regulations – brought about the downfall of Burford and Lavelle (the latter went to prison for six months for perjury and misuse of public funds). All three were replaced by politically savvy operators charged with keeping the administration out of trouble on environmental issues that were in reality peripheral to presidential priorities. Reagan had relearned the lesson that experience in Sacramento should have taught him about the emotional power of environmental concerns. From 1983 onwards, he was careful to avoid giving the impression of not caring about them.

The disappointment of developers with Reagan's pragmatism was nothing compared to that of many evangelical conservatives. To fulfil a pledge made when his 1980 campaign needed a boost, Reagan nominated the first woman to sit on the Supreme Court. With the first vacancy arising in early 1981, the selection of Arizona appeal-court judge Sandra Day O'Connor was unpopular with the Christian Right because of her pro-Equal Rights Amendment position and moderate support for abortion. Favourable vetting of O'Connor by the devoutly Catholic William Clark and attorney general William French Smith reinforced Reagan's determination to stand by her. After speaking in person with O'Connor, he felt reassured that her constitutional views were conservative and that abortion was 'personally repugnant' to her. 'I think she'll make a good Justice,' he concluded in his diary, an opinion also communicated to a sceptical William Buckley. A grateful O'Connor thanked him on behalf of all women, but this did not make her feel beholden to the Reagan Revolution as Supreme Court justice. A conservative stalwart on some issues, notably racial-preference cases, she was often the swing vote on judgements limiting the authority of the states to curtail abortion rights.[67]

Despite his 1980 campaign promises, Reagan did next to nothing about restoring tax exemptions for all-white Christian schools. Initially seeing the issue as one of religious freedom, he assured Representative Trent Lott of Mississippi that the White House would support Bob Jones University and Goldsboro Christian Schools in their current lawsuit against the Internal Revenue Service (IRS) – only to beat a hasty retreat when advised by aides that this meant siding with institutions practising segregation. Seeking a non-existent middle way, Reagan tried to extricate his administration from involvement in the court case by proposing a legislative solution that displeased both evangelical conservatives and civil-rights groups. The Supreme Court finally resolved the matter in an eight-to-one ruling in favour of the IRS in January 1983. By then, Reagan had caused the Christian Right further grief by giving only token support to measures proposed by Senator Jesse Helms of North Carolina to strengthen restrictions on abortions and strip the federal judiciary of the power to review state and local laws permitting prayer in public school, neither of which got anywhere in Congress.

Given this, it is remarkable that evangelical leaders remained so strongly supportive of Reagan. In 1986 Jerry Falwell would describe him as the 'finest president since Lincoln'.[68] In the more cynical assessment of some non-evangelical conservatives, Reagan had hoodwinked the Moral Majority leader and his brethren with symbolism rather than substance. A contrary case can be made that Reagan courted the Christian Right in a way that enhanced its legitimacy. Despite refusing to invest political capital in support of constitutional amendments to outlaw abortion and permit school prayer, he called on evangelicals to campaign for these measures on his behalf. This allowed their leaders to invoke presidential support when urging the faithful to put money into these causes. Reagan's drive to restore America's military power in its struggle with atheistic communism also won him kudos from this constituency. In essence, conservative evangelicals could take comfort that the nation's leader shared their vision of a Christian America opposed to godless forces, one that would in time become the Republican orthodoxy. Accordingly, their decision to back Reagan was shrewder than it initially appeared.

As 1984 dawned, the outlines of the conservative transformation that Reagan had brought about were becoming clear. His principal achievement was the biggest shake-up in federal taxation since the income tax had become a mass tax in World War II. As the coming presidential election campaign would reveal, a multi-class coalition had emerged in support of the ERTA personal-tax cuts.

Whatever they thought of Reagan, most Americans were henceforth unwilling to return to the old regime. Low personal taxes had become a fundamental element of the nation's political culture, locking Reagan's successors into perpetuation of his ideals on this score. Whether the tax changes of the 1980s also embedded unfairness in federal taxation is a matter of dispute. Viewed in one way, the progressivity of the tax structure did not change significantly over the course of Reagan's presidency. The most careful analysis based on Congressional Budget Office data suggests that the effective federal tax rate (the composite of all taxes) for every income quintile registered little change from 1980 to 1991. Nevertheless, the bottom three quintiles saw their tax burden rise somewhat because higher Social Security taxes cancelled out the income-tax cut gained from ERTA. Worst hit was the fourth quintile, populated by non-poor working families of modest means, whose obligations rose from 15.7 per cent to 16.7 per cent of total income in this period. The top two quintiles, in contrast, experienced small declines in their tax payment. The big winners were the top 1 per cent of families, whose tax burden fell from 31.8 per cent to 28.9 per cent of total income, a decline that translated into massive dollar savings for those with most wealth. This would contribute to rising income inequality in American society in the 1980s, a reversal of the prevailing trend since World War II.[69]

At first sight, Reagan enjoyed less success in dismantling the institutions of the liberal political order. The Social Security bill constituted a treaty of surrender to the entitlement state. Not only was this New Deal jewel now sacrosanct, so also were the Great Society pearls of Medicare and Medicaid. In other regards, however, the New Deal tradition, which prioritized the role of government in combatting unemployment, was very much in decline. The political economy of the 1980s was more concerned to ensure price stability even at the cost of recession and chronic unemployment. Federal Reserve monetarism had put the genie of inflation back in the bottle but the Aladdin's cave of prosperity was still shut to many. Unemployment did not fall to the 1980 level until 1986. Two-thirds of the manufacturing jobs lost in the recession never came back, helping to make the 1980s the first decade in American history when numbers employed in this sector declined.

This development was associated with broader structural changes in the national and international economies that had started in the 1970s and speeded up as the United States metamorphosed from being the world's largest creditor in 1980 into its largest debtor in 1985. The fiscal deficits were a key factor in this change of status that was a significant if unwanted element of the Reagan transformation. As budget dissaving eroded national savings – the seed corn for investment – America had to acquire capital from abroad to sustain economic growth. The Federal Reserve accommodated this need by keeping *real* interest rates (the actual rate minus the rate of inflation) high in the post-recession years. This drew in foreign capital like bees to a honeypot. Annual inflows began to exceed outflows, initially by $85 billion in 1983 and eventually by $226 billion in 1986. With demand for US assets pumping up the dollar's value (at one point in 1985, it equalled one British pound), the result was a large trade gap. The strong dollar sucked in cheap imports, creating a consumer boom in the mid-1980s, but damaged the competitiveness of US-made goods at home and abroad.[70] In the hope of getting Reagan to reduce the budget deficit, Arthur Burns, US ambassador to West Germany and a Nobel laureate in economics, communicated European concern that the massive imbalances were distorting the global economy. This elicited a blithe response: 'While I deplore the deficits and am determined to bring them down, I can't accept their view that the deficits are the cause of high interest rates.' Reagan failed to understand that his spend-and-borrow regime weakened the manufacturing sector and strengthened the financial sector. The effects of high real interest rates were another important factor in the rising income inequality evident in the 1980s because they penalized blue-collar industrial workers while benefiting the holders of capital.[71]

As the Reagan presidency approached its halfway point, it seemingly had the potential to build further on the solid conservative foundations of its first-term domestic success. The 1984 State of the Union Address was quite different in tone to its 1983 predecessor. 'America is back,' the president declared, 'standing tall, looking to the eighties with courage, confidence and hope.'[72] Like many of his predecessors, Reagan would discover that his second term would not go as well as the first in advancing his domestic agenda. There were limits to what pragmatic conservatism could achieve and most Americans were uninterested in moving further to the right.

NINE

Cold Warrior

Once his economic programme was in place, Ronald Reagan's next task was to reverse the ascendancy that the Soviet Union had established in the Cold War under cover of détente. In the words of National Security Advisor (NSA) Richard Allen, he set out to confront America's adversary 'intentionally, deliberately, and in slow motion'.[1] In essence, Reagan looked to rebuild US military and economic power, contest the Soviet Union around the globe, and increase pressure on it at home. As a consequence the Cold War heated up to danger point in the early 1980s. The godfather of containment doctrine, George Kennan, lamented that America appeared 'in a state of [...] undeclared war pursued in anticipation of an outright one now regarded as inevitable'.[2] Nevertheless, there was a fourth element in Reagan's Cold War strategy that was little understood at the time. His ultimate goal was to negotiate from a position of strength in order to reduce both US and Soviet nuclear arsenals. Once America had demonstrated capacity to out-build the Soviets in nuclear forces, Reagan told the Vatican secretary of state in late 1981, 'we could invite [them] [...] to join us in lowering the level of weapons on both sides'.[3]

In essence, Reagan envisioned his Cold War strategy as assisting in the historically inevitable process of communism's eventual collapse. In a speech at the University of Notre Dame in May 1981, he declared: 'The West won't contain communism, it will transcend communism [...] It will dismiss it as some bizarre chapter in human history whose last pages are even now being written.'[4]

1 The Reagans – Jack, Nelle, Neil and 'Dutch', 1915.

2 16-year-old 'Dutch' Reagan as a lifeguard in Lowell Park, Dixon, Illinois.

3 Ronald Reagan as a WHO Radio Announcer in Des Moines, Iowa.

4 Reagan as 'the Gipper' in his breakthrough movie for Warner Bros., *Knute Rockne, All American*, 1940.

5   Ronald Reagan and Jane Wyman on their wedding day, 26 January 1940.

6   Ronald Reagan as a P-40 aeroplane pilot in the Army Air Forces training film *Identification of a Japanese Zero*, 1943.

7 Ronald Reagan testifying as Screen Actors Guild president before the House Un-American Activities Committee hearings in Washington DC, 25 October 1947.

8 Ronald and Nancy Reagan cutting their wedding cake, 4 March 1952.

9 Publicity still for Reagan's new role as host of the General Electric Theater television drama series, 1954.

10 Ronald Reagan visiting a General Electric plant in Danville, Illinois, October 1955.

11 Ronald Reagan giving a speech for Barry Goldwater (standing on left) in the 1964 presidential campaign.

12 Ronald and Nancy Reagan at the victory celebration for California governor at the Biltmore Hotel in Los Angeles, 8 November 1966.

13 The Reagan family in 1976. Left to right: Patti, Nancy, Reagan, Michael, Maureen, Ron (and Pogo the dog).

14 At ease: iconic photograph of cowboy-hatted Reagan at Rancho del Cielo, 1976.

15 Reagan giving his acceptance speech at the Republican
National Convention, Detroit, 17 July 1980.

16 Reagan being sworn in on Inauguration Day, US Capitol, 20 January 1981.

17   Chaos outside the Washington Hilton Hotel after the assassination attempt on President Reagan. James Brady and police officer Thomas Delahanty lie wounded on the ground, 30 March 1981.

18   Reagan signs the Economic Recovery Tax Act and Omnibus Budget Reconciliation Act at a misty Rancho del Cielo, 13 August 1981.

19   Reagan meeting with (left to right) David Gergen, Alexander
Haig, Richard Allen, and James Baker to discuss the Senate vote on the
proposed sale of AWACS to Saudi Arabia, Oval Office, 28 October 1981.

20   The president (before he nodded off) and Nancy Reagan
with Pope John Paul II at Vatican City, 7 June 1982.

21   President Reagan and Queen Elizabeth II horseback
riding at Windsor Castle, United Kingdom, 8 June 1982.

22   Holding hands: President Reagan greeting British prime minister
Margaret Thatcher for a bilateral meeting at Schloss Gymnich
in Bonn, Federal Republic of Germany, 5 Febuary 1985.

23 Tragedy: the president and first lady attend a memorial service for Marines killed in Lebanon, 4 November 1983.

24 Triumph: President Reagan speaking at a White House ceremony for medical students from St George's School of Medicine in Grenada, 7 November 1983.

25 The Reagans and Rock Hudson at a White House dinner,
15 May 1984; the movie star's death on 2 October 1985
alerted Americans to the reality of the Aids epidemic.

26 Reagan and Gorbachev's boat-house meeting at
the Geneva Summit, 19 November 1985.

27 So near, yet so far: the faces of disappointment at the
end of the Reykjavik Summit, 12 October 1986.

28 The Red Square
walkabout where the
'evil empire' was laid
to rest, 31 May 1988.

29   Reagan with (left to right) Caspar Weinberger, George Shultz, Ed Meese and Don Regan discussing his press-conference remarks on the Iran–Contra affair, Oval Office, 25 November 1986.

30   The last day as president, 20 January 1989.

31   Nancy Reagan's farewell to her husband just prior to his interment in a vault in the Ronald Reagan Presidential Library grounds, 11 June 2004.

This was also the central theme of the address to the joint session of the UK Parliament at the Palace of Westminster a year later. The Soviet Union, Reagan proclaimed, could not resist 'the march of freedom and democracy which will leave Marxism–Leninism on the ash heap of history'. The triumph of the West was assured because the Cold War was ultimately 'a test of wills and ideas – a trial of spiritual resolve'. During the drafting stage, chief of staff (CoS) James Baker and secretary of state Alexander Haig objected that the content would likely make the Kremlin less open to negotiation. However, Reagan approved conservative speechwriter Anthony Dolan's text, adding several paragraphs of his own in support of its theme. In his view American leaders had too long worried that critiquing 'the empty cupboard' of communist ideology would offend Moscow.[5]

Anticipation that communism would collapse under its own contradictions made Reagan anxious to avoid armed confrontation with the Soviet Union. This was evident in the most important statement of his administration's Cold War goals, National Security Decision Directive (NSDD)-75: 'US relations with the USSR'. Issued in early 1983, it was one of over 120 directives formulated during William Clark's tenure as NSA to convert Reagan's vision into strategy. If there was a 'Reagan Doctrine', a term coined by neoconservative Charles Krauthammer but only ever used once by the president (in remarks at the National Defense University in October 1988), NSDD-75 was its embodiment.[6] The work of a team led by Richard Pipes, head of the National Security Council (NSC) Soviet desk, it opened with the blunt avowal:

> US policy towards the Soviet Union will consist of three elements: external resistance to Soviet imperialism; internal pressure on the USSR to weaken the sources of Soviet imperialism; and negotiations to eliminate, on the basis of strict reciprocity, outstanding disagreements.

Tough but not shrill in tenor, NSDD-75 assumed the need to sustain this strategy over time because a speedy breakthrough in bilateral relations was unlikely. Despite this, it concluded on an optimistic note that administration strategy was not 'a blueprint for open-ended, sterile confrontation with Moscow, but a serious search for a stable and constructive long-term basis for US–Soviet relations'.[7]

The rationale of NSDD-75 confirmed rather than inspired Reagan's approach to the Cold War. He had already fired the opening salvos in employing a brand of anti-Soviet rhetoric not heard from an American president since the early years of the conflict. In his very first press conference, he declared that Soviet leaders were committed to the goal of world revolution, so 'the only morality they recognize is what will further their cause, meaning they reserve unto themselves the right to commit any crime, to lie, to cheat'. Meeting immediately afterwards with Alexander Haig, Soviet ambassador Anatoly Dobrynin, a diplomat accustomed to special treatment in his 20-year service in Washington DC, carped: 'What is the use of all that? Why should he set such a tone for the new administration from the very beginning?' Haig had no comfort to offer. His own message to the Soviets urged realism and restraint because US foreign policy 'has fundamentally and durably changed'.[8]

As well as engaging in a war of words with the Kremlin, Reagan authorized substantive efforts to halt the spread of Soviet influence in the Americas, Africa, and Asia. CIA boss William Casey was his enthusiastic chief lieutenant in the implementation of this strategy. As deputy director Robert Gates recalled:

> Push. Push. Push. Casey never stopped coming up with ideas – or forwarding those of others – for waging war against the Soviets more broadly, more aggressively, and more effectively. From New Caledonia to Suriname, from Afghanistan to Nicaragua, from the Sahara to Cambodia, no report of Soviet, Cuban, Libyan, or Vietnamese activity – no matter how insignificant – escaped his notice and his demands that CIA counter it.[9]

With the CIA doing the heavy – often dirty – work, Reagan employed the language of liberty to glorify the means and ends of its anti-communist operations. Opponents of Soviet acolytes were 'freedom fighters' whom America had a duty to arm, fund, and – if need be – train. This, he told the Irish Dáil in 1984, was a 'forward strategy for freedom' based on understanding that the free world's struggle with communism was 'a test of faith and spirit'.[10]

Such clear-eyed vision blinded Reagan to the reality that some of America's allies in the battle against communism were perpetrators of a different evil. Convinced that Marxist revolution could only advance in the developing world through Soviet support, he failed to understand that indigenous poverty and oppression were its most potent recruiting sergeants. At the very first meeting of his NSC, Reagan expressed determination to support any anti-communist regime, however authoritarian, in marked contrast to his predecessor. 'We must change the attitude of our diplomatic corps so that we don't bring down governments in the name of human rights,' he declared.

> None of them is as guilty of human rights violations as are Cuba and the USSR. We don't throw out our friends just because they can't pass the 'saliva test' on human rights. I want to see that stopped.[11]

The first test of the new approach was in El Salvador, where a civilian–military junta with an appalling record of mass atrocities was in danger of being overthrown by leftist rebels. Reagan was determined to draw a line in the sand in this tiny republic lest Marxist revolution spread out from Central America into the rest of Latin America. As validation of this scenario, he often quoted Lenin's supposed dictum, 'Once we have Latin America, we won't have to take the United States, the last bastion of capitalism, because it will fall into our outstretched hands like overripe fruit.' As a diligent journalist would discover, the source of the Russian revolutionary's alleged words was actually *The Blue Book of the John Birch Society*, compiled by organization founder Robert Welch in 1958. Reagan must have internalized it as gospel during his earlier flirtation with the radical right. Exposure of the Lenin quotation as a canard did not prevent him from repeatedly citing it as proof 'of the stakes we are talking about today'.[12] America's president was incapable of grasping that what was really happening in Latin America was a struggle between insurgent movements representing the impoverished majority and the economic elites who controlled landownership with the support of military regimes, which had seized power all over the continent in the 1960s and 1970s. Nowhere was this more evident than in Central America, where the number of landless peasants had tripled in these decades.[13]

One of the first memos to cross Reagan's Oval Office desk warned, 'Cuba is orchestrating and channeling the arms flow [to El Salvador] and Nicaragua serves as the principal forward staging area.'[14] His determination to stem the cross-border supply would eventually embroil him in an illegal effort to destroy the pro-Soviet Sandinista regime that had come to power in Nicaragua following overthrow of Anastasio Somoza's dictatorship in 1979. More immediately, the new administration propped up the Salvadoran regime with a massive infusion of military aid amounting to $744 million in three years. In 1984 the spigot was turned full on after Christian Democrat José Napoleón Duarte became El Salvador's first freely elected civilian leader in more than 50 years to total $3.5 billion from 1981 until 1991. During this period, however, some 75,000 Salvadorans were killed by massacres, summary executions, landmines, and indiscriminate bombing. A United Nations Commission later documented 22,000 atrocities, attributing 85 per cent of them to the military and its death squads.[15] One of the worst instances was the massacre of several hundred civilians by a US-trained army battalion in Morazán province in late 1981. Contradicting well-documented investigation by American journalists, the Reagan administration consistently denied reports of deliberate slaughter. In remarks that belied reality, the president informed Congress, 'The Salvadoran battalions that have received US training have been conducting themselves well on the battlefield and with the civilian population.'[16] The outcome of his policy was that El Salvador did not fall to Marxism but the cost in innocent blood besmirched any American claim to stand for freedom in that country.

The first direct use of American force that Reagan authorized as commander-in-chief struck at Libyan leader Colonel Muammar al-Gaddafi. The CIA considered this serial purchaser of Soviet weaponry an integral member of a 'Soviet–Libya–Cuban axis' in Africa. William Casey, in particular, suspected him of ambition to threaten Western oil-supply routes by hooking up with Marxist regimes in Ethiopia and South Yemen to destabilize Sudan, Somalia, and Oman, but no conclusive evidence of such a grand strategy was ever discovered. Although Gaddafi preened himself as an Arab hero standing up to the United States, Robert Gates more accurately depicted him as a 'burr under the saddle'. His outlandish claims that Libya's territorial waters extended far beyond the conventional 12-mile limit brought him into direct confrontation with US determination to defend freedom of the seas. The Sixth Fleet was despatched to conduct exercises in the Gulf of Sidra, well inside Gaddafi's so-called 'line of death'. On 20 August 1981, two F-14s engaged in these manoeuvres 60 miles off the coast came under fire from two Libyan planes. In compliance with presidential orders that any aircraft harassing US forces were to be pursued '[a]ll the way into the hangar' if necessary, the American pilots shot down both attackers. Reagan took satisfaction in having sent out the message 'that there was new management in the White House, and that the United States wasn't going to hesitate any longer to act when its legitimate interests were at stake'.[17]

Another episode pertaining to the Arab world had greater Cold War relevance. In March 1981, Reagan approved the largest foreign arms sale in American history to strengthen Saudi Arabia as a bulwark against Soviet advance in the Middle East through surrogates like Syria, draw it away from the Arab coalition against Israel, and safeguard it from the spread of Islamic militancy. In showing even-handedness towards an Arab nation, his ultimate hope was to position the United States as an honest broker for a peace settlement that would guarantee Israel's survival, bring stability to the Middle East, and thwart Soviet efforts to exploit regional divisions.[18] The inclusion of five advanced Airborne Warning and Control System (AWACS) aeroplanes in the agreement proved highly controversial. Vociferous protests by Israel that these would neutralize its air-strike capacity galvanized bipartisan supporters in Congress to oppose the sale. Prime minister Menachem Begin then engaged in personal lobbying on Capitol Hill while on a state visit to Washington – something he had promised Reagan he would not do. In a public expression of displeasure, the president told reporters, 'It is not the business of other nations to make American foreign policy.'[19] Congressional rejection of the AWACS sale, he informed Billy Graham, 'will set us back almost irretrievably in our Middle East peacemaking effort'. An intensive White House counter-lobby did just enough to prevent the Senate joining the House in prohibiting the sale. Believing this 'a battle that *had* to be won', Reagan was actively involved in swaying more than 20 undecided or leaning-against senators to back the sale. With the exception of the 1981 tax and budget bills, he spent more time winning this vote than any other during his entire presidency.[20]

The AWACS sale would do little to facilitate Middle Eastern peacemaking, but it had significant benefits in another regard. As Caspar Weinberger later remarked, 'One reason we were selling the Saudis all those arms was to get lower oil prices.' In 1985, just before delivery of the first AWACS aircraft, Saudi Arabia raised its daily oil output from fewer than 2 million barrels to nearly 9 million, with the consequence that world oil prices dropped from $30 to $12 a barrel. Lower energy costs benefited Western economies, but the oil-exporting Soviet Union lost anywhere between $500 million and $1 billion in hard currency for every $1 of this decline. Given Soviet dependence on oil profits to purchase Western technology, the damage inflicted on its economy was severe.[21]

Meanwhile, the Reagan administration continued Jimmy Carter's strategy of slow-bleeding the Soviet army occupying Afghanistan through provision of military aid for indigenous rebels. It came under pressure from a bipartisan congressional group to ratchet up assistance for the lightly armed Mujahideen fighters taking on the 120,000-strong Fortieth Army equipped with heavy armour and helicopter gunships. For the time being CIA and Pentagon reluctance to supply sophisticated equipment to untrained guerrillas prevented them getting weapons that could truly damage the Soviets. Instead the administration took steps to ensure that Pakistan remained the conduit for US assistance getting to the insurgents. In late 1981 General Muhammad Zia ul-Haq's military regime received a six-year $3.2 billion package of economic aid and military credits, including 40 F-16 fighter planes. Although Zia would never permit free elections in his country, he was now a fellow 'freedom fighter' in Reagan's eyes, one to be celebrated, not criticized. The two met when the Pakistani leader made a state visit to Washington in late 1981. 'We got along fine,' Reagan recorded in his diary. 'He's a good man (cavalry).' Zia also sold him a big lie: 'Gave me his word they were not building an atomic or nuclear bomb.'[22]

As 1981 drew to an end, Reagan was no longer satisfied with merely challenging the Soviets on the periphery. The crackdown on Solidarity, the Polish movement that was part trade union and part indigenous anti-communist protest, precipitated an effort both to weaken the Soviet Union's control of an Eastern bloc country and damage its economy at home. Fearful that growing popular support for democratic reforms would provoke Soviet invasion, as had befallen Hungary in 1956 and Czechoslovakia in 1968, the Warsaw government took pre-emptive action by imposing martial law and interning dissident leaders on 12–13 December 1981. The NSC convened almost daily from 19 to 23 December to discuss the situation in what Richard Pipes called 'an emotionally charged atmosphere inspired largely by Reagan's mounting fury'. These meetings produced agreement to impose economic sanctions on Poland and the Soviet Union if martial law was not lifted within a week. Reagan deemed the crisis a test of America's commitment to act on behalf of freedom. 'We are the leaders of the Western world,' he told the NSC on 21 December. 'We haven't been for years, several years, except in name, but we accept that role now.' That evening, he wrote in his diary, 'I took a stand that this may be the last chance in our lifetime to see a change in the Soviet Empire's colonial policy re. Eastern Europe.'[23]

The impasse over Poland brought about the greatest US–Soviet dispute over European issues since the Berlin crisis in 1961. On 23 December Reagan sent a personal letter warning Soviet leader Leonid Brezhnev that America could not accept 'the pressures and threats which your government has exerted on Poland to stifle the stirrings of freedom'. In reply, Brezhnev accused him of putting 'your personal signature upon the fact that gross interference in the internal affairs of Poland is the official policy of the United States'. A further charge held the president personally responsible for American officials 'uninterruptedly reviling our [Soviet] social and political system, our internal order'.[24] Four days after receiving this, Reagan officially announced that the United States would impose a series of economic sanctions against Poland and the Soviet Union.

Events in Poland convinced Reagan of 'how tenuous was the Soviet hold on the people in its empire'. Accordingly, the economic sanctions on Poland were entwined with an effort to sustain Solidarity as a pro-democracy underground movement. Reagan's comrade-in-arms in this cause was Pope John Paul II, Poland's spiritual leader *in absentia*.[25] At their Vatican meeting on 7 June 1982, Reagan secured papal support for a US plan to smuggle in computers, photo-copiers, printing presses, telephones, and other equipment needed to keep Solidarity alive. Although not engaged in this covert operation, the Vatican pro-vided important intelligence on its impact.[26] In time, the overt sanctions–covert supply strategy achieved Reagan's end. In early 1987 the economic sanctions were lifted after the Warsaw regime agreed to free political prisoners, restore Solidarity's legality, and enter talks with the Catholic Church.

The far stronger sanctions imposed on the Soviet Union launched the eco-nomic warfare campaign that Reagan would wage against it. Convinced that the Soviet economy was fundamentally weak, he wanted to squeeze it till the pips squeaked. The initial target was the 3,600-mile, twin-stranded Yamal pipeline, which was under construction to relay natural gas from Siberia for hook-up into Western Europe's energy system. On completion, it was expected to earn the Soviets $10–12 billion annually in hard-currency funding for military and technology purchases. To Reagan's dismay, a number of Western European gov-ernments – with France in the lead – extended massive credits at low interest for a project seen as a source of jobs and cheap energy for their citizens. 'If the free world had not helped them [the Soviets] and had let their system deteriorate,' he told the NSC, 'we wouldn't have the problems we have today.' The discovery that the Soviets simply purloined the blueprints of the Western technology they could not buy was the final straw. The so-called 'Farewell Dossier', obtained by French intelligence from a mole in the KGB's Technology Directorate and passed on to the CIA, detailed the scale of its industrial espionage against America and other nations. It also revealed that oil and gas technology for the Siberian pipeline topped the KGB's 'must have' list for current operations.[27]

The Soviet sanctions included an embargo on the kind of high-tech products needed for the Yamal project. This aroused a domestic furore because it cost recession-hit American businesses like General Electric and Caterpillar multi-million-dollar contracts. Unwilling to lose jobs amid even harder times across the Atlantic, Western European governments were loath to follow the American lead. Margaret Thatcher, in particular, worried that the issue could undermine the Western alliance. When informed of European leaders' concerns, Reagan had contemptuously dismissed them as 'chicken little's' [*sic*] and bullishly insisted that 'we should let our allies know they too will pay the price if they don't go along'.[28] Nevertheless, he was sufficiently worried about Thatcher's opposition to send Alexander Haig for talks in Downing Street, where the secretary of state got an earbashing from the Iron Lady. When she had calmed down, Thatcher wrote to Reagan suggesting that the NATO allies hold talks to discuss a common way forward, but it required prolonged negotiations to agree this.[29]

As a first step, Reagan would have accepted European agreement to scale back credits, something he pressed for in vain at the G7 meeting in Paris in June 1982. Venting his spleen to the NSC on his return, he avowed that it was time to show enemies and allies alike that America was not 'all rhetoric and no action'. Immediately after the meeting, the White House announced that sanctions would be extended to include equipment produced abroad either by foreign subsidiaries of US companies or under licence to US companies.[30]

A bitterly disappointed Thatcher characterized the episode as 'a lesson in how not to conduct alliance business'.[31] The prime minister made a last appeal to Reagan in the hope of preventing huge job losses at Glasgow's John Brown engineering firm that stood to lose $300 million of business. This only elicited a tough presidential response:

I want you to understand that it is my conviction that what is happening in Poland is not only a human tragedy but an historic test of our will and ability to make the Soviets pay a high cost – if possible a prohibitive cost – for their subjugation of half of Europe. We in the West face no more compelling problem.[32]

The subtext of this communication was clear – Reagan's notion of the so-called special relationship did not extend to accommodating Thatcher's preferences when they conflicted with his. He was the lead actor and she was just one of the supporting players, albeit an important one, in the Western-alliance cast list.

With Western European governments sustaining a common front, American pipeline sanctions could never be effective on their own. Under a compromise negotiated by George Shultz in late 1982, the United States allowed existing contracts to go ahead in return for NATO allies reining in trade and financial subsidies that benefited the Soviets. The Yamal project consequently went ahead, but American opposition delayed its completion by more than a year and restricted it to a single strand. A CIA dirty-tricks campaign had supplemented the embargo in wasting Soviet time and money. Armed with Farewell's exposé of the secret agents involved in technology espionage, the agency arranged for them to be supplied with faulty equipment and misinformation that damaged military and civil projects. Its most spectacular coup was the massive explosion of almost nuclear proportions in Siberia in June 1982 triggered by defective software in computers operating the pipeline.[33]

The fractiousness that characterized the supposedly special relationship between the US president and UK prime minister over economic sanctions was further evident in their disagreements over the Falklands War. A conflict between two allies was the last thing that Reagan wanted because it forced him to choose between Atlanticist and hemispheric interests. Although Britain was America's closest ally in NATO, Argentina was one of the most important nations in Latin America, which was second only to Europe in significance as a Cold War battleground for Reagan. Its reliably anti-communist military dictatorship was cooperating with the CIA to train anti-Sandinista fighters in readiness for counter-revolution in Nicaragua. This was one reason why the Reagan administration turned a blind eye to the junta's dirty war against domestic opponents, which resulted in the death or disappearance of some

13,000 people between its coming to power in 1976 and ouster in 1983. This reign of terror was still insufficient to suppress popular resentment of the economic troubles that engulfed Argentina in the early 1980s. Hoping that an upsurge of nationalism would come to the regime's assistance, junta leader General Leopoldo Galtieri despatched an invasion force to end the long-disputed British dominion of the Falklands Islands and establish Argentinian sovereignty over Las Malvinas. Within a week of its departure for the unguarded territory, Argentina's flag flew above what had been Government House in Port Stanley on 2 April 1982. By then Thatcher had taken the momentous decision to send a naval task force to retake the 8,000-mile-distant islands in order to redress a national humiliation, demonstrate that British power was not in irretrievable decline, and preserve her premiership.

While the task force was being prepared, Thatcher asked Reagan to intercede with Argentina, but his pleas for restraint in an excruciating 50-minute phone call with Galtieri got him nowhere. The president consequently assured the prime minister, 'While we have a policy of neutrality on the sovereignty issue, we will not be neutral on the issue involving Argentine use of force.'[34] What the White House really wanted, however, was a negotiated settlement that would require some compromise on Britain's part. To this end, it sent Alexander Haig on an exhausting, ultimately futile, two-week tour of shuttle negotiations between London, Buenos Aires, and Washington. The president was utterly bemused that Britain could go to war over what he publicly called a 'little ice-cold bunch of land down there'.[35] Some of his public statements even hinted at sympathy for the Argentinians in order to prevent Latin American nations seeing the United States as Britain's crony in the dispute. A message to the Organization of American States on 2 May asserted that 'no American believes that colonisation by any European power is to be accepted in this hemisphere'. Thatcher made clear her anger at these words when hosting the American ambassador to lunch at Chequers the following weekend.[36]

Jeane Kirkpatrick, the pro-Argentinian voice of hemispheric solidarity within the administration, later commented, 'There wasn't any question about where the president stood on this issue, from start to finish.'[37] Nevertheless, Reagan was not the unflinchingly firm ally of Britain that she imagined. When his even-handed shuttle diplomacy got nowhere, Haig put pressure on Thatcher to make lopsided concessions in line with presidential wishes for a settlement.

Fortunately for the prime minister, Galtieri's intransigence came to her rescue. When the junta rejected Haig's final peace plan, which a divided British Cabinet might have forced her to accept, she informed Reagan 'how deeply let down' she would feel if America now failed to 'be seen to be unequivocally on the same side, staunchly upholding those values on which the Western way of life depends'. With hostilities inevitable, the president came off the fence in Britain's favour, but his letter informing Thatcher of this contained a significant qualification that a negotiated settlement would eventually be necessary: 'While it may be possible to forcibly remove Argentine forces,' he warned, 'the future will be fraught with instability, animosity, and insecurity if a mutually acceptable framework for peace is not ultimately found.'[38]

The Reagan administration provided the British with critical intelligence assistance and material support, including the all-important Sidewinder air-to-air missiles, but it never abandoned hope of promoting a settlement that balanced its transatlantic and hemispheric Cold War interests. The sinking of the Argentinian aircraft carrier *Belgrano* on 2 May and of the British destroyer HMS *Sheffield* two days later prompted another effort to mediate. 'We are in a situation,' a memorandum penned by two NSC aides remarked, 'where only an act of sanity may now save not only the belligerents themselves from further loss, but larger US interests as well.' On William Clark's advice, Reagan sent Thatcher a personal appeal to disengage from hostilities, but this only elicited an uncompromising response. A presidential follow-up with personal telephone diplomacy simply provoked a prime ministerial tirade that fundamental issues of self-determination and freedom for the Falkland Islanders were at stake.[39]

Undeterred, Reagan tried again on 31 May just before British forces began their final assault on Port Stanley. A bloody battle with massive Argentinian casualties, the American ambassador in Buenos Aires had warned, 'would produce grave consequences for US interests here and elsewhere in Latin America'. In a conversation Thatcher later described in uncharacteristically understated fashion as having been 'a little painful', she was sharp to the point of rudeness in response to presidential pleas for a settlement. Almost immediately as the call ended, Al Haig was on the line to Sir Nicholas Henderson, the British ambassador in Washington, to reassert more forcefully his boss's message: 'You must help the Argentinians to find a way out, short of total humiliation.'[40]

The surrender of the Argentinian garrison at Port Stanley on 14 June brought the Falklands conflict to its end but did not renew harmony between the White House and 10 Downing Street. On 18 June, Reagan sent a congratulatory message with qualifying remarks that a just peace 'in my judgement must include enhancement of the long-term security of the South Atlantic, mitigation of Argentine hostility and improvement in the relations of both our countries with Latin America'.[41] Some months later, White House support for Argentina's draft resolution to the United Nations calling for a negotiated settlement of the sovereignty issue further angered Thatcher as a ploy to gain by diplomacy what arms had failed to achieve. Visiting her in London, George Shultz was the proxy recipient of a dressing-down aimed at Reagan. This harangue failed to intimidate either the new secretary of state or its intended target. When Shultz reported to the president, 'I found that he, too, was getting a little fed up with her imperious attitude.'[42]

The trials and tribulations of Reagan's first two years in office were as nothing to those of 1983, however, when the world came closer to nuclear catastrophe than at any time since the Cuban Missile Crisis of 1962. Since 1947, the *Bulletin of the Atomic Scientists* had displayed on its cover the so-called 'Doomsday Clock' that symbolically measured mankind's proximity to nuclear destruction. Standing at seven minutes to midnight on the eve of Reagan's election, it was adjusted to a mere three minutes at the end of crisis-ridden 1983. In addition to a war scare, this year of living dangerously featured: the greatest crisis of unity in NATO's history; a Reagan speech that raised Soviet hackles more than any other; a presidential proposal that undermined the principle of nuclear deterrence conventionally thought to underpin world peace; and nearly simultaneous disaster and triumph continents apart for American arms.

The NATO crisis had its roots in alliance approval in late 1979 of a 'dual-track' response to Soviet deployment two years earlier of three-warhead SS-20 intermediate ballistic missiles targeted at Western Europe. This required US counter-deployment of new Pershing II ballistic missiles and ground-launched cruise missiles in 1983 (first to West Germany, the UK, and Italy, then to Belgium and the Netherlands) and simultaneous efforts to negotiate mutual limitations of intermediate nuclear forces with Moscow. Honouring Jimmy Carter's commitment to dual track, the Reagan administration reached agreement with the

Soviets to begin arms-control talks in Geneva in November 1981. However, the president's loose public remarks implying the possibility of a limited nuclear exchange in Europe, in association with similar comments by other administration officials, sparked a transatlantic furore.[43] The European peace movement, which had steadily gained in strength since Reagan's election, now organized massive protests against the Euromissiles in the capital cities of countries where they would be deployed. With West Germany in the forefront of this popular ferment, an embattled Helmut Schmidt renounced the dual-track approach that was largely the product of his personal advocacy to recommend instead a 'zero-zero' approach whereby the Soviets would dismantle their SS-20s in return for US agreement not to deploy Pershing and cruise missiles.

In fact 'zero-zero' was already under White House consideration. Initially conceived by Pentagon aide Richard Perle, it encountered Alexander Haig's opposition on grounds that the Soviets would never agree to being the only ones required actually to dismantle missiles. Seeing an opportunity to reassure popular opinion at home and abroad, Reagan supported zero-zero's adoption at the NSC meeting on 12 November. 'Al, we're not issuing an ultimatum [...] we're negotiating for as long as it takes in good faith,' he reassured Haig.[44] Six days later Reagan made the announcement in a televised address, supplementing it with proposals for talks to limit conventional forces in Europe, guard against accidental nuclear war, and reduce strategic arsenals. Broadcast at 10 a.m. Washington time, this was the first presidential speech beamed live by satellite to Europe, where it was seen by an estimated 200 million people in 16 countries. The Soviets predictably dismissed zero-zero out of hand as 'a formula for unilateral disarmament by our side and, frankly, an insult to our intelligence'.[45] For Reagan, however, this was just the first move towards eliminating the threat of nuclear war. Shortly afterwards, he received a letter from the Pope urging him to do everything possible to prevent superpower tensions escalating into a confrontation that would destroy humanity. The presidential response was unequivocal: 'I fully share your horror at the disastrous consequences of nuclear conflict, the "last epidemic of mankind." I am determined to prevent such a catastrophe.'[46]

In the wake of the Kremlin's rejection of zero-zero, Reagan's insistence on going ahead with the deployment of the so-called Euromissiles made him the target of peace campaigners' moral indignation. In June 1982 the newly established Nuclear Freeze movement staged a rally in New York's Central Park attended by 750,000 people, making it a far larger protest than any during the Vietnam War. Its political clout was reflected in the Democrat-controlled House of Representatives approving a freeze resolution by 278 to 149 votes in May 1983, but there was no chance of the Republican-controlled Senate following suit. Despite presidential insistence that a freeze would simply lock in current Soviet superiority, increasing numbers of Americans now considered the arms race more dangerous than the communist threat – and, opinion polls showed, a majority of them worried that Reagan might start a nuclear war. The Western European public appeared even more convinced of this. Political consensus on Cold War security broke down across the Atlantic when the Labour Party and the Social Democrats ran on anti-Euromissile platforms in the respective British and West German elections of 1983. If the ballots went in favour of either, there was a danger of NATO defence strategy falling apart. Whatever their earlier differences, Reagan's relief at Thatcher's landslide victory on 9 June was palpable – in the first of three letters of congratulation he called it a 'positive shot in the arm to the Western Alliance'.[47] There was further good news with the success of Helmut Kohl's Christian Democrats in West German elections in October. The United States was consequently able to begin Euromissile deployment on 23 November 1983. Although the Soviets withdrew in protest from the Geneva arms-reduction talks just days later, Reagan believed this was nothing more than temporary posturing in the face of NATO solidarity. 'They'd left the ballpark,' he later commented, 'but I didn't think the game was over. We had just changed the rules of the game. And they didn't like it.'[48]

As the Euromissile pot was coming to the boil, the most famous speech of Reagan's entire presidency ratcheted up Soviet–American animosity. Anthony Dolan's draft of the address to the National Association of Evangelicals to be delivered at Orlando, Florida, on 8 March 1983 encountered State Department and White House staff opposition for being too provocative, but Reagan's heavy editing made it even tougher. The primary theme urging faith-based morality rather than secularism in public policy mainly pertained to domestic issues, notably the evils of abortion. In the final section, Reagan turned his attention to how Marxist–Leninist subordination of morality to totalitarian ideology underlay the 'aggressive impulses of an evil empire'. Rubbishing the notion of superpower moral equivalency, the president reasserted his conviction that the Cold War was a spiritual struggle 'between right and wrong and good and evil'. The further condemnation of the Soviet Union as 'the focus of evil in the modern world' took aim at the Kremlin's intent of communist world domination.[49]

New Soviet leader Yuri Andropov immediately denounced the address as proof that Reagan 'can think only in terms of confrontation and bellicose, lunatic anticommunism', remarks echoed by the official Soviet media in the following days.[50] Worried by this reaction, liberal opinion at home accused the president of 'simplistic theology' at best and invoking 'holy war' at worst. The Western European left was even more dismissive. Helmut Schmidt lamented that the speech had undermined 20 years of patient negotiation. Told of this, an unrepentant Reagan remarked that diplomacy had only facilitated the expansion of Soviet power to levels that threatened the West.[51]

The furore obscured Reagan's two purposes in making the speech. In the face of growing support for a nuclear freeze, he was effectively calling for a moral rearmament against communism, a plea that had little effect on public opinion. The speech was more successful if interpreted in relation to what he had earlier told an American citizen living in Europe: 'We are determined to *stop* losing the propaganda war.' The 'evil empire' address was made with 'malice aforethought' to let Kremlin chiefs know that 'I understood their system and what it stood for'. Soviet leaders had long employed much stronger rhetoric in denouncing their American counterparts as 'imperialists' and 'warmongers'. Reagan himself had been singled out for worst epithets, including Andropov's likening him to Hitler. Speaking back in kind challenged communist claims to moral superiority and hit a nerve in the Russian psyche. Following several visits to Moscow in 1983–4, Sovietologist Selwyn Bialer reported that Reagan's 'reduction of Soviet achievements to crimes by international outlaws from an "evil empire"' had damaged the collective self-esteem of the city's political elites.[52]

A fortnight after being attacked with words, the Soviet leadership had something much more substantive to worry about. To understand Reagan's surprise announcement of the Strategic Defense Initiative (SDI) in a television address to the nation on 23 March, it is necessary to review the controversy over deployment of the highly accurate ten-warhead long-range MX missiles, a project initially approved by the Carter administration to replace the ageing Minuteman missiles. At issue was the development of a basing system that would enable these weapons to survive a Soviet first strike. In a nationwide address in November 1982, Reagan insisted that MX was 'the right missile at the right time,' whose emplacement would show the Soviets that 'we are now serious about our own strategic programs.' Though happy to trade what he dubbed the 'peacemaker missile' in an eventual arms-control agreement, such a deal depended in his calculation on the MX being built and deployed.[53] To his dismay, congressional concerns about the viability of the 'dense pack' plan to locate all the MX silos at Warren Air Force base, near Cheyenne, Wyoming, delayed their emplacement for four years and limited missile numbers to 50, half what the administration originally planned.

The MX controversy confirmed Reagan's doubts about the 'mutually assured destruction' doctrine that was the basis of American strategic planning. If domestic politics obstructed nuclear expansion, he feared that the United States would become increasingly vulnerable to Soviet attack. This concern underwrote his support for the SDI programme to investigate the feasibility of developing a space-based defensive system that could intercept and destroy strategic ballistic missiles. Reagan acknowledged that the project might not be accomplished before the end of the twentieth century because of its formidable technical challenges. Nevertheless, he called on America's scientists, 'those who gave us nuclear weapons, to turn their great talents now to the cause of mankind and world peace, to give us a means of rendering these nuclear weapons impotent and obsolete'.[54]

Deriding SDI as a science-fiction fantasy, Democratic critics dubbed it 'Star Wars' after George Lucas' massively popular 1977 movie – a name that probably helped rather than hurt the programme's poll ratings. There were even outlandish suggestions that Reagan had derived the idea from his movie *Murder in the Air* (1940), in which Brass Bancroft safeguarded the Inertia Projector, a new super-weapon capable of destroying enemy planes, but his thinking had far more rational foundations. First and foremost was his utter horror of nuclear war as a conflict that 'cannot be won and must never be fought'. Shortly after becoming president, he received a Pentagon report estimating that 150 million Americans would die in a nuclear war with the Soviets 'even if we "won"'. What life would be like for the survivors Reagan could not begin to imagine.[55] Second was his conviction that reliance on mutually assured destruction to deter nuclear attack made no sense whatsoever. In his memoirs, he likened this doctrine to 'having two westerners in a saloon aiming their guns at each other's heads – permanently. There had to be a better way.'[56] To his mind, a defensive system was an infinitely preferable means of safeguarding American lives, one that could lead eventually to the total elimination of offensive nuclear weapons.[57] Though he had no preconceived notion of the form this would take, the third element in Reagan's thinking on SDI drew on belief in sections of the scientific community that advances in laser technology had enhanced prospects of developing an anti-ballistic shield.

In early 1982 the High Frontier missile-defence advocacy group (later absorbed into the Heritage Foundation think-tank) submitted a report to the White House urging a 'new strategy of Assured Survival'. Citing the precedent of the Manhattan Project, which had developed the atomic bomb within a four-year schedule in World War II, it called for a similarly accelerated pro-gramme to identify and develop a defence system best suited to America's needs.[58] Reagan heard a similar message that missile defence was in reach from Edward Teller, a key figure in the hydrogen bomb's development but now a leading anti-ballistic researcher. 'We should take this seriously and have a real look,' Reagan commented to aides. 'Remember our country once turned down the submarine.' Though not interested in the scheme that Teller had in mind because it operated by nuclear detonation, the possibilities of a defensive system remained fixed in his mind.[59] A White House meeting with the joint chiefs of staff on 11 February 1983 was the moment of SDI's conception. Anxious to resolve the MX controversy, the military brass raised the possibility of missile defence as protection for America's intercontinental ballistic missiles (ICBMs) from Soviet attack, in other words as a means of enhancing deterrence. Reagan had the insight and imagination to envisage its utility to protect people rather than just weapons. After the meeting, he directed deputy NSA Robert McFarlane to work with presidential science advisor George 'Jay' Keyworth to produce a draft speech embodying a 'vision of the future which offers hope'.[60]

Apart from William Clark, other national-security officials were kept out of the loop until two days before Reagan was to address the nation. Their lack of enthusiasm for such an abrupt announcement of a potential revolution in American strategic doctrine on the basis of a technologically questionable pro-ject was palpable. In a robust expression of dissent at an Oval Office meeting on 21 March, George Shultz decried SDI as the unworkable idea of 'a blooming madman'. In his assessment, it would undermine the NATO alliance by decoupling American and Western European security, violate US obligations under the Anti-Ballistic Missile (ABM) Treaty of 1972, which prohibited deployment of comprehensive defensive systems, and destabilize US–Soviet relations by introducing a new dimension into the arms race. To accommodate these concerns, Reagan himself redrafted parts of the speech, paying lip service to the ABM Treaty and deterrence and including a strong paragraph confirming that US and Western European security remained identical, but the basic thrust was unchanged. After delivering it, the president wrote in his diary, 'I felt good,' but the reaction in Washington and foreign capitals was predominantly negative.[61]

Angry liberals condemned SDI as opening a new frontier in the arms race. Leading the charge, Senator Edward Kennedy of Massachusetts accused Reagan of 'misleading red scare tactics and reckless Star Wars schemes' (shortly afterwards he despatched an emissary to Moscow with an offer to hook up Soviet leaders with his American media contacts so that they could counter presidential propaganda, a proposal that was rejected).[62] At a time of escalating fiscal deficits, congressional Democrats and a good many Republicans were aghast at the budgetary implications of a project widely considered unrealizable. Typifying the disdain of the metropolitan press, the *New York Times* editorialized that SDI was 'a pipe dream, a projection of fantasy into policy'. There was comparable incredulity across the Atlantic – Thatcher was utterly sceptical of Reagan's claim that SDI would lead to a nuclear-free world, 'something which I believed was neither attainable nor even desirable'.[63] In Moscow, the Kremlin saw SDI as a sign of the first-strike ambition that it imputed to Reagan. 'Engaging in this is not just irresponsible, it is insane,' declared Yuri Andropov. 'Washington's actions are putting the entire world in jeopardy.' His remarks overlooked Soviet efforts to develop a laser-based defensive system, which had progressed as far as deployment deep in Siberia of a sophisticated radar system to track incoming missiles, something the ABM Treaty forbade. Kremlin outrage was music to Reagan's ears. As he later wrote to a friend, 'I wonder why some of our own carping critics who claim SDI is an impractical wasted effort don't ask themselves, if it's no good, how come the Russians are so upset about it?'[64]

SDI was a rare example of a president – any president – being wholly responsible for creating policy and ensuring its implementation over the objections of not only habitual detractors but also key advisors and allies. George Shultz did not give up hope of delaying the project until Reagan skewered him at a White House meeting in October 1983. After hearing out the secretary of state's reservations, the president reiterated why he considered SDI essential, ending with a sharp reminder of who was boss: 'That happens to be a very gracious man's way of saying thank you, George, but here is the way we go.' Thatcher received a similarly pointed put-down after haranguing a high-level arms-control seminar in Washington in July 1985 about the faulty logic of SDI. Even the notoriously insensitive Iron Lady realized it was time for her to stop talking and start nodding.[65]

Reagan's paternity of SDI is undisputed; its benefits are not. Judged in terms of the ambitious objectives Reagan set – creation of a perfect missile defence that would place nuclear weapons on the scrapheap of history – it was a failure. His statements envisioning total security from attack may seem naive to present-day eyes, but they were recognition of an inescapable reality of the time. As top NSC aide Jack Matlock observed, Reagan oversold SDI to the American public because that was the only way of getting money for it.[66] Despite vast outlays – $22 billion during Reagan's tenure and $60 billion by century's end – the United States has hitherto failed to produce a missile-defence system to protect its people. And instead of the nuclear era passing into history, the late twentieth and early twenty-first centuries witnessed nuclear proliferation beyond the five nuclear-weapons states recognized by the Nuclear Non-Proliferation Treaty of 1970. This was the very opposite of what Reagan had wanted. Non-proliferation, he wrote to Thatcher in 1983, is 'a matter of critical national security concern that we share [...] This is an important priority for me.'[67]

Adjudged in terms of US–Soviet relations, however, the balance sheet weighed heavily in SDI's favour. Despite her initial opposition, Thatcher later adjudged Reagan's pursuit of it as 'central to the West's victory in the Cold War' and 'the single most important [decision] of his presidency'. Nothing else did more to unnerve the Kremlin, producing a reaction that was in the words of a high-level interpreter 'highly emotional [...] in a tone approaching hysteria'. As Robert Gates commented, the possibility that America would create a shield allowing a first strike without fear of retaliation was 'a Soviet nightmare come to life'.[68] Although Russian scientists were sceptical that SDI was technically feasible, the Kremlin could not dismiss it as fantasy. Whatever progress the Soviet Union had made in constructing a partial missile defence, its chances of winning a nuclear-shield race with the scientifically superior and richer United States were effectively nil. SDI therefore had an immense psychological impact in forcing Soviet leaders to confront their country's increasing technological backwardness.

While Reagan pondered the possibilities of space-based missile defence, he received a sharp reminder of America's vulnerability to asymmetrical terrestrial threats in the Middle East. As he would belatedly recognize, the region had its own dynamic, one that did not mesh with his freedom-versus-communism world view. With the chastened wisdom of hindsight, he told conservative commentator William Buckley, the Middle East was 'a complicated place – well, not really a place, it's more a state of mind. A disordered mind.' Shocked by the depth of its historical hatreds, the president told another friend, 'Sometimes I wonder if the Middle East was the cradle of the world's three great religions because they needed religion more than any other spot on earth.'[69] Like his predecessor, he could not avoid being drawn into the region's sectarian webs – and with much graver consequences.

Reagan's well-intentioned but ill-conceived efforts to be even-handed in dealing with Middle Eastern problems planted the seeds of tragedy. In June 1982 Israel launched a full-scale invasion to destroy Palestine Liberation Organization (PLO) forces ensconced in Lebanon. In support of this, its US-supplied aircraft attacked Syria's missile sites in the Bekaa Valley region of east Lebanon, in the process inflicting a heavy defeat on its adversary's Soviet-supplied air force. The Reagan administration could take little pleasure in this triumph of American military technology. Its attention was increasingly fixed on the mounting civilian casualties from Israeli bombardment of Muslim parts of Beirut where PLO fighters were holed up. Despite growing international outrage, Reagan's personal request for a ceasefire initially cut no ice with Tel Aviv, but he stepped up the pressure after King Fahd of Saudi Arabia pleaded with him to stop the slaughter. On 12 August the president telephoned prime minister Menachem Begin to warn that he risked losing America's friendship if the killing continued. 'I was angry,' Reagan recorded in his diary. 'I used the word holocaust deliberately & said the symbol of his war was becoming a picture of a 7 month old baby with its arms blown off.'[70] Although the remarks went down badly with someone whose parents and brother were Nazi victims, Begin halted the barrage.

Thereafter, a US-brokered ceasefire required Israel and Syria to withdraw from Lebanon, something neither fully complied with, and arranged for PLO forces to depart for Tunisia and elsewhere. An over-optimistic Reagan now sensed an opportunity to negotiate a 'land for peace' settlement of the Palestinian problem whereby Israel withdrew from territory captured in the Six Day War of 1967 in return for Arab acceptance of its right to exist. The first ever American endorsement for Palestinian autonomy on the West Bank found no favour with either warring party. Begin peremptorily rejected the initiative just before the president announced it to the American public.[71]

In the absence of a broader peace deal, Lebanon became to Reagan the symbol of America's capacity to do good in the Middle East. The Christian Phalangist massacre of as many as 2,000 Palestinian men, women, and children in the Sabra and Shatila refugee camps in west Beirut on 16, 17, and 18 September, bloodletting in which Israeli forces were complicit, caused him profound shock. Doubtless, too, Reagan shared with George Shultz a feeling of guilt that the recall to ship of 800 US Marines, part of the Multi-National Force (MNF) sent to oversee PLO withdrawal, had made this possible. With the secretary of state's support, the president told the NSC on 19 September: 'We should go for broke [...] No more half way gestures.'[72]

The White House secured agreement from France, Italy, and the UK to send the MNF back in, required Israel to withdraw from Beirut, called on moderate Arab states to pressurize Syria into pulling its forces out of Lebanon, and sought to assist the Lebanese government achieve defence self-sufficiency. A strategy that was pure Reagan in conception, it evinced earnest desire to help Lebanon and naivety that sweet reason could break out with American help. After meeting Lebanon's new leader, Amine Gemayel, he commented, 'I'm impressed, he is modest and apparently totally dedicated to doing his job for the people of Lebanon.'[73] This was an extreme case of wishful thinking. Utterly committed to Maronite Christian interests and closely tied to Israel, Gemayel was incapable of reaching out to Lebanese Muslim factions that increasingly looked to Syria for support.

Following the Israeli pull-out from Beirut in mid-1983, the MNF, and especially its US contingent, was increasingly seen by Gemayel's opponents as his mainstay. No longer regarded as wholly neutral, the Marines came under fire from Syrian-backed paramilitaries ensconced in the hills above Beirut. After two of them were killed on 5 September, an angry Reagan wrote in his diary:

> I can't get the idea out of my head that some F14s [...] blowing hell out of a couple of artillery emplacements would be a tonic for the Marines & at the same time would deliver a message to those gun happy middle east terrorists.

On sober reflection, he understood that any such action 'could be seen as putting us in the war'.[74] Nevertheless, his desire to do something on behalf of the increasingly beleaguered Marines overcame his doubts. On 19 September, Reagan authorized US warships to fire in support of Lebanese operations to clear some hillside positions held by anti-government forces. From his perspective, this was a legitimate response that 'still comes under the head of defense', but the distinction was lost on its targets. As Colin Powell later remarked, 'When the shells started falling on the Shiites, they assumed the American "referee" had taken sides.'[75]

Reagan acknowledged that Lebanon had become a 'nest of adders', but was not prepared to get out. This was precisely what William Clark advocated at the National Security Planning Group (NSPG) meeting of 14 October in opposition to Shultz. Despite the Pentagon also adjudging the situation unwinnable, Reagan decided to hold fast. Some commentators saw this as typifying his incapacity to resolve disputes between aides but these critics arguably underestimated his sincere conviction that the United States had an obligation to stay. What cannot be disputed is that neither Reagan nor his key advisors had read the signs that the geopolitics of Lebanon had become entangled with Shi'i holy war following formation in 1982 of the militant Hezbollah to resist Israel and its US backer. Created by Lebanese Muslim cleric supporters of Ayatollah Khomeini, this organization received funds from Iran and training from a 1,500-strong body of Iranian Revolutionary Guards that Syria allowed to encamp in the Bekaa Valley.[76]

The first warning of the changed situation came when Hezbollah terrorists, with help from Syria, launched a truck-bomb attack on the US embassy in Beirut that killed 63 people, including 17 Americans, in April 1983. 'Lord forgive me for the hatred I feel for the humans who can do such a cruel but cowardly deed,' Reagan wrote in his diary.[77] Worse would follow in the wake of the US shelling of anti-government positions above Beirut. At 2.30 a.m. eastern time on Sunday, 23 October, Reagan was awoken to hear the awful news that another Hezbollah suicide truck-bomber had blown up the Marine barracks at Beirut International Airport. In Robert McFarlane's recall, an ashen-faced president looked like 'a 72-year-old man, who had just received a blow to the chest. All the air seemed to go out of him.'[78] The initial casualty estimate was 100 but this was constantly revised as more information came in. The final count was 241 American service personnel dead – 220 of them Marines, the largest loss of serving men since Vietnam and the deadliest single day for the Marines since Iwo Jima. At the equivalent of 12,000 pounds of TNT, the blast was the largest non-nuclear explosion on record. A simultaneous suicide attack on France's MNF barracks two miles away killed 58 paratroopers in retaliation for its air strike of 23 September against Bekaa Valley missile sites.[79]

Reagan described that Sunday as 'the lowest of the low' points of his presidency. An effective retaliation would have meant a transformational escalation of America's mission in Lebanon that the Pentagon opposed and the president did not want.[80] When Syrian forces fired on an unarmed US reconnaissance aircraft above Beirut, there was a sense of impotent rage in Reagan's insistence on an air strike against their Bekaa Valley base. As military planners had warned, the operation achieved very little of significance, but two planes were downed by surface-to-air missiles.[81] It did nothing to safeguard the remaining US peacekeepers now living underground in dispersed locations as protection against further bombings. In early 1984, amid growing popular disillusion with the enterprise, Tip O'Neill promised a House resolution calling for their prompt withdrawal. The speaker 'may be ready to surrender, but I'm not', was Reagan's tart response.[82] Despite this, his advisors were more willing to face up to the reality that Lebanon was a lost cause. In Reagan's absence, an NSPG meeting on 6 February 1984 concluded that the Marines had to be withdrawn. Informed of this by telephone before a speaking engagement in Las Vegas, the president reluctantly agreed that America's weak hand in Lebanon had become a busted flush.[83]

'The immorality of Vietnam,' Reagan once remarked, 'was asking young men to fight and die for a cause our government had no intention of winning.' If this was so, his despatch of too few Marines to fight but too many to die in

Lebanon repeated the error. A year after the Beirut bombing, Reagan was still trying to reassure grief-stricken parents that their sons had not died in vain, but the truth was different.[84] The premise of the mission had been faulty from the outset. As Colin Powell observed, the United States had stuck 'its hand into a thousand-year hornets' nest with the expectation that our mere presence would pacify the hornets'.[85] Reagan suffered a worse setback over Lebanon than Jimmy Carter over Iran, but did not pay the same price. An official Pentagon report on the Beirut bombing was critical of the administration on two counts – failure to define clearly the Marines' mission and to recognize that changed political conditions would expose them to attacks.[86] White House leaks succeeded in focusing initial media attention on the portions criticizing Marine commanders for not ensuring adequate security arrangements. When fully released, the broader implications of the report never caught up with Reagan because the withdrawal of US forces had satisfied public opinion.

The president had not got off scot-free, however. Just days before the Marine contingent was 'redeployed', the official euphemism for withdrawal, Reagan wrote to MNF allies that 'retreat in the face of terrorism will only embolden those who wish to do us harm'.[87] The denouement of the peacekeeping intervention predictably confirmed to hostile elements in the Middle East that America's regional commitments had blood-cost limits. The lesson that terrorists drew from Lebanon would have dangerous consequences for the United States far beyond Reagan's time as president.

In the immediate aftermath of the Marine massacre, a military intervention undertaken with an overwhelming preponderance of power against a weak foe was a success. The tiny island of Grenada had been on America's radar as a hotbed of Marxist subversion in the Caribbean Basin since the 1979 coup that had brought Maurice Bishop to power. The new regime had promptly invited Cuba to construct military installations, including a 10,000-foot aircraft landing strip, and stockpile munitions in its country. Bishop's murder by ultra-leftists in October 1983 rang alarm bells not only in Washington but also in neighbouring Caribbean states that an escalation of international revolutionary activism was at hand. Among the national-security principals, George Shultz was in favour of immediate intervention but Caspar Weinberger, supported by George Bush, advocated development of a multinational Americas-wide force that would negate charges of imperialism. Reagan cast his decisive voice with Shultz out of concern that 740 American students attending medical school on the island might become the victims of a new hostage crisis. A request for support from the Organization of East Caribbean States (OECS) also weighed on his decision to intervene. 'I could not see how,' Reagan told Australian premier Bob Hawke, 'we could turn down these countries right here that we're trying to help in the Caribbean, and have any credibility left any place in the world.'[88]

At around 4 a.m. on 22 October, while staying at the Eisenhower Cottage on a golfing weekend at Augusta Country Club, Georgia, Reagan ordered an invasion three days hence.[89] This was where he heard the news about the Beirut bombing the following morning. The mounting body count so sickened him that aides thought he might call off the Grenada intervention to avoid further losses, but he remained steadfast. A combined force of Army paratroopers, Marines, and Navy Seals, together with OECS personnel, took almost a week to secure the island, with an American casualty count of 19 dead and over 100 wounded, because of stiffer-than-expected resistance from Grenada's militia and a Cuban construction battalion. According to General Colin Powell, then a senior Pentagon aide, the invasion was 'a sloppy success' marred by poor inter-service coordination. With his habitual esteem for the military now ramped up beyond measure, Reagan would not hear a word of doubt that the operation had been less than perfect. 'I'm so d—n proud of those young warriors of ours, I can't stand it,' he told a California friend.[90]

The liberal media (led by the *New York Times*), academic activists (including Georgetown professor and future secretary of state Madeleine Albright), and a goodly number of Democrats condemned the invasion as immoral gunboat diplomacy. The first post-Vietnam success for America's armed forces generated a surge of popular patriotism that drowned out the critics. Television scenes of the medical students giving thanks for their rescue – the first out of the plane fell to his knees to kiss the ground – when airlifted back to the United States accentuated national pride. The fulsome gratitude they later showed some of their rescuers at a White House South Lawn ceremony especially gratified Reagan. '[I]t was quite a sight,' he declared, 'for a former governor who had once seen college students spit on anyone wearing a military uniform.' Even better was the hero's welcome he received from ordinary Grenadians when visiting the island in 1986. Reagan likened it to how the people of occupied France and Italy greeted their GI liberators in World War II. 'I probably never felt better during my presidency than I did that day,' he wrote in his memoirs.[91]

The Grenada intervention was the first occasion that US military power had rolled back a Soviet ally. Reagan received many plaudits for sending the Kremlin a clear signal that further advances of Marxism would not be tolerated. Typical of these, former Nixon aide Leonard Garment praised him as 'a one-man deterrent' for showing that the United States would not 'flinch from the use of force in those regional areas where the fuses of big power confrontation are being lit'.[92] Pointedly not joining in the back-slapping was Margaret Thatcher, the recipient of an empty promise of consultation before any decision was taken to use force against a Commonwealth nation. Reagan's justification for not honouring this pledge was the need for speed and secrecy to pre-empt any Cuban attempt to reinforce the island.[93] On learning the invasion was imminent, Thatcher telephoned the White House to express her displeasure, insisting the president be summoned from a Grenada briefing for congressional leaders to take the call. Hoping to heal the breach, Reagan called her on 26 October to reassert that secrecy had been vital to the mission. Now it was the prime minister's turn to be inconveniently summoned to the telephone amid an emergency House of Commons Grenada debate wherein the Labour opposition was portraying her as Reagan's poodle. Her manner towards him in this conversation was distant to put it mildly.[94] Thatcher's hurt would take some time to subside, but Reagan was very disappointed in her, too. As George Shultz recalled, the president felt deserving of the prime minister's support in the name of the special relationship over Grenada because of his backing for her in the same cause over the Falklands.[95]

While the Cold War sideshow in Grenada reached a climax, the main event was coming close to boiling point. On the night of 1 September 1983 a Soviet military plane shot down a Korean Air Lines passenger jet, flight KAL007, over Sakhalin, killing all 269 people on board – 61 of them Americans (the flight had originated in New York). Denying responsibility until incontrovertible evidence proved otherwise, the Kremlin then claimed justification on grounds that the airliner had intruded into Soviet airspace on an espionage mission for the United States. Owing to wrongly set computers, KAL007 was certainly far off course. It was also revealed many years later that the US Air Force had been engaged since 1981 in aggressive probes along the edges of the Soviet Union's airspace to test its air defences, manoeuvres that ramped up Kremlin nervousness about a nuclear attack. Nevertheless, Soviet commanders blundered monumentally in ordering KAL007 shot down instead of forcing it to land.[96]

Receiving the news when vacationing at Rancho del Cielo, Reagan's first words were: 'My God, have they gone mad? What the hell are they thinking of?' Cutting short his break, he returned to the White House to deal with the crisis. 'This was the Soviet Union against the world,' the president declared in a national address. 'It was an act of barbarism, born of a society which wantonly disregards individual rights and the value of human life and seeks constantly to expand and dominate other nations.'[97] These tough words were not followed by tough actions to let the Kremlin know it had crossed a line. Reagan stopped well short of what many right-wingers wanted, starting with the mass expulsion of known KGB agents. In reality, the KAL incident had strengthened Reagan's determination to negotiate an arms deal because it 'demonstrated how close the world had come to the precipice'. To him, it signified how the combination of Soviet paranoia and incompetence could have infinitely graver consequences if a missile-launch commander suspected an American attack. This very nearly happened some weeks later, on 26 September, when a defective satellite computer set off a false alarm of Intercontinental Ballistic Missile (ICBM) attack at a Soviet early-warning command centre, Serpukhov-15. Fortunately, the duty officer, Lieutenant Colonel Stanislav Petrov, was aware that the satellite system had been put into service the previous year before being fully ready. His decision to cross-check ground radar rather than pass on the warning to the high command may well have averted accidental nuclear catastrophe.[98]

Though Reagan was blissfully ignorant of this incident, simulations of a Soviet missile attack chilled him to the marrow. On 10 October he had an advance showing at Camp David of *The Day After*, ABC's television movie that graphically portrayed the nuclear obliteration of Kansas City, Missouri, and the post-fallout fate of nearby Lawrence, Kansas. Reviewing it in his diary, he acknowledged that it was 'powerfully done [...] very effective & left me greatly depressed'. ABC's publicity for the movie whipped up popular concerns about nuclear holocaust: schoolchildren deluged the White House with letters; the mayor of Lawrence offered to host peace talks between Reagan and Yuri Andropov; and the nuclear-freeze movement arranged hundreds of teach-ins about the film. Aides contemplated having Reagan rebut the movie but decided this would be counter-productive. Despite being seen by 100 million people, the second-largest television audience in history, when finally aired on 20 November, *The Day After* did not give the nuclear-freeze movement the kind of boost the White House feared – possibly because the advertising breaks were reminders of everyday normality. Nevertheless, it had confirmed the worst fears of its most important viewer. 'My own reaction,' Reagan commented, 'was one of our having to do all we can to have a deterrent & to see there is never a nuclear war.'[99]

Shortly after seeing *The Day After*, Reagan received a Single Integrated Operational Plan (SIOP) briefing on US nuclear response to Soviet attack. This 'most sobering experience', as he called it in his diary, disturbingly projected a sequence of events for the destruction of civilization that 'paralleled those in the ABC movie'.[100] Presidents with analytic minds like John Kennedy, Richard Nixon, and Jimmy Carter could treat SIOP's simulated decision making as an abstract possibility, but Reagan reacted as if it were real. The first one he attended as president had a profound effect. Organized by NSC aide Thomas Reed, one-time gubernatorial campaign assistant, it was held on 1 March 1982 in the Situations Room, located in the White House basement. In the initial session, attended by a large group of national-security officials, Reagan was an observer, while a stand-in acted his role as the Soviet attack came in. With red dots signifying missile strikes, the electronic map of the United States rapidly turned into an obliterated sea of red. In the next session, the president received a full SIOP briefing, alongside only top aides, on the retaliatory destruction of the Soviet Union, entailing selection of missile targets, warhead quantities, and casualty goals. In the final session, accompanied by just William Clark and Reed, he rehearsed procedures to select options from the war plan and authenticate these via the command-authority card carried on his person at all times.[101]

The SIOP briefings confirmed Reagan's long-held conviction about the horrors of nuclear war. The trouble was that Soviet leaders completely misread his mindset in suspecting him of wanting to launch a first strike against their country. In May 1981, then KGB director Yuri Andropov had announced a new programme, codenamed RYAN (acronym for Raketno-Yadernoe Napadenie – Russian for 'nuclear missile attack'), to gather intelligence about US plans for one.[102] In early 1983, Oleg Gordievsky – a British mole within the KGB – told his handlers that the Kremlin was in 'a state of acute apprehension' that Reagan was ready to strike. Veteran diplomat Averell Harriman relayed the same message after a private meeting with Andropov, now the Soviet leader.[103] Reagan's tough talk after the KAL007 incident was regarded as proof of his malign intent – despite the limited actions that accompanied it. US overseas bases going on high alert following the Beirut bombings further fuelled Moscow's fears. Soviet paranoia reached its peak during the NATO war-game exercise in Europe, scheduled to last from 2 to 11 November. Code-named Able Archer 83, this simulated a nuclear-war scenario for training purposes but Soviet intelligence suspected it of being a smokescreen to launch the real thing. Gordievsky later confirmed that the Kremlin put Soviet nuclear forces on high alert in the belief that the moment of attack was at hand.[104]

While some analysts have questioned whether this was more a case of Soviet huffing and puffing, a report by the president's Foreign Intelligence Advisory Board, undertaken in 1990 with unparalleled access to US and NATO files and only declassified in late 2015, indicates that the danger was frighteningly real.[105] In a vain effort to defuse tensions, the White House had scheduled Reagan to visit the Far East while Able Archer was being conducted. Briefed on his return about the signs of Soviet anxiety, he noted in his diary:

> I feel the Soviets are so defense minded, so paranoid about being attacked that without being in any way soft on them we ought to tell them no one here has any intention of doing anything like that. What the h—l have they got that anyone would want.[106]

At the end of three years in office, Reagan had reached the uncomfortable conclusion that Soviet officials 'feared us not only as adversaries but as potential aggressors who might hurl nuclear weapons at them in a first strike'. This realization made him more anxious than ever 'to get a top Soviet leader in a room alone and try to convince him we had no designs on the Soviet Union and Russians had nothing to fear from us'.[107] To his mind, agreement to reduce their nuclear weapons was the surest way to curb escalating superpower tensions. Belying a hawkish reputation at home and abroad, this would be the predominant goal of his remaining years in office. As George Shultz told State Department aides in December 1983, 'The president has noticed that no one pays any attention to him in spite of the fact he speaks about this idea publicly and privately.'[108]

TEN

Morning Man

Ronald Reagan won landslide re-election in 1984 with a campaign that featured one of the most iconic political commercials of all time. Formally entitled 'Prouder, Stronger, Better', the minute-long ad became better known as 'It's Morning Again in America', the opening line that metaphorically expressed national renewal under Reagan. Continuing this theme in his 1985 State of the Union Address, Reagan avowed that 'after 4 years of united effort the American people have brought forth a nation renewed, stronger, freer, and more secure than before'.[1] However, his second-term domestic record turned out to be spotty at best. The morning man encountered increasing opposition from those who did not share his optimism about the present or the future.

There was never any doubt in Reagan's mind that he would seek a second term in order to preserve the achievements of the first and accomplish still-unfulfilled goals. Had it been up to Nancy, he would not have run again. She wanted a settled home after so many years spent in Sacramento and Washington, yearned for privacy, and missed California and her old friends. Above all, she worried about another attempt on her husband's life and sensed that a second term would not turn out so well. After talking it over many times in their White House quarters during 1983 (conversations Reagan overlooked in his memoirs), she went along with his decision to run.[2]

From the moment of his formal announcement on 29 January 1984, Reagan campaigned as the candidate of peace and prosperity, but his image looked stronger on the latter than the former. The election-year economic indicators made good reading for the White House. Although unemployment remained relatively high at 7.5 per cent, it was trending downwards and private-sector job creation was nearly the highest on record; economic growth was a spectacular 6.8 per cent – the fastest rate in 34 years; housing starts were at their highest in six years; inflation was low at 3 per cent; and interest rates were down. The feel-good consequences kept Reagan's approval ratings for economic leadership above 60 per cent throughout 1984. In contrast, his foreign-policy approval hovered around 50 per cent or less in the first half of the year because of continued concerns about conflict with the Soviets. In July, Dick Wirthlin's private polling revealed that nearly four of every ten respondents thought a nuclear holocaust would annihilate mankind in their lifetime.[3]

Reagan had not yet convinced Americans that he could be a peacemaker. The Soviet walkout from the Geneva talks in late 1983 meant that there were no ongoing US–Soviet negotiations on arms control for the first time in 14 years. Kremlin spokesman Georgi Arbatov told *Time* magazine, 'We have come to the conclusion that nothing will come from dealing with Reagan.' To counter such criticism, Reagan expressed hope for a better relationship with Moscow in a nationally televised speech, also beamed live to Western Europe, on 16 January 1984. 'Reducing the risk of war – and especially nuclear war – is priority number one,' he proclaimed. A personally written peroration offered a parable of how American husband and wife Jim and Sally in a chance meeting with Soviet counterparts Ivan and Anya would find their everyday lives had much in common. In particular, their coming together would demonstrate a universal truth: 'People want to raise their children in a world without fear and without war [...] Their common interests cross all borders.'[4] American pundits regarded the address as nothing more than an election-year ploy to counter low approval on foreign policy. No one outside a tight circle of aides understood that Reagan was increasingly attuned to peace now that he had addressed the strength element of his national-security dictum. It was essential, he told Margaret Thatcher, to negotiate with the Soviets because 'East–West relations have entered an even more difficult period'.[5]

In reality there was little prospect of improvement while Yuri Andropov was Soviet leader. Contrary to the Western media's favourable image of him as cosmopolitan, cultured, and progressive, he was a hard-line communist, had been instrumental in crushing the Hungarian Revolution of 1956 and the Prague Spring of 1968, and was deeply hostile to the United States. Andropov's death on 9 February 1984 after prolonged kidney-related illness ended his 15-month tenure. Reagan had no thought of attending the funeral of a man he had come to despise, telling aides, 'I don't want to honor that prick.' Watching the ceremony on television, however, he wondered 'what thoughts people must have [...] when their belief in no God or immortality is faced with death'.[6]

The succession of 73-year-old Konstantin Chernenko was the last hurrah of the Kremlin old guard. After a friendly exchange of communications, Reagan dared to believe that the new man might agree to a summit meeting. 'I have a gut feeling we should do this,' he ruminated. '[M]aybe they are scared of us & think we are a threat.'[7] It became apparent that the Soviets would not consent to a full-blown summit for the time being lest it assist his re-election. A frustrated Reagan yearned to get on with meaningful arms-control talks. 'We are not playing political games,' he told a West German official. The Soviets were doing just that, but realization was dawning that the Geneva walkout had damaged their international standing more than America's. Accordingly, the word went out through various diplomatic channels that foreign minister Andrei Gromyko was prepared to visit the White House following his annual appearance before the United Nations. Advised by George Shultz to give the matter some thought, Reagan's immediate response was: 'No, I don't need to think it over. I think we should definitely do it.'[8]

The 'big day', as Reagan called it, consisted of three hours of talks on 28 September, time that he justifiably believed 'well spent'. He had prepared intensively for this first meeting with a top Soviet official, even devising his own 'talking points' in preference to what the State Department provided. Although the encounter did not produce a breakthrough, Gromyko was impressed that the president's courtesy and lack of frostiness belied his Kremlin image of unremitting hostility. More significantly, the veteran diplomat sensed that Reagan was sincere in wanting to do something to improve bilateral relations – even if his statement on the meeting for the Tass news service gave no hint of this. Reporting to Thatcher, Reagan declared that he was 'prepared to be patient until that time when the Soviet leadership is both able and willing to respond positively to our willingness to negotiate'.[9]

In the meantime, Reagan got on with winning re-election against Walter Mondale, formerly Jimmy Carter's vice-president. According to Wirthlin's polls, the Democrat's tax-and-spend image made him the easiest to beat of all those seeking to become opposition standard-bearer. Mondale's superior organization and relentless courting of liberal interest groups secured the presidential nomination but he ran a woeful campaign against Reagan. Since FDR, Democratic presidential candidates had won the White House through promising to expand jobs and prosperity. Instead of painting himself in these traditional colours, Mondale pledged more pain for a nation just emerged from deep recession. The signature theme of his candidacy rang the alarm bells of national emergency about the mammoth Reagan budget deficits. Addressing the Democratic National Convention on 19 July, he declared: 'We are living on borrowed time. These deficits hike interest rates, clobber exports, cheat our kids, and shrink our future.' If elected, he vowed to cut the budget imbalance by two-thirds within four years through raising taxes. Claiming Reagan would have to do likewise because of the gravity of America's fiscal problems, Mondale asserted: 'He won't tell you. I just did.'[10]

The Reagan camp briefly debated whether to issue a categorical rebuttal or a more cautious statement allowing flexibility for a second-term deficit fix. Ultimately Dick Wirthlin's counsel proved decisive:

> The goal is re-election. That's the big picture. Everything else is small-picture [...] If we want to win – and win big – we need to keep the contrast between the President and Mondale sharp and clear [...] The exigencies of the election force us to solemnly swear that Walter Mondale is the tax-increase candidate and Ronald Reagan is the no-tax increase candidate.

Accordingly, Reagan issued a statement on 12 August: 'I have no plan to raise taxes nor will I allow any plan for a tax increase.'[11] Of course, this formulation still allowed him to do so if circumstances required. Meanwhile, Mondale could not stop digging deeper into the hole of his own making. When finally unveiled, his fair-tax plan damaged his cause in hitting middle-income families as well as the affluent. His claims that a Republican White House would impose even higher burdens on average Americans to protect the rich fell on increasingly deaf ears. By now polls showed that over 80 per cent of respondents preferred to reduce the deficit through spending cuts rather than tax increases.[12]

Reagan could therefore define the election as a choice between prosperity, freedom, and opportunity for all through his low taxes and his opponent's pain-for-everybody approach. This also enabled him to seize the fairness issue from Mondale's inept grasp. At campaign stops, Reagan repeatedly told cheering crowds:

> He sees an America in which every day is tax day, April 15. We see an America in which every day is Independence Day, July 4. We want to lower your and everybody's taxes, so your families will be stronger, our economy will be stronger, and America will be stronger.

Hammering the message home in an election-eve national address, Reagan asked: 'What has happened to the Democratic party's concern for protecting the earnings of working people and promoting economic growth?'[13]

The sole issue where the poll advantage was Mondale's was his 28-point lead as the candidate less likely to start an unnecessary war. To exploit this, he made immediate renewal of arms-control negotiations his foreign-policy priority, voicing support for a nuclear freeze and opposition to the Strategic Defense Initiative to induce the Soviets back to the table. Despite popular concern about nuclear war, polls showed that most Americas still preferred 'peace through strength' to Mondale's 'peace through talk' alternative. What the public seemingly wanted was a leader who would both stand up to and negotiate with the Soviets. With his credentials firmly established on the first requirement, the Gromyko visit enabled Reagan to fulfil the second. Not even the gaffe during a microphone check before his weekly radio broadcast on 11 August could damage his standing. Unaware that he was being recorded, the president joked: 'My fellow Americans, I am pleased to tell you today that I've signed legislation that will outlaw Russia forever. We begin bombing in five minutes.' When leaked to the press, this did not cause any dip in Reagan's poll numbers.[14]

The so-called 'Bear Ad' also undercut Mondale's efforts to promote 'peace through talk'. This 30-second spot presented viewers with the image of a large bear lumbering menacingly through a forest. A voice-over intoned:

There's a bear in the woods. For some people the bear is easy to see. Others don't see it at all. Some people say the bear is tame. Others say it's vicious, and dangerous. Since no one can really be sure who's right, isn't it smart to be as strong as the bear – if there is a bear?

In a visual allegory of 'peace through strength', the final shot showed the bear recoiling from the silhouette of a hunter with a rifle slung over his shoulder. Wirthlin's test audiences loved it and displayed high recall for its message. Reagan was also a big fan – 'I like that one!' he remarked after being shown the spot for approval. Thereafter, the word went out that it was to be aired as regularly as possible.[15]

There was a final glimmer of hope for Mondale when Reagan flopped in the first presidential debate, held at Louisville, Kentucky, on 7 October. It was evident during his preparations for the event that he was uncomfortable having his record come under attack as the incumbent rather than being on the offensive as the challenger in 1980. At one stage, he lost his temper with the aide playing Mondale in mock exchanges, snapping at him, 'Shut up!' In contrast to 1980, he did not do enough preparation for the debate – in part because presidential duties continued to occupy his time. Worried aides mistakenly made a belated effort to cram his mind with facts and figures to make up for this.[16] As a consequence, Reagan gave the worst political performance of his life hitherto. In his wife's words: 'Right from the start, he was tense, muddled, and off-stride. He lacked authority. He stumbled. This was a Ronald Reagan I had never seen before.' By contrast, Mondale was crisp and authoritative in putting his rival on the back foot. A furious Nancy Reagan blamed those in charge of briefing preparations for overtraining her husband, but he knew that the fault was his. With the self-awareness of a performer, a temporarily depressed Reagan understood he had been 'like a fighter leaving his fight in the locker room'.[17]

Wirthlin's polls showed Reagan's lead dipping from 18 points before the debate to 11 points afterwards. More worryingly, the media began focusing on his advanced years as the reason for his poor performance. The normally supportive *Wall Street Journal* ran a front-page article headlined: 'New question in race: is oldest US president now showing his age?' The television networks got into the act by reshowing a clip of him nodding off at the Vatican with the

Pope in 1982. Knowing the second debate at Kansas City on 21 October was now critical, Reagan prepared for it diligently – 'I've been working my tail off,' he remarked in his diary – in between some barnstorming stump appearances that revived his spirits.[18] The second debate, which focused on foreign policy, consequently went much better despite Reagan being cut off by the moderator when his closing remarks ran over the allotted time.

In truth, Reagan only held his own rather than bested Mondale, but this was enough to end doubts that he could handle a second term. The key moment came about 30 minutes into the exchanges when a journalist inquisitor obliquely brought up the age issue by referring to John F. Kennedy going days with little sleep during the Cuban Missile Crisis as a prelude to asking whether Reagan had doubts about being able to function in similar circumstances. Expecting such a query, he had a ready answer of his own making:

> Not at all [...] And I want you to know that, also, I will not make age an
> issue in this campaign. I am not going to exploit, for political purposes,
> my opponent's youth and inexperience.[19]

This elicited a chorus of guffaws from the invited audience – even Mondale laughed. More importantly, television viewers felt reassured that the Gipper had regained his zip.

Thereafter, a big re-election victory was never in doubt. Reagan ended up winning the Electoral College by 525 to 13 votes, a margin only bested by Franklin D. Roosevelt in 1936. Mondale's home state of Minnesota and the District of Columbia were the solitary entries in the Democratic column. Reagan had come even closer than FDR to an all-state sweep – when asked shortly afterwards what he wanted for Christmas, he joked, 'Well, Minnesota would have been nice.' In winning the popular vote by 58 to 42 per cent, he carried every region of the country; he received substantial majorities as expected from male voters and less predictably from female ones (Mondale had named Congresswoman Geraldine Ferraro of New York as his running mate – the first time a woman had featured on a major party ticket – in a vain effort to exploit a supposed 'gender gap'); and he did equally well among Protestants and Catholics. He also won every age group, with voters aged 18–24 giving America's oldest ever president a lopsided 66 to 34 per cent majority in gratitude for making their futures look rosier than four years earlier. Significantly, the biggest audiences for his campaign appearances were at university campuses. After a particularly enthusiastic rally at Ohio State, Reagan wrote in his diary, 'I was so in love with young Americans I was all choked up.' The only groups resistant to him were the lowest-income quintile of voters (46 to 54 per cent), members of labour-union families (48 to 52 per cent), Latinos (34 to 66 per cent) – then only 3 per cent of total voters, and African Americans (9 to 91 per cent).[20]

This was a personal rather than party victory, however. Reagan did little to help the GOP with a campaign that emphasized his leadership and first-term record, a low-risk approach concocted by campaign strategists and White House aides. The president occasionally slipped the leash to come out fighting but fundamentally went along with what William Buckley called 'The blandification of Ronald Reagan'. This incumbency strategy was ill-suited to building a new Republican majority. An 18-seat gain in the House of Representatives still left the GOP in a 253 to 182 minority, and a net loss of two seats in the Senate did not augur well for retaining control of that body in the next midterms, when Reagan would not be on the ticket.[21] 'Reagan did not win a party landslide and that is what his party needed,' observed House Whip Tony Coelho of California. Republican Young Turks were angry about what they considered a missed opportunity. Congressman Newt Gingrich of Georgia, a rising conservative star, declared: 'Reagan should have prepared for re-election by forcing a polarization of the country. He should have been running against liberals and radicals.'[22] It was doubtful that Americans wanted the kind of politics that became the early twenty-first-century norm. Nor was Reagan suited by personality for such a strategy – despite his anger over increasingly bitter Democratic attacks on him as a friend of the rich and a warmonger.

Aside from its insufficiency for mandate creation, the 'Morning Again in America' mood that Reagan invoked was very far from the reality of life for many Americans. For Aids (Acquired Immune Deficiency Syndrome) victims, in particular, it was more a case of dark night. The disease had first appeared in the United States in 1979 but medical awareness of its threat was slow to develop. The discovery that it was transmissible through both sexual contact and blood, with the groups most at risk being homosexuals (especially those with multiple partners), haemophiliacs (from blood transfusions), and intra-venous drug users (from contaminated needles) took another four years. In

April 1984, the Health and Human Services (HHS) Department announced that government researchers had finally identified the source of Aids as a retrovirus they designated 'human immunodeficiency virus' (HIV).[23]

For many gay Americans, Reagan was culpable of homophobic neglect of Aids in deference to the beliefs of moral conservatives that it was God's punishment for the sin of homosexuality. In their view, his refusal to make the epidemic a priority and adequately fund research into finding a cure showed utter disregard for a plague that killed more than 100,000 people in the 1980s and over 300,000 in the following decade.[24] On the 40th president's death in 2004, gay-rights activist Larry Kramer damned him as 'Adolf Reagan' for visiting a holocaust on gays: 'Our murderer is dead. The man who murdered more gay people than anyone in the entire history of the world is dead. More people than Hitler even.'[25]

Reagan's record on Aids was rather more complex than such condemnations suggest. Far from being homophobic, he took a libertarian position that gays and lesbians should not be persecuted. The most accurate summation of his views appeared in a note drafted by an unnamed aide in readiness for possible questions on the subject of homosexuality in the 1980 election. It read: '1) Gays don't bother him; 2) But doesn't want to encourage it and say it's fine.' This explains Reagan's view that the 1984 Democratic platform endorsing gay rights 'was political pandering of the worst kind'. While opposed to criminalization of homosexuality, he told a friend that 'those people [...] are demanding recognition and approval of their lifestyle and no one has a right to demand that'.[26]

The charge made by Kramer and many others that Reagan did not speak out on Aids until the seventh year of his presidency is incorrect. He first mentioned the disease in press-conference remarks on 17 September 1985. More significantly, when speaking to HHS employees in early 1986, he declared:

> One of our highest public health priorities is going to continue to be finding a cure for AIDS. We're going to continue to try to develop and test vaccines, and we're going to focus also on prevention.

To this end Reagan announced that he would charge surgeon general Everett Koop to prepare a major report for the American people on Aids.[27] By now, federal spending to counter the disease was growing rapidly to reach a cumulative total of $5.6 billion from FY1984 to FY1989. Admittedly, the White House was responsible for proposing only half this sum, with the remaining appropriations added by Democratic legislators, but Reagan approved the increases.[28] The first breakthrough in the development of drugs capable of slowing the disease only came in the 1990s, however. It is doubtful that Reagan could have done anything significantly to accelerate their discovery. As one Aids sufferer acknowledged: 'An instant cure for HIV was never going to be possible. Science takes time.'[29]

Nevertheless, Reagan's record on Aids had significant shortcomings. In 1987 he tried to comfort a woman whose family was ravaged by the disease: 'There is no question but that "AIDS" is an emergency calling on all of us to do everything we can in the face of tragedies such as the one you are experiencing.'[30] In light of these words, Reagan should have done all in his power to support the Koop report's call for a wide-ranging prevention campaign, including promotion of condom use and provision of Aids information in schools. Offering a model of what could be done, Margaret Thatcher's Conservative government in 1987 instituted a hard-hitting public-information campaign (headlined 'AIDS: Don't Die of Ignorance') that helped to constrain UK infection rates. An anti-gay fundamentalist Presbyterian, Koop put saving lives above his conservative preferences, a stand that earned him condemnation as a turncoat from moral conservatives, among them secretary of education William Bennett and White House domestic-policy advisor Gary Bauer. This duo combined forces to persuade the president against association with the kind of public information campaign that the surgeon general envisaged.[31]

Had Reagan been willing to use his bully pulpit more forthrightly, he might have helped Americans better understand the crisis, urged sympathy for those living with the stigma of the disease, and shown sufferers that their president grieved for them. Instead of demonstrating his powers of rhetorical symbolism, his most important speech on the disease, delivered at Nancy's prompting to a fundraising dinner for the American Foundation for AIDS Research on 31 May 1987, highlighted the limitations of his Aids leadership. Adopting an uncharacteristically passive approach in the debate over the content of the address, he left Landon Parvin to battle alone against administration conservatives. Surgeon general Koop had suggested inclusion of a passage that read: 'It's […] important that Americans not judge those who have the disease but care for them with dignity and kindness. Passing moral judgments is up to God; our part is to ease the suffering and to find a cure.' This prompted Carl Anderson, a conservative aide in the Office of Public Liaison, to object, 'Failure to make moral judgments on this behavior is why we have this epidemic.'[32] The watered-down version that appeared in the final text lacked the emotive impact of the original. Words of approval for a limited programme of compulsory Aids testing, inserted over Parvin's objections, elicited predictable boos. The audience would have been even more disappointed had it known of the removal of a passage praising the campaign for greater education about the disease waged by Indiana teenager Ryan White, the victim of communal prejudice after contracting Aids from a blood-clotting agent used to treat his haemophilia.[33]

Reagan had already passed up a tailor-made opportunity to promote Aids awareness personally when movie star and closet gay Rock Hudson died from the disease in October 1985. Some months earlier, the dying star, already widely rumoured in the media to have the illness, had desperately sought experimental medical treatment in Paris. Knowing the Reagans were friendly with him since their Hollywood days, Hudson's publicist asked for assistance to get him transferred to a French military hospital where the country's top Aids specialist was based. Taking the decision upon herself, Nancy decided in the words of one aide that this was 'not [...] something the White House should get into'. In her view, such preferential treatment for a celebrity friend was inappropriate – an explanation that Aids campaigners treated with incredulity when it came to light 30 years later.[34] The star's death became the hook by which the media alerted the public to the growing severity of the Aids crisis. It also shook a hitherto complacent president into recognizing that the disease was a killer rather than a virus like measles that sufferers could recover from. Despite this, Reagan spurned the chance to demonstrate sympathy for all sufferers by attending Hudson's memorial service. Asked by celebrity Aids campaigner Elizabeth Taylor for a personal message to be read at the event, Reagan merely put his signature to words drafted by an aide. This followed a perfunctorily brief public statement of sorrow at news of Hudson's death.[35]

After he left the White House, Reagan would show greater boldness in meeting twice with Ryan White in Los Angeles weeks before the teenager's death at age 18 in 1990. 'We owe it to Ryan,' he declared in a moving eulogy, 'to be compassionate, caring and tolerant toward those with AIDS, their families and friends. It's the disease that's frightening, not the people who have it.'[36] Something akin to these post-presidential words would have had much greater significance had he found the courage to deliver them several years earlier when the need for Aids education and his influence were both at their peak.

Aids sufferers were one of the blind spots in Reagan's optimistic vision of America. Another blind spot could be said to be African Americans, a group for whom 'Morning Again in America' was largely a mirage. Having narrowed somewhat in the long postwar boom, the racial gap in wages and employment had started to widen again in the stagflation-hit 1970s, a trend that continued in the supposedly prosperous decade that followed. Inner-city poverty, family breakdown, and gang violence further blighted many black lives. Making matters worse, the police offensive against the crack-cocaine epidemic in the second half of the 1980s and beyond was clearly targeted at young black males. By 1989, one analysis calculated, 23 per cent of African American men aged 18 to 29 were caught up within the criminal justice system – whether in prison, on parole, or on probation (a figure that rose to 32 per cent over the next decade). It was later estimated that a black male born in 1991 had a 29 per cent chance of spending time in prison at some stage of his life, compared to 1 per cent for a white male. Accordingly, many African Americans thought Reagan's celebration of America's renewal manifested wilful disregard for their plight.[37]

Every president from Franklin D. Roosevelt to Jimmy Carter had demonstrated sympathy, albeit to varying extents, for the cause of civil rights, but Reagan broke with this half-century tradition. Despite lacking personal bigotry, he had already proved himself the most successful racial-backlash politician in US history before entering the White House. All of his campaigns, at both state and national level, featured rhetorical assaults on able-bodied welfare cheats that carried strong racial imagery. In the 1976 election he found a perfect target for this demagoguery in the 'Chicago welfare queen' who 'has eighty names, thirty addresses, twelve Social Security cards and is collecting veterans' benefits on four nonexistent deceased husbands' to reap a tax-free cash income of $150,000.[38] Although Reagan never identified her by name or race (black woman Linda Taylor, convicted of fraud in 1977), the not-so-subliminal message of the much-repeated anecdote reinforced a stereotypical view that many white people held of African Americans.

As president, Reagan espoused a colour-blind conservatism that denied any racial intent in his anti-statist agenda, which hit African Americans harder than white people because they relied on government to mitigate the structural inequalities of American society. Lack of interest rather than prejudice blinded him to this reality. Race relations held low priority in his tightly focused political agenda. Taking their cue from his small-government values, however, others in the administration pressed forward with retrenchment of public-assistance programmes that benefited low-income African Americans, unsuccessful efforts to gut a number of 1960s civil-rights initiatives, and regular submissions of hostile legal briefs in high-profile judicial cases regarding racial-preference issues.[39]

Adding insult to injury, Reagan initially opposed legislation to make Martin Luther King's birthday a public holiday, ostensibly on cost grounds that federal workers would gain a tenth annual holiday, but his public and private remarks suggested other motives. Flippant comments at a press conference on 19 October 1983 implied that King might have been a communist sympathizer. 'I almost lost my dinner over that,' White House communications director David Gergen told a journalist.[40] Former New Hampshire governor Meldrim Thomson then released a letter from Reagan saying that he shared this John Birch Society member's reservations about the public holiday because admiration for the civil rights leader was 'based on an image not reality'. An embarrassed president had to telephone Coretta Scott King to offer a convoluted apology-cum-explanation for his remarks about her husband.[41] Faced with overwhelming support for the bill in Congress, Reagan relented to sign it into law on 2 November. Gracious words at the signing ceremony went some way to make up for his earlier comments but it was unclear which ones represented his true feelings.

On a personal level, the 40th president showed many instances of kindness towards African Americans as individuals. As a gesture of solidarity, the Reagans visited with a black family – the husband and wife were government employees – after reading press reports about their racial harassment (including a cross-burning incident) in College Park, Maryland. 'There is no place in this land for the hate-mongers and bigots,' Reagan wrote in his diary. Later, he intervened to help an unemployed black father of eight secure a job after learning of his heroism in rescuing a blind man fallen between the cars on the New York subway. Moreover, to publicize Partnerships in Education, a project encouraging private-sector involvement in educating schoolchildren, Reagan entered into a pen-pal correspondence with a five-year-old African American, Rudolph Lee-Hines. Ruddy, as he was known, was selected for this honour because of his excellent literacy skills, developed at Congress Heights Elementary School in south-east Washington DC with the help of IBM's Writing to Read software.[42]

Nevertheless, Reagan failed to communicate sympathy and support for African Americans in their broader freedom struggle against racism, inequality, and economic disadvantage. Instead of seeking dialogue with black critics, he largely ignored them. In particular, he stopped meeting with the Congressional Black Caucus early in his presidency. At first he tried to rebut in private National Association for the Advancement of Colored People (NAACP) criticisms of his economic policies by pointing out that even low-income African Americans had more purchasing power because of the conquest of inflation. Attempts at bridge building diminished in his second term. Reagan made no response to NAACP chair William Gibson's remarks that he was 'reactionary and [...] racist'.[43] There was one black voice that could not be disregarded. Legendary civil-rights champion Thurgood Marshall, appointed the first black Supreme Court justice in 1968, decried Reagan's record on race as the worst of any modern president. 'I think he's down with [Herbert] Hoover and that group. [Woodrow] Wilson. When we really didn't have a chance,' he declared in a 1987 television interview. Such public criticism of an incumbent president by a sitting justice was almost unprecedented. A worried Reagan invited Marshall to the White House to tell him 'my life story & how there was not prejudice in me'. He reported in his diary that night, 'I think I made a friend.'[44] This was wishful thinking but it reflected Reagan's tendency to see good relations with individual African Americans as an acceptable substitute for broader outreach.

'For all my so-called powers of communication,' Reagan would admit, 'I was never able to convince many black citizens of my commitment to their needs. They often mistook my belief in keeping government out [of] the average American's life as a cover for doing nothing about racial injustice.'[45] Why he should have been surprised that African Americans did not warm to him spoke volumes about his incapacity to understand their problems. One second-term episode in particular highlighted his insensitivity on this score. Civil-rights groups had long clamoured for legislative redress against the Supreme Court's

Grove City v. Bell judgement of 1984 narrowing application of federal civil-rights laws only to educational institutions that accepted national-government funding. When Congress enacted the Civil Rights Restoration Act of 1988 to strengthen anti-bias law, Reagan became the first president since Andrew Johnson (arguably the most racist of all White House occupants) in 1866 to veto a civil-rights bill. His reasoning was consistent with longstanding personal opposition to measures that 'vastly and unjustifiably extend the power of the federal government over the decisions and affairs of private organizations'. Reagan then offered an alternative Civil Rights Protection bill that overturned *Grove City* but exempted religiously affiliated colleges from its provisions. Ignoring this proposal, Congress overrode the veto, with many Republicans crossing the floor to vote with the Democrats.[46]

Despite failing to change Reagan's approach to racial issues at home, African Americans found a way to express their antagonism to his presidency by inflicting one of its greatest foreign-policy defeats. The administration pursued a policy of 'constructive engagement' to persuade the South African government to modify its apartheid policy. 'We must continue,' Reagan declared in a NSC meeting, 'to seek the end of apartheid, but through gradualism in the political process that serves the best interests of all in South Africa who want to avoid bloodshed and revolution.'[47] A tougher stance supposedly ran the risk of generating either bloody revolution or a repressive crackdown by the Pretoria regime. Further weighing on Reagan's calculations, South Africa was a key ally in America's regional Cold War strategy to weaken Angola's pro-Soviet regime.[48]

Gradualism became harder to justify when the South African government in late 1983 began a violent crackdown on anti-apartheid demonstrations that television beamed to a worldwide audience. Backed by the UK, the United States continued to veto UN attempts to impose economic sanctions against it. In December 1984 Cape Town's Anglican bishop and recent Nobel Peace Prize winner, Desmond Tutu, a critic of constructive engagement as 'immoral, evil, and totally un-Christian', visited the White House to plead for sanctions but there was no meeting of minds between the president and the campaigning cleric. Reagan dismissively commented in his diary that Tutu was naive because of his failure to recognize that American firms in South Africa contributed significantly to black economic uplift. In a breathtaking I-know-best comment, he also remarked: 'The Bishop seems unaware, even though he himself is Black, that part of the problem is tribal not racial. If apartheid ended now there still would be civil strife between the Black tribes.'[49]

Going on the offensive, civil-rights organizations formed the Free South Africa Movement (FSAM), which attracted the support of trade unions, churches, campuses, and celebrities to become the most successful protest since the 1960s. Many of its activists went to prison for engaging in civil disobedience while protesting US support for Pretoria.[50] Reagan vainly tried to persuade FSAM's celebrity supporters, like Sammy Davis Jr, that the South African question was 'a much more complex problem than it appears on the surface'. While acknowledging that apartheid was 'an evil that must be eliminated', he insisted that 'we have a better chance of doing so if we maintain contact than if we pick up our marbles and walk away'.[51]

Meanwhile, a sanctions bill sponsored by the Congressional Black Caucus began to make headway in Congress, as public opinion grew increasingly aware of what was happening in South Africa. The White House tried to head it off by ordering limited sanctions on 9 September 1985 but this only provoked Desmond Tutu into denouncing Reagan as 'a racist pure and simple'. Even a major presidential address in July 1986 expressing moral repugnance at apartheid but opposing sanctions because they would primarily hurt black employment in South Africa failed to stem the tide.[52] The Comprehensive Anti-Apartheid Act carried the day with bipartisan support some two months later. Still clinging to the wrong side of history, Reagan issued a veto on grounds that the bill amounted to 'economic warfare' that 'would seriously impede the prospects for a peaceful end to apartheid'. Despite his frantic efforts to corral support, the GOP-controlled Senate overrode him 78 to 21 on 3 October 1986. Speaking for many Republicans, Senate majority leader Bob Dole of Kansas said the vote was a 'litmus test' of support for civil rights at home and abroad.[53]

Doubtless apartheid would have crumbled in time but sanctions certainly hastened its demise, not least because other nations quickly followed America's lead. In 1990 South African president F. W. de Klerk began releasing political prisoners held for challenging apartheid as the first step towards its termination. Among them was Nelson Mandela, who told how FSAM protests had lifted his spirits while in jail. 'It was,' he declared, 'an impressive role for Black Americans to choose arrest.' After Mandela's death in 2013, James Baker declared on

CBS's *Face the Nation* that Reagan came to regret the anti-apartheid veto, but offered no evidence to support this questionable assertion. Far from expressing repentance, Reagan told one correspondent some ten months after casting it, 'I wish my veto of the sanctions bill had been upheld.'[54] Moreover, he blanked the episode, and indeed any mention of South Africa, from his 1990 memoir that was his best opportunity to set the record straight about the success of sanctions.

Though less threatening than Aids and less pernicious than race, the other great shadow over 'Morning Again in America' was the large fiscal deficit that many analysts feared would undermine the nation's future prosperity. Reagan's domestic priority at the start of his second term was to balance the budget by its end.[55] The blithe assumption that landslide re-election constituted a mandate for doing so through spending retrenchment was dispelled within days of his second inauguration. The FY1986 budget plan sent to Congress was declared 'dead on arrival' by Democrats and a goodly number of Republicans for proposing a 6 per cent defence increase alongside large multi-year domestic cuts. Unable to secure the anti-deficit plan he wanted, Reagan fell back on protecting his fiscal priorities against the efforts of other actors to resolve the budget problem. While still condemning deficits as the agency of big government, he only waged phony war against them henceforth.

In contrast, Bob Dole was determined to conquer the new red peril to enhance his presidential credentials for 1988. The Senate leader joined forces with Budget Committee chair Pete Domenici of New Mexico and the administration's leading deficit hawk, Office of Management and Budget director David Stockman, to devise a package of large expenditure economies that spared neither entitlements nor defence. Their assumption was that House Democrats would then insist on tax increases as the price for supporting deficit reduction. In this scenario Reagan would have no option but to accept revenue enhancement as a means of modifying the defence cuts. After months of patient negotiation and no little compromise, Dole won Senate approval for a FY1986 budget resolution featuring a three-year freeze of defence and entitlement spending and domestic programme cuts, enough to halve the FY1985 deficit level of $212 billion by FY1988. However, the House Democrats had no intention of being cast in the role of tax-hikers. In light of Mondale's crushing defeat, speaker Tip O'Neill was determined to make the Republicans take the initiative on this score, a strategy that freed him from having to agree entitlement savings as the price of higher taxes. His lieutenants produced a budget plan that matched the savings in the Senate version but relied on more substantive defence cuts and questionable assumptions about lower interest payments to achieve them.[56]

Learning that Dole was ready to put tax increases on the table to win O'Neill's approval of entitlement cuts, Reagan declared unequivocally, 'I'll repeat it until I am blue in the face: I will veto any tax increase the Congress sends me.'[57] The president eventually met with congressional leaders on the evening of 9 July to discuss the impasse over cocktails on the patio adjoining the Oval Office. After an angry exchange over tax increases, Reagan and O'Neill huddled together to make peace under a nearby oak tree. They made a deal to safeguard their respective priorities – the president agreed to strike out the entitlement economies in return for no tax increases and a defence figure acceptable to him. Taken completely by surprise when the next day's papers carried the news, Dole understood he had been outmanoeuvred. 'There was an agreement under an oak tree,' he complained, 'and it was [my] limb they sawed off.' A disgusted Stockman resigned office in the belief that the last chance of a real offence on the deficit was gone. Congress ended up agreeing a smoke-and-mirrors plan that promised to halve the deficit in three years but the economies supposed to deliver this were never realized. The most significant achievement was to slow rather than stop the expansion of the defence budget.[58]

There was still a political cost in this for Reagan. Republican senators, especially those up for re-election in 1986, were furious that their risky support for entitlement cuts had been for naught. 'People feel they flew a kamikaze mission and ended up in flames and got nothing for it,' remonstrated Warren Rudman of New Hampshire.[59] Unable to rely on Reagan to raise the banner of fiscal responsibility, Rudman teamed up with two fellow senators, Republican Phil Gramm of Texas and Democrat Ernest Hollings of South Carolina, to promote enactment of the Balanced Budget and Emergency Deficit Reduction Act of 1985, better known as Gramm–Rudman–Hollings (GRH). Described by Rudman as a 'bad idea whose time has come', this mandated annually targeted deficit reduction to achieve a balanced budget by 1991 on penalty of annual sequestration of funds by the comptroller general, an agent of Congress, if the imbalance was $10 billion over target in any year. In negotiations to secure GRH's passage, however, the Senate excluded Social Security from its terms and the House followed suit for medical entitlements, thereby removing some three-fifths of spending from sequestration. Far from imposing automatic fiscal discipline, the new arrangement made matters worse because it encouraged optimistic revenue assessments and delays in approving a budget to avoid sequestration of funds that could only be required before the start of the fiscal year.[60]

Despite signing GRH, Reagan repeatedly warned that a defence sequester would only help the Soviet Union and avowed that he would never agree a tax increase to keep deficit reduction on schedule. To safeguard these priorities, the Justice Department supported a suit brought by Representative Mike Synar, an Oklahoma Democrat, challenging the constitutionality of the sequestration process. In early 1986 a federal court ruled in their favour that enforcement should be an executive responsibility, an opinion upheld by the Supreme Court. GRH continued to operate but without any mechanism to compel fiscal discipline. This was a recipe for prolonged stand-off over deficit reduction between the White House and the legislature after the Democrats captured control of the Senate in the 1986 midterm elections. Eventually the opposition party blinked first to protect domestic programmes that served its low-income constituencies. In September 1987 Congress attached a rider to a debt-ceiling extension bill in the form of the Emergency Deficit Control Reaffirmation Act that relaxed GRH targets to achieve a balanced budget by 1993 and empowered the OMB, an executive agency, to formulate any required sequester. This only kicked the deficit can down the road to be addressed when Reagan was no longer president. It gave the White House and Congress the best of both worlds – the appearance of doing something that added up in reality to very little.[61]

Despite the lack of political will to tackle the deficit, continuous economic growth facilitated its decline from 5.1 per cent GDP in FY1985 to 2.8 per cent GDP in FY1989. This was roughly where it had stood in Jimmy Carter's final year when the economy was ravaged by stagflation. What Reagan had then decried as a fiscal mess had now seemingly become acceptable to him after six years of prosperity. Offering an utterly disingenuous defence of his record, he declared in his memoirs: 'Deficits [...] aren't caused by too little taxing [but] by too much spending. Presidents don't create deficits, Congress does. Presidents can't appropriate a dollar of taxpayers' money – only congressmen can.'[62] Yet he had never submitted a balanced-budget plan to Congress, had contributed mightily to spending growth through his defence programme, and had competed with Congress in his second term for the title of artful dodger in their mutual game of fiscal legerdemain.

Reagan left it to the political leaders of the 1990s to bring the deficit under control through tough fiscal measures that involved trade-offs of some partisan priorities. His last roll of the dice in pursuit of this end was the less immediately painful one of promoting a balanced-budget constitutional amendment. Democratic victory in the 1986 midterm elections seemingly ended hopes that Congress would approve such a reform. To pressurize the opposition party, Reagan appeared ready to make common cause with the grassroots movement that had been engaged since the mid-1970s in a campaign to get the required three-quarters of state legislatures to petition for a constitutional convention to adopt such an amendment. With only two more states needed to attain this supermajority, he delivered a speech on the steps of the Jefferson Memorial on 3 July 1987 in sweltering heat to a crowd of 5,000. 'I don't remember ever being hotter than I was on that platform in the sun,' he later remarked. Reagan envisioned a new Economic Bill of Rights that would safeguard economic freedoms in the way the original had protected political ones. Its centrepiece was to be a balanced-budget constitutional amendment containing a tax-limitation provision. This came with a warning that congressional refusal to act would leave him 'no choice but to take my case directly to the States', but the implied threat boomeranged on him.[63]

A constitutional convention – a hitherto untested device – ran the risk of being uncontrollable once called. A *New York Times* editorial took Reagan to task for 'playing with matches […] to push his pet amendment'. Fear that such a gathering would promote wholesale constitutional change had engendered a counter-movement that brought together liberal and conservative groups in a quest to rescind existing state petitions. This drew increased strength from the bicentennial celebrations of the Constitution's founding in 1787 that reminded Americans what they might lose if a convention were called. Alabama and Florida consequently withdrew their petitions in the spring of 1988. The balanced-budget constitutional-convention movement that had entered the 1980s believing victory was at hand was in retreat by its end. Small wonder that one of its leaders adjudged Reagan's contribution to the cause as 'pretty pathetic'.[64]

In contrast, the Tax Reform Act (TRA) of 1986 stood out as the most positive fiscal achievement of Reagan's second term. The announcement in the 1984 State of the Union Address that the Treasury would report on the need for such a measure was widely regarded as nothing more than a pre-emptive strike against Democratic plans to make tax fairness the centrepiece of their presidential campaign. In fact, Treasury secretary Donald Regan was utterly committed to transform a tax system that was, in his words, 'complicated, inequitable, expensive to administrate, and so filled with loopholes that it was entirely unnecessary to cheat on taxes in order to avoid them'. Slowly but surely, he had won Reagan over to the cause of tax fairness by educating him about inequities that needed elimination. Briefing the president in late 1983, he began with a question about his boss's old employer: 'What does General Electric have in common with Boeing, General Dynamics, and fifty-seven other big corporations?' To Reagan's utter amazement and embarrassment, the answer was that none of them paid a cent in federal taxes. On another occasion, the Treasury secretary told his boss that he was a 'sucker' for having paid his full taxes before becoming president when he could have got away with paying nothing by hiring an accountant to exploit the plentiful tax shelters benefiting the rich.[65]

When released in early 1985, the Treasury report received an enthusiastic reception from the press and think-tanks of all hues and the opposite from corporate bodies, both private and public, with stakes in the current system. By now, James Baker had become Treasury secretary and Donald Regan had assumed his old job. The two collaborated to persuade the president to make a revenue-neutral tax reform that would not add to the deficit his principal second-term domestic initiative.[66] Reagan announced his plan 'for fairness, growth and simplicity' in a nationally televised address on 28 May 1985. Having played no part in its formulation, he now became the major salesman barnstorming the country in its support. Framing the issue as a choice between enhancing tax equity or protecting unfair tax breaks made it difficult for the Democrats to oppose him and put Republican objectors in the uncomfortable position of defending special interests.[67] Even so, it took nearly 18 months of legislative manoeuvring to secure TRA's enactment over the opposition of a veritable army of tax lobbyists.[68]

The most thoroughgoing reform of the tax system since World War II, TRA simplified the tax code from 14 brackets to two – 28 per cent for top earners and 15 per cent for everyone else. It also increased personal exemptions and standard deductions to remove 6 million working poor from the rolls and expanded the earned-income credit for low-income taxpayers. Conversely, TRA hit the rich with an increase in capital-gains tax and a reduction or elimination of tax breaks for business and investors, but provided some compensation in reducing the top corporate-tax band from 46 per cent to 33 per cent. In total, 60 per cent of individual taxpayers ended up paying lower taxes, 25 per cent paid the same as before, and 15 per cent paid higher taxes. This was the first time that a tax measure had picked winners and losers. Increasing the burden for the latter, mostly wealthy individuals and businesses whose loss of preferences was greater than their gains from rate reductions, paid for TRA's bounty to lower-band taxpayers.[69]

Of all the political actors who had a part in enacting TRA, the most important was Reagan. Without his backing, the measure would have got nowhere. Presidential appeals to the ideal of fairness trumped special-interest influence that habitually shaped tax legislation. Surprised but delighted at the outcome, Senator Daniel Patrick Moynihan of New York called TRA's passage 'the most ethical event I've ever seen in this place'.[70] Reagan's reward was a tax system that was in line with his political preferences – the top income-tax band that had stood at 70 per cent in 1980 was now a mere 28 per cent, a reduction achieved in the name of fairness. At the same time, TRA's benefits for middle-income taxpayers and the working poor proved very significant in preserving Reagan's low-tax legacy when deficit-reduction took centre stage in the 1990s. It had draped the flag of fairness around lower rates on personal taxes at the price of wiping out the remaining tax preferences that could feasibly be removed. With very limited opportunity to enhance revenue through further loophole closures, future budget-policy makers would need to increase income taxes, a politically risky choice, or cut spending to bring the fiscal ledgers into balance.

The outcome of the 1986 midterm elections confirmed that a new Republican majority would not stand alongside TRA as part of Reagan's political legacy. In contrast to recession-hit 1982, the president was a major asset to the GOP on this occasion, but it could not benefit from his strong Gallup approval scores at a time of peace and prosperity. Midterm bloody noses were the usual fate of a second-term president's party, whose average losses in every such contest since 1918 numbered 41 House seats and seven Senate seats. Reagan helped

Republicans do rather better than this dismal norm by mounting an aggressive campaign schedule that entailed travelling 24,000 miles to make 54 appearances in 22 states. The GOP lost just five House seats but eight senators went down – including freshmen whom presidential coat-tails had carried to narrow victory in 1980. Even so, the Senate outcome was closer than it looked because the Republicans won a higher share of the two-party-vote (49 per cent) than in 1980 (47 per cent). Having announced his political retirement, Tip O'Neill took pleasure in claiming that the historical pendulum had swung back to his party. 'If there ever was a Reagan Revolution, it's over,' he crowed. More accurately, the outcome was the product of the American electorate's divided mind. It certainly did not signify that the Democrats had regained majority status.[71]

As well as clashing with Reagan over the budget deficit, the Democrats resisted his administration's efforts under the direction of the Justice Department to create a conservative federal judiciary. The expansion of appointments to the 13 Courts of Appeal with regionally based jurisdictions and the 94 District Courts to deal with growing caseloads provided the opportunity to put right-minded judges in place. The project gathered momentum when Ed Meese became attorney general in February 1985 with a mission to restore a jurisprudence of original intent, which purported to interpret the Constitution in terms of what those who formulated this document meant it to be. Rejecting any doubt whether the founders had a single, unifying intent that could be accurately perceived two centuries later, this doctrine legitimized rollback of modern judicial policy based on 'living Constitution' theory that the nation's supreme law should be reinterpreted in accordance with changing times. In its name, Justice Department officials instituted a centralized screening and interview process for federal judgeship nominees. Traditional criteria for selection, such as patronage rewards, bipartisanship, and intellectual reputation, went out the window. Henceforth, only the candidates with the required ideological credentials went forward for ultimate approval by the White House Judicial Selection Committee. That said, just over half the Reagan nominees received the American Bar Association's highest ratings (exceptionally well qualified/well qualified), a larger share than achieved by his four immediate predecessors.[72]

The GOP-controlled Senate gave enthusiastic support for administration litmus testing of lower-court nominees. The Democrats, meanwhile, kept their powder dry in readiness to battle changes in Supreme Court personnel. They strongly opposed but could not prevent the promotion to chief justice of this body's most conservative member, William Rehnquist, on incumbent Warren Burger's retirement in 1986. This left them bereft of political capital to challenge the highly conservative Antonin Scalia's nomination to replace Rehnquist as associate justice. The donnybrook was a storm warning of tougher fights ahead once control of the Senate changed hands. The 1987 nomination of Robert Bork to replace retiring justice Lewis Powell became the *casus belli*. A highly regarded conservative jurist, Bork had a broad footprint of public opposition to liberal jurisprudence on race, abortion, and privacy issues. Leading the battle against him, Senate Judiciary Committee chair Joseph Biden of Delaware declared: 'I don't have an open mind. The reason I don't is that I know this man.' Fulminating against 'left wing ideologs [*sic*]', Reagan characterized the assault on Bork as a 'disgraceful, distortion of fact', but this ignored the reality that conservative Democrats and a group of moderate Republicans deemed him too controversial.[73] The 58 to 42 nay vote was the largest ever cast against a Supreme Court nominee. A hurried search for a replacement produced District of Columbia Court of Appeals judge Douglas Ginsburg, an opponent of the 1960s cultural legacy but also a sampler of its forbidden fruit. Revelations of his pot-smoking required the White House to find a more dependable conservative. It was third time lucky for Reagan – Anthony Kennedy sailed through his confirmation after expressing disagreement with the more extreme ideals of original intent associated with the likes of Bork.

In the battle of the bench, the White House emerged points victor as far as the Supreme Court was concerned. Reagan's four appointees weighed in against further expansion of judicial activism on race, gender, and privacy. The embattled bloc of liberal justices now had its work cut out to limit conservative success in undoing past activism. At the lower-court level, in contrast, Reagan was the unambiguous winner – 379 of all 712 federal judges were his nominees by the time he left office. No president had previously secured so many judicial appointees, and only FDR had nominated a higher proportion of the federal bench. The transformation of this arm of the judiciary would prove one of Reagan's most durable legacies.

As Reagan's tenure drew to an end, debate over his domestic legacy increasingly focused on the economy. The valedictory messages delivered from the presidential podium assiduously portrayed the 1980s as an era of renewed prosperity, growth, and optimism about the economic future that only a return of big government could derail. Reinforcing this message, his memoirs recounted that of the many changes that occurred on his watch, 'I'm probably proudest about the economy.' This was also the dominant narrative being developed by conservative publicists of the free market as a means to keep America right with Reagan gone. Former presidential aide Martin Anderson typically trumpeted:

> It was the greatest expansion in history. Wealth poured from the factories of the United States, and Americans got richer and richer [...]
> [The United States] is now an economic colossus of such size and scope that we have no effective way to describe its power and reach.[74]

Not everyone was singing from the same song sheet, however. Most significantly, Paul Volcker led the Federal Reserve into a new round of interest-rate hikes to counter renewal of inflationary pressures in the first half of 1987. The Treasury and the president's economic advisors worried that this change of monetary course would slow down economic growth – or even worse, tip the economy into recession – to the consequent detriment of Reagan's reputation as the manager of prosperity and of GOP prospects in the 1988 elections. Hoping to make Volcker more accommodating, the White House delayed announcing whether he was to be nominated to a third term as Fed chair. Already suspicious that his independence to ensure price stability was under threat from a pro-growth faction of recent Reagan appointees to the central bank's board of governors, Volcker pre-empted matters by announcing his retirement. Delighted that the troublesome priest had fallen on his own sword, James Baker told a friend, 'We got the son of a bitch.'[75]

Virtually the first problem that Volcker's successor, Alan Greenspan, found himself dealing with was the 'Black Monday' Wall Street crash of 19 October 1987 that produced a 22 per cent fall in the Dow Jones industrial average (representing half a trillion dollars in market capitalization), a then record single-day decline. This came after two days of heavy losses on 15 and 16 October, which meant the Dow had lost a third of its value in three days. The roots of the collapse lay in the overvaluation of stocks in the get-rich-quick times, foreign sell-offs of US assets in the face of a declining dollar (the result of the Plaza

Accord that Volcker and Baker had negotiated with G7 partners in 1985 to control the trade deficit), and worry about the effects of the budget deficit on the economy's wellbeing. Reagan remained calm during the crisis but it was a closer run thing than he realized. His diary entry on 20 October recorded that the market had recovered to close at 108.27 up, an observation that did not catch the volatility earlier in the day when many securities firms experienced liquidity problems resulting from the fallen value of their holdings. According to financier Felix Rohatyn, this was 'the most dangerous day' for Wall Street in almost 50 years, one in which meltdown had perhaps been only an hour away.[76]

The crash did not set off a chain reaction because the Fed slashed interest rates to head off a recession and heavy purchase of dollars by foreign central banks put a floor under America's currency. This outcome persuaded Reagan that the stock-market slump was a speculative blip of secondary importance to the key indicators of strong growth, low inflation, and declining unemployment. 'I learned in economics that there's nothing so timid as a million dollars,' he bullishly remarked to British journalist Godfrey Hodgson. Nevertheless, Wall Street's wobble signified that the Reagan economy was not the faultless engine of lasting prosperity that cheerleaders portrayed. It precipitated a counter-narrative from critics that overconsumption, underinvestment, and excessive borrowing from abroad spelled trouble for the post-Gipper United States.[77]

The savings-and-loans (S&L) crisis cast another dark cloud over the new morning that Reagan had promised. S&L 'thrifts' were once heavily regulated institutions that provided low fixed-interest home mortgages. To facilitate their competition for funds with other financial institutions at a time of rising interest rates, Congress relaxed the rules governing their operations in 1980. Two years later another Congress-initiated deregulation allowed them to move into new financial markets. In signing the Garn–St Germain Act of 1982, Reagan commented, 'All in all, I think we hit the jackpot.' Instead, a combination of reckless lending, fraud, and lax federal oversight brought many S&Ls to grief. By early 1989, about a third were insolvent and another third were financially weak. It would require a massive mid-1990s bailout costing the taxpayer some $123 billion to rescue the industry. The bill would have been a fraction of this had the Reagan administration intervened to put S&Ls on a sound footing amid the first wave of thrift failures in the mid-1980s. Industry regulator Edwin Gray, originally a proponent of deregulation, changed his tune to urge stronger supervision, only to be fired for his pains. Blinkered by free-market ideology, administration deregulators regarded any adjustment to deal with complex reality tantamount to reregulation, the ultimate sin in their vision. Sailing serenely above it all, Reagan never acknowledged the scale of the problem, an admission that would have tarnished his legacy.[78]

As the S&L debacle signified, greed and corruption fed off each other in the get-rich-quick atmosphere of the 1980s. In 1983, Reagan had remarked, 'What I want to see above all is that this country remains a country where someone can always get rich.' Many people did get rich during his tenure – the number of millionaires rose from 4,414 in 1980, to 34,944 in 1987, and the 21 billionaires counted in 1982 had risen to 71 by 1991.[79] The accumulation of wealth was not always achieved through legitimate means. Corruption was everywhere but nested most comfortably in New York City, the seat of financial power, and in Washington, the seat of government power. The US attorney for the southern district of New York, Rudolph Giuliani, built a political career by bringing to book a host of Wall Street insider traders. The most notable scalp was that of risk arbitrageur Ivan Boesky, who had famously remarked in 1986: 'Greed is all right [...] Greed is healthy.'[80] In the nation's capital, those trying to live up to the truth of these words had a bipartisan stripe. Their numbers included legislators, political appointees in federal agencies (most notably the Department of Housing and Urban Development), and three men instrumental in building Reagan's political career.

Michael Deaver, a man of modest background, left the White House in early 1985 to establish a lobbying business that he euphemistically labelled a consulting firm in an unsuccessful effort to get round legal restrictions on lobbying by former White House officials. Indicted in 1987 for perjuring himself in grand-jury testimony about his activities, he was convicted and received a one-year suspended prison sentence. Lyn Nofziger, former assistant to the president for political affairs, fell afoul of the same rules in lobbying for WedTech, a Bronx military contractor, but his conviction was overturned on a technicality on appeal. Ed Meese was the subject of a lengthy investigation for habitually using his position in government for financial gain, including loans that were never repaid, failure to pay taxes, and sale of government positions. Only his decision to resign as attorney general in July 1988 and Washington's fatigue with corruption investigations likely saved him from indictment. In

1989 a report by the Justice Department's Office of Professional Responsibility concluded that Meese had engaged in 'conduct which should not be tolerated of any government employee, especially not the attorney general'.[81]

Reagan should have done more to clean house, but he was asleep at the tiller of the ship of state – on one occasion, literally. At a 40-minute Oval Office meeting on 22 April 1988, two senior Justice Department officials who had submitted their resignations in disgust with Meese explained why he should be fired, but the president nodded off before they could finish. By Reagan's final year in office, more than 100 of his appointees were being or had been investigated for corruption. One scandal resulted in 16 convictions being handed down for individuals involved in Department of Housing and Urban Development grant-rigging. Among them was former secretary of the interior James Watt, indicted on 23 counts of lobbying for favourable contracts for Republican contributors and put on probation for five years after pleading guilty to one misdemeanour. Other institutions that fell afoul of corruption investigations included the Environmental Protection Agency, the Department of Justice, and the Department of Defense, where the FBI's Operation Ill Wind investigation resulted in the conviction of 50 officials for corruption in military procurement.[82]

Although much of the wrongdoing was exposed after Reagan left office, it marked his administration as the most corrupt of modern times. The failure to demand higher standards from Meese, Deaver, and Nofziger reflected an unfortunate willingness to believe the best of them. As he told one interviewer:

> I found those individuals to be the soul of integrity in the more than
> 20 years I've known them. I have a feeling there's a certain amount of
> politics involved in all this and that I'm really the target.[83]

This was a comforting retreat from unpleasant reality. Reagan similarly regarded charges against other officials as politically motivated, a perspective that excused him from enquiring into the truth. From this, it may be reasonably concluded that ethics in government was low on his rank of priorities.

As the looting decade ground on, many Americans who lived by the rules were feeling a growing sense of insecurity.[84] The sharp rise in income inequality attested that the fruits of prosperity disproportionately flowed towards the rich. Between 1980 and 1990, the average after-tax income of the top 1 per cent of households had risen by 73 per cent in inflation-adjusted terms, compared with an average gain of 5.6 per cent for the middle quintile of households, and no increase at all for the poorest quintile.[85] Many of the new jobs created in the Reagan era were in low-paid sectors, while the decline of manufacturing employment shrank the supply of well-paid blue-collar work. Millions of ordinary families now had to finance their consumption either by borrowing or by having two adult earners. Meanwhile, job security was diminishing in no small part owing to the record wave of 25,000 corporate buyouts, mergers, and restructuring – especially in the chemicals, oil, food, retailing, and mass-media sectors. In total, $1.3 trillion in corporate assets changed hands in the 1980s – a development facilitated by the Reagan administration's reform of antitrust policy and the abundant availability of loan finance that owed much to the expansion of the fiscal deficit on its watch. Much of this acquisition resulted in the de-conglomeration of large organizations and their replacement with more innovative, wealth-creating enterprises focused on core business. It was largely funded through borrowing, with the result that by 1986 American businesses needed 56 per cent of available earnings just to pay interest compared with the average of 33 per cent in the 1970s. They laid off thousands of workers, pared back wage structures, and transferred operations abroad to ease the debt burden.[86] GE, whose home electrical products Reagan used to promote on television, typified this trend by reducing its workforce from 411,000 in 1980 to 299,000 in 1985, through white-collar cutbacks, shop-floor lay-offs, and sell-offs of some operations. Moreover, its acquisition of other companies, some 600 in the last two decades of the twentieth century, was the prelude to selling off their unprofitable parts and keeping only so-called 'good units'.[87]

Compared with his first presidential term, Reagan's second-term domestic record was a disappointment. He had revived national confidence, helped to restore economic vigour, and changed the terms of political debate in his first four years. There was an element of marking time in the next four years that largely became a defence of his early legacy rather than a constructive engagement with problems that needed resolution. It would be in foreign policy that Reagan would make his main mark in the second term, but this involved a roller-coaster ride that flirted with disaster before culminating in triumph.

ELEVEN
Imperial President

The exposure in late 1986 of illegal and intersecting operations known as Iran–Contra marked the nadir of Ronald Reagan's White House tenure.[1] This might have become his Watergate had not official investigations depicted a detached president unaware that an out-of-control NSC was perpetrating illicit activities. Far from being disengaged from what was going on, Reagan was in reality the central figure driving the policy process of covert operations in the Middle East and Central America. Bizarre in conception and often incompetent in execution, Iran–Contra is most commonly described as a scandal, a term that downplays its significance as an abuse of presidential power. In essence it was a manifestation of what historian Arthur Schlesinger dubbed the 'imperial presidency', which routinely flouted the constitutional limits of executive authority in the name of national security. Born in World War II and consolidated in the Cold War, the imperial presidency had undergone decline as a result of Richard Nixon's Watergate disgrace, but Iran–Contra marked its renewal under Reagan.[2] Never doubting the supremacy of his office in national security, neither the 40th president nor his top officials had any patience with contrary assertions of congressional authority in this domain. Instead of seeing himself as an imperial president, Reagan thought he was battling an imperial legislature. 'Cong. has eroded away much of the Const. authority of the Presidency in foreign affairs matters,' he wrote in his diary. 'They can't & don't have the information the Pres. has & they are really lousing things up.'[3]

Iran–Contra emanated from the Reagan administration's rollback strategy against communism in the third world. In his 1985 State of the Union Address, the newly re-elected president avowed, '[W]e must not break faith with those who are risking their lives – on every continent, from Afghanistan to Nicaragua – to defy Soviet-supported aggression and secure rights which have been ours from birth.'[4] These words heralded the intensification of efforts to best the Soviets and their clients in different parts of the globe. Congress was a willing partner in financing presidential-directed covert operations in Asia and Africa, but no such consensus pertained to Central America. Reagan believed that US support for a ragtag band of Contra guerrillas seeking to overthrow the Marxist Sandinista government of Nicaragua was essential to save the whole of Latin America from communism. In contrast, many Democrats and the Central American peace movement of left-liberal groups that had coalesced in the nation saw the Sandinistas as engaged in a David-versus-Goliath struggle against brutal, anti-democratic cat's paws of Yankee imperialism.[5]

The success of rollback in Afghanistan contrasted with its frustration in Nicaragua. In early 1985 a new Soviet offensive threatened to achieve final victory against the Mujahideen resistance. In response, National Security Decision Directive (NSDD) 166 significantly redefined US objectives in Afghanistan. Abandoning the slow-bleed strategy pursued in its first term, the Reagan administration decided to equip indigenous fighters with the means to inflict heavy losses on Soviet forces. A supportive Congress approved a massive increase of funds to put military hardware directly in Mujahideen hands. The aim was to force the Soviet Union out of Afghanistan by demonstrating that its 'long-term strategy [...] is not working'. The new approach signalled that the United States would 'continue to oppose unacceptable Soviet behavior in other fields' while also pursuing an arms-control agreement with the Kremlin.[6]

A Reagan diary entry noted, 'We are really delivering help to the Afghans who are fighting the Soviets.'[7] The largest covert operation in American history supplied the Mujahideen with huge quantities of heavy machine guns, targeting devices for mortars linked to a US Navy satellite, and wire-guided, anti-tank cannons, all transported to isolated resistance strongholds on mules purchased from China. The Mujahideen's consequent success in beating back the Soviet offensive finally persuaded the Pentagon and CIA that its fighters could be entrusted to make good use of shoulder-fired Stinger anti-aircraft missiles. The 'magic amulets', as their grateful recipients dubbed them, had an immediate effect on the military balance from first battlefield use in September 1986. Thought to have downed in excess of 100 Soviet aircraft by the time the war ended, the Stingers compelled the effective grounding of the hitherto deadly Mi-24 helicopter gunships and forced Soviet planes to fly at out-of-range heights, with adverse consequences for their bombing and ground-support effectiveness.[8] By early 1988 it was evident that the USSR was no longer winning a war that had cost it 15,000 lives and over $100 billion in treasure. Unwilling to commit further resources to staunch what he called a 'bleeding wound', Soviet leader Mikhail Gorbachev announced that the Fortieth Army would quit Afghanistan over the course of the next 12 months.

A continent away, rollback scored another significant success in Angola. A massive expansion of Soviet and Cuban aid had brought the Marxist Popular Movement for the Liberation of Angola (MPLA) government close to victory in its decade-long civil war against National Union for the Total Liberation of Angola (UNITA) rebels by mid-1985. In August the White House persuaded Congress to repeal the Clark amendment of 1976 that had prohibited US aid to any Angola belligerent for fear that this could ultimately lead to direct military intervention in the manner of Vietnam. Reagan's Oval Office meeting with Jonas Savimbi, whom he described as 'a very impressive person', provided reassurance that the UNITA leader was the right man to save his country from communism.[9] Soon afterwards, NSDD-212 decreed that the United States should seek termination of Soviet aid for the MPLA and total withdrawal of Cuban military forces currently fighting as Soviet surrogates in Angola. A cornucopia of covert military aid for UNITA, including Stinger missiles not yet approved for Afghan fighters, restored the military balance between the indigenous combatants. In late 1988 Kremlin reassessment of its third-world interests paved the way for superpower agreement to end all foreign involvement in the Angolan Civil War.[10]

Reagan's commitment to rollback even extended to supporting a Marxist regime in the interests of detaching it from Moscow. To the horror of hard-shell conservatives, he met in September 1985 with President Samora Machel of Mozambique, who wanted US economic assistance for a country ravaged by civil war with South African-backed rebels. 'Turned out to be quite a guy,' Reagan recorded in his diary, '& I believe he really intends to be "non-aligned" instead of a communist patsy. We got along fine.'[11] Although Machel died in a plane crash shortly afterwards, his successor continued the policy of engagement with the United States. Helping Mozambique, Reagan reassured longstanding conservative backer Henry Salvatori, was 'worth a try' to undermine Soviet influence. Nevertheless, ideological purists like New Right leader Paul Weyrich regarded support for any Marxist regime as a betrayal of principle. 'It's amazing how certain they can be when they know so d—n little,' Reagan commented after a turbulent White House meeting with these critics.[12]

This was a storm in a teacup compared to the tempest of controversy that engulfed rollback efforts in Nicaragua. According to veteran diplomat Harry Shlaudeman, the president's special envoy to Central America, this tiny and impoverished country was 'an absolute foreign policy focus of the Reagan administration. Nothing was more important except the Soviet Union itself.'[13] This assessment attested to the exaggerated importance that Reagan placed on Nicaragua as a vital battleground in the global Cold War. In his eyes, the Soviet Union was intent on promoting Marxist revolution in Central America through the agency of Nicaragua's Sandinista regime in order to destabilize Mexico and South America and ultimately threaten the United States.[14] In September 1982, there were unfounded suspicions that Fidel Castro was about to despatch forces at Moscow's behest to assist the Managua regime in this task. Following a meeting of the National Security Planning Group (NSPG), Reagan noted in his diary, 'We have contingency plans leading all the way up to troop involvement if Cuba should send troops to stir the pot in Central Am.'[15] Soviet-bloc weaponry was certainly reaching El Salvador rebels via the Sandinistas, but whether on the massive scale claimed by CIA director William Casey (supposedly $350 million from 1981 to 1985, including tanks and MI-24 helicopters) was questionable. In reality, the Kremlin was more interested in distracting the United States than in establishing a bridgehead in the Americas.[16]

No one could have anticipated the trouble to come when the NSPG met on 10 November 1981 to discuss options for stopping the flow of Cuban weapons to the El Salvador rebels through Sandinista conduits. Reagan himself ruled out anything that could escalate into a Vietnam-style commitment, something he deemed 'the impossible option'. An aversion to the United States being seen in Latin America as 'the Yankee colossus' reinforced presidential resistance to direct military intervention. At the same time, he voiced determination to do something: 'I don't want to back down. I don't want to accept defeat.' To this end, he asked, 'What other covert actions can be taken that will be truly disabling and not just fleabites?' NSPG deliberations eventually resulted in approval of Casey's plan for the CIA to finance a force of 500 Nicaraguan 'Contras' (short for counter-revolutionaries) to conduct cross-border raids from bases in Honduras as a means of pressurizing the Sandinistas into good conduct. After signing a presidential finding authorizing $19 million for this purpose on 1 December, Reagan noted in his diary, 'We're proceeding with covert activity in Nicaragua to shut off supplies to the Guerillas in El Salvador.'[17]

It soon became evident that Contra ambitions extended beyond this limited objective to encompass overthrow of Sandinista rule. Casey was happy to wink at this, as was his boss. Reagan's continued and unqualified support for the Contras signalled that he would have no qualms if the outcome were the destruction of their mutual enemy. The Democrat-controlled House Intelligence Committee (HIC), which shared responsibility with its Senate counterpart for congressional oversight of the covert programme, was of quite different mind. Worried by press reports that more was afoot in Central America than it was being told, this body demanded White House assurance in April 1982 that US aid was not being used to destabilize a government the United States had formally recognized, but this could not be given. As Casey acknowledged to National Security Advisor (NSA) William Clark, '[T]here is a fine line between our purposes and the purposes of those we support.'[18]

Democratic scepticism about White House ends seeped into Republican ranks in late 1982 when a *Newsweek* cover story on Contra aid quoted unnamed US officials as saying that the rebels stood a good chance of overthrowing the Sandinistas.[19] Shortly afterwards, the administration requested additional funding for Contra forces that the CIA had by now built into a 3,500-strong army with bases in Honduras, Costa Rica, and south-eastern Nicaragua. In response, the House of Representatives unanimously adopted an amendment to a defence appropriations bill authored by HIC chair Edward Boland of Massachusetts, an initiative that the GOP-led Senate also approved. This prohibited the CIA and Pentagon from giving the Contras financial assistance to overthrow the Nicaraguan government, but did not preclude support for interdicting arms supplies. Leaked reports that the administration planned to double Contra numbers, vastly increase their aid, and mount large US military exercises off the Honduras coast prompted House Democrats to vote an end to all Contra support in 1983. With Senate Republicans unwilling to go this far, a bipartisan compromise was reached to cap aid at half what the White House had requested.[20]

Reagan resorted to the presidential podium in a vain effort to turn the tide. An almost entirely self-drafted speech to Congress in April 1983 issued a stark warning:

> The national security of all the Americas is at stake in Central America. If we cannot defend ourselves there, we cannot expect to prevail elsewhere. Our credibility would collapse, our alliances would crumble, and the safety of our homeland would be put in jeopardy.

This apocalyptic rhetoric signified Reagan's belief that the stakes involved were immense. 'If the Soviets win in Central Am.,' he wrote in his diary shortly afterwards, 'we lose in Geneva and every place else.' This visceral conviction was undimmed when he wrote in his memoirs that congressional opponents of the covert programme, however well-intentioned, 'were in effect furthering Moscow's agenda in Latin America'.[21]

The Contras 'are our brothers', Reagan once declared, 'and we owe them our help [...] They are the moral equal of our Founding Fathers and the brave men and women of the French Resistance.' This was a sincerely held belief that he also voiced in private: after a House vote rejecting Contra aid, he told the NSC, 'Think how the young men who are the freedom fighters must feel now.'[22] The Central American peace movement, by contrast, depicted the Contras as murderous supporters of Anastasio Somoza's cruel regime, which had long kept Nicaragua in poverty and oppression before its overthrow. The truth was more complex than either side allowed. Neither a monolithic force of freedom-fighters nor one of vicious reactionaries, the Contras were a disparate coalition that included supporters and foes of the former dictator, Indian peasants resentful of Managua's efforts to control them, and disillusioned ex-Sandinistas. Secure in his heroic image of the rebels, Reagan derided their American critics to conservative movie star Charlton Heston, 'We still have a few who can see no threat from the left – only from the right and you don't have to be very far right.' Resentment at being picketed when delivering his

1981 Notre Dame commencement address by Maryknoll Sisters protesting an El Salvador death squad's murder of two of their order the previous year stayed with Reagan throughout his presidency. 'A sizeable number of that order,' he commented in 1987, 'are today supportive of the Communist government of Nicaragua.'[23]

In Reagan's eyes, the failure of many Democrats to share his concerns was due to the slick public-relations outfit the Nicaraguan government had hired to market its cause. 'The pro-Sandinista lobby on the Hill is almost as sophisticated an operation as I've ever seen,' he complained.[24] This conveniently overlooked the propaganda war that the administration was waging on behalf of its clients. As Reagan was well aware, an NSC inter-agency working group was coordinating an expensive pro-Contra public-relations campaign at taxpayer expense. This operation later came under critical scrutiny from the US comptroller general and various congressional committees for expending public funds on purposes not authorized by Congress.[25]

Try as he might, Reagan had limited success in enlisting popular support for Contra aid. Addressing the nation for the first time on Nicaragua in May 1984, he warned of the communist vanguard in America's backyard:

> The role that Cuba has long performed for the Soviet Union is now also being played by the Sandinistas. They have become Cuba's Cubans. Weapons, supplies, and funds are shipped from the Soviet bloc to Cuba, from Cuba to Nicaragua, from Nicaragua to the Salvadoran guerrillas.[26]

This did little to change public attitudes, which generally ran two-to-one against Contra assistance. Most Americans simply did not consider Central America a vital battleground in the global Cold War – indeed a surprisingly large proportion did not know where Nicaragua and El Salvador were located. As Reagan later acknowledged, the yardstick of popular concern was that the United States should not get drawn into military intervention in the region as it had done earlier in South East Asia.[27] If anything, his impassioned pro-Contra rhetoric was counter-productive because it aroused anxiety that Nicaragua could become another Vietnam.

Fearful that Congress would make further cuts in Contra aid, the administration embarked on a politically risky venture to press matters to a conclusion before funds dried up. In September 1983, Reagan approved a CIA plan for covert economic warfare to exploit Sandinista dependence on imports of weaponry, oil, and other materials. With Reagan's full knowledge, CIA contractors – later joined by agency operatives – undertook speedboat attacks on Nicaragua's only oil terminal and its oil-storage facilities and mined some of its harbours to frighten off foreign shipping.[28] The first steps onto the terrain of outright illegality, these assaults handed the propaganda advantage to the Sandinistas. In a suit brought by Nicaragua, the International Court of Justice ruled that the United States was in breach of its obligation under international law not to intervene in the affairs of another state. Anticipating this outcome, the Reagan administration had withdrawn from the case and refused to recognize the judgement.[29]

More significantly, the CIA attacks undermined White House efforts to develop political support at home for its pro-Contra policy. To keep legislators in the dark, the insurgents got the credit for them. In testimony before the Senate Intelligence Committee (SIC), William Casey specifically denied his agency's direct involvement. When the *Wall Street Journal* broke the true story in early April 1984, SIC chair Barry Goldwater of Arizona, Reagan's ideological soulmate for quarter of a century, delivered a withering rebuke in an open letter to the CIA director:

> I've been trying to figure out how I can most easily tell you my feelings about the discovery of the President having approved the mining of some of the harbors of Central America. It gets down to one, little, simple phrase: I am pissed off![30]

The GOP-led Senate promptly voted to condemn the mining, rescinded Contra funding it had recently approved, and eventually joined with the House in October to approve a second Boland amendment. The key section of this measure read:

> During fiscal year 1985, no funds available to the Central Intelligence Agency, the Department of Defense, or any other agency or entity of the United States involved in intelligence activities may be obligated or expended for the purpose or which would have the effect of supporting,

directly or indirectly, military or paramilitary operations in Nicaragua by any nation, organization, movement or individual.[31]

Seeing the writing on the wall, Reagan had taken the decision to circumvent congressional restraint on Contra aid well before enactment of Boland II. In the spring of 1984, he had confidentially issued oral instructions to NSA Robert 'Bud' McFarlane: 'I want you to do whatever you have to do to help these people keep body and soul together. Do everything you can.' The scheme that McFarlane concocted in response to this presidential command was to approach foreign governments in secret for financial assistance. A visit to the Virginia mansion of ambassador Prince Bandar bin Sultan in late May secured agreement that the Saudi royal family would stump up a million dollars a month for the Contra cause. Five days later, McFarlane slipped a note bearing the good news into the president's morning briefing book – this was soon returned to him with 'Mum's the word' scrawled on it.[32]

The first Saudi payment went through to the Miami bank account of a Contra leader on 25 June, the very day that the NSPG discussed whether to seek Contra aid through third parties. Vice-president George Bush, William Casey, UN ambassador Jeane Kirkpatrick, and secretary of defense Caspar Weinberger were in favour. The lone doubter among the national security principals, secretary of state George Shultz communicated the opinion of chief of staff (CoS) James Baker that this endeavour could be 'an impeachable offense'. The NSPG consequently requested a ruling from attorney general William French Smith on the legality of third-party aid. Counselled by Ed Meese about the need 'to give lawyers guidance when asking them a question', it relayed clear indication of wanting a positive opinion. Never letting on that the scheme was already operational, Reagan admonished everyone to keep discussion of it secret. 'If such a story gets out,' he remarked, 'we'll be hanging by our thumbs in front of the White House until we find out who did it.'[33]

Smith duly delivered an oral opinion that third-party funding was permissible provided there was no quid pro quo from the United States. Of course, every donor expected something in return – and got it. Shortly after Saudi funds came through, the White House announced the emergency sale of 400 Stinger missiles to the Riyadh regime. In return for logistical support of Contra operations, Honduras, Guatemala, and Costa Rica all received assurances of generous US economic aid. On 19 February 1985, Reagan signed a presidential directive authorizing enticements for Honduras, the most vulnerable of this Central American trio to Sandinista cross-border raids. George Bush travelled to Tegucigalpa to spell out for President Roberto Suazo Córdova what his country could expect for staying on side. Reagan himself stiffened the Honduran leader's still-wavering resolve with personal assurances of increased aid, initially in a telephone call and then at a White House meeting.[34]

The web of mendacity was woven ever tighter when Boland II came into operation. With Reagan's complicity, the NSC assumed direction of the pro-Contra programme from the CIA on the spurious grounds that not being an intelligence agency put it beyond the scope of this congressional restraint. Such chicanery ignored the NSC's dependence on intelligence to conduct its business. The White House did not even bother to maintain consistency on this score. In 1986, acting in his capacity as attorney general, Ed Meese secured a ruling from the Office of Legal Counsel that the NSC was an intelligence agency in order to legitimize its authorization of arms shipments to Iran.[35]

The NSC aide at the operational centre of what became Iran–Contra was Marine Corps Lieutenant Colonel Oliver North. Deeply committed to Reagan and his goals, this Vietnam veteran was scornful of Congress for abandoning America's allies in South East Asia and determined that the Contras should not suffer the same fate. Possessed of manic energy, the highly ambitious North had proven himself clever, creative, and effective in fulfilling his assignments since joining the NSC as a 38-year-old mid-level official in 1981. His competency, skill at bureaucratic politics, and assiduous self-promotion combined to bring him to the attention of his superiors, including the president. He was also a fantasist who made exaggerated claims of his importance – one NSC colleague assessed him as 'about thirty to fifty percent bullshit'. This meant he was tailor-made for a starring role in the two most madcap operations in NSC history.[36]

North's initial responsibility was to oversee the airlifting of Saudi-funded military supplies to the Contras. In 1985 his brief expanded to helping McFarlane raise new money from Saudi Arabia, South Africa, Israel, Taiwan, and Brunei. Total foreign contributions would eventually aggregate $34 million. North was also active in tapping domestic donors to raise an additional $2.7 million with the help of the National Endowment for the Preservation of Liberty, supposedly a non-profit educational group but in reality an agency that raised funds for right-wing causes from wealthy conservatives. On 30 January 1986 Reagan hosted 19 donors who had each given over $100,000 in the Roosevelt Room of the White House and later attended at least half a dozen photo opportunities for other contributors.[37]

Initially, donors sent contributions to Contra bank accounts, but this fuelled dissension between different rebel groups over the allocation of funds. In July 1985, North assumed direct control of the funds in order to run the supply operation as a NSC venture. William Casey took a strong personal interest in it as a potential model for undertaking other covert initiatives free from congressional restraint. On his advice, North teamed up with arms dealer and former Air Force major general Richard Secord and his Iranian partner, Albert Hakim, to transport aid to the Contras. This duo formed a set of corporations known as 'the Enterprise' to acquire a fleet of ships and planes for the supply venture. Though this vast undertaking was broadly effective, it never functioned like clockwork. There were problems with finding the right sized aircraft, getting clearance for flights, and hooking up with Contras in the field. Moreover, as Casey and North were well aware, some of their principal Contra assets and a number of pilots involved in the supply operation were running drugs back into the United States in the Enterprise's planes.[38]

In the meantime, a covert operation of a different kind was sinking in the quicksand of Middle Eastern politics. The long and bloody war that had started between Iran and Iraq in 1980 had reached a new stage by early 1985. The Iranians were desperate to acquire TOW (Tube-launched, Optically tracked, Wire-guided) anti-tank missiles that were alone capable of penetrating the armour of the Soviet-made T-72 tanks that their enemy had recently acquired. Successive Tel Aviv governments had hitherto kept the Tehran regime resupplied with weapons in order to tie down Israel's deadly foe, Saddam Hussein, in his war with the Islamic Republic. Prime minister Shimon Peres now felt obliged to seek Washington's authorization for the TOW transfer because Israel's entire inventory was US-made and would need replenishment by America. However, a set of legal restraints, most notably the Arms Export Control Act of 1976, barred US arms sales and the resale of US arms by other countries to governments deemed to support terrorism. As an inducement for Israeli support, the shadowy and – it transpired – mendacious arms dealer, Manucher

Ghorbanifar, promised that the TOWs would be supplied to moderate Iranian elements keen on improving relations with the West once the Supreme Leader, the aged and frail Ayatollah Khomeini, was dead. Seeking in turn to induce White House approval of the TOW transfer, Peres required these moderates to demonstrate their goodwill by securing the freedom of all US hostages held by Iranian-backed groups in Lebanon as part of any deal.[39]

At this juncture, the Reagan administration was grappling with a spate of anti-American terrorist attacks and hostage-taking in the Middle East that stemmed from Islamist resentment of the Lebanon intervention of 1982–4. When one kidnap group threatened to try its captives as spies in early 1985, Reagan authorized strong representations warning Tehran that it would be liable for punishment if any harm befell them. This defused the situation but NSPG records indicated that he was more than ready to order air strikes against Iran if required.[40] More often than not, however, violence begat violence. In March 1985 a CIA-sponsored bomb attack on the Beirut base of Hezbollah header Mohammad Hussein Fadlallah killed some 80 people but not the intended target. Revenge for this was probably the motivation for the terrorist hijack of TWA flight 847 bound from Athens to Rome with 109 Americans on board on 14 June. Although the perpetrators freed most of the captives at various stages of the aircraft's enforced shuttling between Beirut and Algiers, they murdered one passenger, US Navy diver Robbie Stethem, and threatened to kill the remaining hostages – 39 American men, including three crew – unless Israel released 766 Lebanese Shi'as taken prisoner during the 1982 invasion. On 17 June, the hijackers disappeared into Beirut after turning the hostages over to militia chief Nabih Berri to conduct negotiations for prisoner exchanges with behind-the-scenes help from President Hafez al-Assad of Syria. With neither the United States nor Israel wanting to be seen as the one backing down to terrorist demands, it took until 30 June to reach a settlement. The final outcome was that the American hostages got their freedom in return for Israel's captives getting theirs.[41]

'America,' Reagan trumpeted amid the crisis, 'will never make concessions to terrorists – to do so would only invite more terrorism – nor will we ask nor pressure any other government to do so.' Following the hostages' release, he repeated the message: 'The United States gives terrorists no rewards and no guarantees. We make no concessions, we make no deals.' Neither claim had any basis in reality. The United States had put considerable pressure on the Israelis to free their prisoners in order to secure the release of its citizens. The TWA crisis demonstrated that Reagan was reluctant to stand up to terrorists at cost of American lives. This was also evident in his increasingly desperate efforts to free seven long-term hostages held by the 'bastardly Hisbollah'.[42]

In early July, Robert McFarlane received representations from various Israeli emissaries about the opportunity to connect with Iranian moderates and the attendant possibility of hostage release in return for arms transfer. The president had several briefings on these exchanges, the second on 18 July while he was in Bethesda Naval Hospital recovering from surgery to remove cancerous tissue from his colon. This was the first time he heard that a possibly illegal transfer of US-made TOWs was the linchpin of any deal. According to McFarlane, Reagan remarked, 'I'm not put off by the idea,' but biographer Edmund Morris questions whether anyone was capable of such a clear-headed response so soon after highly invasive surgery.[43] Reagan was still in recovery when the national-security principals met in the White House residence on 6 August to discuss Israel's request for permission to sell 100 TOWs to Iran on condition of their replacement by the United States. Caspar Weinberger forthrightly questioned the venture's legality and Shultz adjudged it 'a very bad idea'. The president did not show his hand at this gathering but supposedly telephoned McFarlane at home a few days later giving the go-ahead.[44]

This was a strange beginning to such a controversial initiative: there was no formal presidential directive, no record of the decision that standard procedure required, and not even a written note of the phone call by either Reagan or McFarlane. Some analysts have speculated that McFarlane seized the initiative to translate Reagan's inclinations into a policy that he personally favoured.[45] If so, it must be asked why the president did not abort the venture on learning of it. Instead, he sanctioned ever-deeper entanglement in an undertaking that violated legislative prohibitions on arms export to countries supporting terrorism and his own avowed refusal to reward terrorist groups and their sponsors. As recently as 8 July, Reagan had pledged to punish a network of states, with Iran at its heart, that constituted 'a new, international version of Murder, Incorporated' intent on promoting terrorism as a means to 'expel America from the world'.[46]

Why Reagan put his presidency on the line for an illegal arms trade is a further puzzle. His memoirs identified the prospect of reorienting post-Khomeini Iran into the Western orbit as the primary motive: 'Here was a bona fide opportunity to shape the future in the Middle East, take the initiative, and preempt the Soviets in an important corner of the world.'[47] This was nothing more than an attempt to legitimize an ill-conceived venture with a strategic rationale – and a very dubious one at that. It was wholly unclear just who the supposed moderates were and just how US arms were to end up in their hands. In reality, Reagan's objective in sanctioning an illegal weapons transfer was the release of the seven American hostages. While allowing that every human life is valuable, this was a very modest return for the huge risks that he took. Presidents are expected to make cool-headed assessment of their options but Reagan showed an utter lack of emotional intelligence in this case.

For Reagan, the captives were not an abstract problem of geopolitics but flesh-and-blood Americans needing his help. At an NSPG meeting in October 1984 to discuss ways of striking back at Middle Eastern terrorist groups, he had emphasized his 'overriding interest' in release of their hostages.[48] This concern intensified following an encounter with the family of Father Lawrence Jenco, taken by Hezbollah while working as director of the Catholic Relief Service in Beirut. On 28 June 1985, Reagan met with families of soon-to-be-released TWA hostages in a Chicago Heights high-school library. Also present were the Jencos, a blue-collar family from Joliet and seasoned campaigners for the kidnapped priest's release. Angry that the White House appeared willing to cut a deal for the 39 TWA captives, they demanded to know why the same could not be done for the other hostages. The president endured a half-hour harangue that left him visibly upset. 'It was just brutal,' presidential assistant William Henkel commented. 'It was a tough, tough thing for him. It made an indelible impression.' Aides finally extricated Reagan so he could regain his composure in a side room. 'It's an awful thing that these parents and loved ones have to live with,' the shaken president told McFarlane. Thereafter, the captives were rarely far from his thoughts.[49] Fear of appearing inept and powerless like Jimmy Carter in the 1979–80 Iranian hostage crisis haunted him. 'No problem was more frustrating for me,' Reagan would acknowledge.[50]

Israel's first shipment of 96 TOWs to Iran on 20 August 1985 did not produce a single hostage's release. With Reagan's advance knowledge, a second shipment of 408 followed on 15 September, in return for which the Iranian go-be-tweens had promised to get one captive freed. Although McFarlane demanded the release of William Buckley, the CIA's Beirut station chief kidnapped 18 months earlier, Presbyterian minister Benjamin Weir was the hostage set free. It later transpired that Buckley had already died from prolonged torture by Hezbollah captors. Tehran next requested a battery of HAWK anti-aircraft mis-siles for delivery in late November 1985, but on this occasion Israeli shipment procedures ran into difficulties as the deadline for delivery became imminent. At McFarlane's suggestion, Oliver North stepped in to help. With the assistance of senior CIA official Duane Clarridge, a veteran of Contra aid, he contracted a plane secretly owned by the agency to transport 18 HAWKs, the most it could carry but far short of the 120 that Iran had paid for.[51]

This episode had the effect of drawing Reagan deeper into murky waters. Anxious to legitimize CIA involvement in the HAWK transfer, deputy direc-tor John McMahon demanded a retroactive presidential finding to ratify all previous actions by US officials in furtherance of the arms-for-hostages operation. Presidential findings were meant to sanction future actions and by law were supposed to be shared with the congressional intelligence com-mittees. On 5 December Reagan put his signature to a CIA-crafted document that violated both requirements.[52] As was evident in a special meeting of the foreign-policy principals convened in the White House residence two days later, the president was fully aware of the risks he was taking but would not be deterred.

Deputizing for Casey at this conclave, McMahon rubbished the notion that the weapons being traded for hostages would end up in the hands of moderates because there were none left alive in Iran in the wake of the Islamic revolution. Shultz, Weinberger, and a now disillusioned McFarlane – who had resigned as NSA three days earlier – all advised the president to get out before becoming more deeply mired in illegal activities that were certain to be exposed. Even the normally supportive Donald Regan, attending as CoS, advised, 'Cut your losses and get out.' Never again would the president's advisors be so forcefully united in opposition to the Iran initiative, but they could not budge him. Recognizing the possible danger, the president made a gallows-humour quip that if the consequence was going to jail, 'visiting hours are Thursdays'. In Weinberger's account, he proclaimed willingness to answer 'charges of illegality' regarding arms transfer but not the accusation that 'big strong President Reagan passed up a chance to free the hostages'.[53]

The next day Reagan sent McFarlane to London to join North, Ghorbanifar, and the Israelis in discussions about the next step in the Iran initiative. The president wanted to secure release of the hostages as a precondition to agreeing further supply of weapons, a proposal that got nowhere with Ghorbanifar. The arms dealer warned that his moderate contacts needed the weapons in order to build their prestige, so the likely response to Reagan's demand would be: 'To hell with the hostages! Let the Hezbollah kill them.' This was a message coldly calculated to tug at presidential heartstrings. On receiving the bad news, Reagan called another meeting of advisors on 9 December to discuss a way forward, but he was now over a barrel. After attending this, Casey reported to McMahon, 'I suspect he would be willing to run the risk and take the heat if this will lead to springing the hostages.' [54]

The last chance to save Reagan from himself was now gone. The dynamics among his advisors changed significantly after Vice Admiral John Poindexter took over the reins of the NSC in early December. Hitherto, Casey had been the president's bulwark of support against George Shultz and Caspar Weinberger on the Iran initiative, but the new man proved an equally significant ally. A firm believer in presidential supremacy in foreign affairs, Poindexter was more aggressive than his predecessor in pressing for his boss's wishes to be carried out. His lack of interest in having Reagan consider other options accelerated the momentum of the arms-for-hostages operation. On 7 January 1986 a fully fledged NSC meeting discussed an Israeli proposal to ship 4,000 TOW missiles to Iran in return for release for all the US captives. On this occasion, Schultz and Weinberger were the only dissenters – even Donald Regan had changed sides. 'I had an uneasy, uncanny feeling that the meeting was not a *real* meeting,' the secretary of state recalled, 'that it had all been "pre-cooked."' This suspicion was well founded. The previous day, Reagan had signed a Poindexter-submitted draft presidential finding that authorized continuation of the Iran initiative without informing Congress.[55]

On 17 January 1986, Reagan signed another finding, almost identical to that of 6 January, but with a significant procedural change outlined in an accompanying memorandum drawn up by Oliver North and signed by Poindexter. This recommended that the legal requirement of congressional notification could be circumvented 'if the CIA, using an authorized agent as necessary, purchased arms from the Department of Defense […] and then transferred them to Iran directly after receiving appropriate payment from Iran'. Whatever his later claims to the contrary, Reagan was fully aware of what he was approving. His diary entry for this day spoke of 'our effort to get out our 5 hostages out of Lebanon. Involves selling TOW anti-tank missiles to Iran. I gave a go ahead.'[56] What the president may not have known was just how the plan would work – this was Oliver North's brainchild. The NSC aide arranged for the Enterprise, the private network already supplying weapons to the Contras, to do the same for the Iranians.[57] It would fly in shipments of 500 TOWs to Iran on 17 February, 26 February, and 28 October 1986, as well as planeloads of HAWK spare parts.

To White House disappointment, neither February shipment produced a single hostage release. Instead, captive Peter Kilburn was murdered in apparent revenge for US air attacks on Libya on 15 April, ordered in retaliation for its suspected involvement in the bombing of a West Berlin nightclub frequented by American servicemen. A now desperate Reagan approved Robert McFarlane, called back into NSC service, accompanying North on a very risky mission to Tehran in the hope of securing the wholesale release of the remaining captives. They were supposed to meet the Iranian parliament speaker, Akbar Hashemi Rafsanjani, through the good offices of perpetual middleman, Manucher Ghorbanifar. Supported by a CIA technical team and carrying Irish passports (plus cyanide pills if things went badly wrong), the intrepid duo arrived on 25 May in an unmarked plane that also carried HAWK missile parts. Their only contact in the first two days was with very junior officials before an emissary claiming to be from Rafsanjani appeared. McFarlane negotiated with him in vain throughout the night, breaking off to apprise Reagan via a CIA radio of inflated Iranian demands for more weapons in return for release of just two hostages. The outcome, the president recorded in his diary, was that 'Bud told them to shove it […] This was a heartbreaking disappointment for all of us.'[58]

On returning to Washington, McFarlane advised letting the Iranians make the first move if they wanted new weaponry rather than waste time in further approaches. Some two months later, the release of Lawrence Jenco seemed to signal that Tehran was ready to deal. Reagan voiced the hope that the plan initiated by his January presidential directive was nearing fruition, but this was another pipe dream.[59] On 2 November hostage David Jacobsen was freed from

17 months of captivity just days after the third and last TOW shipment reached Tehran. However, Hezbollah had already replenished their stocks of American hostages by kidnapping three more, and they took a further three in January 1987. What Reagan himself had warned of in speeches opposing negotiations with terrorists or their state sponsors had come to pass.

While it was being drawn ever deeper into the arms-for-hostages imbroglio, the White House was growing concerned about the capacity of its other illicit supply programme to sustain anti-Sandinista military operations in Nicaragua. This made it increasingly anxious to regain congressional support for Contra aid. With a vote pending on a $100 million assistance programme in March 1986, Reagan issued apocalyptic warnings of the consequences if dissenting Democrats did not wake up to the communist threat in Central America.[60] This did not stop the House rejecting the bill, but another vote was scheduled for mid-year. With the president doing his bit in public remarks, the administration's propaganda operation changed tack to portray the Sandinistas now as drug barons, anti-Semites, and genocidal murderers of Miskito natives.[61] In combination with the outrage aroused by Sandinista leader Daniel Ortega's visit to Moscow in late April, the new campaign swayed sufficient Democrats in the House to secure approval of military aid for the Contras in late June, but the money was not available until the new fiscal year beginning 1 October.

By then, Contra assistance had become entwined with the arms-for-hostages operation with ultimately disastrous consequences. Commencing with the first HAWK shipment in late 1985, cash from the Iranian weapons sales passed through the same Swiss bank accounts that Oliver North had opened to hold monetary donations for the Nicaraguan rebels. This was the genesis of what he later termed a 'neat idea' to sustain the Contras as a fighting force.[62] It entailed overcharging the Iranians for US weapons and relaying the proceeds to the Contras. In what became known as the 'diversion memo' of April 1986, the contents of which Poindexter was supposed to relay to Reagan, North laid out his scheme to repay Israel $2 million for its 1985 TOW shipments and transmit a projected $12 million for Contra assistance. As he later quipped to 'Enterprise' collaborator Richard Secord, this was what 'put the hyphen in Iran–Contra'.[63]

The wheels came off North's scheme when the Sandinistas shot down an Enterprise plane, taking alive crew member Eugene Hasenfus, on 5 October. Two days later their captive was spilling the beans to the world's media about what he thought was a CIA venture. North heard the news when meeting an Iranian delegation in Frankfurt to negotiate selling another 1,500 TOWs as a means of securing Contra bridging funds. Knowing the game was virtually up, he returned immediately to Washington to begin a mammoth document-shredding operation before investigators came knocking at his door. The other cat was soon out of the bag. On 3 November, picking up on a story put out by a radical Hezbollah faction, the Lebanese magazine *Ash-Shiraa* published an article disclosing US–Iranian arms dealing. Speaker Rafsanjani confirmed the truth of the report within 24 hours, adding the bizarre detail that McFarlane had brought a Bible inscribed by Reagan as a gift for Ayatollah Khomeini on his recent mission to Tehran. In fact, it was North who had presented this to the Iranians he met in Frankfurt. At his behest, Poindexter had got Reagan to handwrite a biblical verse inside: 'And the Scripture, foreseeing that God would justify the Gentiles by faith, preached the Gospel beforehand to Abraham, saying, "All the nations shall be blessed in you." Galatians 3:8.'[64]

Having publicly denied US government involvement in response to the Hasenfus revelations on Contra aid, Reagan similarly pronounced the *Ash-Shiraa* report without foundation. Behind the scenes, however, he was the driving force behind a White House damage-limitation effort. At a meeting of top officials on 10 November, he insisted that the arms sales were undertaken as an opening to Iranian moderates, not a trade for hostages.[65] Everyone present knew better but this was the fiction that the president expected them to support. On the evening of 13 November, Reagan trotted out the same line – adding for good measure the falsehood that Iran had received only 'small amounts of defensive weapons and spare parts' – in a televised address to the nation. This could not halt a precipitous collapse of 21 points in his Gallup approval ratings over the course of November, the largest single-month decline for any president. Dick Wirthlin's private polling also conveyed something that Reagan found very hard to take: '71% of the people like [me] […] But 60% don't think I'm telling the truth.'[66]

The embattled president agreed on 19 November that Ed Meese should conduct an informal inquiry to establish basic facts about what was becoming known as 'Iran–Contra'. On learning that this very cursory investigation had found a smoking gun in the form of North's 'diversion memo', he wrote in his diary, 'This was a violation of the law against giving the Contras money without an authorization by Congress.' Neither North nor Poindexter, he complained, had informed him of the diversion of funds.[67] This was a breathtaking claim of innocence in view of the fact that he had approved the raising of foreign and domestic donations to sustain the Contras from the outset. Aides had likely not kept him in the loop about the diversion of proceeds from the sales of weaponry to Iran, but they had presidential authorization to do everything possible to circumvent legislative restraints on supporting the Nicaraguan rebels. On 25 November, Reagan held a press conference to announce that North had been relieved of his NSC duties and Poindexter had resigned to resume his naval career. After further announcing his intention to establish a presidential commission to review Iran–Contra, he then left Meese to deal with questions from reporters, whom he described in his diary as 'a circle of sharks'. In the same entry, Reagan expressed sorrow at Poindexter's departure, attributing it to the old Navy tradition of accepting responsibility as 'Captain of the ship' – whereas in reality this was his job.[68]

As a creation of the executive branch that it was investigating, the Tower Commission had no constitutional remit as an independent body. The panel also lacked powers to subpoena documents, compel witness testimony, or grant immunity from prosecution. Operating to a very tight schedule, it was required to report within three months of beginning work on 1 December 1986. Nevertheless, the findings of this body (comprising former GOP senator John Tower of Texas as chair, former Carter administration secretary of state Edmund Muskie, and former Ford administration NSA Brent Scowcroft, plus investigatory staff) set the framework that shaped the deliberations of later investigations. Avowing desire for 'all the facts to come out', the president appointed veteran diplomat David Abshire to manage the White House response to the investigation.[69] Of course, the Tower Commission was incapable of turning up the whole truth, but its establishment saved Reagan from appearing to be engaged in a Nixon-style cover-up and lanced the boil of Iran–Contra before it could become his Watergate.

The president did not shine on the two occasions that the panel interviewed him. On 26 January 1987, he admitted having approved the first TOW shipments by Israel in August 1985, a statement that contradicted Donald Regan's evidence. He further claimed to have been so outraged on learning that the Israelis were undertaking an unauthorized shipment of HAWKs to Iran that he had ordered the weapons recalled. This was a figment of his imagination that raised further questions about what had really happened. Recalled to appear on 11 February in the hope of resolving discrepancies in his initial testimony, Reagan received intensive coaching by aides to avoid further revelations that muddied his denials of responsibility. When asked again about the Israeli TOWs, he read verbatim from a cue card – including its prompt: 'If the question comes up [...] you might want to say that you were surprised.' A horrified John Tower terminated the interview in the belief that the president's mental confusion made it useless to question him further. Abshire persuaded the panel to let Reagan make a brief written submission on his recollection of the 1985 TOW shipments but this did not bring enlightenment. Its final words were, '[T]he simple truth is that I don't remember.' When news of this got out, a joke parodying the famous Watergate question about what Nixon knew did the rounds: 'What did the president forget and when did he forget it?'[70]

Granted considerable access to Reagan, official biographer Edmund Morris commented on his state of mind in February: 'RR himself showing signs of depression, failing to read even summaries of important working papers, constantly watching TV & movies.' Nancy later remarked of the period from November to February: 'Ronnie has always had a reputation for integrity, and it went right to his soul to see his character being questioned every day [...] It was a dark and hurtful time.' The new team appointed to clean up White House operations in the wake of the Tower Report was so concerned about Reagan's state of mind that it decided to observe him closely on 2 March with a view to invoking Section IV of the Twenty-Fifth Amendment to the Constitution pertaining to presidential disability if he appeared disoriented.[71]

On the other hand, Reagan continued his habit of regular correspondence throughout the darkest months of the Iran–Contra investigation. Letters of support from old friends like Billy Graham, Charlton Heston, Earl Jorgensen, and George Murphy rallied his spirits. When writing back, he presented himself as the victim of a miscarriage of justice without any acknowledgement of his deep involvement in various misdemeanours. 'I feel like I'm playing in "Oxbow Incident," the role of the fellow who was innocent but was hung anyway,' he told an old Hollywood friend. More often, he was upbeat, as when writing to Marion Grimm (widow of the Chicago Cubs owner whose team he had covered in WHO days): '[The media] are like a lynch mob looking for a victim. I know they've chosen me but I don't think they can get the rope round my neck.'[72]

Recovery from routine surgery on an enlarged prostate gland that required three nights in hospital (5–7 January) offered reassurance that God was still on his side. 'I called on my deep belief in prayer,' he told one correspondent, 'and my prayers were answered.'[73] The self-belief that he had done nothing wrong was unwavering. 'I don't know one d—n thing more than I told them [the press],' he declared, 'and am waiting myself to find out who did what and when.'[74]

The letters present a quite different image of the president from the one conveyed by his Tower Commission testimony. Moreover, the old Ronald Reagan was frequently on display during the course of the inquiry. Despite Reagan's recent surgery, the State of the Union Address was delivered with some style on 20 January. There was no evidence of disengagement when chairing four NSC meetings in February – indeed the very opposite was the case in the 20 February discussion of Central America. The advance briefing from the Tower panel on its findings found the president alert and responsive. Finally, all talk of the Twenty-Fifth Amendment ceased when close scrutiny from the president's new staff found no reason to doubt his mental competence.[75]

It is pertinent to ask whether the old actor had pulled off his greatest performance in hoodwinking the Tower panel into believing that he was too doddery and disoriented to have played the lead in Iran–Contra. This is very unlikely because he resented this image becoming the post-Tower orthodoxy. So why did he appear utterly inept in the face of questioning about what he had authorized? The most likely answer is that Reagan became genuinely confused when his Iran–Contra actions came under close review. Considering himself always to be the good guy, he had at different times in his life invented a truth to confirm that belief when needed. Unable to do so in the complex and highly scrutinized case of Iran–Contra, he likely retreated into confusion and forgetfulness rather than admit to himself and others that he had actively directed illegal operations.

The Tower Commission report rebuked Reagan for devolving responsibility for policy review and implementation to his advisors. 'The NSC system will not work,' it intoned, 'unless the president makes it work [...] and [with] so much at stake, the President should have ensured that the NSC system did not fail him.'[76] Apart from being inaccurate, this criticism proved to be more mitigation than condemnation. At no stage, with the possible exception of North's diversion of funds, had Reagan been anything other than deeply engaged in Iran–Contra operations. Whether he knew every little detail is immaterial – few presidents do – what is not in doubt is that he was willing to break the law and violate the Constitution in pursuit of his ends. The report's focus on the diversion of funds in discussing the Contra dimension of Iran–Contra also worked to Reagan's advantage because this shifted attention from issues in which he was deeply involved. It also concluded quite wrongly that the Iran element had commenced as an effort to develop a strategic opening to moderates and metamorphosed into an arms-for-hostages operation. Fully aware of the report's meaning, Reagan later joked with David Abshire that he had been found not guilty. 'Plainly, there was no smoking gun in the president's hand,' this aide later wrote of his boss's exoneration.[77]

Other dramatis personae – Casey (who never testified because of sudden incapacitation from a brain tumour that eventually killed him in May 1987), North, McFarlane (interviewed in hospital after attempting suicide through barbiturate overdose), Poindexter (who would always maintain that he had never shown North's diversion memo to the president), Shultz and Weinberger (for distancing themselves 'from the march of events') – came in for stronger criticism. However, the report reserved greatest condemnation for Donald Regan, whom it held responsible for the disorder that engulfed the White House over the Iran operation. Having asserted greater personal control over the White House staff, including its national-security component, than any CoS in history, he was singled out for failing to ensure that 'plans were made for public disclosure of the initiative'. What Regan was really guilty of was doing what his boss wanted, but the buck in this instance did not stop at the Oval Office desk.

The president had been under pressure for some months to fire his power-hungry CoS as the necessary first step in the thorough cleansing of White House procedure. Nancy Reagan, a long-time adversary, was the principal advocate of his dismissal. Two old California comrades – Mike Deaver and Stu Spencer – joined forces to relay the same message. At first Reagan was stubbornly resistant to these entreaties, telling Deaver on one occasion, 'I'll be goddamned if I throw someone else out to save my own ass.' Preservation of his credibility would eventually require him to do so, of course. Donald Regan's increasingly open warfare with the first lady became the rationale for his dismissal. The embattled CoS's press briefing that she was vetting new White House appointments proved the final straw for the president. On 23 February Reagan steeled himself to do something he rarely did – ask for someone's resignation, but the meeting ended without a date of departure being fixed. Within days, however, Regan quit in a huff on hearing press reports that his successor, Howard Baker, had already accepted appointment. 'My prayers have really been answered' a relieved president wrote in his diary.[78]

What now remained was for Reagan to address the nation on the Tower Report on 4 March. It required John Tower's confidential insistence, as well as Dick Wirthlin's cogent advice, to persuade him that some statement of regret was the only way to regain popular trust.[79] The key passage read:

> A few months ago I told the American people I did not trade arms for hostages. My heart and my best intentions still tell me that's true, but the facts and the evidence tell me it is not. […] [W]hat began as a strategic opening to Iran deteriorated, in its implementation, into trading arms for hostages. This runs counter to my own beliefs, to administration policy, and to the original strategy we had in mind. There are reasons why it happened, but no excuses. It was a mistake.[80]

The 14-minute address contained shameless untruths. The explanation for the arms-for-hostages operation was entirely false. Reagan said virtually nothing about illicit Contra aid other than to affirm his ignorance of the funds diversion, with the rider that 'as President, I cannot escape responsibility' for this financial impropriety. Focusing on the diversion was itself a diversion from the reality that he had involved the presidency with shady arms dealers, cocaine-smuggling crooks, con artists, illicit money men, and Middle Eastern militants. It was a performance that brought to mind what Democrat Jesse Unruh had remarked of him back in California gubernatorial days:

> Reagan believes himself. He sounds sincere because he is sincere, even when he should know better. Most politicians know when they're lying and so the people sense it. But in his own mind Reagan never lies and the people sense that, too.[81]

Perhaps unsurprisingly, therefore, the speech was a palpable hit with press and public. The once-critical *New York Times* and *Washington Post* applauded Reagan's display of contrition and determination to put things right.[82] Polls also showed his approval ratings recovering from their lows of late 1986. Convinced their man was back on track, friends lined up to congratulate him – with Charlton Heston adjudging the speech the best of his presidency.[83]

To all intents and purposes Reagan was now out of the impeachment-haunted woods. 'Somehow the lynch mob seems to have ridden off into the sunset [...] I think they've lost their rope,' he wrote to publishing tycoon Walter Annenberg.[84] There was still a joint congressional investigation to endure but this did not find a smoking gun with his name on it. Instead, the hearings briefly made a national hero of Oliver North by giving him a platform to overact the patriot. The Democrats on the panel had no stomach to initiate another presidential impeachment process so soon after the Watergate-related one, particularly if it derailed progress towards an arms-reduction agreement with the Soviets. In contrast, most Republican members lined up solidly in support of Reagan and the principle of presidential supremacy in national security.[85] The seemingly endless Independent Counsel investigation, established by the Justice Department in December 1986 in recognition that Tower Commission findings would necessarily be incomplete, eventually produced indictments in the early 1990s against 14 leading participants in Iran–Contra, of whom 11 were convicted. Among these, Caspar Weinberger was charged but was pardoned by President George H. W. Bush before going to trial; Robert McFarlane also received a pardon after pleading guilty to four charges of criminal conspiracy; and Poindexter and North, both convicted on charges of, *inter alia*, perjury and obstruction of justice, had their sentences quashed on grounds that immunized testimony before Congress had prejudiced their trial. Reagan never underwent the ignominy of indictment. Despite admitting that he had been too deferential in his interrogation of the president in the White House, Independent Counsel Lawrence Walsh asserted, 'I never had the feeling that he was going to go down.'[86]

The succeeding investigations followed the Tower Commission's lead in seeking to assess whether the president had direct knowledge of specific illegal operations rather than whether he had been party to constitutional violations. In 1973 special prosecutor Archibald Cox had famously remarked that the

Watergate investigation would determine 'whether ours shall be a government of laws and not of men'. Facing the same test, the Iran–Contra investigators flunked it. At issue, in the words of one eminent constitutional scholar, were matters that 'went to the heart of the president's constitutional stewardship' regarding the obligation to ensure that the laws be faithfully executed, respect the system of checks and balances – even in the foreign-policy domain – and abstain from spending funds unauthorized by Congress.[87] Out of conviction that he was doing good, Reagan may have violated these principles with a pure heart, but in truth his hands were dirty. The serial failure of the Tower Commission, Congress, and the Independent Counsel to establish his wrong-doing resulted in a missed opportunity to stifle the post-Watergate revival of the imperial presidency.

The termination of all arms-for-hostages operations did not mark the end of Reagan's questionable engagement in Middle Eastern affairs because it freed him to support Iraq in its war with Iran. At Kuwait's request, he agreed in early 1987 to 'reflag' its tankers as American and provide US Navy protection to safeguard these vessels, the principal carriers of Iraqi oil exports, against Iranian attack. In May, an Iraqi jet fired two Exocet missiles at the USS *Stark*, killing 37 of its crew. Accepting Saddam Hussein's assurances that the attack was due to pilot error, Reagan declared: 'The villain in the piece really is Iran. And, so, they're delighted with what has just happened.'[88] This judgement ignored the Iraqi dictator's responsibility for precipitating the so-called 'Tanker War' phase of the conflict with Iran in 1984. The US naval operation in the Persian Gulf would later produce an even greater tragedy. On 3 July 1988 the USS *Vincennes*, operating in Iranian waters, shot down an Iran Air civilian jet on its scheduled flight path in Iranian airspace in broad daylight, mistakenly believing that it was a fighter plane. All 290 people aboard were killed, making it the seventh-worst disaster in aviation history at time of writing. In contrast to his public outrage over the Soviet downing of KAL007 in 1983, Reagan offered just perfunctory regrets. In 1996 the United States eventually settled a suit brought by Iran in the International Court of Justice by agreeing to pay $131.8 million in reparations and compensation to victims' families, but never apologized or acknowledged wrongdoing.[89]

Compelled, too, to abandon illicit efforts to arm the Contras, Reagan looked for other ways to help them. In the hope of co-opting the Democrats, he invited

House speaker Jim Wright of Texas to participate in the peace process that President Óscar Arias Sánchez of Costa Rica was seeking to promote. To White House surprise, the Sandinistas agreed to most of what was asked of them. When Wright backed the proposals, Reagan turned on him as a communist dupe. The speaker's retort to this red-baiting was to continue assisting in peace negotiations. 'I'm not afraid of the bastard,' he reportedly remarked of the president.[90] Reagan himself would soon recognize that the winds of change in the Soviet Union had blown away the communist threat in Central America. The White House decided to support the Arias peace initiative once Congress rejected its last serious bid for Contra aid in 1988. This displeased hard-liners in the conservative movement as a step to making the region 'safe for communism'. More willing to put up with liberal criticisms than brickbats from the right, the president dismissively remarked to an aide about his supposed soulmates, 'Those sonsofbitches won't be happy until we have 25,000 troops in Managua, and I'm not going to do it.'[91]

What angered Reagan above all was the decrepit, detached, and disoriented image that had been his salvation during the Iran–Contra investigations. As a consequence, his tongue occasionally strayed from denial of personal wrongdoing. In one exchange with reporters, he objected to being depicted as uninformed and ignorant about everything. 'I was very definitely involved in the decisions about support to the freedom fighters,' he remarked. 'It was my idea to begin with.'[92] Fortunately for Reagan, his success in negotiating arms control with the Soviet Union would soon overshadow his Iran–Contra ignominy and have far greater significance in defining his presidential legacy.

TWELVE

Summit Negotiator

Addressing the United Nations in September 1984, Ronald Reagan declared: 'America has repaired its strength [...] We are ready for constructive negotiations with the Soviet Union.'[1] He did not have long to wait to make good on this declaration. A succession of ageing Kremlin hard-liners had resisted his offers to negotiate in person but the line of old men was running out. When the frail Konstantin Chernenko assumed the post of general secretary of the Communist Party of the Soviet Union (CPSU) following Yuri Andropov's 15-month tenure, a joke circulated in Moscow that Margaret Thatcher had telephoned Reagan after attending Andropov's funeral to say: 'You should have come. They did it very well. I'm definitely coming back next year.'[2] Sure enough, Chernenko died of emphysema on 10 March 1985 after just 13 months in post. 'How am I supposed to get anyplace with the Russians,' Reagan moaned to Nancy on hearing the news, 'if they keep dying on me?'[3] The next day the Soviet press announced the succession of a new breed of leader in the person of 54-year-old Mikhail Gorbachev. If Reagan's most important first-term relationship with a foreign leader was with Thatcher, his second-term one was with Gorbachev. Together they would negotiate an effective end to the Cold War in their various summits and other interactions. Following their final meeting in New York, Reagan remarked, '[Gorbachev] sounded as if he saw us as partners making a better world.'[4]

Gorbachev took over when US–Soviet relations were showing some signs of thaw. Once Reagan's re-election ended Kremlin hopes for being rid of him, Chernenko proposed the renewal of arms-control talks at Geneva. 'They are coming to the table to get at SDI,' Reagan told the NSPG on 17 December 1984. That evening he wrote in his diary, 'I stand firm we cannot retreat on that no matter what they offer.'[5] Almost on cue, a letter arrived from Chernenko warning that continued development of the Strategic Defense Initiative (SDI) would 'make it impossible to conduct serious negotiations'. George Shultz spelled out the American position when meeting Andrei Gromyko at Geneva in early January to discuss protocol for the talks. The Soviets were left with no option but to agree that the negotiations should be conducted without preconditions.[6] The hardheaded conclusion that Reagan drew from this was outlined in a letter to a friend:

> I feel [...] the Soviets came to the table because they finally decided it
> was in their best interests to do so [...] They must be made to realize
> that the alternative will be an arms race which they can't win.[7]

The conviction that America was negotiating from strength enhanced his determination not to surrender SDI just to get a nuclear-weapons agreement.

While some Western leaders greeted Gorbachev's succession with enthusiasm in the expectation that he would be a break from the Soviet past, a sceptical Reagan noted in his diary, 'I'm too cynical to believe that.'[8] Thatcher, by contrast, was something of a cheerleader for the new man. Identifying Gorbachev as a coming Soviet leader, she had invited him for lunch and talks at her Chequers country residence on 16 December 1984. Their encounter convinced the prime minister that here was someone with whom the West, in her famous words, 'could do business'. Briefing Reagan at Camp David a week later about her favourable impression, she also reported the effective ultimatum that Gorbachev had issued on SDI: 'tell your friend President Reagan not to go ahead with space weapons' or the Soviets would respond in one of two ways – build their own defensive shield or, more probably, develop offensive missiles capable of penetrating the American one.[9] Hearing this confirmed Reagan's suspicion that the Kremlin would continue its campaign against SDI whoever was in charge.

On Gorbachev's first day in office, Reagan sent him an invitation to talks in Washington in order to develop 'a more stable and constructive relationship between our two countries'.[10] Top aide Alexander Yakovlev counselled a positive response but not an immediate one lest this create the impression that the US president was the one 'who pushes the buttons of world development'. Gorbachev's reply 12 days later agreed to a meeting without preconditions, but left the venue open for further discussion. While expressing sincere desire to improve relations, he also warned that the inconsistency of friendly words in private and harsh criticisms of the other side in public would impede progress to this end – a clear dig at Reagan.[11] With both leaders equally keen to size each other up, they would eventually hold the first summit since 1979 between a US president and his Soviet counterpart on neutral territory in Geneva in November 1985.

Gorbachev's rise to become Reagan's co-negotiator was an improbable one.[12] The first Soviet leader to have come of age after World War II, he was born in 1931 to peasant parents in Stavropol in the northern Caucasus. His first job was driving a combine harvester on a collective farm. Success in the Komsomol (Young Communist League) earned him a place to study law at the elite Moscow State University, making him the first Soviet leader since Lenin to have a university education. Graduating in 1955, he rose to head the CPSU regional apparatus in Stavropol by 1970. Fast-track promotion saw him become a candidate (non-voting) member of the Politburo in 1979 and the youngest ever full-voting member the following year. Groomed by Andropov for eventual succession, he had only been on the national stage for six years when his chance came. Many of his *shestidesyatnaki* (men-of-the-1960s) generation who had started their rise in the CPSU during the reformist era of Nikita Khrushchev were contemptuous of the Brezhnev-era old guard for presiding over economic and social decay. One of these, Anatoly Chernyaev, soon to become the new general secretary's foreign-policy advisor, commented on his accession: 'Much is expected of Gorbachev [...] I am full of hope and anticipation.'[13]

The reform agenda that Gorbachev initially termed 'new thinking' became better known as *glasnost* (openness) and *perestroika* (restructuring). This began as an effort to preserve communism through reversal of systemic economic decay. According to former NSC Russian expert Richard Pipes, it sought to change 'a totalitarian into an authoritarian regime'. Within a few years of taking power, however, Gorbachev embraced bolder changes to democratize the Soviet Union, but their ultimate effect was to hasten its dissolution. After the Soviet implosion, George Shultz recalled what Thatcher had once told him: 'Gorbachev thinks there are problems with the way the system works; he thinks he can make changes to make it work better. He doesn't understand that *the system is the problem*.'[14] Such thinking arguably underestimated both the Soviet leader's desire to break free from doctrinaire communism and the structural impediments against doing so too quickly. Gorbachev had no bottom-up wellspring of popular support for his project to drag the CPSU and its Soviet state apparatus into a new era. After 70 years of communism, Russians knew no other system and were reluctant to contemplate the unknown.[15]

Whatever failures lay ahead, Gorbachev understood that the arms race had to be curbed if resources consumed by 'the insatiable Moloch of the military-industrial complex' were to be transferred to civil programmes.[16] Within days of his accession, he told the CPSU Central Committee:

> [W]e have an opportunity to concentrate primarily on domestic issues, focus our attention on fulfilling plan objectives, conducting economic experiments, and introducing scientific and technological achievements into the industrial process.[17]

Signalling determination to undo Cold War orthodoxies, he appointed a new team of fellow reformers headed by Eduard Shevardnadze in the foreign ministry, reduced the number of SS-20s targeted at Western Europe, and told military leaders to adapt to new realities. A sceptic from the first regarding the Afghan intervention, Gorbachev informed the Politburo in late 1985 of his determination to end it – though he initially strengthened Soviet forces to give the Kabul regime time to develop defence self-sufficiency.[18]

As their meeting neared, there was considerable anxiety among Reagan's aides that the younger Soviet leader, known to have mastery of detail, would run rings around their ageing boss. Arms Control and Disarmament Agency director Kenneth Adelman recalled: 'It's one thing dealing with Thatcher, and Kohl, and Mitterrand: it's a different thing being at a superpower summit [...] there's an order of magnitude difference. We were very afraid that Reagan wouldn't pull it off.' Aware that Reagan's greatest strength was his optimism, George Shultz worried that being surrounded by uncertainty was doing him no good. Accordingly, the secretary of state took it upon himself to boost presidential confidence of emerging the victor from the summit 'Super Bowl'.[19]

Whether Reagan really needed such encouragement was doubtful. The intensive briefings from worried aides exasperated him. 'I'm getting d—n sick of cramming like a school kid,' he complained in his diary. 'Sometimes they tell me more than I need to know.'[20] Preferring to do things his way, Reagan consulted individuals who had met Soviet leaders, like former presidents Richard Nixon and Gerald Ford, or who were knowledgeable about the Soviet Union and its people, notably author Suzanne Massie. A regular traveller to Russia, the well-connected Massie wangled an invitation to the White House to brief the president on Soviet issues on 17 January 1984, and gained regular access to him thereafter.[21] To Reagan, Massie was 'the greatest student I know of the Russian people', a judgement not shared by other Soviet experts. He was especially impressed by her conviction that 'the Russians are going through a spiritual revival & are completely tuned out on Communism'. Massie also introduced him to the Russian proverb that he would repeat time and again to Gorbachev: '*Doveryai no proveryai*', meaning 'Trust but verify'. In preparation for the first summit with Gorbachev, Reagan read (and took with him to Geneva) her book *Land of the Firebird*, to gain an impression of the Russian people and their history separate from communism.[22]

Building on how he had prepared earlier for meeting Andrei Gromyko, Reagan composed four pages of personal notes to guide his approach in the talks. Contrary to Shultz's exhortations, these repeatedly stressed the importance of not making Gorbachev look the loser lest this weaken his position with 'the Soviet gang back in the Kremlin'. A case in point was human rights. Reagan intended to hit hard on Soviet abuses but only within the negotiating room. On core issues of arms control he was determined to be firm, most notably that SDI would never be bargained away in any deal, something Gorbachev had declared essential during a recent visit to Paris. The summit could be deemed a success, his notes recounted, 'if we fail to arrive at an arms control agreement because I stubbornly held out for what I believed was right for the country'. Notwithstanding such tough words, the aide-memoire concluded with an expression of genuine hope that the talks could be the start of real improvement in superpower relations: 'Let there be no talk of winners and losers. Even if we think we won, to say so would set us back.'[23]

As the summit neared, Reagan became increasingly involved in managing preparations for it. This extended to banning the State Department from calling his private sessions with Gorbachev tête-à-têtes. 'If we're not careful,' he remarked, 'we're going to go from tête-à-tête back to détente. Let's call it a "one-on-one."'[24] More significantly, Reagan refused to follow past practice whereby State Department officials and Soviet counterparts agreed in advance a form of words for the end-of-summit communiqué. With George Shultz's encouragement, he was determined to put a personal stamp on proceedings. 'Let's do things differently,' the secretary of state enthused. 'No precooking [...] Let's make it a *real* summit.'[25] Reagan's insistence that the summary statement had to reflect what actually happened at Geneva proved crucial in allowing the two leaders more scope to interact than was usual at summits, thereby helping them to move beyond entrenched positions.

The American negotiating team headquartered at Maison Fleur d'Eau, a lovely villa on the beautiful Lake Geneva shoreline. The US-hosted opening session got underway on 19 November with a visual triumph for Reagan. On a very cold morning the president bounded out hatless and coatless to greet Gorbachev with the world's media looking on. He was the image of vitality compared to the Soviet leader emerging from his limousine wrapped up against the elements. This gambit was actually the brainwave of aide Jim Kuhn, not the image-conscious Reagan, who needed a lot of persuading to take off the overcoat he had been wearing. More significantly, Reagan sensed something likeable about Gorbachev as the two shook hands for the first time. 'There was warmth in his face and his style,' he recalled, 'not the coldness bordering on hatred I'd seen in most senior Soviet officials I'd met until then.'[26]

The two leaders repaired into a side room for a private meeting that lasted over an hour, instead of the scheduled 20 minutes. Reagan's opening comments emphasized that the United States and the USSR were the only countries on earth 'who could start World War III [or] bring peace to the world'. In response, Gorbachev avowed Soviet commitment to improving relations with the United States through better mutual understanding. Thereafter, the meeting became a rehearsal of points of difference covered in more detail at the big-table sessions that followed. Very unusually for a Soviet leader, Gorbachev used humour to rebut criticism of Moscow's interventions in the third world, saying that Reagan should not think that he awoke every day with the 'thought about which country he would like to arrange a revolution in'.[27]

Mid-afternoon, while experts were discussing the finer points of arms control, Reagan invited Gorbachev to take a walk with him to a nearby boathouse for a breath of fresh air and a private talk. In that informal setting, they talked for another hour or more, mainly about their differences on strategic defence. Staking out his position that SDI should not be considered as part of the arms race, Reagan promised that it would be shared with the Soviets when finally developed. Gorbachev countered that a 50 per cent reduction in offensive missiles should be accompanied by prohibition on development, testing, and deployment of space weapons. Acknowledging that on a 'human level' it was possible to understand how 'the idea of strategic defence had captured the President's imagination', he was adamant about its unacceptability to the Soviet Union.[28]

The two sides continued to remain far apart on substantive matters in the next day's sessions. Their differences on strategic defence, human rights, and regional issues received a full airing. The discord did not prevent them from reaching consensus on the framework of a statement of summit outcomes, however. The final version, reached after a long night's work by backroom negotiators, endorsed the idea of a 50 per cent reduction in each superpower's nuclear missiles. It did not resolve such contentious issues as how to apply this across various classes of weapons so as to leave both sides equal and how to verify implementation. Whatever the disagreements on detail, this still represented significant progress on the principle of nuclear cutbacks – in 1977 Leonid Brezhnev had summarily rejected Jimmy Carter's proposal for a one-third reduction. The statement also asserted the imperative of peaceful coexistence in declaring that 'a nuclear war cannot be won and must never be fought'. Additionally, it called for continued dialogue, regular meetings of foreign ministers, and periodic discussion of regional issues. Reflecting the lack of substantive agreement on human rights, there was a vaguely worded declaration that both sides acknowledged the importance of resolving humanitarian cases 'in the spirit of cooperation'.[29]

This outcome patently did not amount to a diplomatic breakthrough, but it laid the foundations for further summits that both sides had agreed to hold in Washington and Moscow. The principal significance of Geneva was to help Reagan and Gorbachev develop a better understanding of each other. The president told old friend George Murphy:

It would be foolish to believe the leopard will change its spots […] [Gorbachev] believes the propaganda they peddle about us. At the same time he is practical and knows his economy is a basket case. I think our job is to show him […] they will be better off if we make some practical agreements without attempting to convert him to our way of thinking.

He was more forthcoming to Suzanne Massie:

I'm not going to let myself get euphoric but still I have a feeling we might be at a point of beginning. There did seem to be something of a chemistry between the General Secretary and myself.[30]

Addressing the CPSU Central Committee, Gorbachev offered an ambivalent assessment of Reagan's 'manoeuvring' at Geneva but expressed hope that the American people's desire for peace would compel him to move closer to the Soviet position. The opinions shared in private with aides were somewhat more positive. While still critical of Reagan for being 'so loaded with stereotypes that it was difficult for him to see reason', there was acknowledgement of his sincerity in wanting peace and better relations.[31]

This gave Gorbachev grounds for hope that Reagan might join with him in supporting the most far-reaching plan for arms reduction in Cold War history. On 15 January 1986, a Soviet television news announcer droned through a 4,879-word message from the general secretary outlining a three-stage proposal to rid the world of nuclear weapons by 2000. In stage one, the superpowers would cut their strategic arsenals by 50 per cent, eliminate their European-zone medium-range missiles, and renounce 'space-strike weapons'; in stage two, they would be joined by the other nuclear powers (the UK, France, and China) in further reductions, including tactical missiles; and in stage three, all nations would complete the disarmament process and sign a universal pact never to reintroduce nuclear weapons. An enthusiastic Anatoly Chernyaev remarked of Gorbachev's plan:

It seems he really decided to end the arms race *at all costs*. He is going for that very 'risk,' in which he has boldly recognized the absence of risk, because no one will attack us even if we disarm totally.[32]

The general secretary was a man in a hurry because the Soviet economy needed immediate redress. On 24 April, he told top advisors, 'We should do everything not to impoverish our country further through defense spending.' The next day the accident at the nuclear plant near Chernobyl in the Ukraine made him more determined than ever to halt the arms race. The radioactive fallout may have been less lethal than a single warhead, but portended the consequences of a multi-missile attack. 'In one moment,' Gorbachev told the Politburo on 5 May, 'we felt what a nuclear war is.' The multi-billion-rouble cost of the clean-up intensified the pressure on the hard-pressed Soviet treasury. The disaster also revealed the inadequacy of civil defence, the incompetence of regional CPSU officials, and the excessive secrecy of the nuclear establishment about reactor safety. All this underlined the urgency of resolving foreign-policy issues in order to focus on thoroughgoing improvement of domestic operations.[33]

Although Reagan was critical of the Kremlin's initial reluctance to divulge the causes of the accident that generated radioactive contamination far beyond Soviet borders, Chernobyl's horrifying glimpse of nuclear fallout only enhanced his determination to be rid of weapons of mass destruction. He had trouble getting his own national-security team to see the wisdom of doing so, however. The Pentagon, the CIA, and key NSC officials had immediately dismissed Gorbachev's dramatic arms-reduction proposal as nothing more than a propaganda ploy. Despite acknowledging that the plan included 'a couple of zingers [...] which we'll have to work around', Reagan himself was adamant – as the supportive George Shultz told dubious State Department officials – that 'it's a hell of a good idea'.[34] After hawkish advisors had rehearsed their concerns at the NSPG meeting on 3 February, Reagan cut through the discord to insist on a positive response, saying 'we share their goals & now want to work out the details'.[35] This was no easy matter because the 'zingers' kept getting in the way. Like wary suitors, Reagan and Gorbachev exchanged nine letters in the next seven months, always avowing their commitment to make the world a safer place without ever agreeing the formula for doing so.

Worried that the 'spirit of Geneva' was being lost, Gorbachev eventually proposed a quick one-on-one meeting in Iceland or London 'to engage in a strictly confidential, private and frank discussion (possibly with only our foreign ministers present)'. The discussion 'would not be a detailed one' but was intended to demonstrate political will and prepare some issues for the Washington summit.[36]

Hand-delivered by Eduard Shevardnadze on 19 September, the invitation arrived amid a diplomatic rumpus that Reagan insisted on having resolved before he would agree to the meeting. Ten days earlier, the KGB had arrested American journalist Nicholas Daniloff as a spy in retaliation for the FBI's arrest on espionage charges of Gennadi Zakharov, a Soviet scientist working for the United Nations secretariat. This touched off increasingly harsh exchanges between the two governments. Assuring Gorbachev that Daniloff was no spy, Reagan made a personal appeal for his release, only to receive a cold rejection that he deemed arrogant. 'I'm mad as h—l,' he wrote in his diary.[37] Shevardnadze was then treated to a presidential tirade about how Americans valued the individual in contrast to the Soviets. 'I enjoyed being angry,' Reagan remarked afterwards. Suzanne Massie's warning at a lunch meeting a few days later that Gorbachev was under pressure from his own hard-liners helped to pacify Reagan. With both leaders keen to meet, there was never any doubt that the problem would be settled after a face-saving period of delay for the Soviets. Nevertheless, the deal that freed Zakharov and Daniloff had to respect Reagan's unwillingness to hand over a real spy for an American detained on trumped-up espionage charges. Therefore, the Soviets allowed leading dissident Yuri Orlov and his wife to leave the country as the supposed trade for their man's release.[38]

The day after Daniloff flew home to America, Reagan announced that he would meet with Gorbachev in Reykjavik in less than two weeks' time on 11–12 October. The thinking behind the venue selection was that it afforded greater privacy for the talks – the relatively modest facilities would limit delegation sizes and media numbers (over 3,000 had gathered at Geneva). Doubtless, too, a preference not to have Margaret Thatcher close at hand weighed against London. Given the short notice, there was insufficient time to undertake detailed preparations. This time round, Reagan's pre-summit choice of literature was Tom Clancy's techno-thriller *Red Storm Rising*, which gave him the sense of knowing 'every square foot of Iceland'.[39] He had intensive briefings the day before the talks began, including one-to-one sessions in which NSC Soviet specialist Jack Matlock role-played Gorbachev, at the US ambassador's residence where the American delegation headquartered. The trouble was that no one really knew what the Soviet leader wanted from the meeting. It was likely, another NSC aide advised Reagan, that 'you will have to smoke him out during your discussions'.[40]

In fact, Gorbachev intended to 'sweep Reagan off his feet' with a breathtaking offer.[41] The negotiations were held at Hofdi House, once the site of the British embassy but now owned by the Icelandic government. Instead of the lovely lakeside vista of Geneva's Maison Fleur d'Eau, the only view on offer was the grey North Atlantic. The mood of the meeting matched the setting. There was none of the bonhomie of Geneva. Gorbachev got right down to business at the first one-on-one meeting. With Shultz and Shevardnadze called into attendance, he presented Reagan with a stunning package of proposals that included: a 50 per cent across-the-board reduction in all classes of each side's strategic weapons, including heavy intercontinental ballistic missiles; the total elimination of intermediate-range missiles in Europe; and on-site inspection if need be for verification purposes. The fly in the ointment as ever was SDI. However, Gorbachev moved from his position of absolute opposition at Geneva to propose that both sides observe the Anti-Ballistic Missile (ABM) Treaty 'strictly and in full' for an agreed period and reach 'a mutual understanding' that permitted research and testing of space-based weapons only in laboratories.[42]

At lunch, the entire American delegation heard these proposals with a growing sense of excitement of what might emerge from the summit. Veteran Cold Warrior and arms-control expert Paul Nitze remarked, 'This is the best Soviet offer we have received in twenty-five years.' Nevertheless, it still required improvement, not least because 50 per cent across-the-board reductions would not change Soviet superiority in ballistic missiles. In the afternoon session, it was Reagan's turn to seize the initiative by presenting a US-developed SDI shared with the Soviet Union as the route to total ballistic-missile elimination. Shultz deemed this 'a visionary, revolutionary, far-reaching concept', but Gorbachev thought it nothing more than a means of giving the United States first-strike capability from space because of the unlikelihood that a future American president would be willing to share a missile-defence system.[43]

Thanks to expert negotiating teams working long into the night, the two sides moved ever closer on the specifics of ensuring equality of outcome on long-range strategic missile reductions. Another set of teams reached agreement that human rights were a legitimate subject for US–Soviet negotiations – a formal acknowledgement that Gorbachev had resisted at Geneva. The following day Reagan and Gorbachev sustained the momentum in making progress on intermediate-range-missile reductions. Indeed Gorbachev made significant concessions in agreeing to exclude British and French warheads as part of the US total in Europe, reduce the number of Soviet missiles deployed in Asia to 100, and allow US deployment of the same number aimed at Asian parts of his country. In return, he wanted Reagan's acceptance of his position on ABM–SDI in order to justify the compromises he had made on other issues to critics back home. When this was not forthcoming, Gorbachev told aides at the end of the session: 'No, let's go home. We've accomplished nothing.' This was likely a bluff because he immediately accepted an American proposal to see if Shultz and Shevardnadze could produce some form of words to bridge the divide as the prelude for an unscheduled final session.[44]

As the foreign ministers' meeting neared its end without agreement, Shultz on his own initiative suggested an amended version of a proposal that the United States had vainly offered Gorbachev back in July. In his plan, both sides could continue research, development, and testing of defensive weapons permissible under the ABM Treaty for five years while also reducing their strategic arsenals by 50 per cent. Thereafter, they would move to total elimination of their offensive ballistic missiles, both land-based and sea-based, within a further five years. If this goal were attained, either side would then be free to deploy defensive weapons. This very much worked to American advantage in preserving SDI and destroying all ballistic missiles, the weapons class in which the Soviets had a big edge, but not bombers and cruise missiles, in which the United States was superior. The Soviet counter-proposal offered by Gorbachev on his return to the table mid-afternoon was strict adherence to the ABM Treaty for ten years, prohibition on all but laboratory research on space weapons, and elimination of all classes of strategic offensive arms in two five-year stages. After back-and-forth exchanges on this proposal, both sides agreed to take an hour's break to assess where they stood.

With evening now drawing in, the reconvened session would prove remarkable for what it came so close to achieving. Reagan led off with a US counter-counter-proposal that only moved towards the Soviet position in accepting ten-year adherence to the ABM Treaty. While reaffirming absolute insistence on laboratory-only SDI research, Gorbachev seemed genuinely puzzled at the US dichotomization of strategic-missile reduction and ballistic-missile elimination. This gave Reagan the opportunity for a major departure from the script. If the Soviets were saying they wanted to include all classes – ballistic missiles, cruise missiles, battlefield missiles, strategic bombers – 'it would be fine with him if we eliminated all nuclear weapons'. Gorbachev's response was: '[We] can do that. We can eliminate them.' Shultz then chipped in, 'Let's do it.' The secretary of state came under hawkish criticism on his return home for not restraining Reagan's impulsive willingness to set aside deterrence orthodoxy. 'The president,' he responded, 'had taken that position publicly and privately many times […] I knew that no one could stop him from taking this position in which he believed deeply.'[45]

Differences over SDI immediately pulled both leaders back from the brink of agreeing a historic disarmament. Neither man could understand the other's position. Whatever their contrary interpretations of what the ABM Treaty intended, Reagan asked 'what the hell difference did it make' in view of progress on other issues at Reykjavik. In his mind, he owed it to the American people to safeguard the possibility of fully developing SDI because 'some country might come along with a madman who wanted to build nuclear weapons again'. When this cut no ice, Reagan asked Gorbachev's acquiescence as a personal favour. This was evidently something he thought the leader of a totalitarian system could grant without risk of domestic criticism, whereas right-wing critics were 'kicking his brains out' for negotiating with the Soviet Union.

Gorbachev was quick to correct this fundamental misunderstanding of his position. If he returned home having agreed research, testing, and development outside the laboratory for SDI deployment after ten years, 'he would be called a dummy [*durak*] and not a leader'. In his eyes, he was being asked to eliminate his country's nuclear armoury while leaving America free to develop space-based weapons that could threaten the Soviet Union in the future. How would Reagan feel, he wondered, if the same were asked of him? 'It would cause nervousness and suspicion. It was not an acceptable request […] The President was not asking for a favour but for giving up a point of principle.' Laboratory research and testing constituted Gorbachev's final offer. In his reasoning, Reagan had an obligation to accept it in view of Soviet concessions on so many other issues. Gorbachev declared himself ready to sign 'in two minutes' if this was done but everything else was conditional on that.[46]

The meeting ended at 6.50 p.m. without the vital breakthrough. When the two leaders emerged from Hofdi House into the media spotlight, their stricken faces and body language stamped the talks with the image of failure. Inside Reagan was boiling mad because of a mistaken belief that Gorbachev had come to Reykjavik primarily to kill SDI. Watching back home on television, Nancy thought his rage showed through: 'He looked angry, *very* angry. His face was pale, and his teeth were clenched. I had seen that look before but not often – and never on television.'[47] In a brief exchange before parting, Reagan told Gorbachev, 'I still feel we can find a deal.' 'I don't think you want a deal. I don't know what more I could have done,' was the response. The president countered, 'You could have said yes.' The same was true of him, of course. Despite having come so close to agreement for a nuclear-free world, neither man could break wholly free as yet from the mistrust that shaped the Cold War relations of their two nations. As well as overestimating American progress in SDI development, Gorbachev held exaggerated fears of the threat it posed if ever deployed. Reagan conversely underestimated Gorbachev's need to halt the arms race and focus on domestic reform. Whatever his scepticism about SDI's feasibility, George Shultz's conviction that it was the most important leverage at US disposal 'to propel the Soviets moving our way' made him utterly supportive of presidential obduracy regarding its retention.[48]

A distraught Reagan told aides that '[o]ne lousy word' (laboratory) had prevented history being made. Unaccustomed to seeing the president so emotional, staff let him sit alone in his quarters on the flight home but worried about his state of mind. After a few hours of reflection, however, he emerged to say:

> I'm okay now. I gave it a lot of thought. I know I made the right decision
> back there. We couldn't give up SDI, not for America's future. I made
> the right decision. I wasn't sure, but I know now I did.[49]

Reagan was further reassured on getting home to find that the majority of the public supported his stand. He was soon tearing into the Soviets for seeking to deny America the security of SDI in stump speeches for Republican candidates in the midterm elections.

When the dust settled, it was possible to see more clearly the significance of both sides having gone so far in trying to resolve differences at the summit. As Shultz commented: 'The genie was out of the bottle: the concessions Gorbachev made at Reykjavik could never, in reality, be taken back. We had seen the Soviets' bottom line.'[50] Almost immediately on returning from Iceland, Reagan wrote to the pastor of the Presbyterian church he attended while in Los Angeles,

'We felt we made more progress than has been made in years and we'll keep on the effort.' This outlook was evident when Caspar Weinberger presented a proposal to fund a kinetic energy-boosted rocket system that could launch parts of a missile-defence system into space. Before Reykjavik, Reagan likely would have given his enthusiastic backing, but now he queried how it could be reconciled with his verbal commitment to Gorbachev not to bring SDI out of the laboratory for ten years.[51]

The distractions of the Iran–Contra investigations put new overtures to Gorbachev on hold in late 1986 and early 1987. Once his partial *mea culpa* to the nation was out of the way, Reagan saw a Washington summit as the means to rebuild his presidential reputation. With Nancy no less anxious to have one, they began planning possible scenarios with the help of aides. By September, there were three options on the table. The Reagans' preference was for a so-called 'Grand Tour', a week-long spectacle that would begin with White House negotiations and then extend into a multi-stop, westward trip across the United States before ending at Rancho del Cielo. The second option was a 'Washington and California' summit, and the third was 'Washington only' with visits to places of interest outside the Beltway.[52]

Gorbachev's own reflections on Reykjavik convinced him that the meeting had laid the foundations for substantive progress on arms control. The summit report to the Politburo had been predictably critical in describing his American sparring partner 'as a representative of our class enemy, who exhibited extreme primitivism, a cave man outlook, and intellectual arrogance'.[53] Opening up to aides in private, however, he admitted to having been impressed with his co-negotiator's willingness to accept deep cuts in offensive missiles. According to Anatoly Chernyaev, Gorbachev stopped speaking about Reagan within his inner circle in the negative terms routinely employed before Reykjavik. The general secretary 'became convinced that it would "work out" between him and Reagan [...] A spark of understanding was born between them, as if they had winked to each other about the future.'[54] The Soviets had encountered a different Reagan from their stereotyped one at the summit. 'I first saw his human hesitation,' Alexander Yakovlev later commented,

> about what decision to make, and it seemed to me he wasn't acting
> [...] On the one hand [...] he was interested in the idea of universal

nuclear disarmament, on the other hand sticking to the idea of such
a funny toy as SDI.[55]

The general secretary now questioned the wisdom of making arms reduction
conditional on restraint of the SDI projects, especially when informed of his
own scientists' increasing scepticism of its viability. This outlook informed the
announcement on 28 February 1987 that the Soviet Union would no longer
insist on it being part of an arms-control package. With negotiations coming
to a 'dead end', Gorbachev had told the Politburo two days previously, it was
essential to initiate

> a new level of conversation [...] We start from the assumption that
> difficult as it is to conduct business with the United States, we are
> doomed to it. We have no choice. Our main problem is to remove the
> confrontation. That is the central tenet of our entire foreign policy.[56]

These words prefaced further concessions in the following months that laid
the foundations for a far-reaching US–Soviet agreement to eliminate their
intermediate-range missiles not only in Europe but also in Asia. Gorbachev's
ambitions did not stop there, as evidenced by a memorandum he dictated in
preparation for conversations with Reagan. This evinced almost boundless
optimism that the two leaders could reach agreement on further significant
reductions of their nuclear, chemical, and conventional forces and settle outstanding regional issues.[57]

George Shultz's visit to Moscow in April set in motion the process for
negotiating what became the Intermediate Nuclear Force (INF) Treaty that
Reagan and Gorbachev would sign at the Washington summit. The treaty was
not exclusively a US–Soviet concern. America's European allies had to be
brought on board because of their concerns about being left vulnerable to Soviet
conventional-force attack without the protection of US intermediate missiles.
When Margaret Thatcher first heard how far Reagan went at Reykjavik, she
felt 'as if there had been an earthquake underneath my feet'. Cabinet minister
Michael Jopling, present for the briefing, had never seen her 'more incandes-
cent'.[58] As well as exposing Western Europe to conventional Soviet offensive
in her calculation, a Reagan–Gorbachev agreement would have scuppered the

new D-5 Trident submarine-based ballistic-missile programme that the UK government was in the process of buying from the United States. It was ironic that the much-disdained SDI had been Thatcher's saviour on this occasion, but she could not rely on this always being the case. Promptly inviting herself to Washington for talks, the prime minister got thrown a very big bone for making the 14-hour round trip for a three-hour meeting on 15 November. In return for supporting a projected INF Treaty, she was promised America's full support for modernization of the UK's independent deterrent with Trident. A relieved Thatcher still understood that nuclear weapons 'remained the issue on which [...] I could not take the Reagan administration's soundness for granted'.[59]

The other European leader in need of stroking was Helmut Kohl of West Germany. Reagan went to work on him once Shultz returned from Moscow in April with the outline of an INF agreement. A telephone call to the chancellor seemed to go well. 'I think he'll be cooperative,' Reagan remarked in his diary. As predicted, Kohl agreed to back the Reagan–Shultz proposal, but with palpable lack of enthusiasm and on one major condition. To compensate for Soviet superiority not only in conventional forces but also tactical nuclear missiles, he insisted on keeping West Germany's 72 Pershing missiles that carried US warheads if the Americans withdrew theirs from Europe. Though initially acceptable to the White House, Gorbachev's opposition required further presidential diplomacy to make it clear that Kohl could not undermine the US–Soviet arms deal. The chancellor eventually agreed in late August that West Germany would dismantle its Pershings once the US–Soviet treaty went into effect.[60]

Meanwhile, Gorbachev was impatient to lay the foundations for agreement on other missile classes. In early September Shevardnadze arrived in Washington with a letter calling for cuts in strategic offensive weaponry, including space-based ones. This might have been Reagan's chance to make a counter-proposal coupling limitation on such armaments with sharing a space-based defensive system. Pentagon warnings that strategic arms reduction required complex negotiations to secure the best possible terms stayed his hand on this occasion. A nuclear-free world was still Reagan's ideal, however. '[S]ome day,' he remarked in concluding an NSPG meeting, 'people are going to ask why we didn't do something now about getting rid of nuclear weapons.'[61]

Having finalized the details of the INF Treaty with Shevardnadze on his September visit to Washington, Shultz went to Moscow the following month to get agreement on a date for the Washington summit. To his surprise, Gorbachev demanded agreement on SDI restrictions and key provisions of a separate treaty on long-range missiles as preconditions for his attendance. This encounter took place just days after a turbulent CPSU leadership meeting in which the general secretary came under criticism from conservative hard-liners for being too accommodating to the United States. Primarily intent on halting Gorbachev's reforms, these traditionalists attacked his foreign policy in order to weaken his authority and slow down the disarmament that was the essential precondition to domestic change. Needing to shore up his position, Gorbachev likely banked on Reagan's keenness for a summit being so great that concessions would be forthcoming, but this was a vain hope. Holding his ground, Shultz warned that the INF Treaty had to be signed soon or it could not come before the Senate for ratification while Reagan remained in office. The president also refused to blink. Reporting on the Shultz–Gorbachev encounter in his weekly radio address, he declared: 'No date was set for the summit meeting, but we're in no hurry. And we certainly will not be pushed around into sacrificing essential interests just to have a meeting.'[62]

The last thing the Soviet leader wanted was to risk having a new president abandon the INF Treaty. With his bluff called, he agreed to visit Washington sometime during the first ten days of December without requiring conditions for his presence but requesting that 'agreement in principle' be reached on long-range weapons. Nevertheless, Gorbachev wanted a negotiations-only summit without the trimmings envisaged by the Reagans, explaining it would be impossible to make security arrangements for a cross-country tour at such short notice. American officials divined another reason for his reticence. As National Security Advisor (NSA) Colin Powell remarked:

> He came to do business. He didn't come to be a tourist. He also didn't want to be seen as, 'Oh gee, Mr President, if I had only known [what the United States was like], I'd have given up communism.'[63]

One of Reagan's longstanding correspondents, Barney Oldfield, a regular visitor to the Soviet Union on business, relayed that 'the old guys in Moscow' dismissively referred to Gorbachev as 'Mr Yes' because of his concessions on arms reduction. 'It was most interesting,' Reagan responded, 'to hear that the G.S. has some critics that sound like mine.'[64] Other friends, like William Buckley and Charlton Heston, alerted him to the depth of concern among the most fervent supporters of his first-term tough line, receiving assurances in return that he had not gone soft on communism just to get an arms deal. Urged by Heston to avoid 'a Yalta waltz with the Soviet bear', a reference to FDR's alleged surrender of Eastern Europe at the 1945 summit in Crimea with Joseph Stalin, Reagan's response was, 'I'm willing to dance but intend to lead.'[65]

While Reagan tried to reassure friends that he knew what he was doing, there was no way of bridging the divide with his most vehement critics. Among these were the conservative groups that once regarded him as their tribune. Invited to a White House meeting in early 1987, leaders of these organizations denounced the negotiations with Gorbachev and sat in stony silence when the president left the room at the end.[66] The fury of right-wingers built up over the course of the year to reach a crescendo during the Washington summit. Reagan stood accused of misunderstanding that the nature of Soviet communism rather than nuclear missiles constituted the real threat to peace. Howard Phillips of the Conservative Caucus turned nastily personal in denouncing him 'as a very weak man with a very strong wife and a very strong staff', dominated by appeasers like Shultz, and called him 'a useful idiot for Soviet propaganda'. Conservative columnist William Safire was equally harsh in charging: 'The Russians [...] now understand the way to handle Mr Reagan: Never murder a man who is committing suicide.'[67]

Members of the foreign-policy establishment who had shaped national security strategy in the 1970s constituted another group of Reagan critics. Champions of the existing Cold War order based on deterrence, these foreign-policy realists had done battle with Reagan a decade earlier in defence of détente as a geopolitical necessity. Now they opposed him out of belief that competition between the US and Soviet hegemons was an inevitable fact of world politics. The most prominent critics, Richard Nixon and Henry Kissinger, joined forces in an attempt to derail the INF Treaty. After meeting with Gorbachev in Moscow in July 1986, Nixon adjudged him 'the most formidable of all Soviet leaders because his goals are the same as theirs and he will be more effective in achieving them'.[68] Concerted media attacks by Nixon and Kissinger in the spring of 1987 warned that the INF would provoke a crisis within NATO and endanger peace in Europe. More broadly, the duo sought to discredit the idea of total nuclear-weapon elimination as a dangerous fantasy. The Soviets, Nixon admonished, had always played on Western fears of nuclear weapons by urging their abolition. Any American president who fell for this ploy 'courts unimaginable perils'. Kissinger similarly asserted that a president 'must always remember that however he may be hailed in today's headlines the judgement of history would severely condemn a false peace'.[69]

These attacks implicitly portraying Reagan as Gorbachev's poodle caused fury in the White House. On the advice of aides, Reagan agreed to meet with Nixon in secret in the late afternoon of 28 April to explain his position, but drew the line at extending the invitation to Kissinger, whom he had always disdained. The meeting in the residence quarters of the White House did not go well. If Reagan hoped for Nixon's endorsement, there was no chance of him getting it. Instead, Nixon insisted that Gorbachev was the old Soviet wolf in the new lamb's clothing of peacemaker. The ex-president left the meeting thinking that his successor looked 'far older, more tired, and less vigorous in private than in public'. In his assessment George Shultz was pushing a pliant president into making a deal that was harmful to American interests. Reagan's lack of detailed knowledge about arms-control details in contrast to the Soviet leader's mastery of the subject shocked Nixon. The 26-page memoir he drew up of the conversation made a damning indictment: 'There is no way he [Reagan] can ever be allowed to participate in a private meeting with Gorbachev.'[70]

The third group of Reagan's critics resided within the bosom of his own administration. Caspar Weinberger, William Casey, the Pentagon military brass, and a goodly number of NSC officials disliked the rush towards nuclear disarmament. They shared the Nixon–Kissinger stereotype of Gorbachev as a traditional Soviet leader in substance if not in style. NSC aide Fritz Ermarth later commented in embarrassment about how wrong he'd been to think that 'this kindly old gentleman [Reagan] was going to get suckered'.[71] Their positions at the heart of national-security decision making offered hope of influencing the president but also made them vulnerable to his displeasure. With the support of loyalists, Reagan saw off the principal hawks, appointing more dependable replacements in their stead whenever the opportunity arose. On Casey's death from a brain tumour in May 1987, William Webster was put in charge of the CIA instead of deputy director Robert Gates, whose misunderstanding of Gorbachev's intentions was close to total.[72] Citing his wife's ill health but in all likelihood tired of fighting a losing battle, Caspar Weinberger resigned in October. The Department of Defense's top Soviet specialist, assistant secretary Richard Perle, a neoconservative ultra-hawk, followed suit some months later. Reagan put national security advisor Frank Carlucci in charge of the Pentagon and promoted Colin Powell to head the NSC. As well as enhancing administration unity, these changes underwrote Shultz's position as the unchallenged head of the foreign-policy team.

Meanwhile, Reagan turned his attention to proving that he had not turned soft on communism. The opportunity for doing so was the speech delivered in West Berlin on 12 June 1987, ostensibly as part of the celebrations of the city's 750th anniversary. Crafted by speechwriter Peter Robinson, it drew inspiration from John F. Kennedy's 1963 'Ich bin ein Berliner' speech about the city's significance for the free world. There was a prolonged dispute in the drafting stage over the inclusion of the most famous line, which the State Department and NSC regarded as contrary to the new spirit of dialogue with the Soviets. Sharing their concerns, White House staff lobbied strongly for its removal, but Reagan was unrelenting. Dissenting aides were finally silenced with the reminder: 'I'm the president, right?'[73]

Speaking before some 20,000 people just on the west side of the Berlin Wall and with the Brandenburg Gate on the east side in the background, Reagan elaborated on the divided city as a microcosm of the differences between freedom and repression. About halfway through came the dramatic words:

> General Secretary Gorbachev, if you seek peace, if you seek prosperity for the Soviet Union and Eastern Europe, if you seek liberalization: Come here to this gate! Mr Gorbachev, open this gate! Mr Gorbachev, Mr Gorbachev, tear down this wall.[74]

Up until this point, the crowd had been somewhat subdued, but they came to life with the penultimate phrase of this passage. With a seasoned performer's sense of timing, Reagan then repeated Gorbachev's name twice as a sign of what was coming. The next words brought the house down, if not yet the wall.

This passage could be interpreted as an effort to provide political cover against those charging him with readiness to reach an accommodation with communism. If this was the intent, the speech was an abject failure. It was on deeds rather than words that Reagan's critics now judged him. The more likely aim of 'tear down this wall' was to signal that the improvement of US–Soviet relations could not rest wholly on arms-reduction agreements. If the Cold War was truly to end, Reagan was letting Gorbachev know that the Soviet Union had to allow the peoples of Eastern Europe to have real freedom. The true significance of his words did not become apparent until the coming down of the Berlin Wall two years later. The constant television replays of the famous sound bite linked Reagan forever more to the momentous events of November 1989.

Some six months after the Berlin address, the three-day Washington summit got going on 8 December. The first one-on-one meeting in the Oval Office did not start well. Reagan's forceful criticisms of the Soviet Union's human rights record provoked Gorbachev to remark, 'Mr President, you are not a prosecutor here and I am not on trial.' The conversation was more cordial when it turned to reviewing progress on arms control.[75] Reagan held his own during this encounter but then gave probably his worst performance at any summit in the afternoon session. Often disconcerted by sudden changes, he may have been thrown by Shultz's last-minute decision to make it a large meeting with lots of senior aides from both sides in attendance in the Cabinet Room. With the president saying little, the secretary of state had to take responsibility for responding to Gorbachev's review of pending arms-control issues. When Reagan finally interjected, it was a digression on the importance of allowing people to run their own lives, illustrated with one of his anti-Soviet jokes that fell very flat. Colin Powell later remarked of this sally that 'the Americans wanted to disappear under the table, while Gorbachev stared straight ahead, expressionless'. After the meeting, Shultz forthrightly told his boss to up his game, while Powell put NSC staff on an all-night mission to produce talking points for the president.[76] A better-briefed Reagan performed much more satisfactorily in the smaller meetings on 9 December. True to form, he staunchly resisted Gorbachev's continued probing for SDI limits. More significantly, the two leaders reached a sweeping agreement on cutting intercontinental-missile armouries.[77] Negotiating teams would haggle long into the night to put flesh on the bones of this deal but eventually produced a compromise settlement that Shultz proudly hailed as a 'gigantic step forward' on strategic arms.[78]

This was something of an overstatement. The Washington summit had made significantly less headway on arms control than the Reykjavik one had nearly done, but the momentum was still unmistakably in that direction. Although there was still much work to do on strategic missiles, the two leaders signed the Intermediate Nuclear Force Treaty eliminating this entire class of missiles at the White House on 1.45 p.m. on day one of the summit. Unbeknown to Shultz, this was the specific time recommended by Nancy Reagan's astrologer, Joan Quigley.[79] Perhaps the stars were not fully in alignment because Reagan's *'Doveryai no proveryai'* (Trust but verify) line in his signing remarks was once too often for a clearly exasperated Gorbachev.

Despite this being the away leg for Gorbachev, he was clearly the star of the summit, not Reagan. The Soviet leader hosted receptions for various American groups at the Soviet embassy, engaged in many exchanges with journalists and broadcasters, and was the subject of round-the-clock coverage on the relatively new CNN channel. He also pulled off a public-relations coup of the first order on the third day of the summit. With his limousine en route from the Soviet embassy back to the White House, Gorbachev ordered his driver to stop and, to the horror of KGB guards, dived out to work the crowds on Connecticut Avenue like an American politician. This became a huge media event. One of the star-struck people who got to shake his hand told reporters, 'It was like the coming of the second Messiah or something.' Asked just before the summit whether he resented Gorbachev's growing popularity, Reagan laughingly replied that he had no such feeling, adding, 'Good Lord, I once co-starred with Errol Flynn.' At a more serious level, his co-negotiator's celebrity status would prove helpful in the battle to secure Senate ratification of the INF Treaty. The American people liked what they saw of a Soviet leader who defied stereotypes in his evident desire to make the world a more peaceful place. The ABC News–*Washington Post* poll published the day after his departure found that 76 per cent of respondents thought the United States and the Soviet Union were entering a new era.[80]

The minority of disbelievers still had some shots left in the locker. Conservatives launched the Anti-Appeasement Alliance in the hope of persuading the Senate to reject the treaty. Media allies joined them, with the *Wall*

Street Journal leading the charge in branding Reagan a 'utopian disarmer'.[81] Richard Nixon conducted a parallel campaign through continued attacks on Gorbachev's supposedly aggressive intentions, but without his one-time side-kick – Henry Kissinger felt that rejection of the treaty would create more problems than it solved for the Atlantic alliance. Reagan's strategy for dealing with his critics was to reassert his anti-communism without yielding an inch on the treaty. Nackey Loeb's hard-hitting editorials against the INF in her Manchester (New Hampshire) *Union Leader* newspaper drew forth the response: 'I'm still the Ronald Reagan I was and the evil empire is still just that.'[82] The president used a major address before the World Affairs Council in April 1988 to insist that his tough rhetoric about the evil of communism had made the Soviets 'understand the lack of illusions on our part about them or their system'. This speech infuriated Gorbachev because it seemingly handed ammunition to his own conservatives in their increasingly open attacks on him. 'So how am I to explain this?' he asked when Shultz arrived to agree arrangements for Reagan's visit. 'Is this summit going to be a catfight?'[83]

In early March Suzanne Massie brought the president an oral message that she had received from former ambassador and now Central Committee secretary Anatoly Dobrynin, whom she believed was acting on Gorbachev's authority. The go-between conveyed the concerns of Soviet officials that Reagan's views of Russia remained unchanged despite recent developments. She then relayed their request for him to make a public statement that Soviet policy had changed in advance of the Moscow summit. This was accompanied with a query as to what concrete steps they might undertake to prompt this. The suggested trade-off between presidential words and Soviet actions was a remarkable demonstration of the power of Reagan's rhetoric on the Kremlin hierarchy, but nothing came of it.[84]

For the moment, Reagan was more concerned to secure INF Treaty ratification than observe diplomatic niceties. If the renewal of anti-communist rhetoric did not entirely defang the conservative opposition, it still had the effect of weakening its venom. Nevertheless, the treaty continued to face doughty resistance from a group of Republican senators headed by Jesse Helms of North Carolina and Dan Quayle of Indiana. Having done their utmost to slow down hearings in the committee stage, they forced a series of votes on the Senate floor on proposed amendments. The White House peeled off individuals from the conservative bloc through personal lobbying and clarification of treaty issues, but all this took time. At one point, it looked as if Reagan would have to go to Moscow without the INF Treaty being done and dusted. Finally, Democrats and loyal Republicans forced a vote of approval that carried by 93 to five, just two days before he was due to leave.[85]

The INF Treaty's elimination, rather than mere reduction, of this class of nuclear weapons made it the first genuine disarmament agreement of the atomic era. That said, it only got rid of one in 20 missiles in the US and Soviet armouries. The next big step was to eliminate their respective strategic forces. Despite reaching an outline agreement to do so at the Washington summit, this entailed far more complex issues – particularly regarding verification – than did the INF Treaty. Regardless of the lopsided outcome of INF ratification, the battle had been a pointer to the even greater problems that would face a Strategic Arms Reduction Treaty (START). In Shultz's view 'the naysayers' real pint of blood […] was to take the edge off the push for START'.[86] To the disappointment of Gorbachev and Shevardnadze, Reagan was in agreement with his secretary of state that there was no hope of getting treaty terms settled in time for the Moscow summit.

Instead of being the occasion for signing a START agreement, the Moscow summit effectively became a victory lap for a race already run, but this did not make it unimportant as a staging post in ending the Cold War. Reagan took the opportunity to reassure Gorbachev of America's sincere commitment 'to eliminate the distrust that had led to the arms race'. The friendly atmosphere of the talks encouraged the Soviet leader to propose ending with a more robust summit communiqué than the bland one produced by staff negotiators. He was especially anxious to include a statement recognizing 'peaceful coexistence as a universal principle of international relations'. Though Reagan was initially agreeable, George Shultz counselled that the wording of the revised version was all too reminiscent of détente-era agreements binding America 'to leave unchallenged areas of Soviet conquest and control'. The rejection of his initiative provoked a display of temper from Gorbachev in the final plenary session, but it quickly subsided. He had learned by now that Reagan could not be pushed around at the negotiating table.[87]

In many ways what went on outside the talks was more important than what happened within them at Moscow. The competitor in Reagan made him keen to match Gorbachev's Washington triumph. A ten-minute walkabout with Nancy shaking hands with Soviet citizens in the Arbat shopping area was the first step to evening the score. A carefully choreographed visit to the Danilov Monastery, a meeting with nearly 100 invited dissidents at the American embassy residence, and another with Soviet cultural leaders gave Reagan high-profile opportunities to press the need for religious, political, and artistic freedoms. At Gorbachev's alma mater, Moscow State University, he received a standing ovation for an address that envisioned a nuclear-free world in which everyone enjoyed freedom. At a time when few political leaders understood the significance of new information technology, America's president held up a microchip as a symbol of the 'continuing revolution of the marketplace', words spoken beneath a giant bust of Lenin.[88]

The stroll that Reagan and Gorbachev took in Red Square on 31 May became the defining moment of the summit. The president's avowal that the Soviet Union was no longer the evil empire provided the most memorable sound bite of all four summits with Gorbachev. It had immense significance in signalling to the Soviets that he no longer considered them an adversary. A Gorbachev advisor commented, 'Reagan saw that we are not an "empire of evil," but normal people, with a rich history at that, and [...] we are such a giant that you cannot intimidate or dazzle us.' Two decades later, the former Soviet leader would claim that Reagan's words amounted to a proclamation that the Cold War was over.[89] The president's one-time conservative supporters back home greeted them with utter dismay. An irate William Buckley denounced the remarks as exemplifying what George Orwell called 'vaporization' in *1984*. 'Big Brother,' he warned in a *National Review* editorial, 'decides to change a historical or a present fact, and evidence inconvenient to the new thesis is simply made to – disappear.' Such judgements misunderstood that Reagan was looking forward to a new world of mutual US–Soviet trust rather than distorting the past. This would be his message in the summit press conference. Explaining why the evil empire was no more, he declared, 'A large part of it is due to Mr Gorbachev as leader.'[90]

The president's new tone could not have come at a better time for the Soviet leader. Jack Matlock, now US ambassador in Moscow, had briefed Reagan just before the summit that the general secretary was about to issue radical proposals for discussion and adoption at a CPSU conference in July. Officially dubbed the 'Theses', these contained no trace of Marxist–Leninism and incorporated the basic principles of democracy. Many supporters of reform believed that Reagan's visit had given their cause a real boost. The president himself was hopeful that real change was now afoot. '[F]or the first time,' he wrote to George Murphy, 'I believe that there could perhaps one day be a stirring of the people that would make the bureaucrats pay attention.'[91]

Gorbachev's 'Theses' encountered considerable resistance from conservatives when presented to the CPSU conference. His response was to reorganize the party leadership to shore up his position, notably through ousting Andrei Gromyko as chairman of the presidium of the Supreme Soviet and taking this post for himself. Now combining the role of party leader and head of state in his own person, he felt emboldened to advance a dramatic foreign-policy initiative without waiting for Reagan to draw level with him.[92] A sensational address to the UN in New York in December 1988 attempted to lay the Cold War to rest. Gorbachev unilaterally announced reductions of Soviet armed forces by half a million troops and the withdrawal of six armoured divisions as well as 50,000 soldiers from Warsaw Pact countries. Equally important, he signalled a major change in the Soviet Union's outlook on the world in rejecting class and ideology as the basis for its dealings with other nations. Tied to this was a repudiation of the Brezhnev Doctrine that denied the right of any Eastern Bloc country to reject socialism.[93]

In his last personal letter to Reagan, Gorbachev expressed gratitude for the promise given in Moscow to 'do the utmost in the remaining months of your presidency to ensure the continuity and consistency of the fundamental course we have chosen'.[94] This did not elicit any reply, perhaps because Reagan wanted to avoid the appearance of setting the agenda for his soon-to-be-chosen successor. As it transpired, the next occupant of the Oval Office was not ready to show the same trust in the Soviet leader. Despite fulfilling what he considered an obligation to support his boss when vice-president George H. W. Bush personally believed that Reagan had displayed 'sentimentality' towards Gorbachev. Determined to be more hard-headed when president himself, he selected a foreign-policy team of realists that prized order and stability over rapid change in international relations, but caution soon had to be thrown to the winds.[95] Before 1989 was out Gorbachev's willingness to let the Berlin Wall come down and the Velvet Revolution to sweep Eastern Europe without resorting to repression showed that Reagan had been right to trust him as a wholly different Soviet leader. Held just weeks after the momentous events in Berlin, the Malta summit of 2–3 December between Bush and Gorbachev effectively recognized that the Cold War was over.

The two individuals most responsible for their countries getting to this position were Ronald Reagan and Mikhail Gorbachev. Each had the support of astute and influential aides, but they were the ones calling the critical shots. There has been a perhaps inevitable tendency to lionize one man or the other for the great achievement of resolving the Cold War. *Time* magazine made Gorbachev, not Reagan, its 'man of the decade'. In his 5,000 word paean to the Soviet leader, correspondent Strobe Talbott only mentioned Reagan once to criticize the smugness of his Soviet strategy. The 1990 Nobel Peace Prize went to Gorbachev alone (a contrast to the joint award in 1973 to Henry Kissinger and Le Duc Tho for negotiating an end to the Vietnam War).[96] With the implosion of the Soviet Union the following year, however, conservatives began advancing a thesis that belied their earlier disdain of Reagan's negotiations. With the wisdom of hindsight, they now claimed that his ideological offensive, military build-up, and SDI plan had put intolerable pressures on the Soviet system with the consequence that it collapsed and disintegrated. In a lucid but questionable analysis, Dinesh D'Souza acknowledged the significance of both leaders in ending the Cold War, but continued:

> Reagan won and Gorbachev lost. If Gorbachev was the trigger, Reagan was the one who pulled it […] In the cold war, Reagan turned out to be our Churchill; it was his vision and leadership that led us to victory.[97]

The 'Reagan won' thesis is as flawed as the one denying his significance in ending the Cold War. Reagan had no intention of spending the Soviet Union out of existence through an intensified arms race. The principal statement of his administration's Cold War strategy, NSDD-75, declared that the 'primary focus' of America's Cold War policy was to 'contain and over time reverse Soviet expansionism'. One way it saw of doing so was to press for political change within the Soviet Union. Despite this, NSDD-75 also expressed the need to engage the Soviets in negotiations that enhanced and protected US interests. There is nothing in Reagan's public rhetoric or private writing that signified any desire on his part to bring about the Soviet Union's disintegration. Indeed, on a post-presidential trip to Moscow, he went out of his way to support Gorbachev's efforts to prevent its break-up by personally urging the 15 constituent Soviet republics to restrain their passion for independence.[98]

In essence, it was not a case of Reagan winning the Cold War but of Gorbachev abandoning it, yet each leader was equally instrumental in this outcome. Without Reagan deciding that Gorbachev was sincere in his desire to move away from confrontation and being willing to take the heat from realists and right-wing critics to negotiate with him, the United States and the Soviet Union would have remained locked in mutual antagonism. Without Gorbachev's dedication to changing the Soviet Union, Reagan would not have had the opportunity to engage in meaningful negotiations to initiate the process of peace and arms control. In essence, each leader ended up depriving the other's nation of an enemy. Of course, structural factors defined the context in which they were able to do this, but the Reagan–Gorbachev interactions underlined the important roles that individuals could still play on the stage of world politics. Reporting on the Washington summit to the Politburo, Gorbachev remarked: '[P]robably for the first time, we clearly realized how much the human factor means in international politics. Before [...] we treated such personal contacts as simply meetings between representatives of opposed and irreconcilable systems.'[99]

It was indeed remarkable how two leaders steeped in conflicting ideologies could shake off the past to build a new framework for cooperation. Reagan crucially recognized the truth of Thatcher's assessment that Gorbachev was a man he could do business with. In common with the UK prime minister, the Soviet leader thought himself much smarter than the US president, but like her found himself dealing with someone whose convictions, obduracy, and instincts made him more than a match in any talks. All the concessions on the road to the new relationship came from him. Reagan may have had a significantly lesser grasp of detail than Gorbachev but he had a firm understanding of the ideas and principles underlying the Cold War. There was no doubt, too, about the political impact of his words and judgements on the Soviet leader. For all these reasons, Gorbachev would acknowledge in his own memoirs, 'In my view, the 40th president of the United States will go down in history for his *rare* perception.'[100]

EPILOGUE
History Man

Ronald Reagan's presidency came to an end at noon on 20 January 1989 with the swearing in of his successor, George H. W. Bush. Though Reagan had been looking forward for much of his last year in office to being 'a Californian again', the final weeks proved 'a bittersweet time with all the goodbyes'.[1] The last official letter of his presidency was addressed to Margaret Thatcher in response to her gracious private note telling him, 'You have been a great president, one of the greatest, because you stood for all that is best in America.'[2] On his last morning, he received Colin Powell's national-security briefing that 'the world is quiet today'. One of his final White House acts was to place in the top drawer of what would soon be his successor's Oval Office desk a handwritten message on a notepad headed *Don't Let the Turkeys Get You Down*: 'You'll have moments when you want to use this particular stationery. Well, go for it.'[3] With Bush's inauguration, Reagan's presidency became part of history but that did not make it part of the past. Such was the impact of its legacy on American politics and public policy that the United States would live in the Age of Reagan for years to come. In this sense, the history that Reagan made would have a profound influence on the nation's future.

As the debate over his presidency unfolded, Reagan got on with life as a private citizen. Having sold their Pacific Palisades home in 1981, the former president and first lady moved into a new residence, a 7,192-square-foot ranch-style house on a 1.5-acre plot in Bel Air. A relatively modest property for such an exclusive neighbourhood, the Reagans' longstanding backers had purchased it for $2.5 million in 1986 and leased to them with a later option to buy, exercised in late 1989 for a price of $3 million. Another old friend, Lew Wasserman, arranged for Reagan to occupy a magnificent suite of offices atop the newest and highest glass tower on the Avenue of Stars in the Century City area of west Los Angeles. With rent and other expenses funded from the generous federal allowances for ex-presidents, this was where the two Reagans and their staff of 13 conducted post-presidential business.[4]

An important figure in Reagan's pre-presidential life, Wasserman was reportedly the first person that he met with on returning to California as a private citizen. It is likely that the desire to make money during his post-presidency was the main topic of conversation. Wasserman arranged an invitation from Fujisankei Communications Group, one of MCA's biggest overseas customers for syndicated television programmes, movies, and records, to make a short tour of Japan in October 1989. For two 20-minute addresses on Fujisankei-owned television channels, the ex-president earned a fee of $2 million. 'That's what was offered and I didn't protest,' Reagan later remarked. 'I just thought that in sixteen years I hadn't made any kind of money.'[5] Adverse media reaction back home persuaded him to decline further speaking invitations abroad, but he continued to earn $50,000 on average for speaking before Fortune 500 companies and other private-sector groups at home (no charge to charities or schools), less 20 per cent commission to booking agents Washington Speakers Bureau Inc. These engagements grossed him an estimated $1.8 million in his first year out of office. Reagan set a trend for ex-presidents – and many other politicians – to cash in on their celebrity in retirement, but his rewards would soon look modest in comparison to the astronomical earnings of Bill Clinton and George W. Bush.[6]

Eschewing fat fees did not stop Reagan from speaking abroad. His first post-presidential trip overseas was to receive an honorary knighthood from Queen Elizabeth on 14 June 1989. The previous day, he delivered the English-Speaking Union's annual Winston Churchill address amid the Gothic splendour of the Guildhall. A powerful commentary on the global democratic potential of the communications revolution, it was delivered just days after the massacre of Tiananmen Square protesters in Beijing. 'The Goliath of totalitarianism,' Reagan avowed, 'will be brought down by the David of the microchip.'[7] In

September 1990 he was in Europe again for a ten-day visit that took in a tour of the remaining portions of the Berlin Wall, addresses to the Polish parliament and Gdańsk shipyard workers, a meeting with Gorbachev prior to speaking before the International Affairs Committee of the Supreme Soviet in Moscow, and an audience with the Pope in the Vatican. He was back in Britain in December to give a speech to the Cambridge Union Society that captivated the young audience with its celebration of democracy's triumph and communism's failure in Europe. The next day he lunched with the Queen and the Duke of Edinburgh at Buckingham Palace before a bittersweet meeting at Claridge's Hotel – originally scheduled for 10 Downing Street – with Margaret Thatcher, ousted two weeks earlier as prime minister by a rebellion within her own Conservative Party, and husband Denis. As a gesture of solidarity, Reagan invited her to speak at his birthday celebrations the following February.[8]

Reagan's travels underlined his star quality abroad at a time when his reputation was slipping at home. According to the Gallup poll, popular approval of his presidency fell from 63 per cent in his final month in office to 50 per cent in June 1992.[9] This was largely due to the sharp recession of 1990–1 taking the sheen off the much-vaunted prosperity that Reagan's low-tax political economy had claimed to deliver. Meanwhile, the pundits of the left had beaten those of the right to get their assessments of the Reagan era into print. Negative volumes with titles like *Sleepwalking through History, Our Long National Daydream, America: What Went Wrong?*, and *The Bankrupting of America* rolled off the presses in the early 1990s.[10] A surprise bestseller by historian Paul Kennedy warning that the fiscal costs of Cold War victory amounted to 'imperial overstretch' also set off a media blitz that America was doomed to twenty-first-century decline.[11]

Three biographies then wounded the Reagans in different ways. An exceptional and massively researched volume by journalist Lou Cannon offered a less than flattering portrait of a president stage-managed by aides, frequently unable to distinguish between fantasy and reality, fatalistic and passive for the most part, incapable of admitting error, and lacking analytic capacity to understand issues outside his few core beliefs.[12] At a more personal level, Kitty Kelley published a bestselling and highly negative biography of Nancy that purported to be a serious analysis but was described by one British reviewer as full of 'upfront bitchiness' and 'breathless disclosures', few of them verified in a trustworthy manner.

With a number of people cited as sources in actual fact denying any contact with her, Reagan had some justification for telling Richard Nixon, 'Nancy and I are truly upset and angry over the total dishonesty of Kitty Kelley and her book.'[13] Even more hurtful to the Reagans was the publication of daughter Patti's memoir alleging that her father had ignored Nancy's physical abuse of her as a child.[14]

Rather than engage with contemporary critics, Reagan undertook a number of initiatives that would burnish his reputation into the future. The first was to produce a volume of memoirs that encompassed his life but focused on his presidency. Through Lew Wasserman's good offices, he secured the services of New York super-agent Mort Janklow, who promptly negotiated a $5 million advance – a record at the time – from Simon & Schuster to publish two volumes, a collection of speeches with personal commentary and a memoir.[15] The publishing house put editor-in-chief Michael Korda in charge of overseeing the autobiography project and he commissioned journalist Robert Lindsey to act as Reagan's ghostwriter. Quite how much input the supposed author had in shaping the final product is unclear. 'I hear it's a terrific book! One of these days I'm going to read it myself,' he cheerfully quipped at a pre-publication press conference. The idea to open with a brief narrative of the dramatic first encounter with Gorbachev in the Geneva summit was certainly Reagan's, but otherwise his main contributions came from oral reminiscences and his presidential diary. Korda and Lindsey had to press for greater candour on some issues – they eventually persuaded Reagan to make some mention of his marriage to Jane Wyman (in a 38-word paragraph), but could not get real admissions of error over Iran–Contra and the savings-and-loan crisis.[16]

In the annals of publishing, few categories of books are so littered with expensive failures as presidential memoirs, but the prestige of bringing them out means that there are always willing bidders. Simon & Schuster did not come close to making a profit on its Reagan books. The volume of speeches sold poorly but did somewhat better when rereleased following Reagan's death in 2004. Published in 1990, *An American Life* only made it as far as eighth on the *New York Times* bestseller list, initially achieving fewer sales than Nancy's memoir, *My Turn*, brought out by Random House in 1989. A less than favourable critical reception did not help, with the liberal metropolitan press dismissive to the point of contempt.[17] As a literary genre, presidential memoirs tend to be largely inauthentic because they are sanitized versions of reality produced and vetted by many collaborators. Reagan's manages to avoid that trap because it captures his voice and persona surprisingly well despite not being directly penned by him. The volume has plenty of self-serving omissions and misrepresentations, but even these help to reveal Reagan's mindset when checked against the growing (but far from comprehensive) body of administration records released by the National Archives and Records Administration (NARA).

Reagan's legacy enhancement took a giant step forward with the dedication of the Ronald Reagan Presidential Library in Simi Valley, 40 miles west of downtown Los Angeles, on 4 November 1991. Stanford University, home to the Hoover Institution that held Reagan's gubernatorial papers, was the originally intended location. This plan fell through because of faculty and student opposition to the college hosting another icon of the right. There were also environmental concerns over the proposed siting of the library in the foothills above Stanford.[18] Eureka College then offered to become the host site but its most famous alumnus wanted the library in his adopted California rather than his native Illinois.[19] The president and the first lady loved the free-standing Simi Valley site, which they often passed over in Air Force One on flights to Point Mugu Naval Air station, near Oxnard, the alighting point for trips to Rancho del Cielo. The ever-obliging Lew Wasserman was helpful in facilitating its purchase over environmentalist protests that library construction would take place on green-belt land.[20] In political and cultural terms, however, the siting was perfect. The surrounding towns were predominantly Anglo bedroom communities of white-collar workers, who formed the bedrock of Reagan's electoral constituency, and nearby Corriganville was a filming location for old Hollywood westerns.[21]

Perched atop a mountain with magnificent views in all directions, Reagan's library seemed a metaphorical embodiment of his oft-articulated vision of America as 'a shining city on a hill'. The lovely Spanish-style structure, constructed at a cost of $57 million (over $130 million in 2016 values), covered 153,000 square feet, making it the largest of all presidential libraries to date. The Clinton Library in Little Rock, Arkansas, briefly wrested that title when dedicated in late 2004, but the opening of the 90,000-square-feet Air Force One Pavilion in the following year restored the Simi Valley one to pre-eminence. Like all presidential libraries, Reagan's is administered by NARA but was constructed entirely from private funds that the Ronald Reagan Presidential Foundation, established by supporters to promote his legacy, raised with contributions from the likes of publishing multimillionaire Walter Annenberg, Lew Wasserman, media mogul Rupert Murdoch, and venture capitalist Lowden Cook.

Presidential libraries are intended to serve two functions – as a branch of the National Archives, they make available to scholars the documents of presidential history, and their attendant museums provide a popular history of each president's life and record for the general public. In practice, they have increasingly become the instruments for presidents and their supporters to run a final campaign for posterity's positive verdict on their accomplishments. Seeing them as 'presidential temples' that are America's equivalent to what the Pyramids were for the Egyptian pharaohs, cultural historian Benjamin Hufbauer adjudged the Reagan library an extreme example of that tendency owing to its 'baldly propagandistic' museum exhibitions.[22] Visitors are treated to a rosy scenario of Reagan's biography and his time in office, while dark spots like the 1981–2 recession, the massive expansion of public debt, and corruption in public office are given little weight. After its absorption into the federal system in 2007, the Richard M. Nixon Presidential Library and Museum set about mounting an accurate portrayal of Watergate – downplayed when it was privately run. Under academic pressure to do the same for Iran–Contra, hitherto entirely missing from its exhibition, the Reagan museum finally made good that omission but without allocating any responsibility to the 40th president. Thanks to the Reagan Foundation, the voice of conservative donors dedicated to preserving their hero's reputation in aspic, it remained a celebratory monument rather than a dispassionate depiction of a consequential presidency.[23]

Hopes that Reagan would play an active part in the life of his library were doomed to disappointment. On 5 November 1994, he handwrote a note on two sheets of paper embossed with his presidential seal telling the American people that he had been diagnosed as suffering from Alzheimer's disease. After expressing gracious thanks for the opportunity to serve as president, the message concluded on an uplifting note of optimism for the country he loved: 'I now begin the journey that will lead me into the sunset of my life. I know that for America there will always be a bright dawn ahead.' The next day the letter was reproduced in facsimile in newspapers around the world. The Reagans had received confirmation from the Mayo Clinic that he was in the early stages of degenerative cognitive dementia. Knowing this could never be kept secret for long, the former president followed the advice of family, friends, and doctors to write about the illness in his own hand so the whole world would know the words were his. Going public with the news was also intended to promote greater understanding of the illness and its effects on sufferers and their families.

In Nancy's opinion, the onset of her husband's dementia was the result of being bucked off a horse on a rocky trail, falling 15 feet, and striking his head on a stone when he landed. The accident happened on 4 July 1989 during a vacation at former Kitchen Cabinet member Bill Wilson's ranch in Mexico. Though Reagan was flown immediately to a hospital in Tucson, Arizona, he insisted on returning for the celebration of Nancy's birthday two days later. The former president would tell friends that he had only sustained a few bruises from landing on his back, but the injury was far more serious. Undertaken at Nancy's insistence, a check-up at the Mayo Clinic revealed that he was experiencing a swelling of the brain that required surgical drilling of holes in his skull to relieve the pressure.[24] Although Reagan could still function well following surgery, there were times when his cognitive frailty was evident. On the 1990 visit to the Soviet Union, Suzanne Massie was surprised to see Nancy gripping her husband's hand wherever they went so that he could not walk too far away from her. In the summer of 1991, he failed to recognize a trio of longstanding aides – Richard Allen, Martin Anderson, and Ed Meese – at the Bohemian Grove. The first public manifestation that something was wrong occurred at his 82nd birthday celebration at the Reagan library where he toasted guest of honour Margaret Thatcher twice and at length in exactly the same words. 'There was nothing we could do,' biographer Edmund Morris remarked, 'but give her two standing ovations, and not look too closely at Nancy Reagan's stricken face, while Dutch stood obliviously smiling.'[25]

As president, Reagan had occasion to comfort relatives of people afflicted with the illness from which his own mother had suffered. In 1982, he supported the proclamation of National Alzheimer's Awareness Week at the request of Yasmin Aga Khan, daughter of one-time Hollywood great Rita Hayworth, then in the later stages of the disease.[26] Some four years later, a Pennsylvania judge wrote to the president that his Alzheimer-afflicted mother had somehow escaped her cocoon of isolation for a brief moment after recognizing him on television. Reagan responded that Nelle was unable to identify either of her sons during the final years in a nursing home. In his opinion, it was 'a God-given mercy' because his mother was seemingly contented in the little world she now inhabited rather than being miserable at her helplessness.[27] This was a portent of what awaited him a decade or so later.

Although the disease was still undiagnosed, Reagan's cognitive decline necessitated a significant retrenchment of his public schedule after 1990. He made a last trip abroad to address the Oxford University Union in December 1991; he still had one great speech left in him – delivered to the Republican National Convention at Houston in August 1992; and he made a last visit to the White House to receive the Congressional Medal of Honor in January 1993. The announcement of his dementia put an effective end to public appearances, but his mental deterioration thereafter was not uniformly rapid. For a few years, Reagan maintained the routine of going to his office, received visitors – preceded by an aide's explanation of the person's relationship to him, and played a few holes of golf or took accompanied walks.[28] He stopped going to Rancho del Cielo after taking a last ride, an activity now deemed unsafe for him, in early 1995. Nancy put it on the market the following year for an asking price of $5.95 million, but there were few takers for a property with such modest – some would say spartan – living quarters. It was eventually sold in 1998 to the Young America's Foundation, a non-profit conservative youth organization committed, in its leader's words, 'to preserving and protecting both the Reagan legacy and the ranch itself, which will be maintained just as it was when President Reagan lived there'.[29]

Reagan's dementia worsened significantly in the late 1990s. While still capable of physical activity, he would spend hours raking leaves from the pool at his Bel Air home, blissfully unaware they were being replenished by his Secret Service detail. Though there was dim recall of youthful swimming in the Rock River, there was no memory of having been president of the United States. Even the children became unrecognizable to him. A penitential Patti, now returned to the fold in support of her parents, recounted what happened when she told her father, 'Bye. I love you', at the end of one visit:

> His eyes opened wide in surprise and he said, 'Well, thank you. Thank you so much.' He had no idea who I was. He was startled and typically gracious about another human being's telling him she loved him.[30]

Sadly, Reagan himself was in no condition to say goodbye to Maureen before her death from skin cancer in 2001. Though Nancy eventually faded from recognition too, she provided the love and emotional support needed to make the 'long, long goodbye' of his decline as comforting as possible. She would write of her experience:

> You know that it's a progressive disease and that there's no place to go but down, no light at the end of the tunnel [...] Each day is different, and you get up, put one foot in front of the other, and go – and love; just love [...] It's the living out of love.[31]

Medical opinion was initially divided as to whether the disease had been present during the presidential years. Adding his voice to the debate, Ron Reagan claimed in 2011 that his father's stumbling performance in the first presidential debate of 1984 and confusion during the Iran–Contra investigations constituted early indications of Alzheimer's, an assertion that infuriated brother Michael.[32] Substantive resolution of the controversy moved a step closer with the publication in early 2015 of new research based on speech patterns suggesting that cognitive decline had set in while Reagan was in office. The methodology compared the 40th president's use of words in his 46 press conferences with those of George H. W. Bush's in his 101 engagements. In contrast to his successor, there was a noticeable increase towards the end of Reagan's tenure in repetitive words, a growing reliance on 'filler' words (like 'thing', 'well', or 'um') when he struggled to recall more complex terms, and a marked decline in unique words. Whatever else it proves, however, the speech research does not signify that dementia affected Reagan's decision-making capability. Indeed, it is difficult to imagine that the highly personal foreign-policy achievements of the second term would have been possible had this been the case.[33]

Reagan was bedridden and largely comatose for the last three years or so of his life. At an Alzheimer's fundraiser in May 2004, Nancy announced, 'Ronnie's journey has finally taken him to a distant place where I can no longer reach him.'[34] Shortly afterwards he slipped into a final coma from which he never really emerged. At 13.09 PST on the afternoon of Saturday, 5 June, he opened his eyes to gaze up at Nancy's face and breathed his last. The official cause of death was pneumonia. Ron and Patti were also present, but Michael arrived just too late to say a final goodbye. Reagan was 93 years old, making him America's longest-lived president, a record previously held by John Adams and eventually surpassed by Gerald Ford.

Overseen by Nancy, plans had long been in place for a set of elaborate funeral rites. The casket bearing Reagan's corpse was transported to his library on 7 June for display and then flown to Washington on 9 June for public viewing in the Capitol Rotunda. The state funeral service took place at the National Cathedral on 11 June, declared a day of national mourning by President George W. Bush. All four living former presidents and 165 foreign dignitaries were in attendance; Margaret Thatcher delivered the first eulogy (taped some months earlier because of her own frailty after several strokes), followed by former Canadian prime minister Brian Mulroney, George H. W. Bush, and finally the current president. Afterwards, the casket was taken to Andrews Air Base for transportation to Mugu Point, from where it was borne to the final resting place at the presidential library. The flag draped over it was the one that had flown over the Capitol during the 1981 inauguration. There were 700 guests at the library service, among them members of the Reagan administration, California government dignitaries, Margaret Thatcher, representatives of old Hollywood, and first wife Jane Wyman. After final eulogies by the three surviving Reagan children, Captain James Symonds of the USS *Ronald Reagan* folded the flag for presentation to Nancy. Stoic throughout a week of sombre rituals, she finally broke into tears, stroked the casket privately for several minutes, and voiced a final 'I love you'. Ronald Reagan was then laid to rest in a vault with a horseshoe-shaped monument inscribed with words he had uttered in 1991: 'I know in my heart that man is good, that what is right will always eventually triumph, and there is purpose and worth to each and every life.'

Nancy Reagan devoted her remaining years until her death on 6 March 2016 to protecting her husband's historical reputation. This sometimes put her at odds with groups seeking to promote it for their own purposes. By the time of the 40th president's death what has been accurately characterized as a 'conservative commemoration crusade' was already in full swing. The formation in 1997 of the Ronald Reagan Legacy Project under the leadership of eminent conservative activist Grover Norquist effectively signalled its launch. One of this organization's key goals was to give Reagan's memory tangible form by having a monument dedicated to him in each of the 50 states and something named after him in each of the nation's 3,054 counties. It achieved early success in 1998 by getting Congress to rename Washington National Airport as Ronald Reagan National Airport. The same year saw the opening of the Ronald Reagan Building and International Trade Center, the first edifice in the nation's capital designed for both governmental and private-sector purposes. Five years later the commissioning of nuclear-powered supercarrier USS *Ronald Reagan* made Reagan the first living ex-president to have a battleship named after him. Meanwhile, streets, highways, schools, and public buildings in various states were named or renamed in his honour. Other forms of commemoration included Mount Clay (after Henry Clay) in New Hampshire becoming Mount Reagan, and the construction of a record-height 15-foot bronze statue of him in Covington, Louisiana. Amid these successes, the Reagan Legacy Project has three failures to its name: its hope of getting Reagan's visage carved on Mount Rushmore have so far gone unfulfilled; the same is true of its ambition to have a Reagan monument on the National Mall in Washington DC; and in 2003, a bill to replace FDR's head on the dime coin with Reagan's – an initiative disdained by Nancy Reagan – got nowhere.[35]

In the words of one historian, 'commemoration transforms historical facts [...] into objects of attachment by defining their meaning and how people should feel about them'. This was exactly the purpose of the Ronald Reagan Legacy Project. According to Norquist: 'Conservatives have been reticent to promote their heroes, and liberals have been aggressive. If you want to contend for the future, you have to contend for the public understanding of the past.'[36] It must be questioned whether the development of a virtual cult of personality around Reagan was a fitting way of memorializing someone of his humility, modesty, and graciousness. A reverential remembrance of the 40th president on the part of many Americans certainly rose to the fore during his years suffering from Alzheimer's and more particularly after his death. One indication of this was that Gallup polls asking respondents to identify the nation's greatest presidents of all time would find any one of three presidents habitually topped the list – Abraham Lincoln, John F. Kennedy, and Reagan, who came top in 2001, 2005, and 2011.[37] Nevertheless, there is no evidence that this represents a mark of approval for Reagan's conservatism. More realistically, his ongoing popularity is in essence a depoliticized celebration of his personal likeability, optimism, and pride in America.

Setting aside the hagiography of the right and the hatchet jobs of the left, a dispassionate analysis of Reagan must aspire to a 'warts and all' understanding of his achievements and shortcomings, which are often flip sides of each other. A good place to start is by assessing what some commentators regard as his greatest strength – the shining image of America that he carried within him.[38] It was an ideal derived from Midwestern small-town boyhood, nurtured by Hollywood experience, and honed during the speaking tours of the 1950s. Imbuing his public rhetoric from first to last, Reagan's vision of the United States was deeply rooted in its revolutionary tradition of exceptionalism, individual freedom, and sacramental mission. His farewell address as president defined the 'shining city' (the metaphor for America, whose name was never used) as

> a tall, proud city built on rocks stronger than oceans, windswept, God-blessed, and teeming with people of all kinds living in harmony and peace; a city with free ports that hummed with commerce and creativity [...] and the doors were open to anyone with the will and the heart to get here.[39]

Though accused of nostalgic myth-making, Reagan was in reality a futurist in his conviction that the old truths were forever new in their capacity to uplift a free people to ever-greater possibilities. Tom Paine's words of inspiration to the revolutionaries of 1776, 'We have it in our power to begin the world all over again' was one of his favourite maxims. In addressing the Republican National Convention in 1992, his last public speech of note, Reagan avowed:

> We are the country of tomorrow. Our revolution did not end at Yorktown. More than two centuries later, America remains on a voyage of discovery, a land that has never become, but is always in the act of becoming.[40]

The sense of national limits that became an article of faith for many Americans in the troubled 1970s had no place in Reagan's optimistic vision. 'If there is one thing we are sure of,' he avowed in his declaration of presidential candidacy, 'it is [...] that nothing is impossible, and man is capable of improving his circumstances beyond what we are told is fact.'[41] This conviction made him ideally suited to lead the nation out of one of the most pessimistic eras in its history towards renewed recognition of its promise. In 1979, the Gallup organization had found only 53 per cent of poll respondents 'optimistic/very optimistic' and 39 per cent 'pessimistic/very pessimistic' about the nation's future, but the respective scores stood at 75 per cent and 19 per cent in 1991.[42] Reagan told Americans the good things they wanted to believe about the United States. Whether his fellow citizens thought they were actually living in the country that he described is beside the point – more importantly, most of them likely wished that they did.

What Reagan failed to do was empathize with those Americans, whether poor or non-white, who could not share his optimism about their nation's end- less possibilities. The eradication of poverty and racism remained a chimera on his watch. Indeed the 'city on a hill' image became a cruel parody for the growing numbers of young African American men and low-income males of all races who found themselves locked up in the nation's prisons. The policy of mass incarceration that took off with a vengeance at federal and state levels in the 1980s bespoke determination for social control of criminality rather than alleviation of its causes. In presiding over this development, Reagan showed no awareness that Tom Paine, the eighteenth-century revolutionary thinker he claimed to admire so much, had been a passionate critic of the cruel laws that oppressed England's poor in support of property interests.[43]

Supplementing his confident vision of America's future, the second funda- mental element of Reagan's legacy was his restoration of presidential authority. The succession of failed presidencies that preceded his tenure had engendered widespread concern that the office was unmanageable for one man.[44] By the time he departed the White House, the presidency had regained its status as the driving force of national government. Even if Reagan did not achieve everything he wanted, his agenda gave clear direction to national politics and shaped political debate during his tenure. He fulfilled popular yearning for resolute leadership that would resolve economic problems at home and restore the nation's standing abroad. Despite his repomping of the presidency, he still brought it closer to the people, not only through his eloquent articulation of national values but also through his role as celebrant-in-chief in happy times and mourner-in-chief in sad times.

On the other hand, the presidency that Reagan passed on had become more dangerous to the constitutional order. Convinced that Congress had taken advantage of Vietnam and Watergate to infringe on presidential authority in national security, he was blatantly disdainful of what he called 'foreign policy by a committee of 535'.[45] This outlook underlay the Iran–Contra violations of presidential obligation to 'take Care that the Laws be faithfully executed'. The largely unpunished transgression of the letter and spirit of the Constitution created a perilous legacy that would bear bitter fruit in the very early years of the twenty-first century. A link between two imperial presidencies, Dick Cheney defended Reagan's executive authority to conduct national-security policy with minimal interference from the legislature when a Republican congressman in the 1980s and was a powerful articulator of presidential prerogative in this domain when George W. Bush's vice-president. In a foretaste of what would follow, he was a signatory to the minority report of the House select committee investigating Iran–Contra with its assertion that the president could 'exceed the law' if the national interest required.[46]

Other than saving the presidency from the threat of irrelevance, Reagan's historical significance extended to being America's most successful conservative president. As a political spokesman, he defined conservatism in the ideologically pure terms of freedom from big government. As president he understood that pragmatic compromise was sometimes necessary for the wellbeing of American democracy. The expansive anti-statism of his pre-White House days soon contracted in the face of political reality. 'The press is dying to paint me as now trying to undo the New Deal,' he confided to his diary. 'I'm trying to undo the "Great Society." It was LBJ's War on Poverty that led to our present mess.'[47] Once the politically suicidal consequences became evident, he backed away from a frontal assault on entitlement programmes of whatever vintage. Where he was more successful was in shrinking outlays on discretionary programmes with a 1960s pedigree, notably welfare assistance, grants-in-aid to the states, and educational and training programmes, as a percentage of GDP.

Some analysts referred to Reagan as the Roosevelt of the right, an alliterative analogy that was unconvincing. FDR was the liberal progenitor of myriad programmes in the 1930s, but Reagan had a much slighter record in terms of legislating rollback of government. In other regards, however, the 40th president left an enduring legacy that succeeded through indirect means in halting half a century of almost uninterrupted programmatic additions to American government. Reagan's revenge on the liberal state he could not destroy was the overhang of deficit and debt that stifled its continued development. To illustrate the scope of his nearly $1 trillion inheritance of gross federal debt, he told Americans in early 1981 that it was equivalent to a stack of $1,000 notes 67 miles high.[48] By the end of 1988, however, the pile would have been some 200 miles high. Of course, the more accurate measure is the size of the publicly held debt (that excludes debt held in government accounts) in relation to economic output. This had steadily diminished from the World War II-era high of 106.1 per cent GDP in 1946 to 25.5 per cent GDP in 1980. By the end of Reagan's presidency it had climbed steeply to 39.8 per cent GDP, a loss of debt control that the United States has never recovered (excepting temporarily in the final years of the twentieth century when federal coffers benefited from an unsustainable boom on Wall Street). For the most part, the deficit–debt spiral has constrained the fiscal margin needed to fund new domestic programmes to address the needs of a changing America in the years since Reagan left office.

Skyrocketing deficits constituted a paradoxical legacy for a conservative president but Reagan did not pay an electoral price for preserving his political priorities at cost of rising debt. His example encouraged early twenty-first-century Republicans and Democrats to follow suit in putting their programmatic preferences ahead of restoring fiscal responsibility. With the return of large unbalanced budgets on George W. Bush's watch, vice-president Dick Cheney would remark in 2002, 'Reagan proved deficits don't matter.'[49] Perhaps this was once true, but the explosion of fiscal deficits as a result of the Great Recession changed the terms of engagement. Public indebtedness equalled 74 per cent GDP in 2015, a level likely to rise inexorably as the ageing of the post-1945 baby-boomers sends entitlements costs ratcheting upwards. In that event, both Republicans and Democrats will need to set aside their many differences to prevent government borrowing reaching unsustainable levels.

Debate over Reagan's economic record has been ongoing since he left office. The greatest achievement was the conquest of inflation, which created stable conditions for investment in a new computer-driven economy that fully emerged in the 1990s. With the end of the deep recession needed to win this particular war, the United States entered a prolonged period of growth that lasted from 1982 to 2007, interrupted only by brief declines in 1990–1 and 2001.

Despite this, the long-term consequences of Reagan-era economic change for average Americans were more problematic than beneficial. For them, the late 1970s marked what economist James Galbraith has termed 'the end of normal'. Notwithstanding the Great Depression, the US economy had performed remarkably well in the first 75 years of the twentieth century in terms of keeping average income and educational levels mostly rising and economic inequality mainly flat or falling.[50] In contrast, income inequality soared and educational progress slowed in the four decades that followed. In 2015, median household income was not much greater in real terms than in 1979. The principal beneficiaries of economic growth in the intervening years were the wealthy, especially the super-rich. Reagan's bountiful tax cuts for top earners and his deregulatory initiatives assisted this process, but long-term structural changes in the economy that benefited financial-sector growth underlay its development. Reversing the income-inequality gap that has grown inexorably from the 1980s onward is one of the critical challenges facing twenty-first-century America. In 2015 President Barack Obama posed the question, 'Will we accept an economy where only a few of us do spectacularly well?'[51] Always more concerned with the freedom to create wealth than the fairness of its distribution, Reagan would probably have answered that question in the affirmative.

Whether the 40th president would have thought that American politics has changed for the better since his day is unlikely, however. Reagan would probably not have felt at home in the polarized partisan environment of the twenty-first century. His greatest legacy to the Republican Party was its elevation to virtual parity with the hitherto ascendant Democrats. He made conservative ideas more relevant to voters without turning America into a conservative nation. Polls indicated that self-identified conservatives had grown from about a quarter of the electorate to around a third over the course of the 1980s, but they still constituted a minority of voters. As confirmation of this reality, the first survey in what would become Gallup's regular canvass of political ideology – conducted in 1992 – reported that 43 per cent of respondents described themselves as moderates, 36 per cent as conservatives, and 17 per cent as liberals.[52] Aware that the presidency could neither be won nor retained solely with conservative support, Reagan had a pragmatic instinct for how far to press a conservative agenda without alienating centrists. In essence, he would take the half-loaf of compromise but keep trying for more over time. Obama-era congressional

Republicans, in contrast, seemed unwilling to settle for anything less than the whole loaf all at once.

Twenty-first-century Republican presidential aspirants have routinely proclaimed themselves Reagan's heirs, but this did not ring true in Donald Trump's case. It is true that both Reagan and Trump ran against government and promised to return America to greatness after Democratic mismanagement had supposedly laid it low, but there the similarities ended. Reagan grounded his appeal in his long-espoused ideas about freedom; Trump lacks a philosophical core. Reagan's experience as governor of California taught him the value of pragmatism and compromise, but Trump had never held political office before running for president. Reagan practised the politics of inclusion in an effort to create broad coalitions of voter support in his winning races for the state house in 1966 and the White House in 1980, but Trump practised the politics of exclusion to mobilize populist anger against the Washington establishment. The two also differed diametrically in their appreciation of how demography was reshaping the electorate. Just before winning a respectable 34 per cent share of their votes in 1984, Reagan remarked: 'Hispanics are already Republican. They just don't know it yet.'[53] To court this constituency, he signed into law the Immigration Reform and Control Act of 1986, a bipartisan congressional initiative that legalized an estimated 2.7 million undocumented workers in the United States, most of them Latinos. Trump, by contrast, seemed intent on causing Latinos offence with his tough stance against renewed amnesty and deterring illegals from entering the United States.

Arguably the most significant aspect of Reagan's legacy was also its most surprising feature. When he came to office, few analysts would have predicted that he would negotiate a groundbreaking arms-reduction agreement with the Soviet Union to eliminate the threat of nuclear conflict and lay the foundations for ending the Cold War. In pursuing the strategy that culminated in the greatest achievement of his presidency, arguably of any president since 1945, he withstood opposition from hawkish officials within his own administration, the broader conservative movement, and influential voices of foreign-policy realism like Richard Nixon and Henry Kissinger. Any attribution of this success to Gorbachev's need to end the arms race in order to focus on reforming the Soviet economy simply does not do justice to Reagan's strategic vision, sincere commitment to 'peace through strength', and detestation of nuclear weaponry.

Reagan also merits rescuing from neoconservative usurpation of his legacy to justify the 2003 invasion and prolonged occupation of Iraq as striking a blow for freedom. Reassuringly squeamish about incurring American casualties, Reagan only sent troops into action in the case of Grenada, where speedy victory was ensured. Anticipating another easy triumph for US arms, hawkish advisors advocated military intervention to oust drug-running Panamanian dictator Manuel Noriega in early 1988, but the president preferred to strike a bloodless bargain (which later fell through) allowing him to go into exile. Furthermore, in an age in which drone strikes and air attacks, with consequent 'collateral damage', have become regular features of American military operations, it is worth remembering Reagan's admonition that in the case of a retaliatory strike 'in a general direction' against terrorists, 'the result would be a terrorist act in itself and the killing and victimizing of innocent people'.[54]

On the other hand, there were very evident flaws in the 40th president's foreign-policy record. FDR and Reagan deserve recognition for being the great president-liberators of the twentieth century – one helped to free Western Europe from fascism, the other helped free Eastern Europe from communism. Nevertheless, when freedom was struggling for birth against the oppression of authoritarian regimes in Latin America, Africa, and Asia, Reagan was reluctant to lend it a helping hand for fear of assisting the spread of Marxism. With few exceptions, he preferred to align with anti-communist governments with deplorable records on human rights rather than democracy and liberation movements on these continents.

Meanwhile, America's own interventions in these places had adverse effects in the post-Cold War era. Emerging from the anti-Soviet resistance of the 1980s, the Taliban spread its influence to form an Islamic, anti-Western government in Afghanistan in the 1990s. At the same time, the regional threat posed by America's one-time Cold War client Saddam Hussein necessitated military action to drive Iraqi forces out of Kuwait in 1990 and eventually precipitated the invasion of Iraq to oust him in 2003. Finally, the ill-fated peacekeeping mission in Lebanon defined America as anti-Muslim in the eyes of Islamists. Though undertaken with the best intentions, it ultimately fuelled the growth of radical jihadism in the Middle East with very grave consequences for the United States.

The complexity of Reagan's legacy makes assessment of his historical significance a challenging task. The conventional ranking of presidents as 'great', 'near great', 'good', 'average', 'sub-average', and 'failure' is an inherently simplified exercise based on less than objective scorecarding of an individual's record. It cannot do justice to Reagan. If he has to be rated, it should be as a 'consequential president' who changed the nation's course and continued to influence it long after he left office. Arguably, the only other members of this select pantheon are Thomas Jefferson, Andrew Jackson, Abraham Lincoln, Theodore Roosevelt (maybe), and Franklin D. Roosevelt.

Even if political, social, and economic forces of a broad nature are mainly responsible for shaping history, Reagan demonstrates that some remarkable individuals can also be instrumental in directing its course. The United States may have been ripe for change in 1980, but Reagan's leadership was fundamentally influential in shaping the nature of its transformation in the ensuing decade and beyond. It is not claiming too much to say that American history in this critical decade would likely have been different in significant ways with another president at the helm. There is no consensus on whether the Reagan-inspired changes made the United States a better country or not. What is less open to doubt is that his impact will be debated for many years to come because his historical significance is not in question.

Last but not least, Reagan merits remembrance for giving voice to his nation's best values. This, above all, was what made him an American icon. He did not always live up to the ideals he espoused, but perfection is not a human quality. The very opposite of a power-hungry politico, Reagan brought the fundamental qualities of decency, optimism, and belief in individual potential inculcated in the small-town Midwest of the early twentieth century to the White House of the late twentieth century. The words he spoke to his fellow Americans when addressing the Republican National Convention in 1992 serve as a fitting epitaph: 'And whatever else history may say about me when I'm gone, I hope it will record that I appealed to your best hopes, not your worst fears, to your confidence rather than your doubts.'

LIST OF ABBREVIATIONS

ABM	Anti-Ballistic Missile
AFDC	Aid to Families with Dependent Children
AMPP	Association of Motion Picture Producers
ATFP	Alliance of Television Film Producers
AVC	American Veterans Committee
AWACS	Airborne Warning and Control System
CoS	Chief of staff
CPSU	Communist Party of the Soviet Union
CPUSA	Communist Party of the United States
CSU	Conference of Studio Unions
CWA	Civil Works Administration
EPA	Environmental Protection Agency
ERTA	Economic Recovery Tax Act
FBI	Federal Bureau of Investigation
FERA	Federal Emergency Relief Administration
FMPU	First Motion Picture Unit
FSAM	Free South Africa Movement
FY	Fiscal Year
GDP	Gross Domestic Product
GE	General Electric
GOP	Grand Old Party (the Republican Party)
GRH	Gramm–Rudman–Hollings
HHS	Health and Human Services Department
HIC	House Intelligence Committee

HICCASP	Hollywood Independent Citizens Committee of the Arts, Sciences and Professions
HUAC	House Un-American Activities Committee
HUD	Housing and Urban Development
IATSE	International Alliance of Theatrical Stage Employees
ICBM	Intercontinental Ballistic Missiles
INF	Intermediate Nuclear Force
IRS	Internal Revenue Service
JBS	John Birch Society
LSG	Legislative Strategy Group
MCA	Music Corporation of America
MNF	Multi-National Force
MPIC	Motion Picture Industry Council
MPLA	Popular Movement for the Liberation of Angola
NAACP	National Association for the Advancement of Colored People
NARA	National Archives and Records Administration
NATO	North Atlantic Treaty Organization
NSA	National Security Advisor
NSC	National Security Council
NSDD	National Security Decision Directive
NSPG	National Security Planning Group
OBRA	Omnibus Budget and Reconciliation Act
OECS	Organization of East Caribbean States
OMB	Office of Management and Budget
PATCO	Professional Air Traffic Controllers Organization
PCA	Production Code Administration
PLO	Palestine Liberation Organization
RYAN	Raketno-Yadernoe Napadenie (Russian for 'nuclear missile attack')
SAG	Screen Actors Guild
S&L	Savings and loans
SDI	Strategic Defense Initiative
SFSC	San Francisco State College
SIC	Senate Intelligence Committee
SIOP	Single Integrated Operational Plan
START	Strategic Arms Reduction Treaty
TBG	The Brothers for Goldwater
TEFRA	Tax Equity and Fiscal Responsibility Act
TRA	Tax Reform Act
UNITA	National Union for the Total Liberation of Angola

SUGGESTIONS FOR FURTHER READING

R onald Reagan tells his story in *My Early Life, or Where's the Rest of Me?* (London: Sidgwick & Jackson, 1984; originally published in 1965); and *An American Life* (New York: Simon & Schuster, 1990). *Reagan: A Life in Letters*, ed. Kiron Skinner, Annelise Anderson, and Martin Anderson (New York: Free Press, 2003) is a valuable collection of his extensive correspondence. Also illuminating is Nancy Reagan, *My Turn: The Memoirs of Nancy Reagan* (New York: Random House, 1989).

For voluminous biographies, see: *Washington Post* journalist Lou Cannon's indispensable *President Reagan: The Role of a Lifetime* (New York: Simon & Schuster, 1991; updated edition, 2003); Edmund Morris, *Dutch: A Memoir of Ronald Reagan* (New York: HarperCollins, 1999), the official biography criticized for the author's fictional insertions of himself into the narrative; and H. W. Brands, *Reagan: The Life* (New York: Doubleday, 2015). William Pemberton, *Exit with Honor: The Life and Presidency of Ronald Reagan* (Armonk NY: M. E. Sharpe, 1997) is more concise. Anne Edwards, *Early Reagan: The Rise to Power* (New York: Morrow, 1987) covers Reagan up to the 1950s, while Bob Colacello, *Ronnie and Nancy: Their Path to the White House – 1911 to 1980* is a pre-presidential dual biography. Biographies with a thematic approach include: Garry Wills, *Reagan's America* (New York: Penguin, 1988); Paul Kengor, *God and Ronald Reagan: A Spiritual Life* (New York: Regan Books, 2004); and John Patrick Diggins, *Ronald Reagan: Fate, Freedom, and the Making of History* (New York: Norton, 2007).

Marc Eliot, *Reagan: The Hollywood Years* (New York: Harmony, 2008) explores the future president's movie career. Stephen Vaughn, *Ronald Reagan in Hollywood: Movies and Politics* (New York: Cambridge University Press, 1994) is excellent on its political context, and can be supplemented by Steven Ross, *Hollywood Left and Right: How Movie Stars Shaped American Politics* (New York: Oxford University Press, 2011). The standard study of the Hollywood Red Scare is Larry Ceplair and Steven Englund, *The Inquisition in Hollywood: Politics in the Film Community, 1930–1960* (Urbana: University of Illinois Press, 2003). Dennis McDougal, *The Last Mogul: Lew Wasserman, MCA, and the Hidden History of Hollywood* (Boston: Da Capo, 2001) focuses on Reagan's powerful agent.

For Reagan's right turn, see Thomas Evans, *The Education of Ronald Reagan: The General Electric Years and the Untold Story of His Conversion to Conservatism* (New York: Columbia University Press, 2006). For the core principle of his political philosophy, consult: Eric Foner, *The Story of American Freedom* (New York: Norton, 1998). Rick Perlstein, *Before the Storm: Barry Goldwater and the Unmaking of the American Consensus* (New York: Hill and Wang, 2001) and Lisa McGirr, *Suburban Warriors: The Origins of the New American Right* (Princeton NJ: Princeton University Press, 2002) deal respectively with the early 1960s conservative insurgency at national and grassroots southern California levels.

Matthew Dallek, *The Right Moment: Ronald Reagan's First Victory and the Decisive Turning Point in American Politics* (New York: Free Press, 2004) and Gerard DeGroot, *Selling Ronald Reagan: The Emergence of a President* (London: I.B.Tauris, 2015) are illuminating on Reagan's 1966 gubernatorial campaign. The best study of his Sacramento years is Lou Cannon, *Governor Reagan: His Rise to Power* (New York: PublicAffairs, 2003). See, too, Jackson Putnam, 'Governor Reagan: a reappraisal', *California History*, 83/4 (August 2006), 24–45.

For the 1970s growth of conservatism, see Laura Kalman, *Right Star Rising: A New Politics, 1974–1980* (New York: Norton, 2010) and Dominic Sandbrook, *Mad as Hell: The Crisis of the 1970s and the Rise of the Populist Right* (New York: Knopf, 2011). Reagan's role is analysed respectively from liberal and conservative perspectives by Rick Perlstein, *The Invisible Bridge: The Fall of Nixon and the Rise of Reagan* (New York: Simon & Schuster, 2014) and Steven Hayward, *The Age of Reagan: The Fall of the Old Liberal Order, 1964–1980* (Roseville CA: Prima, 2001). See, too, Andrew Busch, *Reagan's Victory: The*

Presidential Election of 1980 and the Rise of the Right (Lawrence: University of Kansas Press, 2005).

For the 1980s, consult: Robert Collins, *Transforming America: Politics and Culture During the Reagan Years* (New York: Columbia University Press, 2006); Sean Wilentz, *The Age of Reagan: A History 1974–2008* (New York: HarperCollins, 2008); and Doug Rossinow, *The Reagan Era: A History of the 1980s* (New York: Columbia University Press, 2015). On Reagan as president, see Richard Neustadt, *Presidential Power and the Modern Presidents: The Politics of Leadership from Roosevelt to Reagan* (New York: Free Press, 1990) and William Leuchtenburg, *The American President: From Teddy Roosevelt to Bill Clinton* (New York: Oxford University Press, 2016). Elliot Brownlee and Hugh Davis Graham, eds, *The Reagan Presidency: Pragmatic Conservatism and Its Legacies* (Lawrence: University Press of Kansas, 2003) is an influential anthology. Also good is Cheryl Hudson and Gareth Davies, eds, *Ronald Reagan and the 1980s: Perceptions, Policies, Legacies* (New York: Palgrave, 2008). See, too, Richard Reeves, *President Reagan: The Triumph of Imagination* (New York: Simon & Schuster, 2006) and Steven Hayward, *The Age of Reagan: The Conservative Counterrevolution 1980–1989* (New York: Crown Forum, 2009).

The Reagan Diaries, ed. Douglas Brinkley (New York: HarperCollins, 2007) (issued in unabridged version in 2009) is indispensable on his presidency. Memoirs by close aides include: James Baker, *'Work Hard, Study... and Keep Out of Politics!' Adventures and Lessons from an Unexpected Life* (New York: Putnam, 2006); Donald Regan, *For the Record: From Wall Street to Washington* (San Diego: Harcourt Brace Jovanovich, 1988); and Edwin Meese, *With Reagan: The Inside Story* (Washington DC: Regnery, 1992). Dick Wirthlin recounts his strategic role as presidential pollster in *The Greatest Communicator: What Ronald Reagan Taught Me about Politics, Leadership, and Life* (Hoboken NJ: Wiley, 2004).

For the different experiences of Reagan's two secretaries of state, see: Alexander Haig, *Caveat: Realism, Reagan, and Foreign Policy* (New York: Macmillan, 1984); and George Shultz, *Turmoil and Triumph: My Years as Secretary of State* (New York: Scribner's, 1993). Their bureaucratic rival, Caspar Weinberger, tells his story in *Fighting for Peace: 7 Critical Years in the Pentagon* (New York: Grand Central Publishing, 1991). Robert Gates, *From the Shadows: The Ultimate Insider's Story of Five Presidents and How They Won the Cold War*

(New York: Touchstone, 1996) discusses CIA operations. For aides with very different perspectives on Reagan's domestic legacy, see David Stockman, *The Triumph of Politics: Why the Reagan Revolution Failed* (New York: Harper & Row, 1986), and Martin Anderson, *Revolution* (San Diego: Harcourt Brace Jovanovich, 1988).

For scholarship on various aspects of Reagan's domestic policy, see: Iwan Morgan, *The Age of Deficits: Presidents and Unbalanced Budgets from Jimmy Carter to George W. Bush* (Lawrence: University Press of Kansas, 2009); Joseph McCartin, *Collision Course: Ronald Reagan, the Air Traffic Controllers, and the Strike that Changed America* (New York: Oxford University Press, 2011); Stephen Shull, *A Kinder, Gentler Racism? The Reagan–Bush Civil Rights Legacy* (Armonk NY: M. E. Sharpe, 1993); and William Turner, '"Adolph Reagan?" Ronald Reagan, Aids, and lesbian/gay civil rights', 13 July 2009, *Social Science Research Network*, available at http://papers.ssrn.com/sol3/papers.cfm?abstract_id=1433567.

For foreign policy, Chester Pach, 'The Reagan doctrine: principle, pragmatism, and policy', *Presidential Studies Quarterly*, 36 (March 2006), 75–88 is a good starting point. Peter Schweizer, *Reagan's War: The Epic Story of His Forty-Year Struggle and Final Triumph over Communism* (New York: Doubleday, 2002) focuses on his anti-communism. Dealings with Britain's prime minister are analysed in Richard Aldous, *Reagan and Thatcher: The Difficult Relationship* (London: Hutchinson, 2012). Malcolm Byrne, *Iran–Contra: Reagan's Scandal and the Unchecked Abuse of Presidential Power* (Lawrence: University Press of Kansas, 2014) is the most authoritative study of its subject. David Hoffman, *The Dead Hand: Reagan, Gorbachev and the Untold Story of the Cold War Arms Race* (New York: Doubleday, 2009) and Jack Matlock, *Reagan and Gorbachev: How the Cold War Ended* (New York: Random House, 2004), an insider account, respectively explore the climax and decline of US–Soviet tensions. Illuminating examples of scholarly studies on Reagan, Gorbachev, and the Cold War's passing include: Don Oberdorfer, *From the Cold War to a New Era: The United States and the Soviet Union, 1983–1991* (Baltimore MD: Johns Hopkins University Press, 1998); James Mann, *The Rebellion of Ronald Reagan: A History of the End of the Cold War* (New York: Viking, 2009), a particularly valuable study; and James Graham Wilson, *The Triumph of Improvisation: Gorbachev's Adaptability, Reagan's Engagement, and the End of the Cold War* (Ithaca NY: Cornell University Press, 2014).

NOTES

SOURCES

Unless specified otherwise, all the archival sources cited in the notes are located in the Ronald Reagan Presidential Library, Simi Valley, CA.

All web references were available online on 20 August 2015 unless otherwise stated.

PRIMARY SOURCE ABBREVIATIONS

AAL	Reagan, Ronald, *An American Life* (New York: Simon & Schuster, 1990)
AMPAS	Margaret Herrick Library, Academy of Motion Picture Arts and Sciences, Beverly Hills, California
APP-PPP	American Presidency Project, Public Papers of the Presidents, online by Gerhard Peters and John Woolley, http://www.presidency.ucsb.edu/
CP:H/CHQ	1980 Campaign Papers: Hannaford/Campaign Headquarters (box number indicated)
FFFD	Reagan, Maureen, *First Father, First Daughter: A Memoir* (Boston: Little, Brown, 1989)
GHP	Godfrey Hodgson Papers, Rothermere American Institute, University of Oxford
MT	Reagan, Nancy, with William Novak, *My Turn: The Memoirs of Nancy Reagan* (New York: Random House, 1989)
MTF	Margaret Thatcher Foundation
NSAEBB	National Security Archive Electronic Briefing Book (declassified documentary collections, variously numbered and published by the National Security Archive, George Washington University)
NSC-ES:CF	National Security Council – Executive Secretariat: Country File

NSC-ES:HoSF	National Security Council – Executive Secretariat: Head of State File
NSC-ES:SF	National Security Council – Executive Secretariat: Subject File
NYT	*New York Times*
PHF:R	Presidential Handwriting File: Records (box number indicated)
RALIL	*Reagan: A Life in Letters*, ed. Kiron Skinner, Annelise Anderson, and Martin Anderson (New York: Free Press, 2003)
RD	Reagan, Ronald, *The Reagan Diaries*, ed. Douglas Brinkley (New York: HarperCollins, 2007)
RIHOH	*Reagan in His Own Hand*, ed. Kiron Skinner and Annelise Anderson, (New York: Free Press, 2001)
ROHO-RRGES	Regional Oral History Office – Ronald Reagan Gubernatorial Era Series, University of California – Los Angeles
RPV	*Reagan's Path to Victory: The Shaping of Ronald Reagan's Vision – Selected Writings*, ed. Kiron Skinner, Annelise Anderson, and Martin Anderson (New York: Free Press, 2004)
RRGP:CSF	Ronald Reagan Gubernatorial Papers – 1966 Campaign Subject Files (box number indicated)
RRGP:GOF	Ronald Reagan Gubernatorial Papers – Governor's Office Files (box number indicated)
RROH-MC	Ronald Reagan Oral Histories – Miller Center, University of Virginia
TRF-NSC	*The Reagan Files, Documentary Collections: National Security Council and National Security Planning Group Meetings*, ed. Jason Saltoun-Ebin, http://www.thereaganfiles.com/
TRF-RGSL	*The Reagan Files, Documentary Collections: Letters between President Reagan and General Secretary Brezhnev, Andropov, Chernenko, and Gorbachev*, ed. Jason Saltoun-Ebin, http://www.thereaganfiles.com/
WBA	Warner Bros. Archive, University of Southern California, Los Angeles
WHSOF	White House Staff & Office File [staff member name and box number indicated]
WTROM	Reagan, Ronald, with Richard Hubler, *My Early Life, or Where's the Rest of Me?* (London: Sidgwick & Jackson, 1984) [original publication – New York: Duell, Sloan and Pearce, 1965]

PREFACE

1 'Reagan recants "evil empire" description', *Los Angeles Times*, 1 June 1988.
2 'Top secret documents reveal NATO training exercise nearly started a nuclear apocalypse with Russia', *Huffington Post*, 12 November 2015. Available at http://www.huffingtonpost.co.uk/2015/11/12/top-secret-documents-reveal-a-nato-training-exercise-nearly-started-a-nuclear-apocalypse-with-russia-_n_8542766.html.

1   YOUNG DUTCH

1 *WTROM*, 1.
2 Reagan to Neil Reagan, 21 June 1984, *RALIL*, 51. On the Irish forebears, see Reagan, Ron, *My Father at 100: A Memoir* (New York: Viking, 2011), 15–28.

3 Edwards, Anne, *Early Reagan: The Rise to Power* (New York: Morrow, 1987), 23–6; Maxine Mertens to Reagan, 1 May 1986, Reagan to Mertens, 28 May 1986, PHF:R–15.

4 Edwards, *Early Reagan*, 26–8.

5 *AAL*, 22.

6 Morris, Edmund, *Dutch: A Memoir of Ronald Reagan* (New York: HarperCollins, 1999), 25–32.

7 Wills, Garry, *Reagan's America* (New York: Penguin, 1988), 17–18; *WTROM*, 41.

8 Reagan to Leonard Kirk, 23 March 1983, PHF:R–6; *AAL*, 28.

9 Edwards, *Early Reagan*, 32, 35; Cannon, Lou, *President Reagan: The Role of a Lifetime* (New York: Simon & Schuster, 1991), 219; *AAL*, 33.

10 *WTROM*, 7–8.

11 *AAL*, 33–4.

12 Gilbert, Robert, 'Ronald Reagan's presidency: the impact of an alcoholic parent', *Political Psychology*, 29 (October 2008), 737–65 [quotation 762].

13 *AAL*, 31.

14 *MT*, 106.

15 *WTROM*, 9.

16 *AAL*, 22.

17 *WTROM*, 63–4; *AAL*, 52; Reagan to Freddie Washington, 23 November 1983, *RALIL*, 12–13.

18 'Remarks at the 1980 presidential campaign debate, Cleveland, Ohio', 28 October 1980, APP-PPP; Morris, *Dutch*, 89.

19 Morris, *Dutch*, 208–9.

20 Edwards, *Early Reagan*, 28–32.

21 Wills, *Reagan's America*, 21; Edwards, *Early Reagan*, 29.

22 *WTROM*, 15; *AAL*, 35.

23 *AAL*, 22; Will, George, 'How Reagan changed America', *Newsweek*, 9 January 1989.

24 Seligman, Martin, *Learned Optimism: How to Change Your Mind and Your Life* (New York: Knopf, 1991), 116–35; *AAL*, 20–1.

25 *MT*, 107–8.

26 Kengor, Paul, *God and Ronald Reagan: A Spiritual Life* (New York: Regan Books, 2004), 10–16.

27 *AAL*, 56; Reagan to Sister Mary Ignatius, 26 November 1984, *RALIL*, 280.

28 Kengor, *God and Ronald Reagan*, 8.

29 *WTROM*, 11.

30 Reagan to Mrs Warne, *c.*1967, *RALIL*, 276; 'Remarks at the Annual National Prayer Breakfast', 3 February 1983, PPP-APP.

31 'The young Reagan's reading', *New York Times Book Review*, 30 August 1981.

32 Wright, Harold Bell, *That Printer of Udell's: A Story of the Middle West* (New York: A. L. Burt Company, 1903).

33 Reagan to Jean B. Wright, 13 March 1984, PHF:R–8; Morris, *Dutch*, 40–2.

34 Words spoken in one of his pre-presidential radio broadcasts, 'Christmas', 9 January 1978, *RPV*, 247–8.

35 Robison, James, 'Remembering Reagan', 8 June 2004. Available at http://archives. jamesrobison.net/columns/060804.htm.

36　Vaughn, Stephen, 'The moral inheritance of a president: Reagan and the Dixon Disciples of Christ', *Presidential Studies Quarterly*, 25 (Winter 1995), 109–27.

37　Reagan to Reverend and Mrs Ben Cleaver, 4 January 1973, *RALIL*, 279.

38　Handwritten notes for *Parade* article, April 1981, PHF:R–1.

39　*AAL*, 27.

40　*WTROM*, 18; *AAL*, 29.

41　*WTROM*, 18–19.

42　Edwards, *Early Reagan*, 63–5.

43　'Reagan takes dive, saves child in pool', *Baltimore Afro-American*, 28 June 1969.

44　'The Lowell Park lifeguard', *Welcome Home Mr President* (Official Souvenir), 6 February 1984, copy in GHP.

45　*WTROM*, 21.

46　Ibid., 21–3; *AAL*, 40–1.

47　'A "refreshing student" recalls North Dixon High School drama coach', *Welcome Home Mr President*.

48　'Reagan the Dixon student', ibid.

49　*WTROM*, 23–4; *AAL*, 45–6.

50　Adams, Harold, *The History of Eureka College, 1855–1982* (Eureka IL: College Trustees, 1982); Miller, John, 'Eureka's Reagan', *National Review*, 31 October 2011.

51　*WTROM*, 26–30 [quotation 29]; *AAL*, 48; Wills, *Reagan's America*, 52–63.

52　*AAL*, 53.

53　Brown, Mary Beth, *The Faith of Ronald Reagan* (Nashville TN: Thomas Nelson, 2011), 52.

54　Blumenthal, Sidney, *The Rise of the Counter-establishment: The Conservative Ascent to Political Power* (New York: Times Books, 1986), 152; *AAL*, 231, 54, 47.

55　*AAL*, 57–8.

56　*WTROM*, 29.

57　'New answer to maidens' prayers', *Motion Picture Magazine*, December 1939.

58　Edwards, *Early Reagan*, 112.

59　*AAL*, 21.

2　RISING STAR

1　*WTROM*, 45.

2　Reagan to Ron Cochran, 12 May 1980, *RALIL*, 31.

3　*WTROM*, 45.

4　Ibid., 45–7.

5　Edwards, Anne, *Early Reagan: The Rise to Power* (New York: Morrow, 1987), 125–6.

6　*WTROM*, 55–9.

7　*AAL*, 71.

8　*WTROM*, 65–7; *AAL*, 72–3.

9　Wills, Garry, *Reagan's America* (New York: Penguin, 1988), 74–6.

10　*FFFD*, 117.

11　Edwards, *Early Reagan*, 142–3, 149.

12　*WTROM*, 139.

13　Reagan to Monte Osburn, 29 March 1982, *RALIL*, 33–4.

14 *WTROM*, 53–4, 59; *AAL*, 68–9, 71.

15 *AAL*, 76.

16 *WTROM*, 67–9.

17 Morris, Edmund, *Dutch: A Memoir of Ronald Reagan* (New York: HarperCollins, 1999), 124–5.

18 *WTROM*, 69–72; *AAL*, 78–9; McClelland, Doug, *Hollywood on Ronald Reagan: Friends and Enemies Discuss Our President, the Actor* (Boston: Faber & Faber, 1983), 154.

19 Eliot, Marc, *Reagan: The Hollywood Years* (New York: Harmony, 2008), 43–6.

20 *AAL*, 79–81; Edwards, *Early Reagan*, 155–6.

21 *AAL*, 82–3.

22 Basinger, Jeanine, *The Star Machine* (New York: Knopf, 2007), 3.

23 Schickel, Richard, and George Perry, *You Must Remember This: The Warner Brothers Story* (Philadelphia: Running Press, 2008); Warner Sperling, Cass, Cork Millner, and Jack Warner Jr, *Hollywood Be Thy Name: The Warner Brothers Story* (Lexington: University Press of Kentucky, 1998).

24 Vaughn, Stephen, *Ronald Reagan in Hollywood: Movies and Politics* (New York: Cambridge University Press, 1994), 32–6 [quotation 35]; Birdwell, Michael, *Celluloid Soldiers: The Warner Bros's Campaign against Nazism* (New York: New York University Press, 2000).

25 Studio Advance Feature, 'Love is on the Air', Ronald Reagan Contracts and Correspondence File [RRCCF], WBA.

26 'Treat for ladies in Ronald Reagan', *New York Daily News,* 14 October 1937.

27 *AAL*, 89.

28 Morris, *Dutch*, 152–3; 'Ex-actress talks about Reagan', *New York Post*, 18 December 1980.

29 *AAL*, 89.

30 Vaughn, *Ronald Reagan in Hollywood*, 67–80 [quotation 70].

31 Parr, Jerry, *In the Secret Service: The True Story of the Man Who Saved President Reagan* (New York: Tyndale Publishing, 2013).

32 Eliot, *Reagan*, 65–7, 70–1.

33 Morella, Joe, and Edward Epstein, *Jane Wyman: A Biography* (New York: Delacorte, 1985).

34 Edwards, *Early Reagan*, 190.

35 Kengor, Paul, *God and Ronald Reagan: A Spiritual Life* (New York: Regan Books, 2004), 49.

36 Morris, *Dutch*, 161–3.

37 Edwards, *Early Reagan*, 197–202.

38 Cannon, Lou, *Governor Reagan: His Rise to Power* (New York: PublicAffairs, 2003), 64–5.

39 Wilson, Earl, *Hot Times: True Tales of Hollywood and Broadway* (Chicago: Contemporary Books, 1984), 219; Eliot, *Reagan*, 153–4.

40 Leamer, Laurence, *Make-Believe: The Story of Nancy and Ronald Reagan* (New York: Harper & Row, 1983), 115.

41 'Making a Double Go of It!', *Silver Screen*, August 1941.

42 *WTROM*, 90–5.

43 Robert Buckner to Arthur Haley, 11 April 1939, Story Department Correspondence, WBA.

44 Vaughn, *Ronald Reagan in Hollywood*, 82–7.

45 Eliot, *Reagan*, 117.

46 Reagan to Chet Sampson, 22 May 1986, PHF:R–15; *RD* (18 January 1989), 691.

47 Mort Blumenstock to Warner Bros. District Managers, 6 September 1940, Publicity Department Correspondence, WBA.

48 *Variety*, 7 October 1940.

49 Vaughn, *Ronald Reagan in Hollywood*, 87–92; Reagan to Michael Palmer, 17 February 1983, *RALIL*, 129.

50 Eliot, *Reagan*, 118, 127–8; *WTROM*, 97–9.

51 *Chicago Herald-American*, 16 September 1941, Louella Parsons Scrapbook, AMPAS.

52 *Hollywood Reporter*, 7 April 1942; *Variety*, 7 April 1942.

53 Northway, Martin, 'Tragic consequences: Fulton, Missouri set the stage for Henry Bellamann novel "Kings Row" and a future for a young Ronald Reagan', *New City Lit*, 27 July 2011. Available at http://lit.newcity.com/2011/07/27.

54 Reagan to George [no surname], draft, n.d. (1970s likely), *RALIL*, 150–1.

55 *WTROM*, 4–6 [quotation 5]; Eliot, *Reagan*, 143.

56 Vaughn, *Ronald Reagan in Hollywood*, 37.

57 Edwards, *Early Reagan*, 255.

58 *WTROM*, 104–5; 'Transcript of Olivia de Havilland interview', 1988, GHP.

59 Reagan and Wyman to Warner, 5 September 1941, RRCCF, WBA.

60 Colonel Horace Sykes (Ninth Corps Area Adjutant General), to R. J. Obringer (Warner Bros. General Counsel), 30 March 1942, Obringer to Jack Warner, 31 March 1942, and to Reagan, 13 April 1942, RRCCF, WBA.

3   FALLING STAR

1 Vaughn, Stephen, *Ronald Reagan in Hollywood: Movies and Politics* (New York: Cambridge University Press, 1994), 109–12.

2 'My soldier', *Modern Screen*, January 1943.

3 Cannon, Lou, *Governor Reagan: His Rise to Power* (New York: PublicAffairs, 2003), 70.

4 Betancourt, Mark, 'World War II: the movie', *Air and Space* (March 2012). Available at http://www.airspacemag.com/history-of-flight/world-war-ii-the-movie-21103597/

5 *RALIL*, 132.

6 Letter from 'Wounded marine', and full-page signed response, *Hollywood Reporter*, 20 and 22 August 1946.

7 Morris, Edmund, *Dutch: A Memoir of Ronald Reagan* (New York: HarperCollins, 1999), 210, 268.

8 R. J. Obringer to Ralph Lewis, 20 September 1944, Ronald Reagan Contract Correspondence File [RRCCF], WBA.

9 *WTROM*, 138.

10 *AAL*, 103.

11 Eliot, Marc, *Reagan: The Hollywood Years* (New York: Harmony, 2008), 260.

12 *WTROM*, 205.

13 Ibid., 193–4; Reagan to Mr and Mrs Lester David, 12 April 1982, PHF:R–3.

14 *Hollywood Reporter*, 22 October 1947; Medved, Harry and Randy Dreyfuss, *The Fifty Worst Films of All Time (And How They Got That Way)* (New York: Warner, 1978).

15   *WTROM*, 212–13.
16   Ibid., 194–6.
17   *FFFD*, 71.
18   Perella, Robert, *They Called Me the Showbiz Priest* (New York: Trident, 1973), 130–1.
19   *FFFD*, 44–5.
20   Ibid., 52–3.
21   Parsons, Louella, 'Last call for happiness', *Photoplay*, April 1948; Hopper, Hedda, 'Trouble in paradise', *Modern Screen*, February 1948.
22   *WTROM*, 201; Cannon, *Governor Reagan*, 74.
23   Reagan to Florence Yerly, 17 December 1951, *RALIL*, 139–40.
24   *Silver Screen,* May 1950.
25   Eliot, *Reagan*, 233–6 [quotation 233]; Kelley, Kitty, *Nancy Reagan: The Unauthorized Biography* (New York: Simon & Schuster, 1991), 85–8, 542–3.
26   Laurie, Piper, *Learning to Live Out Loud* (New York: Crown Archetype, 2011), 60–70.
27   Hodgson, Michael, *Patricia Roc: The Goddess of the Odeons* (Bloomington IN: AuthorHouse, 2010).
28   Stanley, Timothy, *Citizen Hollywood: How the Collaboration Between LA and DC Revolutionized American Politics* (New York: Thomas Dunne, 2014), 167; Ross, Steven, *Hollywood Left and Right: How Movie Stars Shaped American Politics* (New York: Oxford University Press, 2011), 142–3.
29   Morris, *Dutch*, 215–16.
30   *WTROM*, 141.
31   'General Stilwell pins DSC on sister of Nisei hero in ceremony at Masuda Ranch', *Pacific Citizen*, 15 December 1945.
32   'Remarks on signing the bill providing restitution for the wartime internment of Japanese-American civilians,' 10 August 1988, APP-PPP.
33   Reagan, Ronald, 'Fascist ideas are still alive in US', *AVC Bulletin*, 15 February 1946.
34   *WTROM*, 164–6; Morris, *Dutch*, 221–2, 228, 230–1.
35   *WTROM*, 166–9; *AAL*, 111–13; Edwards, Anne, *Early Reagan: The Rise to Power* (New York: Morrow, 1987), 303–4.
36   Parsons, 'last call for happiness'.
37   Ceplair, Larry, and Steven Englund, *The Inquisition in Hollywood: Politics in the Film Community, 1930–1960* (Urbana: University of Illinois Press, 2003), 216–20.
38   Vaughn, *Reagan in Hollywood*, 138–40.
39   Reagan, Neil, 'Private dimensions and public images: the early political campaigns of Ronald Reagan', ROHO-RRGES.
40   Meroney, John, 'Left in the past', *Los Angeles Times Magazine*, February 2012; *WTROM*, 162.
41   Reagan to Brewer, 20 May 1983, *RALIL*, 104.
42   *WTROM*, 171–5.
43   *Los Angeles Times*, 18 May 1947; Dunne, George, 'Christian advocacy and labor strife in Hollywood', ROHO-RRGES.
44   Vaughn, *Reagan in Hollywood*, 141–2.
45   Dales, John, 'Pragmatic leadership: Ronald Reagan as president of the Screen Actors Guild', ROHO-RRGES.
46   *WTROM*, 157; Morris, *Dutch*, 246.

47 *WTROM*, 174; *AAL*, 115.

48 Dunne, ROHO-RRGES; *King's Pawn: The Memoirs of George H. Dunne* (Chicago: Loyola University Press, 1990), 148.

49 *Hollywood Citizen News*, 14 January 1954.

50 Ross, *Hollywood Left and Right*, 150; *AAL*, 110.

51 Edwards, Anne, *Early Reagan: The Rise to Power* (New York: Morrow, 1987), 304–7.

52 Reagan, Ronald, 'How do you fight communism?', *Fortnight*, 22 January 1951.

53 Ceplair and Englund, *The Inquisition in Hollywood*, 125–6, 254–98.

54 House Un-American Activities Committee Testimony: Ronald Reagan 23 October 1947. Available at http://historymatters.gmu.edu/d/6458/.

55 Ceplair and Englund, *The Inquisition in Hollywood*, 324–41; Vaughn, *Reagan in Hollywood*, 153–5.

56 Buhle, Paul, and David Wagner, *Blacklisted: The Filmlovers Guide to the Hollywood Blacklist* (New York: Palgrave, 2003); Ross, *Hollywood Left and Right*, 149–50.

57 Sondergaard to SAG Board, *Variety*, 16 March 1951; SAG Board to Sondergaard, *Hollywood Reporter*, 20 March 1951.

58 Meroney, 'Left in the past'; Douglas Whitney to Knox, 18 August 1952, and Lewis Deakin to Knox, 9 April 1954, Alexander Knox Papers, AMPAS.

59 *MT*, 66–92; Edwards, *Early Reagan*, 375–94.

60 *MT*, 93; Reagan to Florence McHenry, 13 June 1984, PHF:R–10.

61 *MT*, 93–6; *WTROM*, 235.

62 *MT*, 97–103, 108; Reagan, Nancy, *I Love You, Ronnie: The Letters of Ronald Reagan to Nancy Reagan* (New York: Random House, 2000), 9–29.

63 Edwards, *Early Reagan*, 358–61; Dales, ROHO-RRGES.

64 McDougal, Dennis, *The Last Mogul: Lew Wasserman, MCA, and the Hidden History of Hollywood* (Boston: Da Capo, 2001), 184–7.

65 Edwards, *Early Reagan*, 439–40.

66 McDougal, *The Last Mogul*, 224–73.

67 Eliot, *Reagan*, 307–18 [quotation 311]. The full transcript of Reagan's testimony is reproduced in Moldea, Dan, *Dark Victory: Ronald Reagan, MCA, and the Mob* (New York: Viking, 1986).

68 *AAL*, 118–19; Warner to Will Rogers Jr, 23 May 1952, Jack Warner Personal Files, WBA.

69 Graham, Billy, *Just as I Am: The Autobiography of Billy Graham* (New York: HarperCollins, 1997), 528–9.

70 Kengor, Paul, *God and Ronald Reagan: A Spiritual Life* (New York: Regan Books, 2004), 92–7.

71 Leuchtenburg, William, 'Reagan's secret liberal past', *New Republic*, 23 May 1983, 18–25; Vaughn, *Reagan in Hollywood*, 157–8.

72 *AAL*, 119; *MT*, 95–6.

73 *WTROM*, 139, 245; 'Remarks at the Kiwanis international convention', 21 June 1951, in Reagan, Ronald, *Speaking My Mind: Selected Speeches* (New York: Simon & Schuster, 1989), 17–21.

74 R. J. Obringer to Jack Warner, 17 February 1950, Reagan to Warner, 3 May 1950, RRCCF, WBA.

75 'Star to pick future films', *Los Angeles Mirror*, 6 January 1950; Warner to Reagan, 6 January 1950, RRCCF, WBA.

76 R. J. Obringer to Jack Warner, 26 May 1950, and to Steve Trilling, 28 November 1951, RRCCF, WBA.
77 'Reagan's multiple duties', *Christian Science Monitor,* 21 December 1954; *MT,* 125.
78 McClelland, Doug, *Hollywood on Ronald Reagan: Friends and Enemies Discuss Our President, the Actor* (Boston: Faber & Faber, 1983), 134; Eliot, *Reagan,* 259.
79 Edwards, *Early Reagan,* 432–3.
80 McClelland, *Hollywood on Ronald Reagan,* 227; *WTROM,* 247–8.

4   RIGHT STAR

1 *WTROM,* 248–51; Edwards, Anne, *Early Reagan: The Rise to Power* (New York: Morrow, 1989), 446–7.
2 *Los Angeles Daily News,* 24 November 1954.
3 *WTROM,* 251; Eliot, Marc, *Reagan: The Hollywood Years* (New York: Harmony, 2008), 268–9, 275–8.
4 *FFFD,* 108; Morris, Edmund, *Dutch: A Memoir of Ronald Reagan* (New York: HarperCollins, 1999), 304–5; Wills, Garry, *Reagan's America* (New York: Penguin, 1988), 319.
5 Ibid., 319–20.
6 *WTROM,* 257.
7 Ibid., 257–61, 263–5.
8 Cannon, Lou, *Governor Reagan: His Rise to Power* (New York: PublicAffairs, 2003), 108–9.
9 Evans, Rowland, and Robert Novak, *The Reagan Revolution* (New York: Dutton, 1981), 26.
10 *AAL,* 129.
11 Evans, Thomas, *The Education of Ronald Reagan: The General Electric Years and the Untold Story of His Conversion to Conservatism* (New York: Columbia University Press, 2006), 4–5, 92–6.
12 *AAL,* 128–9; Evans, *Education,* 65–6, 74–80.
13 Boyarsky, Bill, *The Rise of Ronald Reagan* (New York: Random House, 1968), 26.
14 Foner, Eric, *The Story of American Freedom* (New York: Norton, 1998), xiii.
15 'Fireside chat', 30 September 1934, and 'Annual message to the Congress on the state of the union', 6 January 1941, APP-PPP; Foner, *The Story of American Freedom,* chapters 9–10.
16 Diggins, John Patrick, *Ronald Reagan: Fate, Freedom, and the Making of History* (New York: Norton, 2007), 268–71.
17 Speech to the Fargo Chamber of Commerce, 26 January 1962, RRGP:CSF-38.
18 Evans, *Education,* 115–16.
19 Nixon to Reagan, 18 June and 6 July 1959, Pre-Presidential Papers, Series 320-Box 621, Richard M. Nixon Presidential Library; Reagan to Nixon, 27 June 1959, *RALIL,* 702.
20 Eliot, *Reagan,* 283–4; *RD* (14 January 1989), 689.
21 Quoted in Hoberman, Jim, 'That Reagan boy', *Village Voice,* 10–16 September 1980.
22 *Los Angeles Times,* 6 October 1966.
23 Reagan to Barney Oldfield, 19 December 1985, PHF:R–14.
24 Wills, *Reagan's America,* 212.

25 *WTROM*, 301; *AAL*, 104.

26 Edwards, *Early Reagan*, 435.

27 McDougal, Dennis, *The Last Tycoon: Lew Wasserman, MCA, and the Hidden History of Hollywood* (Cambridge MA: Da Capo, 2001), 182–3; Wills, *Reagan's America*, 211; Cannon, *Governor Reagan*, 60–1.

28 *WTROM*, 292; *AAL*, 117–18.

29 Mayer, Jane, and Doyle McManus, *Landslide: The Unmaking of President Reagan* (London: Fontana, 1989), 25.

30 Reagan to Patti, 12 July 1954, *RALIL*, 52; Reagan to Nancy Reagan, 13 July 1954, *I Love You, Ronnie: The Letters of Ronald Reagan to Nancy Reagan* (New York: Random House, 2000), 45–6.

31 'California's leading lady', *Look*, 31 October 1967; *MT*, 100, 34.

32 Evans, *Education*, 175–6.

33 *MT*, 128.

34 *FFFD*, 93–4.

35 *MT*, 146–7; *FFFD*, 69, 402; Cannon, *Governor Reagan*, 79–80.

36 See Reagan to Patti, 5 March and 2 April 1968, to Michael, *c.*1971, and to Ron, *c.*1972, *RALIL*, 52–4, 56–8, 60–1.

37 *MT*, 146.

38 *FFFD*, 87–104.

39 *FFFT*, 120–34; Rosenfeld, Seth, 'Reagan's personal spying machine', *New York Times*, 1 September 2012. Available at http://www.nytimes.com/2012/09/02/opinion/sunday/reagans-personal-spying-machine.html?_r=0.

40 *MT*, 155–8; Reagan, Michael, *On the Outside Looking In* (New York: Zebra Books, 1988), 9–11.

41 *MT*, 161–3; Colacello, Bob, *Ronnie and Nancy: Their Path to the White House – 1911 to 1980* (New York: Warner, 2004), 276–8.

42 *FFFD*, 97.

43 Humes, James, *The Wit and Wisdom of Ronald Reagan* (Washington DC: Regnery, 2007), 73.

44 *AAL*, 565–6; Reagan to Ben Cleaver, 17 December 1973, CP:H/CHQ-4.

45 *MT*, 165, 161, 169.

46 Ibid., 169–73.

47 Kengor, Paul, *God and Ronald Reagan: A Spiritual Life* (New York: Regan Books, 2004), 45–8.

48 Reagan to Mrs Hugh Harris, 9 January 1985, *RALIL*, 47.

49 *WTROM*, 280; McDougal, *Last Mogul*, 263–4.

50 Ibid., 264–5; Morris, *Dutch*, 314.

51 *AAL*, 135.

52 Reagan to Nixon, 15 July 1960, *RALIL*, 705.

53 Trumbo, Dalton, 'The Oscar syndrome', *Playboy*, April 1960; Reagan to Hefner, 4 July 1960, *RALIL*, 146–9.

54 'Ronald Reagan warns of Hollywood red invasion', *Hollywood Citizen-News*, 6 March 1961; 'Red threat is cited', *New York Times*, 9 May 1961.

55 'Ronald Reagan pits his voice against JFK's', *Los Angeles Mirror*, 17 June 1961; 'Reagan assails JFK's key plans', *Los Angeles Mirror*, 3 January 1962.

56 The recording can be heard at http://www.youtube.com/watch?v=AYrlDlrLDSQ.
57 Reagan to Lorraine and Elwood Wagner, 13 July 1961, *RALIL*, 578–9.
58 'Encroaching control: keep government poor and remain free', Address to Orange County, California, Press Club, 28 July 1961, *Vital Speeches of the Day*, 1 September 1961.
59 *WTROM*, 297.
60 McDougal, *Last Mogul*, 273–308.
61 *AAL*, 137–8; Evans, *Education*, 161–3.
62 Kelley, Kitty, *Nancy Reagan: The Unauthorized Biography* (New York: Simon & Schuster, 1991), 128–30.
63 Mason, Robert, *The Republican Party and American Politics from Hoover to Reagan* (New York: Cambridge University Press, 2102), chapters 2–6; Critchlow, Donald, *The Conservative Ascendancy: How the GOP Right Made Political History* (Cambridge MA: Harvard University Press, 2007), 41–76.
64 Goldwater, Barry *The Conscience of a Conservative* (Shepherdsville KY: Victor, 1960), 14–15, 91, *AAL*, 138–9.
65 Dallek, Matthew, *The Right Moment: Ronald Reagan's First Victory and the Decisive Turning Point in American Politics* (New York: Free Press, 2004), 64–5.
66 Hopper to Edith Davis, 7 October 1964, Hedda Hopper Papers, AMPAS; Evans, *Education*, 165–6.
67 Dallek, *Right Moment*, 66–7.
68 Evans, *Education*, 168–9.
69 Available at https://www.youtube.com/watch?v=qXBswFfh6AY.
70 *AAL*, 143.
71 *Los Angeles Times*, 11 November 1964.
72 Reagan, Ronald, 'The Republican party and the conservative movement', *National Review*, 1 December 1964.
73 George Murphy with Victor Lasky, *Say... Didn't You Used to be George Murphy?* (New York: Bartholomew Books, 1970); *Los Angeles Times*, 5 November 1964.
74 Smith, William French, 'The evolution of the kitchen cabinet, 1965–1973', ROHO-RRGES.
75 Reagan to Lorraine and Elwood Wagner, 13 July 1961, *RALIL*, 579.
76 Cannon, *Governor Reagan*, 133.

5   CALIFORNIA GOVERNOR

1 D'Souza, Dinesh, *Ronald Reagan: How An Ordinary Man Became an Extraordinary Leader* (New York: Free Press, 1997), 51.
2 Dallek, Robert, *Ronald Reagan: The Politics of Symbolism* (Cambridge MA: Harvard University Press, 1984), 53.
3 'Reagan favorite of GOP', *San Francisco Chronicle*, 23 April 1965.
4 Colacello, Bob, *Ronnie and Nancy: Their Path to the White House – 1911 to 1980* (New York: Warner, 2004), 339–40; Deaver, Michael, *Behind the Scenes: In Which the Author Talks about Ronald and Nancy Reagan and Himself* (New York: William Morrow, 1987), 118; Reagan to Lorraine and Elwood Wagner, May 1965, *RALIL*, 170.
5 Cannon, Lou, *Governor Reagan: His Rise to Power* (New York: PublicAffairs, 2003), 135–6.

6 *Newsweek*, 5 July 1965, 18–19. For Reagan's campaign, see DeGroot, Gerard, *Selling Ronald Reagan: The Emergence of a President* (London: I.B.Tauris, 2015).

7 Reagan to Nixon, 7 May 1965, *RALIL*, 706.

8 *FFFD*, 146–52.

9 John Harmer to Bill Roberts, 12 July 1965, CP:H/CHQ-2.

10 Plog, Stanley, 'More than just an actor: the early campaigns of Ronald Reagan', ROHO-RRGES.

11 *NYT*, 25 July 1965.

12 'Ronald Reagan exits right', *Beverly Hills Courier*, 17 September 1965; 'Statement of Ronald Reagan regarding the John Birch Society', 24 September 1965, RRGP:CSF-31; Reagan to the Editor, *Beverly Hills Courier*, 5 October 1965, *RALIL*, 172.

13 *Los Angeles Times*, 4 January 1966.

14 *Meet the Press*, 9 January 1966. Available at www.nbcnews.com/video/meet-the-press/18765144; McGirr, Lisa, *Suburban Warriors: The Origins of the New American Right* (Princeton NJ: Princeton University Press, 2002), 193.

15 Reagan to Gross, 13 January 1966, CP:H/CHQ-2.

16 Reagan to Goldwater, 13 January 1966, RRGP:CSF-29.

17 'Even nice guys get mad', *Oakland Tribune*, 18 March 1966; Reagan to Jack Rudder, 9 May 1966, RRGP:CSF-32; Diggins, John, *Ronald Reagan: Fate, Freedom, and the Making of History* (New York: Norton, 2007), 148–9.

18 Nofziger, Lyn, *Nofziger* (Washington DC: Regnery, 1992), 222.

19 William Patrick to Reagan, 8 June 1966, Reagan to John McCone, 3 and 10 October 1966, RRGP:CSF-32; 'Reagan endorsed by Goody Knight', *Los Angeles Herald-Examiner*, 2 November 1966.

20 Reagan to Murphy, 19 August 1966, CP:H/CHQ-2.

21 Rarick, Ethan, *California Rising: The Life and Times of Pat Brown* (Berkeley and Los Angeles: University of California Press, 2005).

22 Brown, Edmund G. 'Pat', *Reagan and Reality: The Two Californias* (New York: Praeger, 1970), 130.

23 Dallek, Matthew, *The Right Moment: Ronald Reagan's First Victory and the Decisive Turning Point in American Politics* (New York: Free Press, 2000), 204.

24 McBirnie to Reagan, 30 November 1965, and Reagan speech 'The Creative Society', RRGP:CSF-31.

25 Mark, David, *Going Dirty: The Art of Negative Campaigning* (Lanham MD: Rowman & Littlefield, 2007), 55–74.

26 DeGroot, *Selling Ronald Reagan*, 249–50.

27 Ashbrook to Reagan, 14 March 1967, CP:H/CHQ-2; Wilson, James Q., 'A guide to Reagan country: the political culture of southern California', *Commentary*, May 1967.

28 Edgar Hiestand to Reagan, 9 June 1966, CP:H/CHQ-2.

29 'Reagan demands inquiry', *NYT*, 14 May 1966.

30 'Another opinion: Reagan states his case', *NYT*, 30 October 1966.

31 'Inside report: the anti-welfare state', *Washington Post*, 22 September 1966.

32 'Reagan shuns image of Goldwater in coast race', *NYT*, 1 June 1966.

33 McGirr, *Suburban Warriors*, 204–5; 'Brown assesses backlash', *NYT*, 29 December 1966.

34 Reagan to Brooke, 17 November 1966, RRGP:CSF-29; Reagan to Curtis, 28 November 1966, CP:H/CHQ-2.

35 'Inaugural address', 5 January 1967. Available at www.governors.library.ca.gov/addresses/33-Reagan01.html.
36 Cannon, Lou, *Reagan* (New York: Putnam's, 1982), 20.
37 Cannon, *Governor Reagan*, 184; Reagan to Mrs Lyn Nofziger, November 1966, *RALIL*, 176.
38 *AAL*, 166.
39 Boyarsky, Bill, *Big Daddy: Jesse Unruh and the Art of Politics* (Oakland: University of California Press, 2007).
40 Colacello, *Ronnie and Nancy*, 365.
41 Didion, Joan, and John Dunne, 'Pretty Nancy', *Saturday Evening Post*, 1 June 1968; Cannon, *Governor Reagan*, 234–7.
42 *AAL*, 167–8; Nofziger, *Nofziger*, 84.
43 Cannon, *Governor Reagan*, 177–9; Nofziger, *Nofziger*, 83–8.
44 Cannon, *Governor Reagan*, 253–4.
45 *AAL*, 161.
46 Reagan to Lorraine and Elwood Wagner, 16 April 1970, *RALIL*, 769; Nofziger, *Nofziger*, 78–82.
47 Hamilton, Gary, and Nicole Biggart, *Governor Reagan, Governor Brown: A Sociology of Executive Power* (New York: Columbia University Press, 1984), 182–6.
48 Gordon Smith to Reagan, 12 January 1967, RRGP: Department of Finance Files [DFF]-122.
49 Cannon, *Governor Reagan*, 194; Colacello, *Ronnie and Nancy*, 320.
50 Cannon, *Governor Reagan*, 194–201.
51 Boyarsky, Bill, *Ronald Reagan: His Life and Rise to the Presidency* (New York: Random House, 1981), 157, 159.
52 'Reagan will reveal tax plans today', *Los Angeles Times*, 8 March 1967.
53 'The voice of a conservative, the record of a liberal', *Spotlight*, 4 December 1978; Reagan to Lorraine and Elwood Wagner, 5 February 1979, *RALIL*, 785.
54 Graham to Reagan, 7 March 1967, CP:H/CHQ-2.
55 Reagan to Charles Schultz, 30 July 1970, CP:H/CHQ-3; Reagan to Mrs Stinson, late 1972, Reagan to Kenneth Fisher, circa late 1970s, *RALIL*, 362–3.
56 Doerr, David, *California's Tax Machine* (Sacramento: California Taxpayers Association, 2008), 90.
57 'Good citizen called a "wall" against rioting', *Los Angeles Times*, 31 March 1968.
58 'The race problem and the ghetto', in *Ronald Reagan Talks to America* (Old Greenwich CT: Devon Adair, 1983), 105–13.
59 Cabinet minutes, 28 February and 4 April 1968, RRGP:GOF-23.
60 Livermore to Win Adams, 'Governor Reagan's conservation image', 19 October 1967, RRGP, GOF-23; 'Time is running out', 17 November 1969, RRGP, DFF-122.
61 Cannon, *Governor Reagan*, 297–321.
62 Skelton, George, 'The man who saved the Sierra', *Los Angeles Times*, 28 July 1997.
63 Livermore, Norman, 'Man in the middle: High Sierra packer, timberman, conservationist, and California resources secretary', ROHO-RRGES.
64 'Reagan's cuts called blow to mental health programs', *Los Angeles Times*, 18 September 1967.
65 Putnam, Jackson, *Jess: The Political Career of Jesse Marvin Unruh* (Lanham MD: University Press of America, 2005), 212–13.

66 For transcript, see 'The image of America and the youth of the world'. Available at http:// reagan2020.us/speeches/Reagan.kennedy-debate.asp. A segment of the show can be watched at https://www.youtube.com/watch?v=HMzTcvXk1j4.

67 Kengor, Paul, 'The great forgotten debate', *National Review*, 22 May 2007. Available at http://www.nationalreview.com/article/220949/great-forgotten-debate-paul-kengor.

68 Rosenfeld, Seth, 'Reagan, Hoover, and the UC red scare', *SFGate*, 9 June 2002. Available at http://www.sfgate.com/news/article/Reagan-Hoover-and-the-UC-Red-Scare-2829732.php; 'Governor shelves UC probe', *San Jose Mercury*, 27 January 1967.

69 Cannon, *Governor Reagan*, 279–80; Reagan to Rhodes, 12 January 1967, CP:H/CHQ- 2.

70 Reagan to Hayakawa, 11 January 1971, CP:H/CHQ-3.

71 'The people's park', Address to the Commonwealth Club of San Francisco, 13 June 1969, RRGP: DFF-122; *AAL*, 180.

72 Rosenfeld, Seth, *Subversives: The FBI's War on Student Radicals, and Reagan's Rise to Power* (New York: Farrar, Straus & Giroux, 2012), 516–17 (see Part 3 of this volume for the most thorough coverage of Reagan's response to the campus disorders); Wasserman, Steve, 'Exit stage left: the FBI and student radicals', *The Nation*, 29 October 2012. Available at https://www.thenation.com/article/exit-stage-left-fbi-and-student-radicals/.

73 Reagan to Jack Williams, 17 March 1969, *RALIL*, 190.

74 Hayward, Steven, *The Age of Reagan: The Fall of the Old Liberal Order, 1964–1980* (Roseville CA: Prima, 2001), 327.

75 '"Bloodbath" figure of speech', *Oakland Tribune*, 8 April 1970; 'Reagan remark a campaign issue: "bloodbath" comment fuels oratory in California', *NYT*, 19 April 1970; Reagan to Mrs L. Johsens, April 1970, and to Dave Goble, 14 April 1980, *RALIL*, 191–2.

76 Hayakawa to Reagan, 19 November 1974, 1980 CP:H/CHQ-4.

77 'Reagan on Reagan plus some other views', *Los Angeles Times*, 29 September 1974.

78 Deaver, *Behind the Scenes*, 44.

79 Reagan to Caspar Weinberger, 8 December 1970, CP:H/CHQ -3.

80 Cabinet minutes, 9 November 1967, RRGP:GOF-23.

81 Cannon, *Governor Reagan*, 349.

82 *AAL*, 189; 'Interview with Governor Reagan', *California Journal*, 16 December 1970.

83 'Governor's welfare proposals scored by Democrats', *Los Angeles Times*, 4 March 1971.

84 Cannon, *Governor Reagan*, 353–9.

85 Levy, Frank, *What Ronald Reagan Can Teach the US about Welfare Reform* (Washington DC: Urban Institute, 1977).

86 'Revenue control and tax reduction, submitted to the California legislature by Governor Ronald Reagan', 12 March 1973, quoted in Diggins, John Patrick, *Ronald Reagan: Fate, Freedom, and the Making of History* (New York: Norton, 2007), 175.

87 Boyarsky, *Ronald Reagan*, 161.

88 Uhler, Lewis, *Setting the Limits: Constitutional Control of Government* (Washington DC: Regnery, 1989), 115–16, 177.

89 Putnam, Jackson, 'Governor Reagan: a reappraisal', *California History*, 83/4 (2006), 43.

90 'Address to the American textile manufacturers institute', 29 March 1973, in Reagan, Ronald, *A Time for Choosing: The Speeches of Ronald Reagan, 1961–1982* (Chicago: Regnery, 1983), 115–18.

91 Reagan to Mr and Mrs Clarence Bowman, n.d., *RALIL*, 181.

92 'An offer Californians did refuse', *California Journal*, December 1973.

93 Reagan to James Hayes, 13 November 1973, CP:H/CHQ-4; Reagan, Ronald, 'Reflections on the failure of Proposition 1', *National Review*, 7 December 1973. Available at http://www.nationalreview.com/article/210999/reflections-failure-proposition-1-governor-ronald-reagan.

94 Reagan to Mr Strong, n.d., *RALIL*, 184.

95 'Legacy for state: footprints, but no permanent monuments or scars', *Los Angeles Times*, 29 September 1974.

96 Hamilton and Biggart, *Governor Reagan*, 90.

6 RIGHT MAN

1 Reagan to Goldwater, 11 June 1966, RGP:CSF-29.

2 Colacello, Bob, *Ronnie and Nancy: Their Path to the White House – 1911 to 1980* (New York: Warner, 2004), 377–8.

3 Reagan to Nixon, 10 April 1968, *RALIL*, 707–8; Pemberton, William, *Exit with Honor: The Life and Presidency of Ronald Reagan* (Armonk NY: M. E. Sharpe, 1997), 77.

4 *AAL*, 178; Deaver, Michael, *Nancy: A Portrait of My Years with Nancy Reagan* (New York: Morrow, 2004), 44.

5 Laxalt to Reagan, 12 August 1968, Reagan to Dwight D. Eisenhower, 14 August 1968, Rusher to Reagan, 23 August 1968, CP:H/CHQ-2.

6 Reagan to Sam Harrod Jr, December 1952, quoted in Morris, Edmund, *Dutch: A Memoir of Ronald Reagan* (New York: HarperCollins, 1999), 292–3.

7 Reagan to Nixon, 7 September 1959, *RALIL*, 703–4.

8 Reagan to Patricia Reilly Hitt, 22 June 1971, CP:H/CHQ-3; Morgan, Iwan, *Nixon* (London: Arnold, 2002), 72–5.

9 Imelda Marcos to Reagan, 17 September 1969, Nixon to Reagan, 8 October 1969, CP:H/CHQ-3.

10 Morris, *Dutch*, 378.

11 Reagan to Elwood and Lorraine Wagner, 22 June 1973, *RALIL*, 778.

12 Buckley to Reagan, 24 October 1973, in Buckley Jr, William, *The Reagan I Knew* (New York: Basic Books, 2008), 61; Buckley to Reagan, 6 November 1973, Reagan to Buckley, 6 November 1973, *RALIL*, 708.

13 Transcript of Reagan press conference, 27 August 1974, quoted in Cannon, Lou, *Governor Reagan: His Rise to Power* (New York: PublicAffairs, 2003), 385–6.

14 Ford, Gerald, *A Time to Heal: The Autobiography of Gerald R. Ford* (New York: Harper & Row, 1979), 142–5.

15 Reagan to Senator Strom Thurmond of South Carolina, 4 December 1974, CP:H/CHQ-4; 'Ronald Reagan: building a national organization', 4 November 1974, Deaver and Hannaford Collection [DHC]-1, Hoover Institution Archives, Stanford University; *RPV*, xiii–xiv.

16 'Ronald Reagan: a program for the future', 4 November 1974, DHC-1.

17 *MT*, 179.

18 McDougal, Dennis, *The Last Mogul: Lew Wasserman, MCA, and the Hidden History of Hollywood* (Boston: Da Capo, 2001), 332–3.

19 Cannon, *Governor Reagan*, 304–5.

20 Reagan to Lorraine and Elwood Wagner, 22 October 1975, *RALIL*, 781.

21 *AAL*, 192–4.

22 Rusher, William, *The Making of the New Majority Party* (New York: Sheed and Ward, 1975).

23 Cannon, *Governor Reagan*, 400–1; 'Let them go their way'. Available at http://reagan2020. us/speeches/Let_Them_Go_Their_Way.asp.

24 Hayward, Steven, *The Age of Reagan: The Fall of the Old Liberal Order, 1964–1980* (Roseville CA: Prima, 2001), 450.

25 *MT*, 181.

26 Witcover, Jules, *Marathon: The Pursuit of the Presidency 1972–1976* (New York: Viking, 1977), 75–6; Bell, Jeffrey, 'The candidate and the briefing book', *Weekly Standard*, 5 February 2001. Available at http://stonezone.com/jeffbell2.php.

27 Kiewe, Amos, and Davis Houck, eds, *A Shining City on a Hill: Ronald Reagan's Economic Rhetoric, 1951–1989* (New York: Praeger, 1991), 116–17.

28 Jones, Jerry, 'Memorandum for Don Rumsfeld and Dick Cheney', 26 September 1975, Jerry Jones Files-25, Gerald R. Ford Presidential Library [GRFPL].

29 Cannon, *Governor Reagan*, 406–12.

30 Robert Teeter to Bo Calloway, 'Momentum', 11 December 1975, President Ford Reelection Committee Records-B2, GRFPL.

31 Wirthlin, Dick, *The Greatest Communicator: What Ronald Reagan Taught Me about Politics, Leadership, and Life* (Hoboken NJ: Wiley, 2004), 17–23.

32 Ibid., 23–4.

33 Shirley, Craig, *Reagan's Revolution: The Untold Story of the Campaign That Started It All* (Nashville TN: Thomas Nelson, 2005), 33–57.

34 Anderson, Martin, *Revolution* (San Diego: Harcourt Brace Jovanovich, 1988), 43; Witcover, *Marathon*, 409.

35 Shirley, *Reagan's Revolution*, 158–76.

36 'To restore America', 31 March 1976. Available at https://reaganlibrary.archives.gov/ archives/reference/3.31.76.html.

37 'An explanation of the Reagan victories in Texas and the Caucus states', May 1976, Jerry Jones Files-25, GRFPL.

38 Mike Duval, 'Strategy paper', 21 May 1976, Michael Duval Papers-14, GRFPL.

39 Reagan to Holmes Alexander, December 1979, *RALIL*, 589–90.

40 Critchlow, Donald, *The Conservative Ascendancy: How the GOP Right Made Political History* (Cambridge MA: Harvard University Press, 2007), 149–50; *AAL*, 202.

41 *MT*, 198–200; Shirley, *Reagan's Revolution*, xxii–xxiii.

42 Anderson, *Revolution*, 46–7.

43 Reagan to Ed Hickey, n.d., *RALIL*, 222; *MT*, 202.

44 Reagan to Florence Moore, 2 November 1976, *RALIL*, 223; *MT*, 201.

45 Ford, *A Time to Heal*, 333.

46 Reagan to Ron La Montagne, n.d., *RALIL*, 222.

47 *RPV*, xiv–xvi; 'Reagan's radio producer', *Television/Radio Age*, 8 September 1980, 16; Reagan to Dwight Myers, 5 February 1979, CP:H/CHQ-3.

48 'Reshaping the American political landscape', 6 February 1977, in Reagan, Ronald, *A Time for Choosing: The Speeches of Ronald Reagan, 1961–1982* (Chicago: Regnery, 1983), 181–201.

49 Moynihan, Daniel Patrick, 'Of "sons" and their "grandsons"', *NYT*, 7 July 1980.

50 Gates, Robert, *From the Shadows: The Ultimate Insider's Story of Five Presidents and How They Won the Cold War* (New York: Touchstone, 1996), 194.

51 Phillips-Fein, Kim, *Invisible Hands: The Making of the Conservative Movement from the New Deal to Reagan* (New York: Norton, 2010), 236–62.

52 Blumenthal, Sidney, *The Rise of the Counter-Establishment: The Conservative Ascent to Political Power* (New York: Union Square, 2008).

53 Diggins, John, *Ronald Reagan: Fate, Freedom, and the Making of History* (New York: Norton, 2007), 189–218.

54 Sandbrook, Dominic, *Mad as Hell: The Crisis of the 1970s and the Rise of the Populist Right* (New York: Knopf, 2011), 326–60; Williams, Daniel, *God's Own Party: The Making of the Christian Right* (New York: Oxford University Press, 2010).

55 Anderson, *Revolution*, 7.

56 Kirkpatrick, Jeane, 'Dictatorship and double standards', *Commentary*, 68 (November 1979), 34–45; Reagan, Ronald, 'The canal of opportunity: a new relationship with Latin America', *Orbis* (fall 1977), 560.

57 Schweizer, Peter, *Reagan's War: The Epic Story of His Forty-Year Struggle and Final Triumph over Communism* (New York: Doubleday, 2002), 106–8, 126–7.

58 Drew, Elizabeth, 'Reporter at large: Reagan', *New Yorker*, 24 March 1980, 71.

59 'Strategy II', 4 May 1977, *RIHOH*, 111–13.

60 Kengor, Paul, *God and Ronald Reagan: A Spiritual Life* (New York: Regan Books, 2004), 213–15.

61 Hayward, *Fall of the Old Liberal Order*, 616–17.

62 'What he'd be like as president', *Fortune*, May 1980.

63 'Tax control ballot victory in California', *Washington Post*, 18 June 1978.

64 Phillips-Fein, *Invisible Hands*, 243–6, 248–50; Walker, Charls, 'Summary of discussion', in Feldstein, Martin, ed., *American Economic Policy in the 1980s* (Chicago: University of Chicago Press, 1994), 224–5.

65 'Remarks at the 1980 presidential campaign debate, Cleveland, Ohio', 28 October 1980, APP-PPP; Reagan to William Hoyerman, 10 November 1981, *RALIL*, 300.

66 Domitrovic, Brian, *Econoclasts: The Rebels Who Sparked the Supply-Side Revolution and Restored American Prosperity* (Wilmington DE: ISI, 2009).

67 Anderson, *Revolution*, 161–3.

68 Meese, Edwin, *With Reagan: The Inside Story* (Washington DC: Regnery, 1991), 123.

69 *AAL*, 231.

70 'Taxes', 18 October 1977, *RIHOH*, 277; 'Exchange with reporters on the program for economic recovery', 19 February 1981, APP-PPP.

71 Kemp, Jack, *American Renaissance: A Strategy for the 1980s* (New York: Harper & Row, 1979), 96; Reagan to Representative Clair Burgener, 1 May 1980, CP:H/CHQ-5.

72 Transcript in Buckley, *The Reagan I Knew*, 115–25.

73 Anderson, *Revolution*, 111–21.

74 Reagan, Ronald, 'Editorial: two ill-advised California trends', *Los Angeles Herald-Examiner*, 1 November 1978.

75 'Opening space', *The Advocate*, 7 February 1980; 'Evangelist helps raise a hope, a prayer and money for Prop. 6', *San Diego Union*, 31 October 1978.

76 Williams, Daniel, 'Reagan's religious right: the unlikely alliance between southern evangelicals and a California Conservative', in Hudson, Cheryl, and Gareth Davies, eds, *Ronald Reagan and the 1980s: Perception, Policies, Legacies* (New York: Palgrave, 2007), 137–9.

77   Dochuk, Darren, *From Bible Belt to Sunbelt: Plain Folk Religion, Grassroots Politics, and the Rise of Evangelical Conservatism* (New York: Norton, 2011), 383.

78   'Reagan backs evangelicals in their political activities', *NYT,* 23 August 1980; Williams, 'Reagan's religious right', 140–1.

79   Anderson, *Revolution,* 329–30; *MT,* 205–6.

80   Wirthlin, *The Greatest Communicator,* 44.

81   Reagan to Hank McCullough, March 1980, *RALIL,* 81.

82   Shirley, Craig, *Rendezvous with Destiny: Ronald Reagan and the Campaign That Changed America* (Wilmington DE: ISI, 2009), 108.

83   Wirthlin, *The Greatest Communicator,* 57–61; Reagan to Ambassador John Davis Lodge, 18 August 1980, *RALIL,* 248.

84   Busch, Andrew, *Reagan's Victory: The Presidential Election of 1980 and the Rise of the Right* (Lawrence: University Press of Kansas, 2005), 83.

85   Bush, George, *Looking Forward: An Autobiography* (New York: Doubleday, 1987), 221–2; Sheehy, Gail, *Character: America's Search for Leadership,* rev. ed. (New York: Bantam, 1990), 198; Reagan to Blanche Seaver, 31 July 1980, *RALIL,* 250.

86   Wirthlin, 'Reagan for president campaign plan draft, 6/29/80', 1980 CP, Richard Wirthlin Files-177; Wirthlin, *The Greatest Communicator,* 48–51.

87   'Address accepting the presidential nomination at the Republican National Convention in Detroit', 17 July 1980, APP-PPP; Drew, Elizabeth, *Portrait of an Election: The 1980 Presidential Campaign* (New York: Simon & Schuster, 1981), 220.

88   Cannon, *Governor Reagan,* 482; *MT,* 216–17.

89   Rick Hutcheson to Hamilton Jordan, 'General election', 17 March 1980, Presidential Handwriting File-243, Jimmy Carter Presidential Library.

90   Hayward, *Fall of the Old Liberal Order,* 697–700.

91   Reagan to William Loeb, December 1979, and to Caspar Weinberger, 15 November 1979, *RALIL,* 588, 232.

92   Sick, Gary, *October Surprise: America's Hostages in Iran and the Election of Ronald Reagan* (New York: Times Books, 1991); 'No proof found of an "October surprise" plot, house panel says', *Washington Post,* 14 January 1993.

93   Carter, Jimmy, *White House Diary* (New York: Picador, 2010), 476.

94   'Remarks at the 1980 presidential campaign debate, Cleveland, Ohio', 28 October 1980, APP-PPP.

95   Carter, *White House Diary,* 479.

96   *Time,* 2 February 1981; CBS News/*New York Times,* 'National election day survey', 4 November 1980. Available at http://ropercenter.cornell.edu/polls/us-elections/presidential-elections/1980-presidential-election/.

97   Mason, Robert, *The Republican Party and American Politics from Hoover to Reagan* (New York: Cambridge University Press, 2012), 249.

98   Cunningham, Sean, *American Politics in the Postwar Sunbelt: Conservative Growth in a Battleground Region* (New York: Cambridge University Press, 2014), 191–225.

99   Cannon, *Governor Reagan,* 511.

7   MR PRESIDENT

1   Boone, Pat, *Pat Boone's America: 50 Years* (Nashville: B&H Publishing, 2006), 101–2.

2   Neustadt, Richard, *Presidential Power and the Modern Presidents: The Politics of Leadership from Roosevelt to Reagan* (New York: Free Press, 1990), 269.

3   Ritchie, Donald, 'Who moved the inauguration? Dispelling an urban legend', 22 January 2009. Available at http://blog.oup.com/2009/01/moving_inauguration/.

4   'President Reagan's America', *Washington Post*, 21 January 1980.

5   Blumenthal, Sidney, 'Reaganism and the neokitsch aesthetic', in Blumenthal, Sidney, and Thomas Byrne Edsall, eds, *The Reagan Legacy* (New York: Pantheon, 1988), 251.

6   Wilber, Del Quentin, *Rawhide Down: The Near Assassination of Ronald Reagan* (New York: Macmillan, 2011).

7   Office of Inspection, 'Reagan assassination attempt interview reports', 4 May 1981, United States Secret Service. Previously available at www.secretservice.gov/Reagan-Assassination-Attempt (link no longer works).

8   'Hinckley's 3/30/81 letter to Foster'. Available at http://law2.umkc.edu/faculty/projects/ftrials/hinckley/LETTER.HTM.

9   Audio recording available at https://www.youtube.com/watch?v=ftowIITwmoM.

10 Bush, George, *Looking Forward: An Autobiography* (New York: Doubleday, 1987), 217–25.

11 *RD* (18 February 1981), 5; Kuhn, Jim, *Ronald Reagan in Private: A Memoir of My Years in the White House* (New York: Sentinel, 2004), 81.

12 *RD* (4 November 1983), 194.

13 Kernell, Samuel, *Going Public: New Strategies of Presidential Leadership* (Washington DC: CQ Press, 1986).

14 'Farewell address to the nation', 11 January 1989, APP-PPP.

15 Reeves, Richard, *The Reagan Detour* (New York: Simon & Schuster, 1990), 10; *AAL*, 246–8.

16 Wirthlin, Dick, *The Greatest Communicator: What Ronald Reagan Taught Me about Politics, Leadership, and Life* (Hoboken NJ: Wiley, 2004), 3, 109–13; D'Souza, Dinesh, *Ronald Reagan: How an Ordinary Man Became an Extraordinary Leader* (New York: Free Press, 1997), 249–51.

17 Noonan, Peggy, *What I Saw at the Revolution: A Political Life in the Reagan Era* (New York: Random House, 1990), 124–5.

18 Muir, William Kerr, *The Bully Pulpit: The Presidential Leadership of Ronald Reagan* (San Francisco: ICS, 1992), 78; D'Souza, *Ronald Reagan*, 250.

19 Bates, Toby Glenn, *The Reagan Rhetoric: History and Memory in 1980s America* (DeKalb: Northern Illinois University Press, 2011), 153.

20 Meese, Edwin, *With Reagan: The Inside Story* (Washington DC: Regnery, 1992), 57–9; Pfiffner, James, 'The paradox of President Reagan's leadership', *Presidential Studies Quarterly*, 43 (March 2013), 82–4.

21 Regan, Donald, *For the Record: From Wall Street to Washington* (San Diego: Harcourt Brace Jovanovich, 1988), 137–41.

22 Aberbach, Joel, 'Transforming the presidency: the administration of Ronald Reagan', in Hudson, Cheryl, and Gareth Davies, eds, *Ronald Reagan and the 1980s: Perceptions, Policies, Legacies* (New York: Palgrave, 2008), 195–201.

23 Cannon, Lou, *President Reagan: The Role of a Lifetime* (New York: Simon & Schuster, 1991), 70–1.

24 Baker, James, *'Work Hard, Study... and Keep Out of Politics!' Adventures and Lessons from an Unexpected Life* (New York: Putnam, 2006), 122–41; Cohen, David, 'From the Fabulous

Baker Boys to the master of disaster: the White House chief of staff in the Reagan and G. H. W. Bush administrations', *Presidential Studies Quarterly*, 32 (September 2002), 463–83.

25   Meese, *With Reagan*, 72–3; Baker, *'Work Hard, Study... and Keep Out of Politics!'*, 140 –1; *RD* (14 June 1982), 88.

26   Strober, Gerald, and Deborah Hart Strober, *Reagan: The Man and His Presidency* (Boston: Houghton Mifflin, 1998), 91.

27   Gates, Robert, *From the Shadows: The Ultimate Insider's Story of Five Presidents and How They Won the Cold War* (New York: Touchstone, 1996), 284–5.

28   Cannon, *President Reagan*, 187–9.

29   Weisman, Steven, 'The influence of William Clark', *New York Times Magazine*, 14 August 1983. Available at http://www.nytimes.com/1983/08/14/magazine/the-influence-of-william-clark.html?pagewanted=all.

30   Baker, *'Work Hard, Study... and Keep Out of Politics!'*, 199–202; *AAL*, 448; *RD* (14, 15–16 October, 1983), 187.

31   Regan, *For the Record*, 143.

32   Webster, William, RROH-MC.

33   Baker, *'Work Hard, Study... and Keep Out of Politics!'*, 202.

34   Deaver, Michael, *A Different Drummer: My Thirty Years with Ronald Reagan* (New York: HarperCollins, 2001), 35; Cannon, *President Reagan*, 180–1.

35   Mann, James, *The Rebellion of Ronald Reagan: A History of the End of the Cold War* (New York: Viking, 2009), 342.

36   Dobrynin, Anatoly, *In Confidence: Moscow's Ambassador to America's Six Cold War Presidents* (New York: Times Books, 1995), 494.

37   Haig, Alexander, *Caveat: Realism, Reagan, and Foreign Policy* (New York: Macmillan, 1984), 85; *RD* (25 June 1982), 91.

38   Shultz, George, *Turmoil and Triumph: My Years as Secretary of State* (New York: Scribner's, 1993), 250–3, 274–5, 313; *RD* (14 November 1984), 277.

39   Morris, Edmund, *Dutch: A Memoir of Ronald Reagan* (New York: HarperCollins, 1999), 546; *MT*, 313; Wallison, Peter, *Ronald Reagan: The Power of Conviction and the Success of His Presidency* (Boulder CO: Westview, 2004), 160–4 [quotation 162].

40   *RD* (8 November 1988), 664.

41   *MT*, 315.

42   Grant to Reagan, 7 February 1986, Reagan to Grant, 5 March 1986, Cary Grant Papers, AMPAS.

43   *RD* (4 December 1981), 53, (13 August 1982), 98.

44   *WTROM*, 291.

45   *RD* (24 June 1985), 337, (29 June 1985), 339; Reagan to Lorraine and Elwood Wagner, 25 June 1987, PHF:R–18.

46   'Reagan officials on the March 30, 1981, assassination attempt', RROH-MC.

47   'Cancer found on Reagan's nose', *NYT*, 2 August 1987; Reagan to Don Samuelson, 4 November 1985, PHF:R–14.

48   Reagan to Dr John House, 3 July 1986, PHF:R–16.

49   *FFFD*, 279; *RD* (30 March/11 April 1981), 12; *MT*, 20.

50   Reagan to Ken Duberstein, 28 June 1983, PHF:R–7.

51   *RD* (31 January 1983), 128.

52 Ibid. (30 March/11 April 1981), 12, (23 July 1981), 32, (6 July 1983), 164.

53 *AAL*, 693.

54 *MT*, 21.

55 *RD* (18 and 24–30 November 1981), 50–51; *AAL*, 291; Kilgore, Andrew, 'The Libyan "hit squad" hoax', *Washington Report on Middle East Affairs*, December 2000. Available at http://www.wrmea.org/the-libyan-hit-squad-hoax.html.

56 *MT*, 21, 44–52; Cannon, *President Reagan*, 583–5; Regan, *For the Record*, 3–5, 70–1, 73–4, 367–70.

57 'The 80s are over: greed goes out of style', *Newsweek*, 4 January 1988; Reagan to Otis Carney, 23 February 1982, PHF:R–2.

58 *MT*, 28–34, 39–43, 139.

59 Mann, *The Rebellion of Ronald Reagan*, 228.

60 Reeves, Richard, *President Reagan: The Triumph of Imagination* (New York: Simon & Schuster, 2005), 163; Shultz, *Turmoil and Triumph*, 312, 317.

61 Loizeau, Pierre-Marie, *Nancy Reagan: The Woman Behind the Man* (Huntington NY: Nova, 2003), 168.

62 *MT*, 152–5; *FFFD*, 280–91, 322–9.

63 *MT*, 148–9, 157–61; *RD* (26 November 1984), 281, (12 April 1987), 489.

64 Davis, Patti, 'My body, then and now', *More*, 17 May 2011. Available at http://www.more.com/patti-davis-naked-body; *RD* (6 December 1982), 117; Reagan to Patti Davis, 23 May 1983, PHF:R–5.

65 Davis, Patti, *Home Front* (New York: Crown, 1986); 'The problem of being Patti', *People*, 24 February 1986; *MT*, 166–7.

66 *RD* (18 May 1981), 20, (18 July 1987), 517.

67 *MT*, 169, 177.

68 'Memorandum of a conversation with Chancellor Helmut Schmidt, May 21, 1981', NSC-ES:SF-48; *RD* (20 July 1981), 31; Kengor, Paul, and Patricia Clark Doerner, *The Judge: William P. Clark: Ronald Reagan's Top Hand* (San Francisco: Ignatius Press, 2007), 176–80.

69 Thatcher, Margaret, *The Downing Street Years* (London: HarperCollins, 1993), 156–7; Aldous, Richard, *Reagan and Thatcher: The Difficult Relationship* (London: Hutchinson, 2012), 11–17.

70 Urban, George, *Diplomacy and Disillusion at the Court of Margaret Thatcher* (London: I.B.Tauris, 1996), 20–1, 27.

71 *RD* (27 February, 1981), 5; Speeches at the British Embassy Dinner for President Reagan 27 February 1981, MTF, docid=104581; Henderson, Nicholas, *Mandarin: The Diaries of Nicholas Henderson* (London: Weidenfeld & Nicolson, 1994), 390.

72 *RD*, 27 February, 21 July 1981, 5, 32; Aldous, *Reagan and Thatcher*, 49.

73 Reagan to Hannaford, 3 May 1983, PHF:R–3; *RD* (16 November 1988), 667.

74 *RD* (27 May 1983), 155, (9 June 1984), 246, (3 May 1985), 322.

75 'Mitterrand and Duras on Reagan's America', *Harper's*, August 1986, 12; Reagan to Mitterrand, 7 July 1986, PHF:R–16.

76 *RD* (14 September 1981), 38, (12 August 1982), 98; Cannon, *President Reagan*, 486–8.

77 Kuhn, James, RROH-MC; Aldous, *Reagan and Thatcher*, 108–9, 127–8; *AAL*, 354.

78 Kengor, Paul, *God and Ronald Reagan: A Spiritual Life* (New York: Regan Books, 2004), 209–12; Bernstein, Carl, 'The holy alliance', *Time*, 24 February 1992; 'The Pope

and the president: a key adviser reflects on the Reagan administration' (interview with William Clark), *Catholic World Reporter*, November 1999.

79 *Travels of President Reagan*, Office of the Historian, US Department of State. Available at https://history.state.gov/departmenthistory/travels/president/reagan-ronald; *RD* (26 April 1984), 234; Kuhn, *Reagan in Private*, 102, 251–2.

80 'Remarks at a ceremony commemorating the 40th anniversary of the Normandy Invasion, D-Day', 6 June 1984, APP-PPP; Cannon, *President Reagan*, 483–5.

81 Hayward, Steven, *The Age of Reagan: The Conservative Counterrevolution 1980–1989* (New York: Crown Forum, 2009), 434–5; *RD* (19 and 22 April, 5 May 1985), 317–18, 323; Reagan to Lisa Zenatta Henn, 22 May 1985, PHF:R–12.

82 Peter Aviles to Reagan, 2 January 1985, Reagan to Aviles, 28 January 1985, PHF:R–11; '"Honorary marine," 13, gets last wish', *Long Beach Press Telegram*, 5 March 1985.

83 Reeves, *President Reagan*, xiii.

8 PRAGMATIC CONSERVATIVE

1 'Remarks at the Conservative Political Action Conference Dinner', 20 March 1981, APP-PPP.

2 Evans, Rowland, and Robert Novak, *The Reagan Revolution* (New York: Dutton, 1981).

3 'What he'd be like as president', *Fortune*, 19 May 1980, 78.

4 *RD* (20 May 1982), 86.

5 Hayward, Steven, 'Is the "age of Reagan" over?', in Dunn, Charles, ed., *The Enduring Reagan* (Lexington: University Press of Kentucky, 2009), 150.

6 Barrett, Laurence, *Gambling with History: Reagan in the White House* (Garden City NY: Doubleday, 1983), 7, 62.

7 White House Staff, *President Ronald Reagan's Initial Actions Project* (New York: Threshold, 2009), 5–6.

8 *AAL*, 333.

9 Ibid., 244; Greenberg, David, 'Hot for Coolidge', *Slate*, 10 November 2011. Available at http://www.slate.com/articles/life/history_lesson/2011/11/calvin_coolidge_why_are_republicans_so_obsessed_with_him_.html.

10 Hayward, Steven, *The Age of Reagan: The Conservative Counterrevolution 1980–1989* (New York: Crown Forum, 2009), 68–70.

11 'Address to the nation on the economy', 5 February 1981, APP-PPP.

12 'White House report on the program for economic recovery', 18 February 1981, APP-PPP.

13 Stockman, David, *The Triumph of Politics: Why the Reagan Revolution Failed* (New York: Harper & Row, 1986), chapters 1–3.

14 Sloan, John, *The Reagan Effect: Economics and Presidential Leadership* (Lawrence: University Press of Kansas, 1999), 122.

15 *AAL*, 233; Farrell, John, *Tip O'Neill and the American Century* (Boston: Little, Brown, 2001), 7; O'Neill, Tip, *Man of the House: The Life and Political Memoirs of Speaker Tip O'Neill* (New York: Random House, 1987), 330–1.

16 *AAL*, 250–1; Farrell, *Tip O'Neill*, 558, 563–70.

17 James Wright Diary [JWD], 29 April 1981, Texas Christian University [TCU]; *RD* (7 May 1981), 18.

18 Darman to Reagan, 'Meeting with the Legislative Strategy Group, June 18, 1981', 17 June 1981, WHSOF: Craig Fuller-OA10972.

19 *RD* (18 June, 1981), 25–6; Darman, Richard, 'Next steps on budget reconciliation', 18 June 1981, WHSOF: Craig Fuller-OA10972; 'Suggested talking points in telephone calls to congressmen (June–July 1981)', PHF: Telephone Calls-1.

20 Barrett, *Gambling with History*, 160–1.

21 *RD* (24–29 June 1981), 27; 'Remarks in Los Angeles at the taxpayers' association luncheon', 24 June 1981, APP-PPP.

22 James Wright Oral History, 13 February 1986, TCU.

23 Morgan, Iwan, *The Age of Deficits: Presidents and Unbalanced Budgets from Jimmy Carter to George W. Bush* (Lawrence: University Press of Kansas, 2009), 89–90.

24 Hayward, *Conservative Counterrevolution*, 161; Ippolito, Dennis, *Deficits, Debt, and the New Politics of Tax Policy* (New York: Cambridge University Press, 2012), 115–20.

25 Weidenbaum, Murray, 'Reagan and economic policy-making', in Thompson, Kenneth, ed., *Reagan and the Economy: Nine Intimate Perspectives* (Lanham MD: University Press of America, 1994), 7; David Gergen to Jim Baker, Mike Deaver, and Ed Meese, 'The tax cut', 18 May 1981, WHSOF: Craig Fuller-OA10972.

26 *RD* (25, 26, 27, 28, and 29 July 1981), 33–4; 'Address to the nation on federal tax reduction', 27 July 1981, APP-PPP; 'Tracking the great persuader', *Time*, 10 August 1981.

27 JWD, 29 July 1981; Farrell, *Tip O'Neill*, 561; Hayward, *Conservative Counterrevolution*, 163.

28 McCartin, Joseph, *Collision Course: Ronald Reagan, the Air Traffic Controllers, and the Strike that Changed America* (New York: Oxford University Press, 2011).

29 *AAL*, 282–3; Reagan to Mrs Browning, September 1981, PHF:R–1.

30 'Monetary policy: Paul Volcker', in Feldstein, Martin, ed., *American Economic Policy in the 1980s* (Chicago: University of Chicago Press, 1994), 162.

31 McCartin, *Collision Course*, 348; Lehmann, Chris, 'Winging it: the battle between Reagan and PATCO', *The Nation*, 21 March 2012. Available at http://www.thenation.com/article/winging-it-battle-between-reagan-and-patco/.

32 Tolchin, Martin, 'The troubles of Tip O'Neill', *NYT Magazine*, 16 August 1981.

33 Stockman, *Triumph of Politics*, 269–99; Darman, Richard, *Who's in Control?: Polar Politics and the Sensible Center* (New York: Simon & Schuster, 1996), 93–7.

34 Baker, James, *'Work Hard, Study... and Keep Out of Politics!' Adventures and Lessons from an Unexpected Life* (New York: Putnam, 2006), 179–82; Darman, *Who's in Control?*, 98–100; Stockman, *Triumph of Politics*, 306–21 [quotation 319].

35 Stockman, *Triumph of Politics*, 6.

36 Greider, William, 'The education of David Stockman', *Atlantic Monthly* (December 1981), 27–54.

37 Morgan, Iwan, 'Monetary metamorphosis: the Volcker Fed and inflation', *Journal of Policy History*, 24 (October 2012), 546–71.

38 Donald Regan to the president, 'Current monetary policy', 12 May 1981, White House Office of Records Management [WHORM]: Cabinet Meetings-FG010-01.

39 Volcker, Paul, and Toyoo Gyohten, *Changing Fortunes: The World's Money and the Threat to America's Leadership* (New York: Crown, 1992), 175; Lawrence Kudlow to James Baker, 30 January 1982, WHSOF: Craig Fuller-OA13258.

40 Regan, Donald, *For the Record: From Wall Street to Washington* (San Diego: Harcourt Brace Jovanovich, 1988), 172–3, 178; Reagan to Justin Dart, 12 April 1982, and to Alfred Kingon, 25 June 1982, PHF:R–3.

41 Stockman, *Triumph of Politics*, 353.

42 'A test of wills', *US News & World Report*, 22 February 1982.

43 'GOP fears loss of senate: Reagan told rising deficits pose a threat to majority', *Kansas City Times*, 17 March 1982; Transcript of Dole remarks on *Face the Nation*, 28 February 1982, Robert J. Dole Senate Paper [RJDSP]-28, Robert J. Dole Institute of Politics [RJDIP].

44 *RD* (9, 10, 18, 19 August 1982), 97–9; Farrell, *Tip O'Neill*, 589.

45 Reuss, Henry, 'Supply-side's sunk', *NYT*, 30 August 1982.

46 House Republicans (61 signatories) to Reagan, 27 July 1982, WHSOC: M. B. Oglesby-OA8619.

47 *AAL*, 314–15; Meese, Edwin, *With Reagan: The Inside Story* (Washington DC: Regnery, 1992), 143–7.

48 Senator Ernest Hollings to Reagan, 10 March 1982, WHSOC: Craig Fuller-OA10972; *RD* (28 April 1982), 82; Reagan to Dole, 2 June 1982, RJDSP-7, RJDIP.

49 'Address to the nation on federal tax and budget reconciliation legislation', 16 August 1982, APP-PPP.

50 Transcripts of Federal Open Market Committee Meetings, 18 May, 5 October 1982. Available at http://www.federalreserve.gov/monetarypolicy/fomc_historical.htm; 'Radio address to the nation on the economy', 28 August 1982, APP-PPP.

51 Cabinet Council on Economic Affairs to Reagan, 'Balanced budget-tax limitation constitutional amendment', 19 April 1982, WHORM: Cabinet Meetings-3; 'Remarks at a rally supporting the proposed constitutional amendment for a balanced federal budget', 19 July 1982, APP-PPP; 'Making amends', *Time*, 12 August 1982.

52 Farrell, *Tip O'Neill*, 596–7.

53 Greenspan, Alan, *The Age of Turbulence: Adventures in a New World* (New York: Penguin, 2007), 94–6; Derthick, Martha, and Steven Teles, 'Riding the third rail: social security reform', in Brownlee, Elliot, and Hugh Davis Graham, eds, *The Reagan Presidency: Pragmatic Conservatism and Its Legacies* (Lawrence: University Press of Kansas, 2003), 196–204.

54 'Remarks on signing the social security amendments of 1983', 20 April 1983, APP-PPP.

55 Martin Feldstein to Reagan, 'The new economic forecast', 30 December 1982, and 'Alternative deficit forecasts', 13 January 1983, WHSOF: Martin Feldstein-OA9815; Darman, *Who's in Control?*, 118.

56 'Big deficit cut urged by US leaders', *NYT*, 20 January 1983; 'The federal deficit', *NYT*, 23 January 1983.

57 Darman, *Who's in Control?*, 118–19.

58 Sloan, *Reagan Effect*, 229–32.

59 Moynihan, Daniel Patrick, 'Reagan's bankrupt budget', *New Republic*, 31 December 1983, 18–21; Moynihan to Wright, 27 January 1984, James Wright Papers-724, TCU; Morgan, *Age of Deficits*, 92.

60 Darman, *Who's in Control?*, 64.

61 *RD* (7 January 1982), 61.

62 Richard Williamson to James Baker and Michael Deaver, 'Our deteriorating relations

with state and local officials', 16 November 1981, WHSOF: Michael Deaver-OA7621; Snelling to Reagan, 4 December, 16 December 1981, PHF:R–1.

63   *RD* (11 January 1982), 61, (3 January 1983), 123.

64   Wirthlin to Meese, Baker, and Deaver, 'Federal deficits', 30 August 1983, WHSOF: Michael Deaver-OA11584; Morgan, *Age of Deficits*, 105.

65   Feldstein, Martin, Memorandum to the President, 'Tax increases and economic recovery', 18 October 1983, 'Deficits and inflation', 8 January 1984, 'Tax rates and tax revenues', 10 January 1984, WHSOF: Martin Feldstein-OA9815; *RD* (9 January 1984), 210.

66   Allitt, Patrick, *A Climate of Crisis: America in the Age of Environmentalism* (New York: Penguin, 2014), 161–5.

67   *RD* (6 July 1981), 40; Reagan to Buckley, 15 July 1981, O'Connor to Reagan, 13 October 1981, PHF:R–1.

68   'US conservatives on the march: religious right optimistic', *Christian Science Monitor*, 19 March 1986.

69   Steuerle, Eugene, *The Tax Decade: How Taxes Came to Dominate the Public Agenda* (Washington DC: Urban Institute, 1992), 194–6.

70   Morgan, 'Monetary metamorphosis', 561–2.

71   Burns to Reagan, 20 January 1984, Reagan to Burns, 22 February 1984, PHF:R–8; Krippner, Greta, *Capitalizing on Crisis: The Political Origins of the Rise of Finance* (Cambridge MA: Harvard University Press, 2011).

72   'Address before a joint session of Congress on the state of the nation', 25 January 1984, APP-PPP.

9   COLD WARRIOR

1   Allen, Richard, 'The man who changed the game plan', *The National Interest* (summer 1996). Available at http://nationalinterest.org/article/the-man-who-changed-the-game-plan-471.

2   Kennan, George, *The Nuclear Delusion: Soviet–American Relations in the Atomic Age* (New York: Pantheon, 1982), xxiv.

3   'Memo of conversation: president's working lunch with Agostino Cardinal Casaroli', 15 December 1981, *TRF-NSC*.

4   'Address at commencement exercises at the University of Notre Dame', 17 May 1981, APP-PPP.

5   'Address to members of the British Parliament', 8 June 1982, APP-PPP; Reagan, Ronald, *Speaking My Mind: Selected Speeches* (New York: Simon & Schuster, 1989), 108.

6   Krauthammer, Charles, 'Essay: the Reagan doctrine', *Time*, 1 April 1985, 54–5; Pach, Chester, 'The Reagan doctrine: principle, pragmatism, and policy', *Presidential Studies Quarterly*, 36 (March 2006), 75–88.

7   NSDD-75, 17 January 1983. Available at https://www.reaganlibrary.archives.gov/archives/reference/NSDDs.html.

8   'The president's news conference', 29 January 1981, APP-PPP; Dobrynin, Anatoly, *In Confidence: Moscow's Ambassador to America's Six Cold War Presidents* (New York: Times Books, 1995), 490–1; Haig to Reagan, 'My forthcoming meetings with Soviet Minister Gromyko', 18 September 1981, NSC-ES:HoSF-37.

9   Casey to Reagan, 'Progress at the CIA', 6 May 1981, PHF:R–1; Gates, Robert, *From the*

Shadows: The Ultimate Insider's Story of Five Presidents and How They Won the Cold War (New York: Simon & Schuster, 2007), 256.

10   'Address before a joint session of the Irish parliament', 4 June 1984, APP-PPP.

11   NSC-1: 'The Caribbean Basin; Poland', 6 February 1981, *TRF-NSC*.

12   NSC-142: 'South American democracy', 13 March 1987, *TRF-NSC*; Meyer, Karl, 'The elusive Lenin', *NYT*, 8 October 1985; *AAL*, 474.

13   Smith, Christian, *Resisting Reagan: The US Central America Peace Movement* (Chicago: University of Chicago Press, 1999), 9.

14   Richard Allen to Reagan, 'El Salvador: external assistance to the left', 28 January 1981, NSC-ES:CF-30.

15   *From Madness to Hope: The 12-Year War in El Salvador, Report of the UN Truth Commission on El Salvador*, 1 April 1993. Available at http://www.derechos.org/nizkor/salvador/informes/truth.html.

16   'Address before a joint session of the Congress on Central America', 27 April 1983, AAP-PPP.

17   Gates, *From the Shadows*, 254–5; *RD* (5 August 1981), 35; *AAL*, 288–91.

18   *AAL*, 410–12.

19   *RD* (14 September 1981), 38; 'The president's press conference', 1 October 1981, APP-PPP.

20   Reagan to Billy Graham, 5 October 1981, PHF:R–1; *AAL*, 411, 416.

21   Schweizer, Peter, *Reagan's War: The Epic Story of His Forty-Year Struggle and Final Triumph over Communism* (New York: Doubleday, 2002), 239–41.

22   Gates, *From the Shadows*, 251; *RD* (7 December 1982), 117.

23   Pipes, Richard, *Vixi: Memoirs of a Non-Belonger* (New Haven CT: Yale University Press, 2003), 171; NSC-33: 'Poland', 21 December 1981, *TRF-NSC*; *RD* (21 December 1981), 57.

24   Reagan to Brezhnev 23 December 1981, Brezhnev to Reagan, 25 December 1981, *TRF-RGSL*.

25   'Memo of conversation: president's working lunch with Agostino Cardinal Casaroli', 15 December 1981, *TRF-NSC*; Reagan to Pope John Paul II, 17 December, 29 December 1981, Pope John Paul II to Reagan, 10 January 1982, William Clark to Reagan, 'Reply from the Pope on Poland', 11 January 1982, NSC-ES:HoSF-41.

26   Weigel, George, *Witness to Hope: The Biography of Pope John Paul II* (New York: HarperCollins, 1991), 441.

27   NSC-23: 'East-West trade controls, USSR, oil', 16 October 1981, *TRF-NSC*; Reed, Thomas, *At the Abyss: An Insider's History of the Cold War* (New York: Ballantine Books, 2004), 266–70.

28   NSC-34: 'Poland', 22 December 1981, *TRF-NSC*.

29   Thatcher, Margaret, *The Downing Street Years* (London: HarperCollins, 1993), 253–6; Haig to Reagan, 29 January 1982, Thatcher to Reagan, 29 January 1982, NSC-ES: HoSF-34.

30   NSC-51: 'East–West sanctions', 18 June 1982, *TRF-NSC*; 'Statement on the extension of United States sanctions on the export of oil and gas equipment to the Soviet Union', 18 June 1982, APP-PPP.

31   Aldous, John, *Reagan and Thatcher: The Difficult Relationship* (London: Hutchinson, 2012), 67–8; Thatcher, *The Downing Street Years*, 256.

32 Thatcher to Reagan, 25 June 1982, Reagan to Thatcher, 2 July 1982, NSC-ES:HoSF-35.
33 Weiss, Gus, 'Duping the Soviets: the Farewell dossier', *Studies in Intelligence*, 39/5 (1996), 121–6.
34 Reagan to Thatcher, 1 April 1982, MTF, docid=109265.
35 James Rentschler's Falklands Diary, 1 April–25 June 1982 (8 April), MTF; 'Remarks at a question-and-answer session on the program for economic recovery with editors and broadcasters from Midwestern states', 30 April 1982, APP-PPP.
36 Freedman, Lawrence, *The Official History of the Falklands Campaign* (London: Routledge, 2005), Vol. II, 359.
37 The Falklands Roundtable, RROH-MC.
38 Thatcher to Reagan, 29 April 1982: MTF, docid=122038; Reagan to Thatcher, 29 April 1982, MTF, docid=122041.
39 James Rentschler and Roger Fontaine to William Clark, 'The Falklands Islands: What Now? What Next?' James Rentschler's Falklands Diary, 1 April–25 June 1982 (4 May), MTF; Thatcher, *The Downing Street Years*, 221; Aldous, *Reagan and Thatcher*, 97–8.
40 'UK–Argentine War', NSC Paper, n.d., WHSOF: Dennis Blair-OA90223; Thatcher, *The Downing Street Years*, 231; Henderson, Nicholas, *Mandarin: The Diaries of Nicholas Henderson* (London: Weidenfeld & Nicolson, 1994), 466–7.
41 Reagan to Thatcher, 18 June 1982, MTF, docid=109363.
42 Reagan to Thatcher, 2 November 1982, MTF, docid=109269; Shultz, George, *Turmoil and Triumph: My Years as Secretary of State* (New York: Scribner's, 1993), 162–3.
43 'Remarks at a question-and-answer session at a working luncheon with out-of-town editors', 16 October 1981, APP-PPP; 'Nuclear war a real prospect to Reagan hard-liners', *Chicago Sun-Times*, 4 October 1981.
44 NSC-25: 'Theater nuclear forces, NATO, strategic forces', 12 November 1981, *TRF-NSC*.
45 'Remarks to members of the National Press Club on arms reduction and nuclear Weapons', 18 November 1981, APP-PPP; Hayward, Steven, *The Age of Reagan: The Conservative Counterrevolution 1980–1989* (New York: Crown Forum, 2009), 241.
46 Pope John-Paul II to Reagan, 25 November 1981, Reagan to the Pope, 11 January 1982, NSC-ES:HoSF-41.
47 Reagan to Thatcher, 15, 16, and 20 June 1983: MTF, docid = 109273, 109330, 109331.
48 *AAL*, 586.
49 Morris, Edmund, *Dutch: A Memoir of Ronald Reagan* (New York: HarperCollins, 1999), 472; Dolan, Anthony, 'Premeditated prose: Reagan's evil empire', *The American Enterprise* (March/April, 1993), 24–6; 'Address to the National Association of Evangelicals', 8 March 1983, APP-PPP.
50 Kengor, Paul, *God and Ronald Reagan: A Spiritual Life* (New York: Regan Books, 2004), 254–5.
51 'Onward Christian soldiers', *NYT*, 10 March 1983; 'Reverend Reagan', *New Republic*, 4 April, 1983; Weinberger, Caspar, RROH-MC.
52 Reagan to Barton Hartzell, 11 January 1982, PHF:R–2; *AAL*, 569–70; Bialer, Selwyn, 'Danger in Moscow', *New York Review of Books*, 16 December 1984.
53 'Address to the nation on strategic arms reduction and nuclear deterrence', 22 November 1982, APP-PPP.
54 'Address to the nation on defense and national security', 23 March 1983, APP-PPP.

55   Reagan to Dr Gerald Broussard, 15 February 1988, PHF:R–20; *AAL*, 550.

56   *AAL*, 547; Lettow, Paul, *Ronald Reagan and His Quest to Abolish Nuclear Weapons* (New York: Random House, 2005).

57   Reagan to Roy Innis, 20 June 1983, to Patrick Mulvey, 20 June 1983, PHF:R–6, and to Lawrence Beilenson, 25 July 1983, PHF:R–7.

58   Michael Berta to Richard Allen, 'Space-based lasers', 23 April 1981, and 'Final report to the president of the high frontier panel', 8 January 1982, NSC-ES:SF-13.

59   Teller, Edward, *Memoirs: A Twentieth Century Journey in Science and Politics* (Cambridge MA: Perseus, 2002), 509, 525–33; Teller to Reagan, 23 July 1982, Reagan comment written on George Keyworth to William Clark, 29 July 1982, PHF:R–4.

60   McFarlane, Robert, *Special Trust* (London: Cadell & Davies, 1994), 230–2.

61   Keyworth, George, RROH-MC; Shultz, *Turmoil and Triumph*, 252–3; *RD* (23 March 1983), 139–40.

62   Kengor, Paul, *The Crusader: Ronald Reagan and the Fall of Communism* (New York: HarperCollins, 2006), 179–80, 205–8, 317–20.

63   Shultz, *Turmoil and Triumph*, 259; Thatcher, *The Downing Street Years*, 463.

64   'Excerpts from the interview with Andropov', *NYT*, 27 March 1983; Reagan to Victor Krulak, 5 September 1985, PHF:R–13.

65   Keyworth, George, RROH-MC; Aldous, *Reagan and Thatcher*, 193–6.

66   Strober, Gerald, and Deborah Hart Strober, *Reagan: The Man and His Presidency* (London: Houghton Mifflin, 1998), 248.

67   Reagan to Thatcher, 19 August 1983, NSC-ES:HoSF-35.

68   Thatcher, *The Downing Street Years*, 463; Palazchenko, Pavel, *My Years with Gorbachev and Shevardnadze: The Memoir of a Soviet Interpreter* (University Park: Pennsylvania State University Press, 1997), 41; Gates, *From the Shadows*, 264.

69   Reagan to William Buckley, 5 January 1984, and to Paul Trousdale, 20 February 1984, PHF:R–8.

70   *AAL*, 425–9; *RD* (2, 4, and 12 August, 1982), 95–8.

71   Reagan to Fred Ehrman, 25 October 1982, PHF:R–4; *AAL*, 430–5; 'Address to the nation on United States policy for peace in the Middle East', 1 September 1982, APP-PPP.

72   Shultz, *Turmoil and Triumph*, 105; *RD* (19 September 1982), 101.

73   *RD* (19 October 1982), 106.

74   Ibid. (7 September 1983), 177, (11 September 1983), 178–9.

75   Ibid. (19 September 1983), 180; Powell, Colin, *My American Journey* (New York: Random House, 1995), 291.

76   Norton, Augustus Richard, *Hezbollah: A Short History* (Princeton NJ: Princeton University Press, 2007).

77   *RD* (19 April, 23 April, 1983), 146–7.

78   Hoffman, David, *The Dead Hand: Reagan, Gorbachev and the Untold Story of the Cold War Arms Race* (New York: Doubleday, 2009), 93.

79   Frank, Benis, *U.S. Marines in Lebanon 1982–1984*. Available at http://www.ibiblio.org/hyperwar/AMH/XX/MidEast/Lebanon-1982-1984; Geraghty, Timothy, *Peacekeepers at War: Beirut 1983 – The Marine Commander Tells His Story* (Dulles VA: Potomac Books, 2009).

80   *AAL*, 464–5; *RD* (1 December 1983), 201.

81 *RD* (3–4, 5 December), 202–3.
82 'Interview with the *Wall Street Journal* on foreign and domestic issues', 2 February 1984, APP-PPP.
83 Cannon, Lou, *President Reagan: The Role of a Lifetime* (New York: Simon & Schuster, 1991), 454–7.
84 Reagan to Reverend Andrew Carhartt, 12 March 1982, PHF:R–2; Reagan to Mr and Mrs Joseph Smith, 3 November 1984, PHF:R–10.
85 Powell, *American Journey*, 280.
86 *Report of the DoD Commission on Beirut International Airport Terrorist Attack on October 23, 1983*, 20 December 1983. Available at http://www.ibiblio.org/hyperwar/AMH/XX/MidEast/Lebanon-1982-1984.
87 Reagan to MNF heads of state, 3 February 1984, NSC-ES:HoSF-35.
88 Shultz, *Turmoil and Triumph*, 329; *AAL*, 449–50; 'President's telephone conversation with Prime Minister Hawke of Australia', 25 October 1983, *TRF-NSC*.
89 *RD* (21 [*sic*] October 1983), 189.
90 Powell, *American Journey*, 292; Reagan to Justin Dart, 17 November 1983, PHF:R–7.
91 *AAL*, 456–7.
92 Leonard Garment to Reagan, 21 December 1983, PHF:R–8.
93 Reagan to Thatcher, 24 October, 24 October, and 25 October 1983, MTF, docid=109428, 109429, 109430; Thatcher, *The Downing Street Years*, 328–32.
94 *RD* (24 October 1983), 190; Reagan telephone call to Thatcher, 26 October 1983, MTF, docid=109426; Thatcher, *The Downing Street Years*, 332–3.
95 Shultz, *Turmoil and Triumph*, 336–40.
96 Hoffman, *Dead Hand*, 72–6.
97 *MT*, 260; *RD* (5 September 1983), 176–7; 'Address to the nation on the Soviet attack on the Korean civilian airliner', 5 September 1983, APP-PPP.
98 *AAL*, 584–5; Hoffman, *Dead Hand*, 6–11.
99 *RD* (10 October 1983), 185–6; 'An audience of 100 million – how ABC built it', *US News & World Report*, 5 December 1983.
100 *RD* (18 November 1983), 199; *AAL*, 586.
101 Hoffman, *Dead Hand*, 136–40.
102 Andropov to Leonid Brezhnev, 'Report on the work of the KGB in 1981', 10 May 1982, and Andropov to Victor Chebrikov, 'Report on the work of the KGB in 1982', 15 March 1983, Document [D]-8, 'The 1983 war scare: "the last paroxysm" of the Cold War', NSAEBB-426, Part I. Available at http://nsarchive.gwu.edu/NSAEBB/NSAEBB426/.
103 Hoffman, *Dead Hand*, 54–6; KGB Headquarters Moscow to the London KGB Residency, 'Permanent operational assignment to uncover NATO preparations for a nuclear missile attack on the USSR', plus enclosures, 17 February 1983, Top Secret, D-9, NSAEBB-426, I; 'Memorandum of a conversation between General Secretary Yuri Andropov and Averell Harriman, 3.00 PM, June 2, 1983, CPSU Central Committee Headquarters, Moscow', D-14, NSAEBB-426, I.
104 Gates, *From the Shadows*, 270–3; Hoffman, *Dead Hand*, 86–100.
105 'The Soviet "war scare"', 15 February 1990, in 'The 1983 war scare declassified and for real', NSAEBB-533. Available at http://nsarchive.gwu.edu/nukevault/ebb533-The-Able-Archer-War-Scare-Declassified-PFIAB-Report-Released/.
106 *RD* (18 November 1983), 199.

107 *AAL*, 588–9.

108 Shultz, *Turmoil and Triumph*, 376.

10 MORNING MAN

1 'Address before a joint session of the Congress on the state of the union', 6 February 1985, APP-PPP.

2 *AAL*, 325; *MT*, 264–5.

3 Wilcox, Clyde, and Dee Alsop, 'Economic and foreign policy as sources of Reagan support', *Western Political Quarterly*, 44 (December 1991), 941–58; Wirthlin, Dick, *The Greatest Communicator: What Ronald Reagan Taught Me about Politics, Leadership, and Life* (Hoboken NJ: Wiley, 2004), 138.

4 'Men of the year', *Time*, 1 January 1984, 32; 'Address to the nation and other countries on US–Soviet relations', 16 January 1984, APP-PPP.

5 Reagan to Thatcher, 15 January 1984, NSC-ES:HoSF-35.

6 Matlock, Jack, *Reagan and Gorbachev: How the Cold War Ended* (New York: Random House, 2004), 87; Reagan to Suzanne Massie, 15 February 1984, PHF:R–8.

7 McFarlane, Robert, 'Chernenko letter of February 23, 1984, and the paper on a framework for US–Soviet relations', 28 February 1984, NSC-ES:SF-12; *RD* (14 June 1984), 247.

8 'Summary of president's meeting with German Defense Minister Woerner, 13 July 1984', NSC-ES:SF-52; Oberdorfer, Don, *From the Cold War to a New Era: The United States and the Soviet Union, 1983–1991* (Baltimore MD: Johns Hopkins University Press, 1998), 84–7.

9 *RD* (28 September 1984), 270; Gromyko, Andrei, *Memoirs* (New York: Doubleday, 1989), 308–9; Reagan to Thatcher, 3 October 1984, NSC-ES:HoSF-36.

10 'Address accepting the presidential nomination at the Democratic National Convention in San Francisco', 19 July 1984, APP-PPP.

11 Wirthlin, Richard, 'The tax issue', n.d., WHSOF: James Baker-OA10514; 'Statement expressing opposition to a federal tax increase', 12 August 1984, APP-PPP.

12 Morgan, Iwan, *The Age of Deficits: Presidents and Unbalanced Budgets from Jimmy Carter to George W. Bush* (Lawrence: University Press of Kansas, 2009), 106–7.

13 'Address to the nation on the eve of the presidential election', 5 November 1984, APP-PPP.

14 Yankelovich, Daniel, and John Doble, 'Nuclear weapons and the USSR: the public mood', *Foreign Affairs*, 63 (fall 1984). Available at https://www.foreignaffairs.com/articles/russian-federation/1984-09-01/nuclear-weapons-and-ussr-public-mood; Oberdorfer, *Cold War to New Era*, 85–6, 95.

15 Wirthlin, *The Greatest Communicator*, 143–5, 149–50.

16 Ibid., 150–3; Baker, James, *'Work Hard, Study… and Keep Out of Politics!' Adventures and Lessons from an Unexpected Public Life* (New York: Putnam, 2006), 207–8.

17 *MT*, 266; *RD* (6–7 October 1984), 271; Reagan to Earl Smith, 30 October 1984, PHF:R–10.

18 *RD* (20 October 1984), 273.

19 'Debate between the president and former Vice President Walter F. Mondale in Kansas City, Missouri', 21 October 1984, APP-PPP.

20 'Minnesota heads Reagan's wish list', Associated Press, 4 December 1984; *RD* (21–24 October 1984), 272; Roper Center, 'How groups voted in 1984'. Available at

http://ropercenter.cornell.edu/polls/us-elections/how-groups-voted/how-groups-voted-1984/.

21 Buckley, William, 'The blandification of Ronald Reagan', *National Review*, 6 April 1984; Mason, Robert, *The Republican Party and American Politics from Hoover to Reagan* (New York: Cambridge University Press, 2012), 263–4.

22 Hayward, Steven, *The Age of Reagan: The Conservative Counterrevolution 1980–1989* (New York: Crown Forum, 2009), 389.

23 Andriote, John-Manuel, *Victory Deferred: How AIDS Changed Gay Life in America* (Chicago: University of Chicago Press, 1999), 27–8, 48–9.

24 'HIV and AIDS – United States, 1981–2000', Center for Disease Control, MMWR [Morbidity and Mortality Weekly Report], 1 June 2001. Available at https://www.cdc.gov/mmwr/preview/mmwrhtml/mm5021a2.htm.

25 Kramer, Larry, 'Adolf Reagan', *The Advocate*, 6 July 2004. See also White, Allen, 'Reagan's AIDS legacy/silence equals death', 8 June 2004. Available at http://www.sfgate.com/opinion/openforum/article/Reagan-s-AIDS-Legacy-Silence-equals-death-2751030.php.

26 Turner, William, '"Adolph Reagan?" Ronald Reagan and lesbian/gay rights', 13 July 2009, *Social Science Research Network*. Available at http://papers.ssrn.com/sol3/papers.cfm?abstract_id=1433567; handwritten note, no author, n.d., in folder 'Homosexuals/gay rights', WHSOF-Doug Bandow-6; Reagan to Victor Krulak, 30 October 1984, PHF:R–10.

27 Cannon, Carl, 'Ronald Reagan and AIDS: correcting the record', *Real Clear Politics*, 1 June 2014. Available at http://www.realclearpolitics.com/articles/2014/06/01/ronald_reagan_and_aids_correcting_the_record_122806.html; 'The president's news conference', 17 September 1985, and 'Remarks to employees of the department of health and human services', 5 February 1986, APP-PPP.

28 Shilts, Randy, *And the Band Plays On: Politics, People, and the AIDS Epidemic* (New York: St Martin's Press, 1987), 297; Johnson, Judith, *AIDS Funding for Federal Government Programs: FY1981–FY 2001* (Washington DC: Congressional Research Service, 2000).

29 Sullivan, Andrew, 'Reagan did not give me HIV', *The Advocate*, 18 June 2004.

30 C. Peters to Reagan, 7 October 1987, Reagan to C. Peters, 21 October 1987, PHF:R–19.

31 Rossinow, Doug, *The Reagan Era: A History of the 1980s* (New York: Columbia University Press, 2015), 212–14.

32 Anderson to Mari Maseng, 28 May 1987, in Geidner, Chris, 'Nancy Reagan turned down Rock Hudson's pleas for help nine weeks [*sic*] before he died', *BuzzFeed News* (posted 3 February 2015). Available at https://www.buzzfeed.com/chrisgeidner/nancy-reagan-turned-down-rock-hudsons-plea-for-help-seven-we?utm_term=.gg4YPEZ2X#.vipn4vmwq.

33 Cannon, Lou, *President Reagan: The Role of a Lifetime* (New York: Simon & Schuster, 1991), 816–18.

34 Mark Weinberg, Memorandum for Bill Martin, 24 July 1985, in Geidner, 'Nancy Reagan'.

35 Elizabeth Taylor to Reagan, 9 October 1985, Reagan to Taylor, 16 October 1985, PHF:R–13.

36 Reagan, Ronald, 'A tribute to a life cut short', *Washington Post*, 15 April 1990.

37 Bound, John and Richard Freeman, 'What went wrong? The erosion of relative earnings and employment among young black men in the 1980s', National Bureau of Economic Research Working Paper, 3778 (July 1991). Available at http://www.nber.org/papers/w3778; Mauer, Marc, 'The crisis of the young African American male and the criminal

justice system', April 1999. Available at http://www.sentencingproject.org/wp-content/uploads/2016/01/Crisis-of-the-Young-African-American-Male-and-the-Criminal-Justice-System.pdf.

38   Edsall, Thomas, and Susan Edsall, *Chain Reaction: The Impact of Race, Rights, and Taxes on American Politics* (New York: Norton, 1991), 148.

39   Schull, Stephen, *A Kinder, Gentler Racism? The Reagan–Bush Civil Rights Legacy* (Armonk NY: M. E. Sharpe, 1993).

40   Cannon, Lou, *President Reagan: The Role of a Lifetime* (New York: Simon & Schuster, 1991), 462.

41   Reagan to Thomson, 3 October 1983, PHF:R–7; 'Reagan calls Mrs King to explain', *Washington Post*, 22 October 1983.

42   *RD* (3 May 1982), 83, and (21 December 1982), 121; *RALIL*, 747–8.

43   Reagan to NAACP executive director Benjamin Hooks, 12 January 1983, PHF:R–5; 'Rights group leader calls Reagan racist', *NYT*, 19 May 1985.

44   'Justice Marshall rips Reagan', *NYT*, 9 September 1987; *RD* (17 November 1987), 549.

45   Reagan, Ronald, *Speaking My Mind: Selected Speeches* (New York: Simon & Schuster, 1989), 163. See also Reagan to Donald Wilson, 28 January 1985, PHF:R–11.

46   Graham, Hugh Davis, 'The storm over Grove City College: civil rights regulation, higher education, and the Reagan administration', *History of Education Quarterly*, 38 (Winter 1998), 407–29.

47   NSC 119: 'South Africa', 26 July 1985, *TRF-NSC*.

48   Reagan to Joan Joyce Sellers, 28 January 1985, PHF:R–11, and to Henry Salvatori, 15 October 1985, PHF:R–14.

49   'Hill panel gives Tutu rare ovation', *Washington Post*, 5 December 1984; *RD* (7 December 1984), 285.

50   Nesbitt, Francis Nuji, *Race for Sanctions: African Americans against Apartheid, 1946–1994* (Bloomington: Indiana University Press, 2004), 123–56.

51   Reagan to Sammy Davis Jr, 24 June 1986, PHF:R–16.

52   'South Africa gets off too easy under Reagan's limited sanctions', *Washington Post*, 10 September 1985; 'Remarks to members of the World Affairs Council and the Foreign Policy Association', 22 July 1986, APP-PPP.

53   'Message to the House of Representatives returning without approval a bill concerning apartheid in South Africa', 26 September 1986, APP-PPP; 'Senate, 78–21, overrides Reagan's veto and imposes sanctions on South Africa', *NYT*, 3 October 1986.

54   'Nelson Mandela: a special message to African Americans', *Ebony*, May 1990; 'Reagan regretted vetoing sanctions against pro-apartheid South Africa', *New York Daily News*, 8 December 2013; Reagan to John Kehoe, 10 August 1987, PHF:R–18.

55   *AAL*, 325; Reagan to Charles Price, 29 November 1984, PHF:R–10.

56   Morgan, *The Age of Deficits*, 107–9.

57   'Radio address to the nation on the federal budget', 22 June 1985, APP-PPP.

58   Morgan, *The Age of Deficits*, 109; 'GOP rift widens as Dole criticizes Reagan and House', *NYT*, 13 July 1985.

59   Rudman, Warren, *Combat: Twelve Years in the US Senate* (New York: Random House, 1996), 79–80.

60   Farrier, Jasmine, *Passing the Buck: Congress, the Budget, and Deficits* (Lexington: University Press of Kentucky, 2004), 82–128.

61 Morgan, *The Age of Deficits*, 110–12.

62 *AAL*, 336.

63 *RD* (3 July 1987), 513; 'Remarks announcing America's bill of economic rights', 3 July 1987, APP-PPP.

64 'A convention that's uncalled for', *NYT*, 13 August 1987; Morgan, *The Age of Deficits*, 117–18; author's interview with David Keating, National Taxpayers Union vice-president.

65 Regan, Donald, *For the Record: From Wall Street to Washington* (San Diego: Harcourt Brace Jovanovich, 1988), 192–6, 212–13.

66 Regan to Reagan, 27 November 1984, PHF:R–10, and Baker to Reagan, 10 May 1985, PHF:R–11.

67 'Address to the nation on tax reform', 28 May 1985, APP-PPP; Beryl Sprinkel to Donald Regan, 'Tax reform priorities', 9 July 1986, WHSOF: Beryl Sprinkel-OA17746.

68 Birnbaum, Jeffrey, and Allan Murray, *Showdown at Gucci Gulch: Lawmakers, Lobbyists, and the Unlikely Triumph of Tax Reform* (New York: Vantage Books, 1988).

69 Brownlee, Elliot, and Eugene Stuerle, 'Taxation', in Brownlee, Elliot, and Hugh Davis Graham, eds, *The Reagan Presidency: Pragmatic Conservatism and Its Legacies* (Lawrence: University Press of Kansas, 2003), 168–74.

70 Niskanen, William, *Reaganomics: An Insider's Account of the Policies and the People* (New York: Oxford University Press, 1988), 99.

71 Hayward, *The Conservative Counterrevolution*, 513–14.

72 Ibid., 411–17; Wilentz, Sean, *The Age of Reagan: A History 1974–2008* (New York: HarperCollins, 2008), 190–4; Cannon, *President Reagan*, 802–3 n.

73 *RD* (6 July 1986), 513; Reagan to Lynn Siegel, 21 October 1987, PHF:R–19; 'Bork's nomination rejected 58–42: Reagan "saddened"', *NYT*, 23 October 1987.

74 *AAL*, 333; Anderson, Martin, *Revolution* (San Diego: Harcourt Brace Jovanovich, 1988), 175–6.

75 Morgan, Iwan, 'Monetary metamorphosis: the Volcker Fed and inflation', *Journal of Policy History*, 24 (December 2012), 562–3; Beryl Sprinkel to Reagan, 'Avoiding recession in 1988', 15 October 1987, WHSOF: Beryl Sprinkel-OA17737.

76 *RD* (20 October 1987), 540; 'Terrible Tuesday: how the stock market almost disintegrated', *Wall Street Journal*, 20 November 1987.

77 'Transcript of interview with President Reagan (1988)', Godfrey Hodgson Papers, Rothermere American Institute, Oxford; Friedman, Benjamin, *Day of Reckoning: The Consequences of American Economic Policy under Reagan and After* (New York: Random House, 1988).

78 'Remarks on signing the Garn–St Germain Depository Institutions Act of 1982', 15 October 1982, APP-PPP; Cannon, *President Reagan*, 824–8.

79 'The president's news conference', 28 June 1983, APP-PPP; Sloan, John, 'The economic costs of Reagan mythology', in Longley, Kyle, Jeremy Mayer, Michael Schaller, and John W. Sloan, *Deconstructing Reagan: Conservative Mythology and America's Fortieth President* (Armonk NY: M. E. Sharpe, 2007), 67.

80 Rossinow, *The Reagan Era*, 125, 208–9.

81 Cannon, *President Reagan*, 800–2.

82 Johnson, Haynes, *Sleepwalking through History: America in the Reagan Years* (New York: Norton, 1991), 170–84.

83 'Interview with the president', *Washington Post*, 25 February 1988.

84   Barlett, Donald, and James Steele, *America: What Went Wrong?* (Kansas City, MO: Andrews & McMeel, 1992); Peterson, Wallace, *Silent Depression: The Fate of the American Dream* (New York: Norton, 1994).

85   Congressional Budget Office, *Trends in Distribution of Household Income Between 1979 and 2007*, 25 October 2011. Available at https://www.cbo.gov/publication/42729.

86   Friedman, *Day of Reckoning*, 99–102; Collins, Robert, *Transforming America: Politics and Culture during the Reagan Years* (New York: Columbia University Press, 2007), 110–15.

87   See CEO Jack Welch's memoir, co-written with John Byrne, *Jack: Straight from the Gut* (New York: Warner, 2003).

11   IMPERIAL PRESIDENT

1   The most authoritative study is Byrne, Malcolm, *Iran–Contra: Reagan's Scandal and the Unchecked Abuse of Presidential Power* (Lawrence: University Press of Kansas, 2014).

2   Schlesinger, Arthur, *The Imperial Presidency* (Boston: Houghton Mifflin, 1973). See also Rudalevige, Andrew, *The New Imperial Presidency: Renewing Presidential Power after Watergate* (Ann Arbor: University of Michigan Press, 2005).

3   *RD* (26 April 1983), 148.

4   'Address before a joint session of the Congress on the state of the union', 6 February 1985, APP-PPP.

5   Smith, Christian, *Resisting Reagan: The U.S. Central America Peace Movement* (Chicago: University of Chicago Press, 1996). See too Witham, Nick, *The Cultural Left and the Reagan Era: US Protest and Central American Revolution* (London: I.B.Tauris, 2015).

6   NSDD-166: 'US policy, programs, and strategy in Afghanistan', 27 March 1985. Available at https://www.reaganlibrary.archives.gov/archives/reference/NSDDs.html.

7   *RD* (26 March 1985), 311.

8   Gates, Robert, *From the Shadows: The Ultimate Insider's Story of Five Presidents and How They Won the Cold War* (New York: Touchstone, 1996), 348–50.

9   Reagan to Henry Salvatori, 12 February 1986, PHF:R–14.

10 NSDD-212: 'US policy toward Angola', 10 February 1986. Available at https://www.reaganlibrary.archives.gov/archives/reference/NSDDs.html; Gates, *From the Shadows*, 346–7, 433–4.

11 *RD* (19 September 1985), 354.

12 Reagan to Henry Salvatori, 15 October 1985, PHF:R–13; *RD* (12 April 1988), 595.

13 Oral History Interviews, Association for Diplomatic Studies and Training. Available at http://adst.org/oral-history/oral-history-interviews/.

14 *AAL*, 474.

15 *RD* (24 September 1982), 102.

16 NSC 128: 'Review of US policy in Central America', 10 January 1986, *TRF-NSC*; Brutents, Karen, 'A new Soviet perspective', in Smith, Wayne, ed., *The Russians Aren't Coming: New Soviet Policy in Latin America* (Boulder CO: Lynne Rienner, 1992), 66–80.

17 NSC-24: 'Strategy towards Cuba and Central America', 10 November 1981, *TRF-NSC*; *RD* (1 December 1981), 52.

18 Gates, *From the Shadows*, 245–9 [quotation 247].

19 'A secret war for Nicaragua', *Newsweek*, 8 November 1982.

20 Byrne, *Iran–Contra*, 18–21, 24–5.

21 'Address to a joint session of Congress on Central America', 27 April 1983, APP-PPP; *RD* (26 June 1983), 163; *AAL*, 478.

22 'Remarks at the annual dinner of the Conservative Political Action Committee', 1 March 1985, APP-PPP; NSC-129A: 'Aid to the Nicaraguan Democratic Resistance', 20 March 1986, *TRF-NSC*.

23 Reagan to Charlton Heston, 10 May 1983, PHF:R–3; Reagan to William Wilson, 3 March 1987, PHF:R–17.

24 Reagan to Earl Smith, 4 April 1985, PHF:R–11.

25 For documentary evidence, see 'Public diplomacy and covert propaganda: the declassified record of Ambassador Otto Reich', NSAEBB-40. Available at http://nsarchive.gwu.edu/NSAEBB/NSAEBB40/.

26 'Address to the nation on United States policy in Nicaragua', 9 May 1984, APP-PPP.

27 *AAL*, 479.

28 White House, 'Presidential finding on covert operations in Nicaragua (with attached Scope Note)', Secret, 19 September 1983, Document [D]-1 in 'The Iran–Contra affairs 20 years on', NSAEBB-210. Available at http://nsarchive.gwu.edu/NSAEBB/NSAEBB210/; Oliver North and Constantine Menges, memorandum to Robert McFarlane, 'Special activities in Nicaragua', 2 March 1984, with notation 'RR briefed, 3/5, RCM', D-38 in 'Science, technology and the CIA', NSAEBB-54. Available at http://nsarchive.gwu.edu/NSAEBB/NSAEBB40/.

29 George Shultz to Reagan, 'Nicaragua ICJ case', 26 January 1984, and Nicholas Platt to Robert McFarlane, 'Decision to withdraw from ICJ case', 18 January 1985, NSC-ES:CF-33; *Nicaragua v. United States of America*, judgement of 27 June 1986. Available at http://www.icj-cij.org/docket/?sum=367&p1=3&p2=3&case=70&p3=5.

30 'Text of Goldwater's letter to the head of the CIA', *NYT*, 11 April 1984.

31 Public Law 98-473, Section 8066 (A), 1984.

32 McFarlane, Robert, *Special Trust* (New York: Cadell & Davis, 1994), 68–70.

33 NSPG 91: 'Central America', 25 June 1984, *TRF-NSC*.

34 Robert McFarlane, Memorandum for the President, 'Approach to the Hondurans regarding the Nicaraguan resistance', 19 February 1985, D-IC00858, National Security Digital Archives, http://nsarchive.gwu.edu/; Independent Counsel, Court Records, 'US government stipulation on quid pro quos with other governments as part of contra operations', 6 April 1989, D-11 in NSAEBB-210; McFarlane to Reagan, 'Recommended telephone call', Secret, 25 April 1985, D-5 in NSAEBB-210; *RD* (21 May 1985), 329.

35 Walsh, Laurence, *Iran–Contra: The Final Report* (New York: Times Books, 1994), 67–9, 455–6.

36 Mayer, Jane, and Doyle McManus, *Landslide: The Unmaking of President Reagan* (Glasgow: Fontana/Collins, 1989), 107–12.

37 Memorandum from Oliver North to Robert McFarlane, 'Fallback position for the Nicaraguan resistance', 16 March 1985, Top Secret, NSAEBB-210; Cannon, Lou, *President Reagan: The Role of a Lifetime* (New York: Simon & Schuster, 1991), 716.

38 NSC, 'Diagram [by Oliver North] of "Enterprise" for contra support', July 1986, D-7 in NSAEBB-210; Byrne, *Iran–Contra*, 49–53, 132–4. See also 'The Contras, cocaine, and covert operations', NSAEBB-2. Available at http://nsarchive.gwu.edu/NSAEBB/NSAEBB2/index.html.

39 Byrne, *Iran–Contra*, 33–8, 66–9.

40 NSPG-105: 'Response to threat to Lebanon hostages', 18 January 1985, *TRF-NSC*.
41 *AAL*, 493–9; Reeves, Richard, *President Reagan: The Triumph of Imagination* (New York: Simon & Schuster, 2005), 259–64.
42 'The president's news conference', 18 June 1985, and 'Remarks announcing the release of the hostages from the Trans World Airlines hijacking incident', 30 June 1985, APP-PPP; *RD* (29 June 1985), 339.
43 McFarlane, *Special Trust*, 26; *The Tower Commission Report: The Full Text of the President's Special Review Board* (New York: Bantam, 1987), 131; Morris, Edmund, *Dutch: A Memoir of Ronald Reagan* (London: HarperCollins, 1999), 604–7.
44 Byrne, *Iran–Contra*, 70–1.
45 Mayer and McManus, *Landslide*, 194–5.
46 'Remarks at the Annual Convention of the Bar Association', 8 July 1985, APP-PPP.
47 *AAL*, 505.
48 NSPG-97: 'Lebanon', 3 October 1984, *TRF-NSC*.
49 Mayer and McManus, *Landslide*, 155–8; McFarlane, *Special Trust*, 21–3.
50 *AAL*, 490
51 Byrne, *Iran–Contra*, 101–2.
52 CIA, Draft Presidential Finding, 'Scope: hostage rescue – Middle East' (with cover note from William Casey), 26 November 1985, D-3, NSAEBB-210.
53 Cannon, *President Reagan*, 629–31; *RD* (7 December 1985), 374–5; Diary entry, Caspar Weinberger, 7 December 1985, D-14, NSAEBB-210.
54 McFarlane, *Special Trust*, 47–51; *RD* (9 and 10 December 1985), 374–5; Casey, Memorandum to John McMahon, 10 December 1985, in Tower, John, Edmund Muskie, and Brent Scowcroft, *Report of the President's Special Review Board* (Washington DC: Government Printing Office, 1987), B-50.
55 *Report of the Congressional Committees Investigating the Iran–Contra Affair*, abridged edn (New York: Random House/Times Books, 1988), 203; Shultz, George, *Turmoil and Triumph: My Years as Secretary of State* (New York: Scribner's, 1993), 803–4.
56 John M. Poindexter, Memorandum to President Reagan, 'Covert action finding regarding Iran' (with attached presidential finding), 17 January 1986, D-15, NSAEBB-210; *RD* (17 January 1986), 384.
57 *Report of the Congressional Committees Investigating the Iran–Contra Affair*, 155–6, 302.
58 *RD* (27 and 28 May 1986), 414–15.
59 Ibid. (26–7 July 1986), 427.
60 'Message to Congress on United States assistance for the Nicaraguan Democratic National Resistance', 19 March 1986, APP-PPP.
61 'Remarks and a question-and-answer session with the American Society of Newspaper Editors', 9 April 1986, APP-PPP; 'Reagan's pro-Contra propaganda machine', *Washington Post*, 4 September 1988.
62 *Report of the Congressional Committees Investigating the Iran–Contra Affair*, 271.
63 Oliver North Memorandum, 'Release of American hostages in Beirut' (so-called 'Diversion memo'), *c.*4 April 1986, D-16, NSAEBB-210; Secord, Richard, *Honored and Betrayed: Irangate, Covert Affairs, and the Secret War in Laos* (New York: Wiley, 1992), 229.
64 'White House verifies Reagan did write in Bible sent to Iran', *NYT*, 30 January 1987; *RD* (11 February 1987), 474.

65 Caspar Weinberger, Memorandum for the Record, 'Meeting on November 10, 1986 in the Oval Office', D-20, NSAEBB-210.

66 'Address to the Nation on the Iran Arms and Contra Aid Controversy', 13 November 1986, APP-PPP; *RD* (1 December 1986), 455.

67 Ibid. (24 November 1986), 453.

68 Ibid. (25 November 1986), 454.

69 'Remarks announcing the review of the National Security Council's role in the Iran arms and Contra aid controversy', 25 November 1986, APP-PPP.

70 Wallison, Peter, *Ronald Reagan: The Power of Conviction and the Success of His Presidency* (Boulder CO: Westview, 2004), 241–66; *RD* (11 February 1987), 474.

71 Morris, *Dutch*, 620; *MT*, 320.

72 Reagan to A. C. Lyles, 24 November 1986, PHF:R–16; Reagan to Marion Grimm, 15 January 1987, PHF:R–17.

73 Reagan to Madeleine Fraser, 13 January 1987, PHF:R–17.

74 Reagan to Clark Mollenhoff, 10 December 1986, PHF:R–17.

75 Cannon, *President Reagan*, 729; Morris, *Dutch*, 622–3.

76 *Excerpts from the Tower Commission's Report*, APP-PPP. All quotations from 'Part IV: what went wrong'.

77 Abshire, David, *Saving the Reagan Presidency: Trust Is the Coin of the Realm* (College Station: Texas A&M Press, 2004), 133.

78 Cannon, *President Reagan*, 719–32; *RD* (21–2, 23, 26, and 27 February 1987), 476–9.

79 Cannon, *President Reagan*, 734–5; Wirthlin, Dick, *The Greatest Communicator: What Ronald Reagan Taught Me about Politics, Leadership, and Life* (Hoboken NJ: Wiley, 2004), 192–3.

80 'Address to the nation on the Iran arms and Contra aid controversy', 4 March 1987, APP-PPP.

81 Quoted in Nofziger, Lyn, *Nofziger* (Washington DC: Regnery, 1992), 285.

82 'The Reagan White House: in a spirit of contrition', *NYT*, 5 March 1987; 'The president's speech', *Washington Post*, 5 March 1987.

83 Heston to Reagan, 5 March 1987, PHF:R–18.

84 Reagan to Annenberg, 11 March 1987, PHF:R–18.

85 Byrne, *Iran–Contra*, 279–84, 289–306.

86 Woodward, Bob, *Five Presidents and the Legacy of Watergate* (New York: Simon & Schuster, 1999), 168–70.

87 'Transcript of interview with Philip Bobbitt, legal counsel to the Senate select committee on Iran–Contra (1988)', GHP.

88 'Question-and-answer session with area reporters in Chattanooga, Tennessee', 19 May 1987, APP-PPP.

89 'Statement on the destruction of an Iranian jetliner by the United States Navy over the Persian Gulf', 3 July 1988, APP-PPP; Kaplan, Fred, 'America's flight 17', *Slate*, 23 July 2014. Available at http://www.slate.com/articles/news_and_politics/war_stories/2014/07/the_vincennes_downing_of_iran_air_flight_655_the_united_states_tried_to.html.

90 LeoGrande, William, *Our Own Backyard: The United States in Central America, 1977–1992* (Chapel Hill: University of North Carolina Press, 1998), 522.

91 Falcoff, Mark, 'Making Central America safe for communism', *Commentary* (June 1988); Cannon, *President Reagan*, 337.

92   'Remarks and a question-and-answer session with southeast regional editors and broadcasters', 15 May 1987, APP-PPP.

12 SUMMIT NEGOTIATOR

1   'Address to the 39th session of the United Nations general assembly in New York', 24 September 1984, APP-PPP.
2   Brown, Archie, *The Gorbachev Factor* (Oxford: Oxford University Press, 1996), 83.
3   *AAL,* 611.
4   *RD* (7 December 1988), 675.
5   NSPG-104: 'Substantive issues for Geneva', 17 December 1984, *TRF-NSC; RD* (17 December 1984), 287.
6   Chernenko to Reagan, 20 December 1984, *TRF-RGSL*; Shultz, George, *Turmoil and Triumph: My Years as Secretary of State* (New York: Scribner's, 1993), 514–19.
7   Reagan to Alan Brown, 22 January 1985, PHF:R–11.
8   *RD* (24 June 1985), 337.
9   Thatcher, Margaret, *The Downing Street Years* (London: HarperCollins, 1993), 459–63; 'Meeting with Prime Minister Thatcher, Camp David, 22 December 1984', MTF, docid=109185.
10 Reagan to Gorbachev, 11 March 1985, Document[D]-2, *To the Geneva Summit: Perestroika and the Transformation of U.S.–Soviet Relations*, NSAEBB-172. Available at http://nsarchive.gwu.edu/NSAEBB/NSAEBB172/.
11 Yakovlev, Alexander, 'On Reagan: memorandum prepared on request for M.S. Gorbachev and handed to him on March 12, 1985', and Gorbachev to Reagan, 24 March 1985, D-3 and D-6, NSAEBB-172.
12 For insightful interpretation, see Brown, *The Gorbachev Factor* and Sandle, Mark, *Gorbachev: Man of the Century?* (London: Hodder, 2008).
13 *The Diary of Anatoly Chernyaev 1985* (11 March), ed. Savranskaya, Svetlana. Available at http://nsarchive.gwu.edu/NSAEBB/NSAEBB192/.
14 Pipes, Richard, 'Gorbachev's Russia: breakdown or crackdown?', *Commentary* (March 1990), 18; Shultz, *Turmoil and Triumph*, 568.
15 Brown, *The Gorbachev Factor*, xiii–xv, 106–29.
16 Gorbachev, Mikhail, *Memoirs* (New York: Doubleday, 1994), 444.
17 'Minutes of Gorbachev's meeting with CC CPSU secretaries', 15 March 1985, D-5, NSAEBB-172.
18 *The Diary of Anatoly Chernyaev 1985* (17 October), NSAEBB-192.
19 Adelman, Kenneth: RROH-MC; Shultz, *Turmoil and Triumph*, 475–6.
20 *RD* (26 September 1985), 355.
21 Mann, James, *The Rebellion of Ronald Reagan: A History of the End of the Cold War* (New York: Viking, 2009), 61–7; *RD* (17 January 1984), 213.
22 *RD* (20 May 1986), 412; Massie, Suzanne, *Land of the Firebird: The Beauty of Old Russia* (New York: Simon & Schuster, 1980).
23 Matlock, Jack, *Reagan and Gorbachev: How the Cold War Ended* (New York: Random House, 2004), 150–4.
24 Mann, *The Rebellion of Ronald Reagan*, 90.
25 Shultz, *Turmoil and Triumph*, 596–7.

26 Kuhn, James, RROH-MC; *AAL*, 635.

27 'Geneva Summit memorandum of conversation. November 19, 1985 10:20–11:20 a.m. First private meeting', D-16, NSAEBB-172.

28 *AAL*, 636; 'Geneva Summit memorandum of conversation. November 19, 1985 3:40–4:45 p.m. Second private meeting', D-19, NSAEBB-172.

29 'Geneva Summit memorandum of conversation. November 20, 1985, 2:45–3:30 p.m. Fourth plenary meeting', D-22, NSAEBB-172; Shultz, *Turmoil and Triumph*, 603–6.

30 Reagan to Murphy, 19 December 1985, and to Massie, 10 February 1986, PHF:R–14.

31 'Gorbachev speech at the CC CPSU conference, November 28, 1985', D-27, NSAEBB-172; Chernyaev, Anatoly, *My Six Years with Gorbachev* (College Park: Pennsylvania State University Press, 2000), 52–3.

32 *The Diary of Anatoly Chernyaev 1986* (18 January), NSAEBB-220, ed. Savranskaya, Svetlana. Available at http://nsarchive.gwu.edu/NSAEBB/NSAEBB220/.

33 Hoffman, David, *The Dead Hand: Reagan, Gorbachev and the Untold Story of the Cold War Arms Race* (New York: Doubleday, 2009), 244–53.

34 Matlock, *Reagan and Gorbachev*, 178; *RD* (15 January 1986), 385; Shultz, *Turmoil and Triumph*, 699–702.

35 NSPG-127: 'Responding to Gorbachev', 3 February 1986, *TRF-NSC*; *RD* (3 February 1988), 388.

36 Gorbachev to Reagan, 15 September 1986, D-1, *The Reykjavik File*, NSAEBB-203. Available at http://nsarchive.gwu.edu/NSAEBB/NSAEBB203/.

37 Reagan to Gorbachev, 4 September 1986, *TRF-RGSL*; *RD* (7 September, 1986), 355.

38 *RD* (19 and 24–6 September 1986), 439–41; Shultz, *Turmoil and Triumph*, 746.

39 Reagan to Barney Oldfield, 30 September 1986, PHF:R–16. See also Reagan to Charlton Heston, 15 October 1986, PHF:R–16.

40 Shultz, George, Memorandum for the President, 'Subject: Reyjkavik', 2 October 1986, D-4, and Sestanovich, Stephen, 'Gorbachev's goals and tactics at Reykjavik', 4 October 1986, D-6, NSAEBB-203.

41 Chernyaev, *My Six Years with Gorbachev*, 82–3.

42 'US memorandum of conversation, Reagan–Gorbachev, first meeting, 11 October 1986, 10:40 a.m.–12:30 p.m.', D-9, NSAEBB-203.

43 Shultz, *Turmoil and Triumph*, 760–1; 'US memorandum of conversation, Reagan-Gorbachev, second meeting, 11 October 1986, 3:30 p.m.–5:40 p.m.', D-11, NSAEBB-203.

44 Shultz, *Turmoil and Triumph*, 762–8; 'US memorandum of conversation, Reagan-Gorbachev, third meeting, 12 October 1986, 10:00 a.m.–1:35 p.m.', D-13, NSAEBB-203.

45 'US memorandum of conversation, Reagan–Gorbachev, final meeting, 12 October 1986, 3:25 p.m.–4:30 p.m. and 5:30 p.m.–6:50 p.m', D-15, NSAEBB-203; Shultz, *Turmoil and Triumph*, 772.

46 D-15, NSAEBB-203.

47 *AAL*, 679; *MT*, 345.

48 Shultz, *Turmoil and Triumph*, 773.

49 Ibid., 774; Kuhn, James: RROH-MC.

50 Shultz, *Turmoil and Triumph*, 775.

51 Reagan to Donn Moomaw, 15 October 1986, PHF:R–16; Talbott, Strobe, *Master of the Game: Paul Nitze and the Nuclear Peace* (New York: Knopf, 1988), 330.

52 Memorandum, 'Options for Gorbachev's visit', 23 September 1987, WHSOF: Kenneth Duberstein-1, RRL.

53 'USSR CC CPSU Politburo session on results of the Reykjavik Summit, 14 October 1986', D-21, NSAEBB-203.

54 Chernyaev, *My Six Years with Gorbachev*, 85.

55 Oberdorfer, Don, *From the Cold War to a New Era: The United States and the Soviet Union, 1983–1991* (Baltimore MD: Johns Hopkins University Press, 1998), 209.

56 'Politburo session [excerpt], 26 February 1987', D-3, *The INF Treaty and the Washington Summit 20 Years Later*, NSAEBB-238. Available at http://nsarchive.gwu.edu/NSAEBB/NSAEBB238/.

57 'Plan of conversation between M. S. Gorbachev and the president of the United States R. Reagan before the first trip to Washington, May 1987' (dictated to Anatoly Chernyaev), D-8, NSAEBB-238.

58 Thatcher, *The Downing Street Years*, 471; Dale, Iain, *Memories of Margaret Thatcher: A Portrait* (London: Biteback, 2013), 144.

59 Aldous, Richard, *Reagan and Thatcher: The Difficult Relationship* (London: Hutchinson, 2012), 222–5; Thatcher, *The Downing Street Years*, 772.

60 *RD* (12 May 1987), 495; *AAL*, 686; Mann, *The Rebellion of Ronald Reagan*, 238–40.

61 'Letter from General Secretary Gorbachev to President Reagan, September 10, 1987', *TRF-RGSL*; NSPG 165: 'United States arms control positions', 8 September 1987, *TRF-NSC*.

62 'Memorandum of conversation between M. S. Gorbachev and US secretary of state G. Shultz [excerpt]', 23 October 1987, D-15, NSAEBB-238; Shultz, *Turmoil and Triumph*, 995–1002; 'Radio address to the nation on the economy and Soviet–United States relations', 24 October 1987, APP-PPP.

63 Gorbachev to Reagan, 28 October 1987, *TRF-RGSL*; Mann, *The Rebellion of Ronald Reagan*, 261.

64 Oldfield to Reagan, 26 August 1987, Reagan to Oldfield, 8 September 1987, PHF:R–19.

65 Buckley to Reagan, 5 April, 1987, Reagan to Buckley, 5 May, 1987, in Buckley Jr, William, *The Reagan I Knew* (New York: Basic Books, 2008), 199–202; Heston to Reagan, 29 June 1987, Reagan to Heston, 9 July 1987, PHF:R–18.

66 Kuhn, James, RROH-MC.

67 Phillips, Howard, 'The treaty: another sellout', *NYT*, 11 December 1987; 'An offer they can refuse', *Time*, 14 December 1987; Safire, William, 'Secrets of the summit', *NYT*, 6 December 1987.

68 'Memorandum on conversation with General Secretary Gorbachev, at the Kremlin, July 18, 1986' [quotation 12], Ronald Reagan Postpresidential Correspondence [RRPC], Richard Nixon Library.

69 Nixon, Richard, and Henry Kissinger, 'A real peace', *National Review*, 22 May 1987, 32–4; 'An interview with Richard Nixon', *Time*, 4 May 1987, 23; 'Kissinger: how to deal with Gorbachev', *Newsweek*, 2 March 1987.

70 Nixon, 'Memorandum to the file, meeting with President Reagan at the White House, 5 p.m., April 28, 1987' [quotations 9], RRPC.

71 Mann, *The Rebellion of Ronald Reagan*, 48.

72 Gates, Robert, Memorandum: 'Gorbachev's game plan: the long view', 24 November 1987, D-20, NSAEBB-238.

73 Robinson, Peter, '"Tear down this wall:" how top advisers opposed Reagan's challenge to Gorbachev – but lost', *Prologue* 39 (summer 2007). Available at http://www.archives. gov/publications/prologue/2007/summer/berlin.html.

74 'Remarks on East–West Relations at the Brandenburg Gate in West Berlin', 12 June 1987, APP-PPP; *AAL*, 680–3.

75 'Memo of conversation between President Reagan and General Secretary Gorbachev, 10.45 a.m.–12.30 p.m.', 8 December 1987, D-23a, NSAEBB-238.

76 Powell, Colin, *My American Journey* (New York: Ballantine, 1995), 350–1; Shultz, *Turmoil and Triumph*, 1010–11.

77 'Draft memo of conversation between President Reagan and General Secretary Gorbachev, 10.55 a.m.–12.35 p.m., 9 December 1987', D-24b, NSAEBB-238.

78 'Telegram: secretary's 12/11 NAC [North Atlantic Council] briefing on Washington Summit', D-27, NSAEBB-238.

79 Shultz, *Turmoil and Triumph*, 1005.

80 'The summit: as "Gorby" works the crowds, backward reels the KGB', *NYT*, 11 December 1987; 'Remarks and a question-and-answer session with area high school seniors in Jacksonville, Florida', 1 December 1987, APP-PPP; 'Poll: Americans believe summit had important achievements,' *Washington Post*, 11 December 1987.

81 'Mad momentum', *Wall Street Journal*, 13 April 1988.

82 Reagan to Loeb, 18 December 1987, PHF:R–19.

83 'Remarks to the World Affairs Council of Western Massachusetts in Springfield', 21 April 1988, APP-PPP; Shultz, *Turmoil and Triumph*, 1097.

84 *RD* (11 March 1988), 585; 'National Security Council Memorandum of Conversation, NSC Meeting with Suzanne Massie', 11 March 1988, D-4, The Moscow Summit 20 Years Later, NSAEBB-251. Available at http://nsarchive.gwu.edu/NSAEBB/NSAEBB251/

85 Shultz, *Turmoil and Triumph*, 1081–6.

86 Ibid., 1085.

87 Memorandum of a conversation, 'President's second one-on-one meeting with General Secretary Gorbachev', 31 May 1988, and Memorandum of a conversation, 'Second plenary meeting between President Reagan and General Secretary Gorbachev', 1 June 1988, NSAEBB-251; Shultz, *Turmoil and Triumph*, 1104–5.

88 *RD* (29–31 May, 1 June 1988), 613–14; 'Remarks and a question-and-answer session with the students and faculty at Moscow State University', 31 May 1988, APP-PPP.

89 *Anatoly Chernyaev Diary*, 19 June 1988, D-28, NSAEBB-251; Gorbachev, Mikhail, *Ponyat' Perestroiku… Pochemu eto vazhno seichas* [To understand perestroika… why it is important now] (Moscow: Alpina Business Books, 2006), 161.

90 'So long, evil empire', *National Review*, 8 July 1988; 'The president's news conference following the Soviet–United States summit meeting in Moscow', 1 June 1988, APP-PPP.

91 Matlock, Jack, *Autopsy on an Empire* (New York: Random House, 1995), 124–5; Reagan to George Murphy, 8 July 1988, PHF:R-20.

92 Gorbachev, *Memoirs*, 459–60.

93 'The Gorbachev visit: excerpts from speech to UN on major Soviet military cuts', *NYT*, 8 December 1988.

94 'Letter from General Secretary Gorbachev to President Reagan, September 20, 1988', *TRF-RGSL*

95 Matlock, *Reagan and Gorbachev*, 306, and *Autopsy on an Empire,* 590–1.

96 'Man of the decade', *Time*, 1 January 1990.

97 D'Souza, Dinesh, *Ronald Reagan: How an Ordinary Man Became an Extraordinary Leader* (New York: Free Press, 1997), 197. For a rebuttal, see Brown, Archie, 'Perestroika and the end of the Cold War', *Cold War History*, 7 (March 2007), 1–17.

98 'NSDD-75: US relations with the USSR', 17 January 1983. Available at https://www.reaganlibrary.archives.gov/archives/reference/NSDDs.html; 'Reagan urges Soviet Republics to let reason prevail over passion', Associated Press, 17 May 1990. Available at http://www.apnewsarchive.com/1990/Reagan-Urges-Soviet-Republics-to-Let-Reason-Prevail-Over-Passion-With-AM-Soviet-Gorbachev-Bjt/id-dcf391f4c852707a18563fa94e a6fe76.

99 'Politburo session', 17 December 1987, D-29, NSAEBB-238. For illuminating analysis of the significance of the two leaders in changing US–Soviet relations, see Wilson, James Graham, *The Triumph of Improvisation: Gorbachev's Adaptability, Reagan's Engagement, and the End of the Cold War* (Ithaca NY: Cornell University Press, 2014).

100 Gorbachev, *Memoirs*, 457.

EPILOGUE: HISTORY MAN

1 Reagan to Victor Krulak, 11 July 1988, PHF:R–20, and to William Rusher, 17 January 1989, PHF:R–21.

2 Thatcher to Reagan, 19 January 1989; MTF, docid=110359; Reagan to Thatcher, 19 January 1989: MTF, docid=110358.

3 *AAL*, 722.

4 'Reagans settle in at 668 Saint Cloud', *NYT*, 23 January 1989; *RD* (27 December 1989), 683.

5 McDougal, Dennis, *The Last Mogul: Lew Wasserman, MCA, and the Hidden History of Hollywood* (Boston: Da Capo, 2001), 469–71.

6 'Reagan's fall from grace', *Los Angeles Times Magazine*, 4 March 1990. Available at http://articles.latimes.com/1990-03-04/magazine/tm-2327_1_nancy-reagan-foundation; 'Hillary Clinton isn't alone: former politicians rake it in on speaker circuit', 11 July 2013. Available at https://www.washingtonpost.com/news/post-politics/wp/2013/07/11/hillary-clinton-isnt-alone-former-politicians-rake-it-in-on-speaker-circuit/.

7 'Reagan gets a red carpet from the British', *NYT*, 14 June 1989.

8 'Reagan's jolly good speech', *Washington Post*, 6 December 1990; Aldous, John, *Reagan and Thatcher: The Difficult Relationship* (London: Hutchinson, 2012), 274.

9 'Ronald Reagan from the people's perspective: a Gallup poll review', 7 June 2004. Available at http://www.gallup.com/poll/11887/Ronald-Reagan-From-Peoples-Perspective-Gallup-Poll-Review.aspx?g_source=Ronald%20Reagan%20From%20the%20People's%20Perspective&g_medium=search&g_campaign=tiles.

10 Blumenthal, Sidney, *Our Long National Daydream: A Political Pageant of the Reagan Era* (New York: HarperCollins, 1990); Johnson, Haynes, *Sleepwalking through History: America in the Reagan Years* (New York: Norton, 1991); Barlett, Donald, and James Steele, *America: What Went Wrong?* (Kansas City: Andrews & McMeel, 1992); and Calleo, David, *The Bankrupting of America: How the Federal Budget Is Impoverishing Our Nation* (New York: Morrow, 1992).

11 Kennedy, Paul, *The Rise and Fall of the Great Powers: Economic Change and Military Conflict from 1500 to 2000* (New York: Random House, 1988).

12 Cannon, Lou, *President Reagan: The Role of a Lifetime* (New York: Simon & Schuster, 1991).

13 Kelley, Kitty, *Nancy Reagan: The Unauthorized Biography* (New York: Simon & Schuster, 1991); Colley, Linda, 'At least they paid their taxes', *London Review of Books*, 25 July 1991; Reagan to Nixon, 11 April 1991, *RALIL*, 822.

14 Davis, Patti, *The Way I See It: An Autobiography* (New York: Putnam, 1992); 'A daughter's lament', *People*, 18 May 1992.

15 *Publishers Weekly*, 10 February 1989, 34; Reagan, Ronald, *Speaking My Mind: Selected Speeches* (New York: Simon & Schuster, 1989), and *An American Life: The Autobiography* (New York: Simon & Schuster, 1990).

16 Korda, Michael, 'Prompting the president', *New Yorker*, 6 October 1997.

17 Dowd, Maureen, 'Where's the rest of him?', *NYT*, 18 November 1990; Hertzberg, Hendrick, 'The child monarch', *New Republic*, 9 September 1991.

18 'Plan for Reagan library at Stanford is dropped', *NYT*, 24 April 1987.

19 Reagan to President George Hearne of Eureka, 16 June 1987, PHF:R–18, and 27 January 1988, PHF:R–19.

20 *RD* (31 August, 1988), 643, (3 October 1988), 660; 'Disputes over land common to presidential libraries', *Chicago Tribune*, 10 February 2015.

21 '"Reagan country" gets put on the map', *Los Angeles Times*, 27 October 1991.

22 Hufbauer, Benjamin, *Presidential Temples: How Memorials and Libraries Shape Public Memory* (Lawrence: University Press of Kansas, 2006), and 'The Ronald Reagan Presidential Library and Museum', *Journal of American History*, 95 (December 2008), 786–92.

23 'What's a presidential library to do?', *NYT*, 12 September 2011.

24 Reagan, Nancy, *I Love You, Ronnie: The Letters of Ronald Reagan to Nancy Reagan* (New York: Random House, 2000), 179–80; Reagan to Lorraine Wagner, 13 July 1989, and to Helen Lawton, 16 September 1989, *RALIL*, 812–14.

25 Mann, James, *The Rebellion of Ronald Reagan: A History of the End of the Cold War* (New York: Viking, 2009), 339; Morris, Edmund, *Dutch: A Memoir of Ronald Reagan* (New York: HarperCollins, 1999), 656.

26 Khan to Reagan, 15 November 1982, Reagan to Khan, 19 November 1982, PHF:R–5.

27 Reagan to Leonard McDevitt, 17 July 1986, PHF:R–16.

28 Barrett, Laurence, 'Alzheimer's and the Reagans: an inside report on how they're coping', *New Choices*, July/August 1996, 23–6.

29 'Keeping Reagan's legacy alive at his old ranch', *NYT*, 24 May 1998.

30 'Grace under fire: Patti Davis on her father's final years', *Time*, 6 February 2011. Available at http://content.time.com/time/magazine/article/0,9171,2044769,00.html. See too, Davis, Patti, *The Long Goodbye* (New York: Knopf, 2004).

31 Reagan, Nancy, *I Love You, Ronnie*, 184–8.

32 Reagan, Ron, *My Father at 100: A Memoir* (New York: Viking, 2011), esp. 217–19; 'Ronald Reagan had Alzheimer's while president, says son', *The Guardian*, 17 January 2011.

33 Berisha, Visar, Shuai Wang, Amy LaCross, and Julie Liss, 'Tracking discourse complexity preceding Alzheimer's disease diagnosis: a case study comparing the press conferences

of Presidents Ronald Reagan and George Herbert Walker Bush', *Journal of Alzheimer's Disease*, 45 (January 2015), 959–63.

34   'Ronald Reagan dies at 93', *CNN International*, 6 June 2004. Available at http://edition.cnn.com/2004/ALLPOLITICS/06/05/reagan.main/index.html.

35   Bjerre-Poulsen, Niels, 'The road to Mount Rushmore: the conservative commemoration crusade for Reagan', in Hudson, Cheryl, and Gareth Davies, eds, *Ronald Reagan and the 1980s: Perception, Policies, Legacies* (New York: Palgrave, 2008), 209–28; Bunch, Will, *Tear Down This Myth: How the Reagan Legacy Has Distorted Our Politics and Haunts Our Future* (New York: Free Press, 2009), 18–21.

36   Schwarz, Barry, *Abraham Lincoln and the Forge of National Memory* (Chicago: University of Chicago Press, 2000), 12; 'In search of Mount Rushmore', *US News & World Report*, 15 December 1997, 35.

37   'Americans say Reagan is the greatest US president', 18 February 2011. Available at http://www.gallup.com/poll/146183/Americans-Say-Reagan-Greatest-President.aspx?g_source=Americans%20Say%20Reagan%20is%20the%20Greatest%20US%20President&g_medium=search&g_campaign=tiles.

38   Cannon, Lou, 'Why Reagan was the "great communicator"', *USA Today*, 6 June 2004.

39   'Farewell address to the nation', 11 January 1989, APP-PPP.

40   'Republican National Convention address', 17 August 1992. Available at https://www.youtube.com/watch?v=WxL3OU1dwml.

41   'Ronald Reagan's announcement of presidential candidacy', 13 November 1979. Available at https://www.reaganlibrary.archives.gov/archives/reference/11.13.79.html.

42   'Majority of Americans optimistic about US in the future', 4 January 2010. Available at http://www.gallup.com/poll/124910/majority-americans-optimistic-future.aspx.

43   Kaye, Harvey, *Tom Paine and the Promise of America* (New York: Hill & Wang, 2006).

44   'One more "disposable president"', *US News & World Report*, 17 November 1980; Cutler, Lloyd, 'To form a government', *Foreign Affairs* (fall 1980), 126–43.

45   *RD* (21 May 1985), 329.

46   *Report of the Congressional Committees Investigating the Iran–Contra Affair*, 110th Congress, 1st Session (Washington DC: Government Printing Office, November 1987), 865.

47   *RD* (29 January 1982), 65.

48   'Address before a joint session of the Congress on the Program for Economic Recovery', 18 February 1981, APP-PPP.

49   Morgan, Iwan, *The Age of Deficits: Presidents and Unbalanced Budgets from Jimmy Carter to George W. Bush* (Lawrence: University Press of Kansas, 2009), 219.

50   Galbraith, James, *The End of Normal: The Great Crisis and the Future of Growth* (New York: Simon & Schuster, 2014).

51   Kristof, Nicholas, 'Reagan, Obama, and inequality', *NYT*, 22 January 2015; 'State of the union address', 20 January 2015, APP-PPP.

52   'US Liberals at record 24%, but still trail Conservatives', *Gallup*, 9 January 2015. Available at http://www.gallup.com/poll/180452/liberals-record-trail-conservatives.aspx?g_source=US%20Liberals%20at%20Record%2024%%&g_medium=search&g_campaign=tiles.

53   Navarrette Jr, Ruben, 'Remembering Reagan', *Latino Magazine* (fall 2011).

54   'The president's news conference', 18 June 1985, APP-PPP.

INDEX